A KINGDOM DIVIDED

CONFLICTING WORLDS

New Dimensions of the American Civil War

T. Michael Parrish, *Series Editor*

A KINGDOM DIVIDED

EVANGELICALS, LOYALTY, AND SECTIONALISM IN THE CIVIL WAR ERA

April E. Holm

LOUISIANA STATE UNIVERSITY PRESS
BATON ROUGE

Published by Louisiana State University Press

Manufactured in the United States of America
FIRST PRINTING

DESIGNER: *Mandy McDoanld Scallan*
TYPEFACE: *Text: Whitman; Display: Franklin Gothic Extra Condensed*
PRINTER AND BINDER: *Sheridan Books, Inc.*

Library of Congress Cataloging-in-Publication Data
Names: Holm, April E., 1981– author.
Title: A kingdom divided : evangelicals, loyalty, and sectionalism in the Civil War era / April E. Holm.
Other titles: Conflicting worlds.
Description: Baton Rouge : Louisiana State University Press, [2017] | Series: Conflicting worlds : new dimensions of the American Civil War | "A kingdom divided is the first comprehensive study of white evangelical Protestants in the border region during the nineteenth century"—Introduction. | Includes bibliographical references and index.
Identifiers: LCCN 2017019257| ISBN 978-0-8071-6771-7 (cloth : alk. paper) | ISBN 978-0-8071-6772-4 (pdf) | ISBN 978-0-8071-6773-1 (epub)
Subjects: LCSH: Protestantism—United States—History—19th century. | Evangelicalism—United States—History—19th century. | United States—History—Civil War, 1861–1865—Religious aspects—Christianity.
Classification: LCC BR525 .H635 2017 | DDC 277.3/081—dc23
LC record available at https://lccn.loc.gov/2017019257

The paper in this book meets the guidelines for permanence and durability of the Committee on Production Guidelines for Book Longevity of the Council on Library Resources.♾

For my parents, Don and Suzanne, who got me started,
and my husband, Will, who saw me to the finish.

CONTENTS

ACKNOWLEDGMENTS

I could not have written this book without generous help from many people. Eric Foner, who advised my dissertation, has guided me through the ups and downs of research and writing in graduate school and beyond. I am grateful for his steady encouragement throughout this project. Elizabeth Blackmar's interest and insight were indispensable in motivating me and clarifying my thinking. I appreciate Barbara Fields's thought-provoking comments and matchless editorial advice. I would also like to thank Harry Stout and Randall Balmer for their comments.

I am grateful for the funding that made it possible for me to devote my time to this book. A Beinecke Scholarship, a Doris Quinn Fellowship, and a Whiting Fellowship helped fund the early stages of research and writing. A Schwartz Postdoctoral Fellowship at The New School and the New-York Historical Society supported me for a year. Summer research grants from the University of Mississippi College of Liberal Arts made manuscript revisions possible. I am indebted to the archives and archivists who were essential to this project. I received warm welcomes and helpful suggestions everywhere I worked. I would particularly like to thank the staff at Emory University, the Filson Historical Society, the Library of Congress, the Partee Center, and the University of Kentucky. As I traveled for research, many strangers took me into their homes. I admire and appreciate all of them for taking that leap of faith.

I feel fortunate to have found so many friends among my colleagues. I am grateful to have shared the graduate experience with Jenna Feltey Alden, Sarah Bridger, Alex Cummings, Megan Doherty, Courtney Fullilove, Julie Golia, Beth Pillsbury, Rachel Van, and Neil Young. I owe a special debt of gratitude to Nicole Hemmer, who has staved off many doubts, given many pep talks, and never failed to offer wisdom and inspiration. Few could hope to find as warm and collegial a place to work as the Arch Dalrymple III Department of History at the University of Mississippi. Many thanks to my friends and colleagues, especially Joshua First, John Neff, John Ondrovcik, Anne Twitty, Joe Ward, and Noell Wilson. A surprising number of friends who are not historians have also provided thoughtful feedback and a sympathetic ear throughout this process. I owe particular thanks to Erica Nofi, Catherine Rzepniewski, and Naomi Beckman-Straus.

My loving families, both by marriage and by birth, have had unflagging faith in me throughout this project. Nobody could ask for better parents-in-law than Janet and Tom Murray, who have always offered excellent advice. Thank you to my sister, Ali Aguilar, and my sister-in-law, Elizabeth Murray. The day was saved more than once by my parents, Don Holm and Suzanne Toaspern-Holm, who taught me persistence—the most important asset for a historian to have. My daughters, Julia and Eleanor, both arrived in the course of writing this book. The best moments of every day are spent with them.

There is nobody to whom I owe a larger debt of gratitude than my husband, Will Murray. This book would not exist without him. His insightful observations and incisive editing have made their mark on every page of this book. He not only makes me a better thinker, he also makes me a better person, and I am lucky to share my life with him.

A KINGDOM DIVIDED

INTRODUCTION

A KINGDOM DIVIDED

In 1864, Robert L. Stanton published *The Church and the Rebellion*, the first study of religion and the Civil War. Stanton, a professor of theology in Danville, Kentucky, did not hesitate to draw conclusions about a war still in progress. "Men in all classes of society, freely lay the blame of this Rebellion," he observed, "at the door of the Church." He had no doubt that "future Bancrofts" would "write the elaborate histories of the rebellion," and when they did, they would note "the agency of the Church" and the "zeal of the ministers of religion" in promoting secession.[1]

While elaborate histories were indeed forthcoming, most American historians did not follow Stanton's lead in blaming churches for the Civil War. Quite the opposite: over the course of the nineteenth century, religion gradually dropped out of mainstream accounts of the era.[2] It is easy to read Stanton's concerns as the vindictive hairsplitting of a man who could not see past denominational spats during a great national crisis. Little wonder that narratives like Stanton's did not become canonical. However, histories like his—and the events they chronicle—are far from irrelevant. In fact, a fresh look at these seemingly marginal squabbles reveals a great deal about the war and about how people respond to moral and political dilemmas. This book uses religion as a critical lens through which to analyze sectionalism, war, and reunion. More than simply gauging the church's role in causing secession, it examines how religion, politics, and morality interacted in a time of political crisis to create lasting institutional and cultural divisions in American Christianity.

While Stanton focused on the war years, I begin much earlier, covering the period from the end of the Second Great Awakening to the Gilded Age. In the early nineteenth century, Baptist, Methodist, and Presbyterian churches experienced spectacular growth. However, in the 1840s and 1850s, the slavery controversy divided all three denominations into separate sectional branches. In the border region—made up of Kentucky, Missouri, Maryland, and portions of surrounding states—congregations were riven with conflict. While northern and southern evangelicals struggled bitterly over border churches, many border evangelicals sought to avoid conflict, developing a border theology of "spirituality" and political neutrality.

The divided denominations grew increasingly sectionalized and politicized during the secession crisis and Civil War. Northern denominations embraced the Union cause, and southern branches fervently supported the Confederacy. Meanwhile, many border evangelicals continued to profess neutrality. For both practical and political reasons, border evangelicals rejected patriotic sermons, conspicuous flag displays, and prayers for the Union during the Civil War. Northern evangelical patriotism and loyalty tests, as well as secular pressure to swear loyalty to the Union, made neutrality nearly impossible to maintain. Wartime loyalty oaths, banishment, and redistribution of church property alienated border Christians who had maintained loyalty to the North.

After the war, southern churches were financially weak and bereft of the institutions they had defended: slavery and the Confederacy. Southern evangelicals sought a compelling defense of denominational distinctiveness in the face of northern pressure to reunite. Over the next decade, disaffected border evangelicals joined southern churches, bringing along the doctrine of spirituality and neutrality honed through years at the center of conflict. Ironically, the failed border strategy for preventing denominational division became a key element in perpetuating sectional denominational branches after the Civil War. Southern branches adopted both the disaffected border churches and their doctrine of spirituality, using it to give sectional division a theological basis. Southern evangelicals promoted a version of the past in which churches had divided, not over the politics and morality of slavery, but in order to preserve theological purity. In maintaining separate faiths, southern evangelicals romanticized and naturalized the distinctiveness of their denominations, while downplaying the importance of both slavery and politics in their formation.

Between 1876 and 1894, sectional hostilities ceased in all three denominations as northern branches formally recognized the legitimacy of their southern counterparts. Once aligned, politics and theology powerfully reinforced each other, perpetuating division. In contrast to national northern and southern postwar reconciliation, the end of the nineteenth century saw these denominations more firmly sectionally divided than they had been at the close of the Civil War.

A Kingdom Divided is the first comprehensive study of white evangelical Protestants in the border region during the nineteenth century. This analysis of border-state Christianity uses institutional history to provide new insights into four key spheres of scholarship on the nineteenth-century United States. First, I delineate the relationships between religion, morality, and politics in a contested region. Border moderates attempted to use a strategy of neutrality to navigate the moral and political quandaries of the Civil War era. But neutrality proved an unsustainable and problematic approach. In my assessment of religion and politics, I offer a model for a new institutional history of religion—one that takes seriously the structures that evangelicals, themselves, invested with so much significance. Second, I complicate and reperiodize sectionalism and regionalism during the Civil War era. Third, I investigate a series of little-studied debates over the relationship between church and state in wartime. Finally, in this account of war in the churches, I challenge existing narratives of reunion and memory during the postwar period.

Despite—or, perhaps, because of—the First Amendment's provisions separating church and state, religion and politics have a long, tangled history in the United States. The present volume focuses on clergy and lay leaders in America's three largest evangelical denominations. Methodists, Baptists, and Presbyterians all experienced tremendous growth during the Second Great Awakening. From 1776 to 1860, the number of Americans who actively belonged to Protestant churches rose from 17 to 34 percent. In 1860, over 1.7 million Americans were members in full standing of one of these three denominations. This amounted to nearly 70 percent of the Protestant population.[3] Many more Americans attended church and identified with a particular denomination without being full members. In sum, evangelical Protestantism colored the way most nineteenth-century Americans viewed their nation and understood the world around them.[4]

The denominations at the center of this study shared certain characteristics common to American evangelicals. These included: a literal reading of the Bible and belief in its ultimate authority; emphasis on the personal conversion experience and living a holy life; certainty that Christ would return to earth; and, of course, a focus on evangelism. They also built institutions to support their endeavors.[5] These characteristics directly shaped the way evangelicals interacted with national politics.

Much of the scholarship on religion and the Civil War era wrestles with the intertwined nature of religion and politics and leans toward one of three broad categories of interpretation. In the first of these are works that seek to determine the role of religion in contributing to sectionalism, secession, and the coming of war. For example, scholars like C. C. Goen and Mitchel Snay argue that sectional division in the churches contributed to national divisions more broadly.[6] Other scholars in this tradition have debated the extent to which the development of a biblical defense of slavery contributed to secession.[7] Still others have investigated the place of religion on the battlefield, during Reconstruction, and in the process of reunion.[8] A second group of scholars approaches the topic from the opposite angle—asking how the great crisis influenced American religion. They question whether secession, the Civil War, and the war's aftermath constituted a turning point for American Christianity and how the war influenced theology and the content of faith.[9]

A third approach to religion and the Civil War—using church and denominational history—has fallen out of favor and now seems old-fashioned.[10] However, as Laurie Maffly-Kipp reminds us, the seemingly "antiquated intricacies of denominations" mattered deeply to nineteenth-century Americans, and we must take them seriously.[11] Religious institutions united Americans across sections and regions at a time when few other national organizations existed.[12] The networks they forged across the antebellum West both unified the region and laid the groundwork for later sectionalization. The newspapers they published disseminated highly influential stories of clergy apprehended by federal authorities in wartime. And their denominational meetings were the venues for agreements that would formalize religious sectionalism in the postwar decades. Throughout this period, networks of capital—invested in seminaries, publishing houses, church buildings, and missions—tied evangelical institutions together. They were also centrally important in the lives of hundreds of thousands of clergy and lay leaders who had both a professional and a spiritual commitment to their denominations, and were enmeshed in institutional bonds.[13] When denominations divided, it was a traumatic experience for those involved. This was the case for Jonathan Palmer Finley, a Missouri Presbyterian who lived through secession and war but considered the day in 1866 when his presbytery divided "the most marked day in my life."[14] Finley devoted many more pages of his diary to that event than to the national crisis unfolding around him. In considering the ties that motivated people to act and determined loyalty in the

Civil War era, a fresh look at the power and influence of religious institutions is warranted.

Because religion and politics were deeply intertwined in American culture during the Civil War era, I draw from all three of these approaches to show how political debate, morality, and religious institutions interacted in the border region to determine responses to sectionalism, war, and reconstruction. The unfolding of denominational division and the development of religious sectionalism placed border evangelicals at the center of national political conversations, but I do not argue that denominational schisms caused political secession. Many American contemporaries, however, certainly thought they did, as Stanton's claim in *The Church and the Rebellion* makes clear. The schisms within the churches were a response to the same destabilizing debate over slavery that would later divide the nation. Denominational institutions grew more sectionalized in response to the events of the era, but my goal is not merely to chronicle church history. By studying evangelicals who lived on the contested border between North and South, I offer a perspective on how religion intersected with politics at the regional level. Communities and congregations divided not just over national political debates, but also over local religious concerns.

Border conflicts were the product of profound ethical quandaries. What was the Christian's obligation toward the enslaved? What was his duty to the state in times of crisis? To what degree should Christians concern themselves with solving material problems in this world? These questions consumed and divided evangelicals throughout the nineteenth century. They shaped the evangelical relationship to the West in the 1830s, and led directly to the sectional denominational divisions of the 1840s. They divided border congregations during the Civil War, and helped to perpetuate division between northern and southern denominational branches in the postwar period and beyond.

In order to effectively analyze these issues, I treat the moral and the religious as separate but related factors. Their nuanced interaction with each other—and with the political debates of the era—point to the difficulty of generating a single, cohesive, religious narrative of the Civil War.

In response to the slavery debate and sectional crisis, moderate border evangelicals attempted to avoid local controversy by embracing a position of neutrality. This tactic had evident appeal: border evangelicals were deeply divided over the issue of slavery, and choosing one side or the other inevitably meant alienating friends and fellow congregants. Indeed, it was debates over slavery that had set off wrenching divisions in beloved church institutions in the decades preceding the war. Consequently, these divisions—and not slavery itself—came to seem like the most pressing problem facing border moderates. From this vantage point, remaining neutral—and thereby preserving the church—was conceived as a morally superior choice. However, neutrality in the face of a complex moral problem like slavery came with its own ethical perils. For one thing, opting to be neutral was a privilege. African Americans, for example, had no such option open to them. But far from recognizing this privilege, neutral clergy felt beleaguered by those who pressed them to choose a side. This sense of victimhood helped propel them toward affiliation with southern evangelicals, who continued to defend slavery even after it was abolished. Neutrality in the face of the slavery conflict and civil war was ultimately unsustainable.

In addition to untangling these complex moral threads, *A Kingdom Divided* challenges prevailing definitions of sectionalism. Historians often approach sectionalism as a phenomenon limited to conflict between North and South during the decade before the Civil War. I address sectionalism as a phenomenon that persisted throughout the nineteenth century, before the war and after. Although sectionalism was constant, it was not static. For example, it did not simply divide North from South. In the early antebellum decades, division between the East and the West pervaded the major evangelical denominations.[15] This division was exacerbated by the heightened significance of the West to the evangelical project of shaping the United States into a Christian nation. I provide a religious narrative of sectionalism to explain how conflict over slavery eventually dissolved the earlier debate over the role of evangelicals in the West. Sectionalism persisted into the postwar era. Unlike political institutions that reunited along with the nation, evangelical denominations did not reunite, and Union victory did not herald an end to evangelical sectionalism. In fact, sectionalism defined the structure of America's largest evangelical denominations well into the twentieth century.

The border region is usually treated as peripheral to the events of the Civil War era. I place the border at the center—where North and South met not just on the battlefield, but also in the ordinary transactions of daily life. In doing so, I join other historians who have increasingly turned to the border region to understand the era.[16] I contend that we must consider the border as a discrete, distinctive region in nineteenth-century America—just as we do the North and South.

There are two common ways that scholars approach the study of the United States in the era of the Civil War. The so-called "lumpers" view the nation as a whole, and they frame their analyses in terms of a generalized North versus a generalized South. This approach divides all of the states into one of two vast sections.[17] It has the advantage of allowing us to see the sectional conflict in broad perspective and to make large generalizations, but it obscures regional variation. The differences between Indiana and Massachusetts, for example, are lost in the work of lumpers. Another category of historians, the "splitters," study the Civil War at the state level.[18] This approach avoids the problem of glossing over differences within each section, but it introduces a new challenge: state borders can make for rather arbitrary interpretive containers. There is often very little that distinguishes the experience of people living on either side of a state line. In the present study, the border is differentiated as a region separate from the North as a whole (or, for that matter, the South). However, it is not determined by state borders. Instead, I define the border as the area in which, when faced with divisive political conflicts, evangelicals struggled with the question of whether they were northern or southern. This flexible regional approach offers a middle way between the "lumpers" and the "splitters" of Civil War scholarship. Using this method, I define the border as encompassing all of Delaware, Maryland, western Virginia, Kentucky, and Missouri, as well as portions of every neighboring state. This region boasted a population of over six million and was the site of some of the era's most violent conflicts.[19]

The boundaries of this border region shifted and evolved in response to national growth and the sectional crisis. Nevertheless, it retained identifiable features that distinguished it from either the North or the South. In addition to quarreling over sectional denominational affiliation, border residents tended to think of themselves as neither northern nor southern and therefore occupying a moderate political position. Many viewed themselves as westerners, which is why, in discussing the Ohio Valley region west of the Appalachians, I use the terms "border" and "West" somewhat interchangeably. Later, as the slavery conflict divided the nation, the border between slavery and freedom became increasingly significant. As sectionalism increased, I more frequently included eastern states like Maryland and Virginia. During and after the Civil War, as the Union gained control of the border, occupied areas of upper South states like Tennessee followed border-like patterns.

The relationship between church and state is another key topic. During the Civil War era, questions about how evangelicals should relate to the state were ubiquitous. From the antebellum denominational divisions through Reconstruction, clergy and church leaders dealt with the state in numerous ways. In many cases, the carefully drawn lines between the religious and the secular were brought under close scrutiny and found to be less distinct than they had first appeared. For example, numerous disputes over church property made their way into secular courts both during antebellum divisions and in the aftermath of war.

As Amanda Porterfield has pointed out, the internal church governments of the major evangelical denominations constituted a "parallel government" in the nineteenth-century United States.[20] These "parallel governments," which sometimes took precedence over secular authorities, resolved internal disputes over church property. This was the solution that both church and state officials favored. However, beginning with denominational schisms in the 1840s, conflicts over church property became too contentious to be resolved internally, and they spilled into secular courts. In fact, even though they resisted cases that required a secular court to rule on the legitimacy of a denominational branch, courts continued to render verdicts in property disputes well into the era of Reconstruction.[21]

The courts were not the only places where secular authorities intervened with churches and clergy. A similarly complex dynamic played out in the chaos and uncertainty of war. The Civil War led Union officials to police civilian loyalty—including loyalty within the churches. Using oaths, arrests, banishments, and the seizure of property, federal officials attempted to enforce a Unionist message in border pulpits. They monitored sermons and denominational newspapers for signs of disloyalty, required prayers for Union victory, and expected the U.S. flag to fly over congregational meetings. Special orders even authorized Union officials to strip control of church buildings away from disloyal preachers. This dramatic, if brief, instance of state intervention in church affairs has received relatively scant attention from historians.[22] It reveals the importance of securing clergy loyal to Union war efforts and the limits of neutrality in the contested border region. Monitoring by federal agents profoundly shaped the postwar experience of border evangelicals and their denominations.

The enduring sectional rift in the major evangelical denominations has largely been ignored in explanations of the failures of Reconstruction and the limits of reunion. The southern churches played a critical part in these failures insofar as they remained strongholds of southern exceptionalism. Continued division in the churches is evidence that reunion did not happen evenly and equally across all facets of civil society. Nineteenth-century evangelicals never reunited. Rather, they actually deepened and codified their sectional divisions in the decades following the end of the war.

Continued sectionalism within white evangelical denominations stemmed from two related processes that began in the aftermath of war: the development of the myth of the Lost Cause, and the reconciliation and reunion of the North and South. Historians have amply demonstrated how white southerners constructed a history that cast Confederate objectives as just, moral, and honorable. At the same time, they romanticized slavery and the antebellum South. The churches often appear in these narrative histories as key sites for the creation of Lost Cause mythology.[23] Myth-making within the churches did more than just contribute to the civil religion of the white South—it also shaped the organizational structure of American Christianity. The nation's three largest evangelical denominations remained sectionally divided long after the war had ended. What's more, the churches developed internal, denomination-specific myths about the past that remained robust even as reconciliation occurred elsewhere in southern society. These myths denied that the southern branches had withdrawn in defense of slavery. Instead, the persecution of border evangelicals and the attack on spirituality were at the center of Lost Cause church histories.

Historians of the postwar era describe a national reconciliation process through which both the North and the South reunited by agreeing on mutually acceptable versions of the past, usually at the expense of civil rights and social justice. Most scholars of reunion emphasize a dominant narrative of white unity built upon forgetting all aspects of the war other than "the pathos and endearing mutuality of sacrifice among soldiers."[24] But the persistent institutionalized sectionalism within the major evangelical churches is at odds with these narratives of postwar national reunion and white unity.[25] A superficial reunion could only occur because so much sectionalism still existed. Cross-sectional fraternity was acceptable precisely because institutions like the churches remained sectionally distinct. It was easier for white southerners to accept reunion in some areas when churches remained distinctly southern. Late nineteenth-century agreements between northern and southern evangelicals did not so much hasten meaningful reunion as prolong the process. They served to curtail overt sectional antagonism while protecting and acknowledging sectional difference. *A Kingdom Divided* uncovers a vital chapter in American religion, the Civil War, and Reconstruction, the effects of which lasted well into the twentieth century and still echo in current debates over the relationship between religion and politics in the United States.

My focus in this book is white evangelical Protestant ministers and lay leaders in the border region—in particular, border moderates—who attempted to remain neutral through the slavery debates, sectional denominational schism, and the Civil War. By no means was every evangelical on the border a moderate who attempted neutrality. Throughout the nineteenth century, some evangelicals living on the border instead identified with the views and goals of the northern or southern branches. I refer to these sectionalized border residents as "northern-affiliated" or "southern-affiliated." Evangelicals who lived outside the region are referred to simply as "northern" or "southern."

I focus on Baptists, Methodists, and Presbyterians because these three denominations were widely popular—in 1860, close to two million Americans were members of one of the three. These denominations were also structured in a way that made them particularly vulnerable to sectional conflict. All three developed national organizations that brought together denominational leaders from different regions. However, authority within the organizations was not so centralized as to prevent internal dissent.[26] This combination of circumstances created intense sectional conflict within the churches. African American churches on the border followed a different path through sectional conflict, war, and Reconstruction. Their trajectory differs significantly from that of white border evangelicals and is therefore not the direct subject of this study. It is important to note, however, that the choices black evangelicals made during the crisis of war and Reconstruction played a key role in shaping sectionalism in white churches. White evangelicals, who considered black coreligionists their wards, did not anticipate the swift postwar withdrawal of black congregants. Their departure undermined the northern rationale for postwar missions to the South.[27]

This study is as concerned with ordinary ministers and lay leaders as it is with prominent denominational leadership. I have examined material from all ranks of church organizations. This literate group produced a wealth of written sources, ranging from private papers to published volumes. Their writings provide a window into how denominational organizations conceived of their relationship to section and to nation over the course of the nineteenth century. In the confines of private correspondence and on the pages of public journals, these men maintained lively debates over regional identity, the relationship between church and state, the demands of loyalty in wartime, and postwar denominational structure.

Local and denominational leaders were comparatively elite, all white, and mostly male. As such, they do not represent the entire range of religious expression in the border region. Indeed, historians have long recognized that women made up a majority of converts and church members during the Second Great Awakening.[28] As Ann Braude has argued, American religious history is distorted by the assumption of men as the norm despite the preponderance of women in organized religion. This distortion has been perpetuated by the fact that, in organized religion, men have had a "monopoly on institutional authority," even though women made up a numerical majority.[29] The congregations in this study were no exception; women belonged to border churches in greater numbers than did men. Male power—in denominational leadership, as clergy, and as lay leaders—depended upon the presence of women in the pews, especially during the war, when many men were absent for military service. However, as this is a work of institutional history, my subjects—those in positions of "institutional authority"—are almost entirely men. Certainly, women were involved in sectionalized conflict—as witnessed, for example by the thirty Southern Methodist women who, after the Civil War, occupied a Missouri church that was under Northern Methodist control and refused to leave, spending the day "knitting and sewing" in the pews.[30] Still, while pious women sometimes asserted their sectional affiliation publicly and frequently remarked privately on political matters, deliberation and decisions about denominational affiliation were recorded and made by men.

In addition to examining personal papers, letters, and diaries, I rely heavily on denominational newspapers published in the border region. Religious periodicals abounded in the nineteenth century. Edited by ministers or pious laymen, published daily or weekly, and intended for regional circulation, these publications commented extensively on events in the border churches. Although most were produced for a specific denominational readership, they were not official mouthpieces of the denomination itself. I also make use of theological reviews, intended for a scholarly readership. These journals were usually published by prominent theological seminaries and edited by nationally known figures.[31]

I consulted the minutes of major denominational organizations and nineteenth-century polemical histories produced by evangelicals, both of which provide information about how evangelicals responded to national political controversy, as well as debates and changes within their own churches. Methodists, in particular, generated a great deal of literature—first about their schism in the 1840s, and then in defense of each branch's behavior before, during, and after that conflict. (Robert L. Stanton's *The Church and the Rebellion* is an example of the genre.)

Within nineteenth-century evangelicalism, one can find a bewildering array of denominational differences and theological disputes. One great challenge in writing religious history is to strike the right balance between respecting the idiosyncrasies of each denomination and creating an accessible narrative that is useful to scholars who do not specialize in religion. I aim for the latter objective. Therefore, I gloss over some differences in terminology, deliberately simplify denominational branch names, and equate analogous—but not always identical—structures within different denominations.[32] Wherever possible, I use the general terms "northern" and "southern" to denote sectional branches. If some distinctive features are obscured by this approach, I hope my readers will agree that the narrative perspective gained is worth the sacrifice in detail.[33]

A Kingdom Divided begins in the 1830s, at the tail end of the Second Great Awakening. The first chapter establishes the significance of the border region in the period before North-South sectionalism dominated politics. During this period, many border residents identified as westerners. The West, centered on the Ohio Valley, symbolized the nation's future and was central to the evangelical plan to convert the nation. During the 1830s and early 1840s, evangelicals rushed to bring Christianity to the West, sending missionaries, distributing printed material, and building seminaries. As their empires grew, western evangelicals developed an identity distinct from that of their eastern brethren. The strain of this growth prompted the first partially sectional evangelical schism: the 1837 divide between Old and New School Presbyterians. Western development—educational institutions, property, and strong local ties—also made evangelical denominations vulnerable to emerging conflicts over slavery.

The Presbyterian schism of 1837 foreshadowed the sectional denominational divisions of the 1840s. Chapter 2 introduces the subsequent Methodist and Baptist schisms over slavery. Both national denominations divided into northern and southern branches because leaders could not agree on whether slave ownership constituted a sin. Northern and southern evangelicals prioritized their position on slavery over their commitment to denominational unity. In contrast, many border Methodists and Baptists—faced with divided congregations—prioritized church unity and argued that the slavery question was political, not a moral or theological matter. Therefore, they reasoned, discussion of the topic should be tabled to prevent division. But these border moderates could not halt a schism, nor could they forestall the strife and local upheaval that came with it. Out of this turmoil, some border evangelicals began to adopt and refine the doctrine of the "spirituality of the church." They argued that politics had no place in the pulpit.

After denominational division, local conflicts arose along the border between slave and free states. Chapter 3 describes how, once divided, these denominations struggled to demarcate the line dividing northern and southern churches. Christians with proslavery and antislavery sentiments worshipped together in the same congregations, shared membership in regional associations, and jointly administered church property. Northern evangelicals pushed south, and southerners pushed north in a flurry of lawsuits, violent confrontations, and underhanded maneuvers designed to assert control over the region. Local ministers fought for control of churches, newspapers, seminaries, meetings, and missionary resources. Antagonists on both sides located the root cause of the disputes in political questions, rather than in theological differences. Local conflicts exacerbated the division between northern and southern branches on the national level. In the border region, evangelicals acquired a greater appreciation of how local disputes could damage congregations and disrupt worship. These struggles contributed to an emerging border evangelical style defined by political neutrality and the doctrine of spirituality.

In the 1850s, mounting political controversy, generated by debates over the expansion of slavery, subsumed other matters in the churches. In chapter 4, I show how, as the nation drew closer to war, northern and southern evangelical leaders increasingly spoke out in support of either the Union or the Confederacy. Meanwhile, many evangelicals in the border region attempted to remain neutral. Neutrality was both a survival strategy and the product of theological opposition to mixing politics with religion. By the end of the decade, both branches of the Presbyterian Church divided between North and South.

In chapter 5, I argue that border evangelicals employed the idea of spirituality—developed during the antebellum schisms—to navigate wartime conflicts. During the Civil War, secular authorities contributed to the conflict and tension in border communities. Federal agents enforced displays of loyalty in northern and border churches. They targeted ministers who did not explicitly profess loyalty to the Union cause. This short-lived program of federal intervention included transferring church property from disloyal to loyal ministers and monitoring the patriotism of local church services. Military involvement that was intended to increase patriotism had the ironic effect of alienating border moderates from their northern brethren and generating more sympathy for southern denominations.

This trend continued into the postwar era. The combination of northern evangelical patriotism and support from secular authorities laid the groundwork for religious Reconstruction. Chapter 6 is an account of the unanticipated sectional conflicts among border-state evangelicals during this period. Initially, Union officials supported loyalty oaths, the redistribution of church property, and assistance with missions to freedpeople. Union authorities, however, did not have a long-term investment in supporting loyal churches and loyal ministers. Secular involvement encouraged northern evangelical plans for denominational reunion, and at the same time, it dashed border hopes that the churches would return to the prewar status quo. Evangelical reactions to Union victory profoundly shaped the American religious landscape in the postwar years.

Northern evangelicals did not rely solely on military assistance to begin religious Reconstruction. The most concerted efforts to ensure a shared political position among all northern-affiliated brethren came from within the churches. After the war, Union-sympathizing evangelicals viewed loyalty to the government as a divine mandate. Northern denominations sent missions to the South and to border states, attempting to establish churches for both white and black southerners. Bolstered by Union victory and secular support, northern evangelicals administered loyalty tests, imposed membership conditions, and confiscated property in regions suspected of disloyalty. This proved even more infuriating to border evangelicals than loyalty tests imposed by a secular authority. Ultimately, religious Reconstruction further alienated border evangelicals from the northern mainstream.

Chapter 7 concerns the religious realignment that took place in the final quarter of the nineteenth century. During this period, border evangelicals in all three denominations increasingly aligned with the southern churches. Realignment benefited the southern denominations, which had, after the war, struggled to defend their independence despite the abolition of slavery. Southern evangelicals had made claims to spirituality and a nonpolitical church, but their overt support for the Confederacy during the Civil War undermined these claims. However, since many border evangelicals had refused to publicly support either side during the war, southern churches found border history useful and adopted it as their own, along with the border evangelicals themselves. This realignment helps explain the strength and duration of the southern evangelical denominations, all of which lasted into the twentieth century, and sometimes beyond.

The final chapter traces the relationship between northern and southern branches after it became clear that reunion was not forthcoming. As the possibility of reunion receded, evangelicals in both sections sought to establish the "true" record of their sections' role in the conflict. Evangelical polemicists created sectionalized denominational histories—rich sources which historians have largely ignored. Southern books and articles recast denominational division as a matter of doctrinal difference, not as a defense of slavery. These narratives presented southern denominations as nonpolitical and "spiritual." Northerners also sought to create a flattering history of their role in the sectional conflict. Revisionist narratives cast mainstream northern evangelicals as heroic abolitionists. Both sides drew on the mid-century border conflict to support their arguments. As southerners perfected a defense of independence, northerners continued to seek rapprochement on northern terms. In this war of words, southerners defended their independence and successfully paved the way for the agreements that would preserve denominational autonomy into the coming century.

During the last quarter of the nineteenth century, all three major evangelical denominations formally established fraternal relations. This meant that northerners recognized the legitimacy and equal standing of the southern branches. The atmosphere of cooperation between northern and southern churches corresponded with a general spirit of reconciliation in the late nineteenth-century United States. However, these agreements led to even more deeply inscribed divisions between evangelicals in the two sections, and provided a home for an enduring strain of southern nationalism.

"Every kingdom divided against itself is brought to desolation; and every city or house divided against itself shall not stand."[34] Lincoln used this verse in his 1858 "House Divided" speech to help explain why the United States could not "endure, permanently, half slave and half free."[35] Steeped as they were in evangelical culture, Lincoln's listeners would have immediately recognized the reference. His use of scripture reminds us that, in the minds of American evangelicals, the United States was more than an earthly nation—it also embodied the divine promise of a Kingdom of God on earth. Robert L. Stanton, the Presbyterian who wrote the first history of the churches in the Civil War, hoped to see the United States "restored to those principles which were the glory of the earlier and better days of the Republic, and prepared for that great mission to which we have always fondly believed they were destined by the Ruler of the whole earth."[36]

Slavery and war divided the American Kingdom in the first half of the nineteenth century, and it remained divided well into the twentieth. Politically, the nation reunited and became one, but the imagined Christian Kingdom did not. At the heart of this book—and at the heart of religious reunion's failure—stand the evangelicals of the border states. They thought they had found a way to preserve the Kingdom: political neutrality and the spirituality of the church. But neutrality could not prevent the division of the churches before the war, and it could not eliminate strife during the war. Ironically, however, when adopted by the southern churches with which border evangelicals aligned during Reconstruction, spirituality did help southern denominations remain independent. This ensured that the rift in the Kingdom of God would outlast the circumstances that led to its formation.

— 1 —

WATCHMEN ON THE WALLS OF ZION

The Evangelical West

Cincinnati Methodist Thomas Morris knew he played a vital role in God's plan for the United States. "Providence has placed some of us as watchmen on the walls of Zion in the great 'Valley,'" he wrote in 1834. The Ohio Valley, Morris continued, "is already peopled with millions of fallen, yet rational beings; and. . . may be some day, as populous as the Chinese empire."[1] The region was indeed rapidly expanding. By the 1830s, the greater Ohio Valley boasted sufficient economic strength and a population large enough for its occupants to consider themselves distinct from their neighbors to the east.

White evangelical Christians in the Ohio Valley forged a particularly strong regional identity because of the West's strategic importance for their mission to evangelize the nation. The major evangelical denominations carried that mission into the West and created institutions to advance it in the Ohio Valley. The 1837 Presbyterian schism resulted from disputes over this effort to evangelize the West. In the 1830s, the possibility of sectional division between northern and southern evangelicals seemed remote. As evangelical churches took root and flourished in the West, clergy concentrated on winning the region for Christ. Eventually, however, the very growth and institution-building that made churches strong, swiftly growing, and popular also rendered them vulnerable to fractures over slavery and sectionalism.

Evangelical conceptions of the West as both symbol and site of the nation's future were of more significance than pinpointing its exact boundaries. Historians have defined the antebellum West in various ways—as a frontier, a border, an economic system, and a sphere for the growth of federal influence.[2]

For evangelicals, however, it was a physical space where national growth and Christ's cause were inextricably intertwined. Evangelism was patriotism. In the 1820s, evangelical interest thus focused on the Ohio Valley region.

The Ohio River begins in western Pennsylvania and flows westward to the Mississippi, forming part of the borders of what are now West Virginia, Ohio, Kentucky, Indiana, and Illinois. It drains most of Tennessee, parts of Maryland and Virginia, and small areas of other states. At the southern tip of Illinois, the Ohio joins the Mississippi, which flows south along the eastern border of Missouri. The Ohio River served as a natural extension of the Mason-Dixon Line, which had marked the border between Pennsylvania and Maryland—and the divide between slavery and freedom—since the eighteenth century. The Ohio River did not always demarcate a significant cultural divide, however. Residents of the western valley of the Ohio—both north and south of the river—shared much in common despite their different labor systems.[3]

In the late eighteenth century, the first white Americans arrived from the upland South to settle in the Ohio Valley region. Hailing from Virginia, Maryland and North Carolina, they moved westward and north into Tennessee and Kentucky, displacing Native American inhabitants. While southerners led the way, settlers from New England and the Mid-Atlantic states soon followed. Most of these immigrants were not large plantation owners. Rather, they sought to establish farms and gain the independence that came with land ownership.[4]

Yankees and southerners who had settled in the West did not forget their regional origins, but their common interests and frequent interactions gave rise to a new western ideal: "manly, politically astute, and egalitarian."[5] Several elements of western life helped to forge this identity. The Ohio River itself, as a transportation route and communication system, unified residents more than it divided them. In addition, westerners were drawn together by a common political culture that valued local control and rejected the elitism and paternalism associated with the East. Matthew Salafia argues that westerners "developed a regional counternarrative that emphasized a tradition of compromise" in contrast to both North and South. Westerners also united against the East to defend economic interests, such as access to markets through internal improvements and the need for access to banks and credit.[6]

White westerners on both sides of the Ohio River shared a racist anxiety about the growth of the black population in the region. This is not to say that western views of slavery were monolithic. Despite early talk of abolishing slavery in Kentucky, whites living south of the Ohio and in Missouri embraced the institution. For their part, many residents of free western states associated slavery with the eastern elite and opposed its expansion into the region. Most of all, they feared that slavery nearby would mean the presence of free blacks who would threaten the western ideal of an egalitarian white society. Westerners in free and slave states generally shared an abhorrence of free blacks and abolitionists—both threatened the existing racial hierarchy in the region. This fragile racist consensus could not withstand the sectional conflict of the late 1840s and 1850s.[7]

The region was hardly homogenous or static. Latent differences in the population never disappeared entirely and would eventually contribute to later conflicts. Nonetheless, a recognition of western distinctiveness—and a sense of being above the fray of sectionalism—survived into the middle of the century. "Say to the Northern and Southern cadets," wrote a Missourian to his son at West Point in 1858, "that you belong to *neither section*—that you are a true son of the great West."[8]

THE SECOND GREAT AWAKENING

From the 1790s to the 1830s, America's major evangelical denominations rapidly expanded during a tide of evangelism and revivals we now know as the Second Great Awakening. Both the deism that thrived among the Revolutionary generation and New England Calvinism lost ground to the energetic, upstart evangelicals, particularly Methodists and Baptists. Presbyterians also adopted evangelical tactics. By the end of the Second Great Awakening, Richard Carwardine argues, "evangelical Protestantism was the principal subculture in American society."[9] Unlike their Calvinist forebears, nineteenth-century evangelicals believed that through an experience of conversion—being "born again"—and living a continued life of morality, any sinner could achieve salvation and eternal life in heaven. The message of salvation for all greatly appealed to the unsettled and changing American population.[10]

Baptists, Methodists, and Presbyterians all shared an imperative to evangelize which inspired missions to the West. The Methodists were the most zealous and organized group to pursue this missionary mandate, and they did so with great success, helping to produce a pervasive evangelical culture in the United States. "Methodists," argues Nathan Hatch, "injected vernacular Christianity into the bloodstream of America, faith incarnate in popular culture." Methodism's power and appeal derived from the use of vernacular preaching to spread a message of grace: God did not predestine a select few to heaven and condemn all others to damnation. The use of popular language and the message of possible redemption for all appealed powerfully to nonelites and the emerging middle class.[11]

The spectacular growth and popularity of Methodism compelled other denominations to adopt Methodist missionary methods. These methods included the use of itinerant clergy and lively, emotional preaching—both of which helped to quickly form new congregations. Baptists and Presbyterians adopted these methods, and Methodists served as their "example, prod, and guide," argues Donald Matthews. "The constant visitation of evangelical preachers and their preaching the same values, norms, and vision of society throughout the United States helped create a distinct moral community."[12]

Missionaries from all three denominations placed particular emphasis on the importance of evangelizing the West and building institutions there. However, in the early years, it was difficult to obtain funds and secure ministers to take positions, and the denominations competed fiercely, sometimes in the face of local hostility. The internal organizational structure of each denomination—Presbyterian, Methodist, and Baptist—affected their responses to these challenges and the institutions they built. For this reason, it is worth discussing the structure of each group individually.

Methodists

Following the flood of conversions that took place during the Second Great Awakening, Methodists enjoyed enormous popularity. From 1820 to 1830, the number of Methodists in the United States doubled, rising from a quarter-million to a half-million adherents. By the middle of the nineteenth century, the denomination claimed 1.5 million members and was the largest religious organization in the country.[13] Part of this success was due to its hierarchical structure.

Methodist evangelism depended on the circuit rider, an itinerant preacher assigned to a set of communities within a region. These preachers rode these "circuits" on a regular basis, ministering to the people who lived in the area. This approach to evangelism was well suited to the sprawling Ohio Valley region. But by the 1830s and 1840s, the itinerant model began to wane as Methodism became more respectable and established. As towns grew and prosperous residents built handsome brick and stone churches, some larger communities were appointed permanent ministers. Nevertheless, the romantic vision of the hearty itinerant survived late into the nineteenth century, as did the effectiveness of the Methodist system of spreading religion.[14]

The circuit riders and ministers received their appointments from regional bodies called "conferences," which met once a year. These "annual conferences" did not necessarily follow political borders. Rather, they were designed to best meet the needs of the areas they served. This meant that the bounds of some of the conferences, particularly in the West, crossed state lines. The Ohio Conference, for example, included a large portion of western Virginia and only the southern half of Ohio itself. The Baltimore Conference contained most of Maryland, but also the central third of Pennsylvania and a generous portion of northern Virginia, while the Philadelphia Conference included eastern Pennsylvania, all of Delaware, and Maryland's eastern shore.[15]

A bishop presided over each annual conference. Bishops held the highest rank in the Methodist Church. Methodist bishops were active public figures who communicated regularly with one another. They traveled extensively to attend multiple conferences each year. At the 1852 General Conference, for example, Bishop Matthew Simpson reported, "It was arranged for me to take Western Virginia, Pittsburgh, and Erie Conferences and to accompany Bishop Janes to Ohio and Cincinnati and if convenient to Missouri and to go in fall of 1853 to California."[16] This Episcopal leadership structure knit the church together and formed the ties that connected North and South, making Methodism a truly national denomination.

Every four years, Methodist bishops and other prominent denominational figures convened for a General Conference, which made major decisions about doctrine and policy. The General Conference was one of the few nongovernmental assemblies that convened at the national level in the nineteenth century.[17] As such, the conference was one of the first places, outside of Congress, where conflict over slavery had material consequences.

Baptists

In the early decades of the nineteenth century, Baptist Church membership also flourished. Like the Methodists, the Baptists practiced an emotional, personalized faith, but they emphasized the primacy and centrality of individual congregations. This decentralized structure made organizing missions difficult. In the mid-eighteenth century, some Baptist congregations began to form regional associations for this purpose. Missionary associations did not have authority over their constituent congregations, which were at liberty to join and leave as they saw fit.[18] Still, Baptist congregations remained distrustful of centralized organizations in a way that Methodists, by virtue of their structure, were not.

The value of missionary associations soon became evident to wary congregations, however. In 1845, the General Association of Baptists in Kentucky sent an agent on a journey of 2,820 miles, during which he "visited about 30 counties, attended five associations," and collected nearly fifteen hundred dollars in contributions from formerly dubious Kentuckians. These funds were to be used to send missionaries to underserved parts of the state. The Kentucky Association served as a clearinghouse to assist in distributing the products of ecumenical religious presses. The association urged missionaries to sell inexpensive theological books and Baptist newspaper subscriptions to "as many families as possible." Missionaries also carried "religious tracts for gratuitous distribution among the destitute." All of these activities would have been impossible to coordinate at the congregational level.[19]

By the early nineteenth century, Baptists were keenly aware of the extraordinary success of the more hierarchically organized Methodists. In response, they introduced a new kind of organizational body: the society.[20] Reflecting their commitment to congregational autonomy, society members joined as individuals. Even so, Baptist evangelization was hampered by this aversion to national institutional organizations. For foreign missions, this problem was resolved in 1814 through the creation of the General Missionary Convention of the Baptist Denomination in the United States for Foreign Missions.

To coordinate missionary efforts across the nation, Baptists established the American Baptist Home Mission Society (ABHMS) in 1832. It organized funding and appointed missionaries within states and territories. Like earlier Baptist societies, the ABHMS was composed of individuals, not congregations, and did not oversee individual churches. By the 1830s, well-connected Baptist leaders met regularly at a convention that drew membership from across the nation.[21]

Presbyterians

Presbyterians—the oldest and most conservative of these three denominations—possessed the most centralized ecclesiastical structure. A single ruling body oversaw and communicated with every congregation. This ensured that Presbyterian theology remained comparatively consistent from region to region, even during the fervor of the Second Great Awakening. While not conducive to explosive popular growth, this strong, centralized government generated a well-connected, powerful, and highly literate Presbyterian elite.[22]

Although hierarchical, the Presbyterian system of government was largely democratic. The church, which constituted the smallest organized unit of government and worship, elected lay elders to govern the congregation along with the clergy. This governing body then elected certain ministers and ruling elders to serve as part of a presbytery—a local organization of ministers and lay elders that administered churches and resolved theological disputes. Presbyteries, for example the Presbytery of Louisville, oversaw the churches within a specified area or community.

Each presbytery belonged to a synod. These larger regional bodies, such as the Synod of Kentucky, generally corresponded with a state, territory, or missionary field and met annually. The General Assembly, which convened at a different location each year in May, was the highest governing body. At the General Assembly, the leading figures in every synod met in person to resolve theological and organizational questions.[23] The hierarchical Presbyterian chain of command, which replicated itself in miniature at each level, ensured uniformity of church proceedings across the vast and rapidly expanding nation. It also brought local issues to the attention of national leadership.

Nineteenth-century Presbyterians took particular pride in this system, celebrating it as "a fine specimen of a spiritual republic."[24] Presbyterians believed that their government most closely approximated the structure of Christ's true church. And, as custodians of a tradition they believed to have been handed down from the apostles, the Presbyterian ministers and ruling elders took seriously the task of preserving church doctrine and organization. To alter church structure was to second-guess Christ's plan.

Calvinism set nineteenth-century Presbyterians apart from other popular Protestant denominations. Presbyterians subscribed to the Westminster Confession of Faith, a Calvinist statement of belief in the doctrine of predestination, which held that faith did not assure salvation—man was saved by the grace of God alone. Under the terms of the confession, God determined who would receive eternal life, and no quantity of good works could affect this fate. The severity of this doctrine proved alienating to many potential converts, and in the first half of the nineteenth century some Presbyterian leaders, inspired by Methodist success, began to soften the strict tenets of the Confession of

Faith and even ordain ministers who did not adopt it. These changes led to schism as Presbyterians spread into the West.[25]

VISIONS OF A WESTERN MILLENNIUM

In 1845, New York newspaper editor John L. O'Sullivan proclaimed that it was the nation's "manifest destiny to overspread the continent allotted by Providence for the development of our yearly multiplying millions."[26] But even before he penned those famous words, national expansion and divine will were yoked in the American mind. Evangelicals along the Atlantic seaboard shared this high estimation of the importance of the West and focused institutional resources on the region. All three denominations invested the West with the potential to spark the conversion of the nation. To save the souls of the West for Christ was both to save the nation and to hasten the coming of the millennium. "The West—The Great West—are words of magic power, and wondrous import," wrote the Kentucky Baptist editor John Waller in 1844. "We look upon the West as among the most important and interesting missionary fields upon the earth," Waller continued, "pregnant with the greatest consequences to the kingdom of the Messiah."[27] A proponent of building western seminaries wrote, "we stand at a point of amazing interest in our country, and to the world—at the formation of the character of the Great West: the crisis of the destiny of its teeming millions perhaps for ages and ages."[28]

The millennial conviction that Christ would return to earth and reign over a thousand-year era of peace and perfection had long pervaded American religion. Most mainstream churches were postmillennialist—meaning they believed that Christ would return only after a period of Christian dominance on earth. As James Moorhead explains, nineteenth-century Protestants believed that "America was not merely an extrinsic token of the impending millennium, but an intrinsic instrument of its coming."[29] In postmillennial thought, therefore, it was of utmost importance to convert the American nation as it "overspread the continent." A vast nation of believers would be part of the golden age that would hasten the coming of Christ. Therefore, the evangelization of the West was a religious imperative, and an unconverted West was an obstacle to the millennium.[30]

The virulent anti-Catholicism of the period added additional urgency to competition for the West. Without Protestant churches regularly dotting the landscape, it seemed entirely possible that Jesuits could establish a foothold and destroy evangelical hopes for the region.[31] Presbyterian minister Lyman Beecher, who had moved from Boston to Cincinnati in 1832, provoked Protestant anxieties and spurred missionary zeal with his *Plea for the West.* Beecher cast the region as critical to the salvation of humanity and under siege by Catholicism. He believed the United States was "destined to lead the way in the moral and political emancipation of the world." Furthermore, "it is equally plain that the religious and political destiny of our nation is to be decided in the West. . . . the West is destined to be the great central power of the nation, and under heaven must affect powerfully the cause of free institutions and the liberty of the world." Beecher warned, though, that "the foreign emigrants whose accumulating tide is rolling in upon us" threatened this vital region. "THE CATHOLIC CHURCH IS ACCOUNTABLE," Beecher claimed, for "deeds of persecution and blood, JUSTIFIED BY THEIR PRINCIPLES and *perpetuated by Catholic power.*" This foreign "tide," under the sway of the "Catholic power," would overtake the West, dashing Protestant millennial hopes. Beecher's call to arms encouraged anti-Catholic violence as well as missionary fervor.[32] Although their numbers were far fewer, Mormons, who moved westward in response to local violence and hostility, also seemed to pose a threat to Protestant control of the West.[33]

A shared fear of Catholics and Mormons, however, could not quell interdenominational competition. Theoretically, all evangelicals desired a merger of denominations in the name of Christian unity. Christ himself had warned against the sin of schism and prayed of the churches "that they might be one; as thou, Father, art in me."[34] However, each denomination remained convinced that its own brand of Christianity best approximated the true church. It was one thing to desire unity—it was quite another to change one's practices in order to achieve it. "The union of all who love their Savior is an object which has engaged the attention of Christians for successive ages," a Kentucky Baptist editor wrote. However, "the followers of Zuinglius and Luther, of Calvin and Knox, of Cameron and Erskine, and of Whitfield and Wesley have much to do before they concur in common ground upon which to share the Lord's table."[35] Unsurprisingly, the editor proposed that other denominations change to become more like Baptists. In the face of denominational differences, each church rushed to stake claims in the West, and ministers and missionaries saw themselves as competitors for the salvation of the nation.[36]

"Among the *chief* evils threatening the cause of truth and the best interests of Zion is Methodism," an alarmed Presbyterian minister wrote. He warned against the "power for evil" that attended Methodism. "As an organization," he wrote, "it is almost as perfect and effective as that of the Jesuits," reflecting his suspicion of both Catholicism and the highly efficient Methodist system of expansion and church building.[37] "It is highly desirable that this field be occupied *now*," wrote George Brenhoke, another Missouri Presbyterian. "The Methodists, Baptists . . . appear to understand the advantages of pre-occupancy." Brenhoke cautioned against any slackening of Presbyterian efforts in his state and warned about "the schemes of the Methodists and Baptists." The stakes were high. "If they had all Missouri in their churches," he warned, "I fear there would be no millennium."[38]

These urgent millennial hopes and fears led eastern organizations to dedicate missionary resources to the West. And westerners themselves felt that the attention they received was well justified. One Kentucky Baptist proudly wrote, "The West is to us of more importance than any other portion of the earth—more even than the original thirteen states. The West is to sway our national destinies—the center of power is moving westward."[39] George Callanhan, a Methodist minister, reminded readers of the Cincinnati *Western Christian Advocate* in 1839 that God desired westerners to "spread the victories of his kingdom over the wide empires of the Earth."[40]

However, as the West developed, westerners began to resent eastern intrusions. One common complaint was that, while easterners were eager to fund missions to the underserved West, they were far less inclined to allow westerners themselves to direct how resources would be employed. "We lift up both of our hands and cry aloud against being always treated as a COLONY!" protested one editorial.[41] All the major denominations shared similar complaints.

Locals saw easterners as hopelessly different from the rugged, individual, yet spiritual, western population, which, as a Cincinnati Methodist put it, had "more pure and undefiled religion in a corncrib" then did eastern congregations."[42] By the late 1830s and 1840s, the population of the Ohio River Valley had grown large enough that residents could propose greater independence from eastern missionary aid. In 1840, a Louisville editorial called for "more efficient organization amongst Western Baptists" who "placed too much dependence on our Eastern brethren supplying our wants."[43] A Missouri congregation had dismissed a minister "on the grounds, that he was an abolitionist, Yankee, an Eastern man, with Eastern habits and did not suit the West, &c."[44] In 1840, the Kentuckian John Waller visited New York City and remarked of the Baptist leaders there that "they do not exactly understand the wants of the West."[45]

These men spoke with the voice of an emerging western evangelicalism.

Westerners wanted their own regional institutions and sought to establish newspapers, seminaries, and publishing houses. Through these efforts, western evangelicals amassed a considerable amount of property. The names of their endeavors—*Western Christian Advocate, Baptist Banner and Western Pioneer, Western Presbyterian, Western Christian Journal,* Western Methodist Book Concern, Western Baptist Theological Institute—all reflected their regional orientation. As one historian explains, "frontier preachers strove for every agency possessed by anyone else."[46] These institutions formed a network of people and ideas, through which the millennial vision of the evangelical West took concrete form. The institutions themselves made the idea manifest. Paradoxically, however, institutional strength become a weakness that fueled animosity when churches divided.[47]

THE WESTERN PRESS

The press was a powerful instrument for building a western evangelical identity and creating institutional networks.[48] During the first several decades of the nineteenth century, sectional evangelical newspapers flourished. The pages of western evangelical newspapers praised the robustness of western Christianity and the virtues of the region. Methodists in particular embraced periodicals, publishing numerous newspapers and journals. These papers, the *Christian Advocates,* took root in every major city in the Ohio Valley. The *Christian Advocates* carried news, both religious and secular, edifying articles, and scriptural pieces. "A *religious newspaper* would have been a phenomenon not many years since," remarked the editor of the *Methodist Magazine* in 1823. "But now the groaning press throws them out in almost every direction."[49]

The *Western Christian Advocate* provides an example of such success. It was founded in Cincinnati in 1834 to serve as "a religious paper of Methodist influence in the West." The first issue beseeched Methodists in the region to drum up "a large list of subscribers, with punctual payments," as well as "a large and rich variety of materials to fill its columns." To do otherwise, the editors warned, would be "to sleep at our posts, and incur the 'wo[e]' which the prophet applies 'to them who are at ease in Zion.'"[50] Readers apparently took these instructions to heart; by 1840, the paper had fifteen thousand subscribers.[51]

Sometimes the quantity of publications seemed almost nonsensical. "Dr. Elliott is beginning to think that we *have too many papers,*" fretted William

Hunter, the editor of the Pittsburgh *Christian Advocate*. Elliott edited the *Western Christian Advocate* and was "the Daddy of the whole of us," according to Hunter.[52] By 1848, Cincinnati was home to forty different religious periodicals. In 1834, Dr. Samuel Bolles estimated that the Baptist press had used "2500 reams of paper" in the printing of "7,000,000 pages" of Baptist literature. Nevertheless, the religious papers across the United States thrived. The New York *Christian Advocate and Journal* had the largest circulation of any newspaper in the world, with twenty-five thousand subscribers by 1830.[53]

Aside from their missionary purpose, journals and newspapers also strengthened institutional ties among northern, southern, and western evangelicals. And, like national denominational meetings, the newspapers became a forum in which sectional differences surfaced and conflicts first flared. Newspapers were central to the growth and coherence—and later the dissolution—of all three denominations. Reverend Phelps, a Maryland Methodist, estimated very highly "the *influence* of the periodical press—and the responsibility connected with its patronage. Phelps also worried about "the evils of a corrupt and licentious press."[54] Later, when denominational conflict arose, these newspapers became platforms for sectional attacks and recriminations.

Evangelicals' "infatuation with the printed word" involved more than just newspapers.[55] All three denominations maintained publishing houses that produced religious tracts. Itinerant clergy served as traveling salesmen of this modestly priced Christian reading material. These salesmen were a staple feature of the evangelical West. David Paul Nord argues that their efforts produced "a frontier of publication" that drew together far-flung readers through literary consumption. Sales of evangelical texts in turn helped fund evangelical growth in the West.[56]

The most successful antebellum evangelical publishing operation was the Methodist Book Concern—a combined printing press, publishing house, and distribution system. Based in New York City, the Book Concern was originally established at the 1789 Methodist General Conference. Despite a rocky start, it blossomed in the new century as tireless Methodist itinerants marketed books on their rounds, and it became "Methodism's most effective agency in the general education of its people."[57] By 1836, the concern was worth $250,000.[58] One historian deems the New York concern the single most financially successful denominational publisher of the nineteenth century.[59]

Asserting their regional interests, westerners called for a Book Concern of their own, "to meet the wants and wishes of the brethren of the West."[60] Thus, in 1820, the Methodist General Conference established a publishing house known as the "Western Book Concern" in Cincinnati, Ohio. It was designed to operate in tandem with the New York Book Concern.[61] The Cincinnati Concern began as a small affair. One minister sentimentally recalled that it was the size of "the log cabins of our fathers." But soon it too had expanded and could "send out work that loses nothing from comparison with any other west of the mountains."[62] In 1836, the Western Concern, with the approval of the General Assembly, purchased a "large and eligible lot" in Cincinnati and began construction of a "substantial" brick edifice to house the booming establishment.[63]

WESTERN SEMINARIES

In addition to newspapers and publishing houses, western evangelicals also desired their own regional educational institutions. They were particularly keen to establish western seminaries, since seminary graduates were thought to make better ministers. Kentucky Presbyterian Joel Lyle recalled with displeasure the "ranting and fanaticism of ignorant preachers" who had not attended seminaries. He noted approvingly that "now all the leading denominations seem to be vying with each other to excel in making learned preachers. The Baptists and the Methodists see they cannot get along without learned preachers."[64] Lyle's comments reflect the broader secularization of evangelical denominations and the general rise of middle-class respectability following the emotional enthusiasm of the Second Great Awakening.[65] They indicate the centrality of seminaries to the project of creating an evangelical West.

Seminary-building became a source of regional pride and spurred interdenominational competition in the West. Ohio Methodist Lucian Berry, the future president of Indiana Asbury University, fretted about Methodism's late entry into founding seminaries. "I have no little anxiety that the Methodist Church should be represented both in talents and numbers," Berry remarked of an upcoming education convention. He feared that, without a Methodist presence, Presbyterians would "convince scores of persons in the Legislature . . . that Presbyterians have all the talent."[66]

Millennial hopes, sectional pride, the formalization of preaching styles, and interdenominational competition all contributed to the proliferation of religious educational institutions in the West. For example, in 1827, Presbyterians founded Hanover College in southern Indiana and, two years later, established Lane Seminary outside Cincinnati. In 1822, Methodists from Ohio and Kentucky cooperated to establish Augusta College in northern Kentucky along the Ohio River, and Methodists opened Indiana Asbury (now DePauw) in 1837. Like publishing houses, seminaries required a tremendous outlay of capital and extensive institutional organization, and they were valuable assets to the denominations. They could also generate conflict because stakes were so high: as a training ground for leaders, seminaries could shape the future of the denomination. Seminary graduates became newspaper editors and college presidents—often both—as they pursued careers in church leadership.[67]

The Western Baptist Theological Institute exemplifies evangelical motivations for founding seminaries in the West and the challenges such projects faced. The story of the Institute begins in 1833, when a rush of sectional zeal inspired the formation of the Western Baptist Convention. "The grand ultimate object" of this convention was to promote "the cause of Christ, as connected with the interests of the Baptist Denomination in the Western States."[68] During its first meeting, the convention created the Western Baptist Education Society, whose purpose was "the establishment of a theological institution in some central portion of the Mississippi valley."[69] The Education Society resolved to construct "an institute designed for the benefit of the whole West."[70]

All agreed, in principle, with the idea of founding an institute for the whole region. But the proposed location of the institute was in contention. Which state should be home to the seminary? While the vision of a united evangelical West had prompted the formation of the Western Baptist Education Society, the members of that society were sensitive to the potential fault line that crossed the region: the border between slavery and freedom. They were eager to keep this political divide from threatening the cohesion of western Baptists. In his recollection of the first Baptist Convention meeting in 1833, John Stevens recalled a deliberate sanction against discussion of "*everything which might awaken prejudice and opposition*. . . . And hence, especially every allusion and every topic was studiously avoided which might awaken the mutual prejudices and antipathies of North and South."[71]

The Education Society sought a location that would please Baptist constituents from the Northwest and the Southwest. It found a solution in a parcel of Kentucky land lying directly across the Ohio River from the booming city of Cincinnati, Ohio. Covington lay on Kentucky soil, but was essentially part of the city of Cincinnati. Society members congratulated themselves on their choice: "Kentucky will feel pleased that it is hers; Ohio will feel pleased that it is hers; while, in fact, *it belongs to neither; but it is to be looked upon as a great institution, devised for the benefit of the West.*"[72] The society, however was long on vision but short on funds. Before its doors could open, its founders faced the challenge of raising an endowment.

For a decade, individual fundraising agents traveled the West, urging the faithful to subscribe to the new venture in Baptist education. In 1840, while Baptists worked to raise the endowment money, the Kentucky legislature granted a charter to the Western Baptist Theological Institute. The institute opened its doors in 1845.

PRESBYTERIAN SCHISM OF 1837

Institution-building endeavors such as seminaries, missionary organizations, newspapers, and publishing houses created an evangelical West. However, they also placed demands on denominational infrastructure. Methodists and Baptists flourished in this environment. The more conservative Presbyterian denomination did not adapt so easily. Presbyterianism foundered amid the social changes and expansion of the Second Great Awakening. The lure of the unconverted West and the power of revivals led some Presbyterians to adopt evangelical techniques. The renowned revivalist Charles Grandison Finney, for example, began his career as a Presbyterian and generated tremendous religious enthusiasm in the 1820s and 1830s. However, conservative Presbyterian theologians looked askance at his emotional preaching style and his rejection of certain Calvinist principles. While Finney eventually abandoned the Presbyterian Church in 1835, his success as an evangelist contributed to a rift in the denomination.[73]

Presbyterians who embraced the emotional, enthusiastic style associated with Methodists clashed with those who rejected it. This conflict established an internal division between conservative (Old School) and liberal (New School) Presbyterians. New School Presbyterians were more open to uneducated lay preaching, emotional displays, women speaking in public, and antislavery activity. Adherents were willing to sacrifice some doctrinal purity to capitalize on the opportunities for growth these social changes offered. In contrast, James Moorhead explains, "the Old School sought to claim a smaller domain but one with more secure boundaries."[74]

Presbyterians differed over three strategies used to help develop the evangelical West. First, while New School Presbyterians accepted reinterpretations of the Westminster Confession of Faith designed to appeal to a broader audience, Old School leaders rejected this relaxation of Calvinist standards. New School Presbyterians displayed less concern over the maintenance of Calvinist purity and more distress over divisions between the Christian churches of the world, which violated the "fundamental doctrine of Presbyterianism, that the Church is *one*."[75] Second, Old and New School Presbyterians also disagreed over cooperation with nondenominational Christian organizations. Old School Presbyterians abhorred involvement in these organizations, which, they argued, sacrificed theological soundness and wasted resources on ameliorating earthly existence when true Christian duty lay in saving the immortal soul. In contrast, New Schoolers were eager to join in "moral reform" ventures and "interdenominational cooperation" with other Christian institutions.[76]

Finally, extensive debate revolved around joint pastoral appointments with other denominations. The Presbyterian Church had long collaborated with Congregationalists, especially in the West, where people could not afford to be particular about which denomination supplied their minister. The 1801 Plan of Union with Congregationalists, for example, authorized missionary cooperation and shared funds for the West. By the early nineteenth century, some Synods accepted Congregationalist members who continued to follow Congregationalist practices. These cooperative endeavors helped Presbyterians compete with the more charismatic Methodists, but they ultimately led to schism. Old School leaders feared that the denomination had sacrificed doctrinal purity in the name of growth. At the 1837 General Assembly, a slim Old School majority voted to repudiate the Plan of Union and expelled synods who appeared to have compromised Calvinist standards.[77] Presbyterians thus formally divided into the New and Old Schools.

Each school represented one of two distinct strands of Presbyterian doctrine. The New School, expansionist and inclusive, admitted change and valued the incorporation of the greatest possible number of souls into Christian unity over doctrinal purity. The Old School, internalist and exclusive, favored the maintenance of secular distinctiveness and tradition over the expansion of the church.[78] Many western Presbyterians longed for a neutral position. "I cannot go with the New School Presbytery—and I do not well relish the Old School Assembly," wrote one Presbyterian.[79] A preacher from Palmyra, Missouri, wrote that he was "heartily disapproving" of the division. Still, he felt, "I cannot at present unite with the Old School Synod."[80] Fincelius Gray, an itinerant Presbyterian missionary who preached in Missouri and Kentucky, declared that he was "with those of a middle ground." He believed that much acrimony could be avoided if all concerned did not "make too much noise" about the points of difference between Old and New School Presbyterians.[81]

While "the slavery question" fueled acrimony in the Presbyterian schism, it was not the sole cause of division, as would be the case in the Baptist and Methodist schisms that came a decade later. Both older tension raised by western evangelization and rising conflicts over slavery fueled acrimony between the two schools within the Presbyterian Church. James Moorhead argues that it is "misleading" to draw "a sharp distinction between concern for proper doctrine" and disputes over slavery. Old School Presbyterians shared a "common fear . . . rooted in the entire range of intellectual, religious, cultural, social, and political changes of the 1830s. It was an anxiety that legitimate authority was under assault and collapsing."[82] Prominent Louisville Presbyterian Robert J. Breckinridge, for example, favored the Old School, arguing that "some central body or individual must wield the power."[83] Still, the split relieved tensions over slavery: the New School tended to attract Presbyterians who were not opposed to admitting antislavery members, while the Old School attracted Presbyterians who opposed any discussion of slavery and emancipation. In the West, along the border between slavery and freedom, many Presbyterians ultimately joined the Old School.

If the two new Presbyterian branches that emerged in 1837 could not be easily identified as either proslavery or antislavery, they did separate the extremes of belief within the Presbyterian Church, relieving latent hostility that might otherwise have led to a sectional division. Both branches continued to draw on a national membership until the Civil War—but "the majority of Presbyterian Abolitionists . . . cast their lot with the New School."[84] Likewise, many Presbyterians, like one Missouri minister, characterized the Old School as "in favor of the *divine right of slavery*."[85] The conflict over the 1837 schism gave western Presbyterians living close to the border between slavery and freedom a sense of the tremendously divisive potential of the slavery controversy.

SLAVERY, ABOLITION, AND RACISM IN THE WEST

The boundary between slave and free states was a latent fault line beneath early nineteenth-century evangelical endeavors in the West. Slavery was prohibited in Ohio, Illinois, and Indiana, but it was legal south of the Ohio River and in Missouri. The presence of a fixed border between slavery and freedom suggests that views of slavery north and south of the Ohio diverged sharply.

This was far from the case, however. Rather, the prevailing white attitudes toward slavery in the region are best summarized as either mild support or mild opposition to slavery, paired, in either case, with intense antiblack racism. The West boasted both abolitionists and outspoken slavery supporters, but they did not represent the majority view.[86]

Before the cotton boom, enthusiasm for expanding slavery into the West was at a low ebb. During this period, a conservative strain of abolitionism—favoring gradual emancipation and colonization—briefly surfaced in parts of the upper South, but it drew the most support from white racists "who had a profound aversion to the Negro," even in the role of slaves.[87] In the same vein, the Missouri and Kentucky legislatures of the 1830s and 1840s debated laws for gradual emancipation, coupled with deportation of free black residents. These conservative abolition efforts, however, did not lead to any legislative action.[88]

In fact, slavery was already enmeshed in the upper South. There were relatively few large plantations in Kentucky or Missouri, and the region was too far north to produce cotton. However, the area was suited to the production of hemp, and plantations in Kentucky and Missouri raised this material, which southerners used to bale cotton. Slavery and white supremacy were therefore deeply embedded in the border region, even if plantation agriculture did not dominate the landscape. Modern scholars dismiss the notion that slavery in the border and upper South was "milder" than slavery elsewhere in the South, even if it was different. Enslaved people tended to live and work on smaller farms and had closer everyday contact with their owners (a situation that could often bring additional difficulties for slaves). Masters also frequently "hired out" slaves to people who needed labor. This system gave nonslaveholders a stake in the institution.[89]

For their part, most white westerners in free states did not welcome either abolitionists or free black residents. In Ohio, for example, the 1804 and 1807 "Black Laws" restricted free black employment options and voting rights and mandated that all free African Americans post a prohibitively expensive five-hundred-dollar bond. Residents of Indiana and Illinois enacted similar laws. Some of those who lived north of the Ohio River even welcomed the idea of extending slavery into their states in order provide labor for corn farms. White Ohioans, Illinoisans, and Indianans made it perfectly clear in the first three decades of the nineteenth century that, while they did not want slavery in their state, neither did they want free black residents.

This attitude formed the basis of the western free-soil ideology that would flower as the century progressed.[90]

At the national level, views of slavery began to diverge. After 1804, emancipation plans were in place in every northern state.[91] As gradual emancipation slowly diminished the already small population of enslaved people in the North, slavery flourished along with cotton in the South. These demographic and economic shifts led to increasingly opposed attitudes regarding slavery in the North and the South. Nevertheless, a majority of residents in the West—in slave states and in free states—continued to harbor mildly proslavery or antislavery sentiments and a deep racism against African Americans. In addition, they shared a growing antipathy toward abolitionists, who were regarded as dangerous troublemakers in both slave and free states.[92]

Initially, these tempered views on slavery and abolitionists were shared by a majority of the members of the Baptist, Methodist, and Presbyterian churches nationwide. Most evangelicals were mildly antislavery but objected more strenuously to abolitionism than to slavery.[93] No matter what private opinions a northerner may have held about slavery, the activities of abolitionists usually seemed a greater threat to the church than the membership of slave owners ever would.

"The Methodist church will *never* be divided by the abolitionists—*never!*" wrote northern Methodist LaRoy Sunderland. "We go for the whole Church—we *dread* a division."[94] One Kentucky Baptist complained that, when he made his antislavery views known, he was shunned and felt "the weight of abolition intolerance."[95] In Cincinnati, a Methodist minister "could not have his license renewed because he is an Abolitionist."[96] An Illinois Presbyterian described his "objections against the anti-slavery agitation" in 1837. "We are too weak for it," he explained. "It seems to me like loading a piece of artillery with a charge too great."[97]

Active moral opposition to slavery—the conviction that slaveholding or profiting from slavery constituted a sin—was a minority position within the evangelical churches of the 1830s and 1840s. Most would have agreed with a Pennsylvania Methodist who explained, "I think holding property in man is not *necessarily* sinful, but at the same time [it is] *dangerous*."[98] Similarly, southern evangelicals, while proslavery, were not, at this point, strenuously so. In sum, neither northerners nor southerners commonly held that slavery was actually a sin—they may have diverged in the degree to which it was undesirable, but these sectional differences posed no immediate threat to denominational unity across the North and South.

When abolitionists within each denomination began to demand more explicit condemnation of slavery, however, southerners responded by demanding denominational approval of slavery. In response, national organizations of each church changed their strategies and adopted a policy of avoiding the subject of slavery and explicitly condemning abolitionists. Consequently, during the first four decades of the nineteenth century, many abolitionists split from the main branches of their denominations.[99]

The gradual departure of the most ardent abolitionists from the mainstream evangelical churches in the 1820s and 1830s muted conflict over slavery in those years. Since the late eighteenth century, abolitionists within the Methodist Church had put pressure on the General Assembly to condemn slavery. The majority backlash against the abolitionist (Wesleyan) Methodists prompted their complete withdrawal from the General Assembly by 1842.[100] Likewise, the divide between the Old and New Schools relieved tensions in the Presbyterian Church.

Baptist conflicts over slavery during the first three decades of the nineteenth century tended to occur on the congregational level, in keeping with their denominational structure. In these conflicts, individual congregations split over the question of slavery's sinfulness.[101] Abraham Lincoln's family moved from Kentucky to Illinois in 1809, prompted in part by conflict over slavery in the South Fork Baptist Church, where his parents were members. Siding with the antislavery wing, Lincoln's parents "went out of the church on account of slavery."[102] In the 1820s and 1830s, debates over abolitionism and the sin of slavery in the church tended to be localized and did not override all other areas of conflict. Still, discord over slavery was already a component, if not yet the direct agent, of disunion in national denominational organizations.

THE LIMITS OF THE EVANGELICAL WEST

In the 1830s, the evangelical West reached its peak—both as an idea and as a network of institutions and investments. During this time, residents of the Ohio Valley region saw themselves as different from easterners, both North and South. Evangelicals argued that the West was essential to the nation's future. They insisted that the evangelization of the region was the key to the conversion of the nation and the coming of the millennium. Evangelicals in the West also argued that the people of their region had spiritual needs that differed from those to the East and that these needs warranted separate regional institutions. Westerners invested great sums in missionary projects, regional publishing houses, and seminaries. Tensions over slavery and abolition were present in the evangelical West, but did not fracture regional unity. In fact, while denominational conflict and division would overshadow regional identity later during the events of the 1840s and again in the 1860s, the sense of difference from the East never entirely disappeared.

White evangelicals in the West generally shared a conviction that abolitionism was a great evil. However, in the churches, sectional tension increased as abolitionists denounced slaveholders, and southerners responded with demands for an unequivocal statement that slavery was not a sin. The major evangelical denominations were among the few national organizations in this period. When they convened, people from the North, South, and West regularly came into direct contact. In these instances, regional differences in belief about slavery, abolition, and sin were too pronounced to ignore.

— 2 —

THE GREAT SECESSION

Slavery and Schism on the Religious Border

Through the winter of 1844 and the spring of 1845, Henry Bascom's pen seldom rested. That spring, he had participated in the 1844 Methodist General Conference, where he signed an address declaring that "the Southern Conferences are to have a distinct and independent organization of their own, in no way subject to Northern jurisdiction."[1] Having signed on behalf of the Kentucky Conference, however, Bascom now faced the challenge of persuading the members of that conference that a "distinct and independent" organization was really desirable. As the rhetorical bluster faded, Bascom, a former circuit rider who was now president of Transylvania University in Lexington, Kentucky, surveyed his region with concern. Among his coreligionists, quite a few deplored the division of 1844 and remained skeptical of Bascom's claim that "the separation proposed is *not* schism, it is *not* secession."[2]

Through that anxious summer, Bascom kept up a correspondence with Reverend William Wightman of South Carolina, who also favored division. Bascom did not fail to remind Wightman that, ensconced in his southern stronghold, he need never fear for his state's loyalty to the cause of the new southern organization. Bascom however, living on the border, dared not rest, as he feared "the whole tribe of Northern writers might have a chance to destroy the effort of my work before the Convention." His work concerned "the whole border section, from Maryland to Missouri." Bascom wrote, "I leave no item of importance untouched and I feel some confidence in the result. Still I need some assistance."[3] His efforts included authoring a book, *Methodism and Slavery,* in which he insisted that "Northern prejudice, on the subject of slavery" drove the church apart. Prior to this rising prejudice, Bascom argued, Methodists from all sections had practiced "mutual concession and forbearance" regarding slavery in order to "prevent division and ruin."[4] Bascom feared that, if they did not win the border, the campaign for a separate, Southern Methodist Church would fail.

Several months later, Matthew Simpson, a tirelessly active Methodist minister residing in Indiana, also traveled the border region, making his way to the very conference for which Bascom had so assiduously prepared. Simpson, like Bascom, was an educator who would become an editor and a bishop. He had opposed the division of the Methodist Church in 1844. But, in the months following, it was clear that division was inevitable, so he now worked against Bascom to keep the Kentucky Conference affiliated with the North. Simpson expressed uncertainty over how to interpret border sentiments regarding slavery and schism. In his diary, he recorded his varied impressions. He hopefully asserted, "the antislavery feeling seems to be deepening and widening." Simpson recalled meeting with a man who declared, "sink or swim, live or die, survive or perish, I will throw myself into the antislavery movement in Kentucky." Simpson next visited a Methodist publishing house in Cincinnati, only to learn that "a strong feeling in favor of the South has prevailed." Simpson considered the implications: "If the feeling continues to increase at the same ratio for two or three years more, the line of *feeling* will be deep and broad between the North and South."[5] Bascom's and Simpson's divergent encounters reflect how debates over slavery divided denominations into northern and southern branches, polarized western evangelicals, and frayed their regional unity. These conflicts highlighted the divide between freedom and slavery that ran through the region. The schisms of the 1840s transformed the evangelical West into an evangelical border.

Churches were among the first American institutions to feel the divisive power of the slavery question. All three major evangelical Protestant denominations experienced sectionalized conflict between northern and southern members during the 1840s and 1850s. Methodists and Baptists divided into separate sectional branches. The process of division, which was straightforward in the North and South, became a protracted and troublesome affair in the border region. These divisions reshaped evangelical denominations.

Border communities and congregations experienced physical manifestations of the national tension much sooner than did their counterparts in the North or South. These conflicts, whether originating among congregants, in the pages of the religious press, or among esteemed church leaders, displayed certain common characteristics. Antagonists tended to attribute instability and conflict within the church to political pressure and influence from the outside—from either abolitionists or defenders of slavery. Disputes most often resulted in a breakdown of regional denominational bodies in the border region.

Inhabitants of the border attempted to downplay dissention and avoid discussion of slavery and abolition in favor of denominational unity. Many border residents viewed themselves as intermediaries between irrational actors in the North and the South. During the same summer that the Reverends Bascom and Simpson concerned themselves with the proceedings of Kentucky Methodists, a convention of Kentucky Baptists faced a similar denominational division. Foreshadowing regional political trends of the 1850s, they resolved that "the Baptists of Kentucky, and of the West generally, occupy a position between the North and the South, which imposes weighty responsibilities; and we should see to it that we do nothing that will increase the strife, already existing by reason of those who delight in agitation."[6] For these and other border evangelicals, the debate was less about human liberty or the morality of slavery than it was about preserving harmony in the church (an end many defended as a moral imperative).[7]

Western evangelicals may have sought to avoid divisive slavery debates during the 1840s, but evangelicals in other parts of the nation raised the question—and the specter of schism. At the national level, leaders in all three denominations recognized that slavery debates in national meetings created dangerous fissures in denominational unity—but the strength of feeling on both sides rendered compromise on the topic unachievable. American Methodists divided sectionally in 1844. Baptists followed suit in 1845. Even Presbyterians engaged in contests between Old and New School adherents—and within each school—over slavery and abolition. In 1845, after eight tense years of debate, Old School Presbyterians overwhelmingly voted that they could not exclude slave owners or pass legislation condemning slavery in the future.

The schisms of the 1840s demonstrated that national religious organizations could not withstand debates over slavery and abolition. The lessons to be learned were these: A church could be wholly abolitionist or entirely proslavery in the antebellum political climate. But it could not accommodate both views. A debate over slavery was incompatible with preserving the unity of the church. For those who feared division, then, allowing abolitionism in the church was a greater threat than slavery itself.

To approach slavery from this perspective required the assumptions that slavery was a purely political, this-worldly issue, not a problem with moral or theological dimensions.[8] This view of slavery could only be sustained if one also believed that the churches should not play a role in ameliorating material conditions in this world. In other words, the church had no place promoting equality and freedom, or opposing racism and slavery. In theory, this was neutrality. In practice, it was proslavery. Despite the efforts of abolitionists, the laws of the United States protected slavery. Avoiding debates of the subject would help to keep slavery alive.

METHODIST RUPTURE

Both denominational schisms of the 1840s developed out of conflict over slave-owning clergy. Since 1796, Methodists, in a concession to "localism," granted each Annual Conference the authority to determine the qualifications for admission to official positions within the church. Therefore, within slaveholding states, ministers and lay members could own slaves. Most clergy avoided slave ownership, and the buying and selling of slaves by bishops was prohibited. But many Methodists in the South owned, bought, and sold slaves throughout the first half of the nineteenth century.[9]

During the 1830s, as Methodist abolitionism expanded in the North, opposition to abolitionism increased as well. Abolitionists, unlike the antislavery Methodists who stopped at the belief that slavery was sinful, called for a change in political and legal institutions outside the church, even if it meant disruption. "Are there no interests to be consulted besides the peace of the Church?" asked Orange Scott, a Methodist abolitionist. Scott argued that the Methodist Church should not "give herself any peace till she cleanses the skirts of her garment from 'blood guiltiness!' . . . If public opinion is wrong, it ought to be braved."[10] When abolitionists periodically brought their cause to the Methodist General Conferences in the 1820s and 1830s, they were rebuffed with the argument that the church had no place disputing slavery in states where the institution was legal.[11] The conferences resisted issuing a general censure against slavery or slave ownership. At the 1836 General Conference in Cincinnati, for example, delegates resolved "that they are decidedly opposed to modern abolitionism and wholly disclaim any right, wish, or intention to interfere in the civil and political relation between master and slave."[12] The message of the 1836 conference rang loud and clear: abolitionism, not slavery, posed the greatest danger to the unity of the church.[13]

Four years later, when the 1840 General Conference convened in Baltimore, little had changed in the majority attitude toward slavery. Again responding to petitions from abolitionists, the pastoral address defined slavery as a political, not a theological, matter. Charles Elliott, a Cincinnatian who opposed denominational division, remarked, "The General Conference is an assembly of Christian pastors, not of legislators; [it is] not authorized to make laws."[14] This construction of the problem, it was hoped, would prevent a ruling on the moral propriety of slaveholding. Such a conclusion satisfied border residents like Elliott. But for those determined to resolve the moral dilemma, this sort of evasion was unsatisfying.

Condemnation of abolitionism had been intended as part of a moderate, conciliatory strategy, but it did nothing to appease the two most deeply opposed groups within the Methodist Episcopal Church: abolitionists and those who owned slaves or ministered to slaveholders. In this early trial, the middle road proved ineffectual—although Methodist conservatives, who desired denominational unity, continued to promote it. Prolonged arguments over the sinfulness of slavery persisted, exasperating those who valued the unity of the church. Reverend James Flay compared Methodist abolitionists to "the bird that fouls its own nest." Flay continued, "Did not our Bishop advise us *wholly to refrain* from any intermeddling with this matter?"[15] Far better, Flay reasoned, to classify abolition as a political question about private property than to take a direct stand on the issue.[16]

Until well into the Civil War, moderate border Methodists continued to hope that "intermeddling" could be avoided. Charles Elliott blamed abolitionists for unrest among Methodists. As long as the abolitionists remained within the main branch of the Methodist church, the major fault line in the denomination lay between abolition and anti-abolition parties.[17] During the 1830s and 1840s, most Methodists, North and South, agreed that abolitionism was wrong. James Flay ruefully remarked that he had lost influence within the church after being unjustly "tainted with the bloodied principles of Abolition."[18]

Following the 1840 conference, abolitionist Methodists—thwarted in their attempts at reform from within—chose the purity of their theological convictions over the unity of the church. By 1842, the abolitionist wing of the Methodist Church had been expelled or withdrawn from the General Conference.[19] But their departure did not result in the hoped-for harmony. Rather, it narrowed the spectrum of acceptable opinions on slavery among mainstream Northern Methodists. Those who were only mildly antislavery came to occupy, de facto, the extreme position regarding the institution.[20] Ironically, without a shared distaste for abolitionists to hold the conference together, national sectional division swiftly severed Methodists in slaveholding states from those in free states. The spark that triggered sectional divide—the first among American evangelical denominations—was the second marriage of a slaveholding bishop.

In 1844, Bishop James O. Andrew, a resident of Georgia, owned at least fourteen slaves. Andrew and other Southern Methodists claimed that he had unwillingly come to own these people through remarriage and remembrance in a will. In reality, while the state laws of Georgia did prohibit emancipation, Andrew had owned slaves since the 1830s and continued to do so for the rest of his life. Andrew might not have violated local conventions, but northern members of the conference were perturbed by the idea of a slave-owning bishop presiding over Methodists in free states. This case challenged the "localism" compromise by elevating a slaveholder to a national office.[21]

The Andrew case was the sensation of the 1844 General Conference. Still, attendees avoided direct discussion of the sinfulness of slavery. Instead, in a structure redolent of secular language surrounding federalism, they framed their debates around the question of whether the General Conference had ultimate authority over the appointment of bishops. If the conference had this authority, it could, with its northern majority, remove Andrew from the episcopacy. Northeasterners, styling themselves as the Conference Party, favored this solution. In contrast, the majority of southerners and westerners—the Constitution Party—claimed that the bishops themselves held joint power with the conference, meaning that the General Conference party could not dictate who could or could not serve as a bishop.

Northerners encouraged Andrew to resign, citing the interests of peace and unity. But southerners argued that Andrew's resignation would set a precedent that would make it impossible for southerners to remain within the church. Ultimately, the General Conference delegates voted that Bishop Andrew should relinquish his office as long as he owned slaves.[22] The decision fell short of a definitive statement for or against the sinfulness of slavery, but was enough to sever the increasingly tenuous bonds of the Methodist Church. Southern Methodist leaders met in Louisville in May of 1845 to organize a separate Southern Methodist Church.

Throughout the dispute, border Methodists displayed an "anxiety for consensus," again raising a cry against the divisive question and remaining "anxious to prevent strife by preventing schism."[23] John McClintock, a border resident, wrote, "I can hardly keep down my indignation at Bishop Andrew for involving the church in such a difficulty with his eyes open. He might, like an honorable man, to have resigned."[24] McClintock took no issue with Andrew owning slaves per se. Rather, he directed his outrage at the fact that Andrew had brought this controversial issue to the General Conference. Causing discord, not owning slaves, was the true offense.[25]

In anticipation of such a divide, Northern and Southern Methodists had begun work on a "Plan of Separation" that would dictate the terms of sectional division within the denomination. The Plan of Separation was a unique document among sectional denominational divisions: Methodists attempted to preempt the problems arising from schism should such an event occur. Despite good intentions, the plan was a fiasco. It led to drawn-out property disputes and contributed to much of the border unrest that followed division.[26] The plan provided for two things: it called for the equitable division of property between the two branches, and it determined the border between them. The latter concern was addressed in a single, disastrously ambiguous paragraph:

> The following rule shall be observed with regard to the Northern boundary of such connection: all the societies, stations, and Conferences adhering to the Church in the South, by a vote of the majority of the members of said societies, stations, and Conferences, shall remain under the unmolested pastoral care of the Southern Church; and the ministers of the Methodist Episcopal Church [North] shall in no wise attempt to organize churches or societies within the limits of the Church South, nor shall they attempt to exercise any pastoral oversight therein; it being understood that the ministry of the South reciprocally observe the same rule in relation to stations, societies, and Conferences bordering on the line of division, and not to the interior charges, which shall in all cases be left to the care of that church within whose territory they are situated.[27]

It must have seemed a simple and fair proposition to the creators: individual congregations and local bodies on the border between the northern and southern branches would hold a vote to decide upon their affiliation.

But the plan contained two false assumptions. First, its authors assumed that all proslavery (or anti-abolition) Methodists lived south of a certain geographic line and all antislavery Methodists lived to the north. However, the border was not a fixed line, but a region. Attempts to put the plan into effect revealed this geographic complexity. Many congregations in the western border region protested being denied a vote over affiliation.[28] Although not located on a state line, members of the so-called "interior societies" considered themselves border residents.

The plan's second flaw was even more shortsighted: it did not indicate precisely where division should occur, leaving that up to local congregations. Methodist leaders presumed, but never clearly specified, that the dividing line would fall along the political boundary between slave and free states, a boundary that bisected several large conferences. By allowing any congregation along this line to vote on its affiliation, each vote, even a peaceful one, moved the border north or south by one congregation, placing a new congregation on the border and entitling it to vote over its own affiliation. Bishop Thomas Morris of Cincinnati, a moderate who ultimately remained with the northern church, presciently remarked, "some very hard cases may arise under the practical operation of these rules, especially as to interior societies and minority members of border societies."[29]

Adding to the chaos, the Northern Methodists—realizing how much territory and property they stood to lose now that schism was a reality—repudiated the plan entirely at their General Conference of 1848. They argued that the plan violated the constitution of the church and that it had never been "confirmed or established" in the North. Even if the plan were valid, Elliott argued, southerners did not respect its terms. In particular, he claimed, border residents had not all been allowed a vote: "the majorities of the votes of Church members in the border conferences of Virginia, Kentucky, and Missouri, were never taken in any fair or ecclesiastical manner."[30] Northern Methodists argued that because border conferences had never officially adopted the plan—and because each individual congregation had not held a vote—the northern church was still free to evangelize in the border region. Meanwhile, southerners decried "the Northerners in their revolutionary movements upon our territory."[31]

Over the next decade, unrest plagued border Methodists. Between the institution of the Plan of Separation in 1844 and the next General Conference, in 1848, conflicts requiring mediation arose in over thirty Methodist churches and congregations in Bascom's "whole border section from Maryland to Missouri." Churches fought over property, the ministry, and sectional affiliation. Hardly a meeting passed anywhere in the region that did not erupt in contentious debate. By the time of the 1856 General Conference, several dozen ministers had suffered harassment and threats to their families, and many had been driven out of town.[32]

The incidents spanned the entire border region. Following the 1844 General Conference, congregants in Chapel Creek, Bethesda, Campbellsville, Maysville, and Louisville, all in Kentucky, passed resolutions strenuously opposing the division.[33] On the eastern shore of Virginia, in the summer of 1846, half the churches in the Salem circuit voted to join the South and half favored the North. When Valentine Gray, a Northern Methodist, preached in Salem, an angry mob pulled him from his pulpit. A similar crowd ejected James Hargis from his church in Guilford, Virginia. In 1847, in Hannibal, Missouri, where a majority of the local Methodist Church favored the North, southern preachers nonetheless took possession of the church and selectively disqualified voters until they had a majority in favor of joining the southern church.[34] In 1845, a bold group of Southern Methodists in Cincinnati—a city that was presumed to fall within the bounds of the northern church—formed a congregation. When they bought a building and established a Southern Methodist church in the heart of the city, northerners cried foul. In the fall of that year, however, the same scenario played out in reverse when a group of northerners established a congregation in St. Louis, a city generally accepted as Southern Methodist. All along the "border territory," Methodism was indeed, in the words of border resident Jesse T. Peck, a "distracted Church."[35]

The authors of the Plan of Separation of 1844 erroneously assumed that it would be easy to determine whether any given congregation should affiliate with the northern or southern branch of the denomination. Methodists from Massachusetts or Georgia found this decision easy enough to make, but it was nearly impossible for congregations in places like Kentucky or Missouri. The authors also assumed that each branch would conceive of itself as confined to a particular geographic region, which was contrary to the expansive evangelism that characterized Methodism. The stage was set for a clash of missionaries in contested areas.

BAPTIST BREAKDOWN: DIVISION AND CONSOLIDATION

As the Methodists worked out the terms of their division, slavery debates generated similar acrimony in the Baptist Church. Although decentralized, Northern and Southern Baptists still met and sparred over slavery at national missionary-society meetings. Before 1845, the board of the national Baptist

General Convention oversaw boards for Home and Foreign missions. By the early 1840s, Baptists from New England and from the deep South began to pressure the boards to take a stance on the propriety of Christian slave ownership. An 1845 letter from Basil Manly Jr. of Alabama, then a student at Princeton Seminary, illustrates the divergence between abolitionist Baptists and Baptists from the slaveholding states. Manly recalled reading an antislavery Baptist editorial denouncing the pronouncement that "the salvation of one soul is of more consequence than the liberation of all the slaves in America." Manly agreed with the assertion, and wrote, "judge what was my astonishment at finding that he *denied* it [the truth of the above sentence] flatly and declared the sentiment to be the offspring of a blind fanaticism, which left out of view entirely the important and vital sinfulness of slavery."[36]

Southern Baptists, like Manly, perceived the missionary boards to be increasingly antislavery. They were convinced that southern states received a disproportionately small number of missionaries because the boards held slavery to be a sin. At the same time, Southern Baptists became increasingly outspoken in defense of slavery. "We have examined the matter and come to the deliberate conclusion that it is not wrong to hold property in slaves," Basil Manly's father wrote from Alabama. "There we mean to stand." As for northerners, "it is for them to say whether, with this understanding, they are willing to work with us on equal terms—acknowledge us as brethren and *let us alone*."[37]

The controversy came to a head when the Georgia Baptist Convention brought a test case to the Foreign Mission Board in 1844, asking that the board appoint a known slaveholder as a missionary. As Methodists did in the Bishop Andrew case, the board initially evaded the test, but Alabama Baptists quickly followed up with a direct demand that the General Board affirm that slaveholders were morally equal and had the right to "receive any agency, mission, or other appointment within the scope of its operations and duties."[38] These demands, dubbed the Alabama Resolutions, delivered the fatal blow to national Baptist cooperation. After much equivocation, the General Board declared that it could not appoint a missionary who actively owned slaves. Baptists in the South responded with outrage. "The society should hereafter act in separate organizations at the South and at the North," concluded delegates at a May 1845 meeting of Southern Baptists in Augusta, Georgia.[39]

Like the Southern Methodists who swiftly withdrew from the national denomination following the Plan of Separation, it was easy for Baptist congregations located far below the Mason-Dixon Line to join the Southern Baptist

Convention. Likewise, congregations in northern states knew that their allegiance lay with the Northern Baptists.[40] Baptists living in divided states such as Ohio, Kentucky, Missouri, and Indiana faced a difficult decision. Where exactly *was* the division between Northern and Southern Baptists? The editor of the Louisville *Baptist Banner* reported: "Brother Owen, of the *Christian Messenger* . . . comes out the decided advocate of a state-line division between the slaveholding and non-slaveholding states." The Louisville editor continued, "we think our good brother of the *Messenger* mistaken." Unlike Owen, he advocated "sustaining the unity of the churches," and denounced denominational division as "evil."[41] There was no neat line between North and South, and, unlike the Methodists, with their "Plan of Separation," the decentralized Baptists did not attempt to formally establish how congregations in the border would determine their allegiance. The question became a matter of extended debate. "It seems to me that in whatever company I am thrown the subject of the separation of North and South comes up" wrote Basil Manly Jr.[42]

Baptist organizations in the border reacted to the division with uncertainty. Some, hoping to avoid conflict, left the issue unresolved. In 1849, the General Association of Baptists in Kentucky had not yet confirmed their affiliation with the South, and the board reported that "the unsettled condition in which we are placed in reference to North and South" tended to "greatly impede the prosperity of the society." The report continued: "The denomination in the state are uneasy upon this subject, and until the question is finally settled, and the Society shall either retain its connexion with the parent Society, or dissolve such connexion, and become united with the South, little will be accomplished."[43]

National denominational divisions have been credited with deepening sectionalism throughout the nation, hastening the onset of the Civil War, and eliminating the last checks on the articulation of distinctly proslavery theology in the South.[44] These, however, are national rather than regional consequences. In the border region, the division was experienced not as a culmination, but as the beginning of years of discord. Throughout the latter half of the 1840s, following these sectional divisions, Baptist and Methodist congregations, institutions, and regional bodies participated in acrimonious disputes over affiliation.

Caught in this unrest, many border evangelicals longed for peace and church unity. Their views of church division paralleled a general dismay over political sectionalism. "We cannot contemplate, without deep emotion, the discordant elements which at present disturb the fellowship of our churches," wrote George Walker, from Louisville. He concluded that western Baptists bore the responsibility to act as mediators.[45] Walker struck the same note as other border residents who attempted to resolve political strife. Such impulses did nothing to halt sectional division, but they did form the basis of later border responses to secession and the Civil War.

PRESBYTERIAN TENSION

As Methodists and Baptists divided, the border region continued to be a focal point for disputes between Old School and New School Presbyterians. Despite schism in 1837, conflicts again arose in Presbyterian churches during the 1840s and 1850s. Schism had separated the primary antagonists in the slavery debates, allowing Presbyterians to avoid a national denominational debate over the institution in the 1840s. Disputes that did occur suggest that, had it not been for the 1837 split, the Presbyterian Church would have divided into "northern" and "southern" branches before the end of the 1840s.

The Old School defined itself as more orthodox than the New School. This conservative position corresponded with stronger anti-abolition and proslavery sentiment than in the New School.[46] In 1838, a Missouri Presbyterian wrote that a faction opposing his work was both "ultra Old School and in favor of the divine right of slavery."[47] Still, Old School Presbyterians prized unity over adopting an official position on slavery. The Old School leadership resolved, after 1837, not to discuss slavery in any capacity at the General Assembly. Because of this policy, Old School Presbyterians maintained unity until the beginning of the Civil War, longer than any other Protestant denomination, including the New School branch, which divided in 1857. While the two branches had not yet divided North from South, as had the Methodists and Baptists, local clashes between the two Presbyterian schools—often freighted with proslavery or antislavery overtones—took place throughout the border region in the 1840s and 1850s.

The expansive and inclusive New School was less hesitant to take on social and political issues. Their General Assembly swiftly declared slavery an "evil" and condemned the institution. Despite this policy, the New School retained a significant number of southern members until the eve of secession.[48] Southern New School Presbyterians consciously chose their doctrinal affinity over their sectional interests until 1857. Through the 1840s and 1850s, the New

School continued to send ministers and missionaries to the border states and into slaveholding areas. Missionary boards made an effort, however, not to send avowedly antislavery ministers below the Mason-Dixon Line. When John Fee, an abolitionist New School minister preaching in Cabin Creek, Kentucky, began barring slaveholders from membership in his church, home mission leaders swiftly removed him. Local residents made it clear that Fee "will not be recommissioned to labor in our commission."[49] Incidents like this made it difficult to keep the area supplied with preachers.

The divide between the Old and New Schools had relieved Presbyterian sectional tension in most of the United States. However, places where both Old School and New School Presbyterians resided together in significant numbers—and regions lacking ministers altogether—attracted missionaries from both branches. In the western border region, which fit both these criteria, conflicts arose frequently. Kentucky and Missouri saw many instances of hostility between Old and New School ministers. "The conflict of opinion in Kentucky among the ministers and elders, and among *the whole church, is great*, and it is increasing," one minister reported. Another wrote from Missouri, "I am anxious to preoccupy the ground and keep out Old Schoolism." In 1848, another Missouri minister remarked that a "hostile feeling" persisted between Old School and New School Presbyterians. The discord, he reported, had divided the church and led to "lies and slanders" as well as "mischief" from the Old School faction. "While all these things are going on," he complained, "the multitude are going to the Methodist and Campbellite Ch[urche]s." The minister, a New School Presbyterian, blamed "*Old Schoolism*," whose "chief and most abundant fruit is Bigotry and hate—contention and discord."[50]

DIVIDING A CONTESTED REGION

By the middle of the 1840s, all three denominations were well on their way to sectional division. Whether under a formalized (though dysfunctional) system in the case of the Methodists, or through unregulated skirmishes, as with the Baptists and Presbyterians, the border churches went through the physical process of turning one denomination into two. The border, and particularly the western border, was not a line but a region—a region containing many thousands of Americans who belonged to one of these three denominations and held diverse opinions on the sinfulness of slavery, politics in the pulpit, and whether they were northern or southern. As one historian has argued, the boundary between freedom and slavery did not cleanly divide "two separate worlds."[51] Residents of the region represented a jumble of affiliations, often within a single congregation. Under these conditions, defining the border—let alone deciding if, when, and how to divide the church—constituted a challenge to clergy and laypeople alike.

The debates that took place in regional organizations reveal how border evangelicals classified themselves as well as what was at stake in those decisions. Favoring northern affiliation meant rejecting division—but it also implied approval of "northern" and "southern" political and moral positions on slavery. In the same vein, supporting the South, in practice, meant endorsing the division of the denomination into two separate branches. These were the terms of the debate for many border evangelicals. But, regardless of whether they favored northern or southern affiliation, border evangelicals consistently blamed abolitionism for the troubles leading to division. This belief continued to dominate border explanations for sectional division through the 1850s. Those who favored northern affiliation made it clear that they did so in spite of the increasing abolitionist (or at least antislavery) tendencies of mainstream northern evangelicals. And those who preferred division and joining the southern church accused their opponents of raising "the war cry of abolition."[52]

This consummate dislike of abolitionism—even among those who disapproved of slavery—spanned all three denominations. A Louisville *Baptist Banner and Western Pioneer* editorial declared abolition was "treason." Likewise, Methodists at an 1844 Springfield District meeting in Missouri convened an "investigation before a public meeting" to examine a preacher charged with the "odium of abolitionism." A Baltimore Methodist denounced northern abolitionist "agitators," asserting that they "will have an awful account to settle at the high Tribune for the injury they have done to the church." John Fee, an abolitionist, lost much of his audience and was the subject of "extended persecution and threatened violence" in Kentucky.[53] John Waller, a Kentucky Baptist, demanded "the exorcism of the demon of revolution and anarchy, nurtured in the bosom of abolitionism." Waller himself "opposed drawing lines between the North and the South," but placed the blame for the regrettable breach on "the hypocritical cant of the abolitionists." An 1846 Louisville editorial declared, "To our minds it is clear that abolition, and that alone, is the cause of the spiritual dearth which prevails in all the Northern churches." Therefore, the author concluded, "ABOLITIONISM IS A SIN."[54]

A majority of border evangelical leaders favored continued union during this period of division. However, prominent border evangelicals could be found in significant numbers on both sides of the debate. Those who opposed division styled themselves conservatives, constructing a theological argument against schismatics. Separation into two branches within one nation expressly violated Christ's imperative for unity of the church: "that they might be one; as thou, Father, art in me."[55] Any party that supported division dealt a blow to Christian unity.

Some border evangelicals did favor the split. The argument in favor of division was at root about protecting the right of slaveholders to hold full fellowship in the church. But it, too, had a scriptural basis: the mandate to separate religion and politics. The church belonged to a "kingdom not of this world."[56] None of the three major denominations stipulated that slaveholding was incompatible with full fellowship in the church or with holding an office. To devise such a rule would be to write politics into church discipline, or, for Baptists, to impose excessive church government on individual congregations. Slaveholding had not been a sin in the past; no modern political controversy should change that. Proponents of division argued that separation would preserve the purity of the church and protect it from corruption by politics. "The cause of God will be advanced," wrote Kentucky Baptist William Buck, if southern and border Baptists "withdraw from our friends in order to avoid collision with our foes."[57]

For their part, Southern Methodist and Southern Baptist leaders repeatedly argued that southern withdrawal was not caused by doctrinal differences and therefore did not constitute schism. Doctrine remained unchanged in the southern branches. This continuity, southerners argued, meant the divisions were not sinful. "It appears to be the settled policy of the Northern Connection to hold us as seceders," wrote Southern Methodist Bishop William Capers. Quite the contrary, he insisted: the southern church held to "the same articles of faith and doctrines of religion to the smallest particular." The split was merely the result of "the naked fact of a difference of opinion about slavery and abolition."[58] At the first meeting of the Southern Baptist Convention in Augusta, Georgia, in May 1845, delegates issued a resolution affirming that they were not guilty of schism: "A painful division has taken place in the missionary operations of the American Baptists," the resolution began. "Let not the extent of this disunion be exaggerated. . . . Northern and Southern Baptists are still brethren. They differ in no article of the faith. They are guided by the same principles of gospel order." The southern message was clear: the disagreement was over slavery, not theology. This interpretation of the schism prevailed in southern churches until after the Civil War.[59]

In contrast, most border debates about the division of the church took place in the language of doctrinal differences. The use of this language did not mean that slavery was not the underlying issue driving the debate. Rather, it meant that a straightforward conversation about the acceptability of slavery never took place in the church. Such a discussion would have recalled too vividly the protests of the abolitionists, and avoiding the taint of abolitionism was the only way to retain churchgoers. Try as they might, vocal opponents of slavery in northern churches could not formally cast the division as a dispute over the sinfulness of slavery itself—abolition remained the focus.[60]

This dynamic was at play in the aftermath of Baptist schism. At the Baptist General Convention of 1845, following division, one Maine minister proposed a resolution to formally define the recent split as one between "free and slaveholding missions."[61] The members of the convention quickly and unanimously tabled this resolution. Baptist abolitionists fruitlessly protested the fact that, even after division, slaveholders still held membership in the society and that some slaveholding missionaries were still being appointed. Most galling, the church maintained an official stance of "neutrality" on the slavery question, even though neutrality had been ineffective in preventing division. Still, this so-called neutrality allowed them to claim the moral high ground as conservative and nonpolitical. It would not alienate the many border Baptists who did not oppose slavery, and valued the unity of the church.[62]

In 1845, as the schism debate reached its peak, the Louisville *Baptist Banner and Western Pioneer*—a paper that pointedly held a position of "neutrality upon the abolition controversy"—reviewed the Boston board's controversial decision regarding the Alabama Resolutions. The editorial expressed hope that northern churches would censure the decision, not out of opposition to slavery, but in order to "sustain the union of the churches and thereby ward off the tendency of ultra-abolitionism and the dissolution of our political compact."[63] In the same issue, a self-proclaimed "Baptist of the Old School" laid out his case for the preservation of Baptist unity on the grounds that the ABHMS Board, as an institution, was sound. It was only the present members, those who had passed the Alabama Resolutions, who should be removed. "Let the old association remove their present unfaithful servants and put others in their stead. . . . it is the course of wisdom and of sound policy. The cause of truth, peace, and missions alike demands it."[64]

Another correspondent to the same paper, however, argued in favor of a sectional division. "While no person," he wrote, "would be more pleased to see the Board removed from Boston and union and harmony of action upon our foreign mission preserved than myself, I must frankly avow that I conceive such a desirable object unattainable." He went on to remark: "I can see no just reason why the Baptists of the South and West should continue dependent upon the East. . . . The strongest objection I have against the course you recommend arises from its tendency to encourage and perpetuate a spirit of strife, at war with the gospel, and calculated to disgrace the Christian character."[65]

In October of 1845, the General Association of Baptists in Kentucky met and voted to "dissolve our auxiliary connection with the American Baptist Home Mission Society, and become auxiliary to the Southern Baptist Convention."[66] However, since Baptists coordinated their missionary endeavors through several national societies, the General Association of Kentucky Baptists continued to contribute to other national organizations that organized Baptist missions. One border Baptist who identified himself only as "a member of the Convention," argued that "having withdrawn from the Home Mission Societies, we should also do so from the Am[erican] and For[eign] Bible Society and the Baptist Pub[lication] Society."[67] In contrast, John Waller maintained that, even through "the Rubicon was passed" when it came to the Home Mission Society, "*we will go no further at present*. . . . We are opposed to any more divisions. We wish to see no further alienation of feeling between the North and the South." Waller feared that further division was "contributing to the disruption of our Federal Union. . . . we would not go to the judgment with the sin of such a schism upon our soul for all the treasures of the universe."[68] Despite professing sympathy for the South, Waller received a stinging response from the *Christian Index* of Georgia, whose editor admonished him to "be as faithful in maintaining *Southern rights* as you are in defending our *denominational views*."[69]

Such disagreements typified the border response to national divisions. Despite consensus on the necessity of dividing from the Home Mission Society, Kentucky Baptists were at odds about completely severing ties with all northern organizations. Accounts of the annual meeting of the Board of the Kentucky and Foreign Bible Society reveal some of this ambivalence. In his annual report from Louisville, Corresponding Secretary A. D. Sears noted, "the Board would impress upon the minds of the Society the melancholy truth that the Bible Society is now one of the very few ligaments which bind in benevolent action American Baptists."[70] Ultimately, the majority of Kentucky Baptists identified with the Southern Baptist Convention but continued to affiliate with other missionary societies until the eve of the Civil War.[71]

The events that followed the Methodist General Conference of 1844 also provide a dramatic example of the struggles over affiliation that took place on a regional level. The Kentucky Annual Conference was the first to meet after the divisive events of 1844, and the nation's Methodists, North and South, turned their attention to the meeting. In Kentucky and in Missouri, where the Annual Conference followed shortly on the heels of Kentucky's, delegates expressed regret at the events of the General Conference. They created a Committee on Division, charged with plotting a course of action. The committee recommended delegates for a planned meeting to be held in Louisville in 1845 for the purpose of creating a Southern Methodist Church. Neither conference finalized a decision to leave the northern church, although they concluded that there would be a division and that Missourians and Kentuckians would go South.[72] Similarly, while they did not ultimately send delegates to the Louisville Convention, a strong, vocal, and organized minority in the Baltimore conference of Maryland Methodists also favored adherence to the proposed Southern Church.

Methodist conferences erupted in acrimonious debates, and during the following year, a significant number of Methodists left the conferences that had elected to go South and formed their own, or joined existing northern conferences. Seemingly neat divisions concealed great disagreement. In the Kentucky and Missouri conferences, a significant minority strongly opposed adhering to the proposed Church South. Conversely, the Baltimore conference, which voted to remain in the northern church but denounced "fellowship with abolitionism," received numerous petitions from members wishing to join the Church South.[73] And in all three conferences, tension ran high.

The Methodist leadership on both sides worried about retaining control of the border region. Between the end of the General Conference and the meetings of the annual conferences, the fate of that region remained uncertain. This was what prompted Bascom and Simpson's tireless travel through the region. Religious leaders wondered how many conferences would send delegates to the Louisville Convention. Jesse T. Peck wrote to Matthew Simpson in Indiana, "I am anxious to be informed particularly from you what is the state of things in our distracted church in your section of the border territory." Peck went on to note, "They are greatly distracted in the Philadelphia Conference—Lord preserve them!"[74] Meanwhile, Reverend Thomas Bond, editor of the *Christian Advocate and Journal*, first observed that in Baltimore "there seemed to be a pretty general disposition among both preachers and people to remain where they were" (in the northern church). Bond went on to note that "on my late visit to Baltimore I found the brethren in great difficulties" over the decision to go with the South or remain with the North. "If we go with the South, they will force a slave-holding ministry upon us, and if we go with the North they will force upon us a rule excluding all slaveholders from the Church. Either the one or the other would ruin us, and nothing seems left for us but to set up for ourselves," Bond remarked.[75]

The effects of these regional debates sometimes rippled across state lines. "I have reason to believe the final conclusion of the Baltimore Conference is doubtful," a Pennsylvania minister remarked. "They will be much divided among themselves, but it is hoped that the majority will be with the North. In this case the Philadelphia Conference will be safe: but if Baltimore should go with the South then it is uncertain what Philadelphia will do."[76] Southerners fretted over the decisions of conferences on the state border as well. In a letter to a colleague in South Carolina, Henry Bascom wrote, "I am preparing for action at the Kentucky Conference . . . I feel some anxiety about Missouri, and shall try to secure a deputation from the Kentucky Conference, lest things go wrong there."[77]

This apprehension was also evident in Bishop Thomas Morris's accounts of his episcopal tours. Morris hailed from western Virginia and edited the *Western Christian Advocate*. He had been a circuit rider in the Ohio and Kentucky annual conferences and now presided over annual conferences in the border region. He toured an area that included Louisville, western and central Virginia, Baltimore, Cincinnati, Illinois, and Indiana.[78] Morris deeply desired to prevent a schism and remained in friendly contact with an ardent southern organizer, Bishop Joshua Soule, well into the fall of 1845. Born in Maine and descended from a Mayflower Pilgrim, Soule nevertheless sided with the South in the Methodist schism.[79] Morris wrote to Soule as he traveled to Cincinnati and St. Louis, where he sought to gauge the feeling of the people. He found, predictably, division and confusion—some preferred South, some preferred North, others still hoped for a resolution. Morris wrote that, if division could not be prevented, "my chief concern is that our worse than needless controversy should be speedily terminated" by a split.[80]

Further travels revealed to Morris that even a speedy fracture would entail a degree of cooperation and consensus that did not exist in the border. Everywhere Morris went, he found that, whichever affiliation a group favored, a significant minority could be found inclined in the other direction. This held true in Cincinnati, in St. Louis, and in Illinois. Having decided that, lamentably, a separation was to occur, and having hoped to make it occur "at a comparatively narrow point," Morris then encountered a large and angry minority of Missourians wanting to go North and a large minority of Illinoisans wanting to go South.[81] Several ministers in these states vacillated in a manner that the exasperated Morris deemed "unreasonable." Morris also received, from St. Louis area Methodists, a resolution requesting that northern Bishops "visit Ky. and Mo. this fall and hold conference with the minority preachers." Morris, sticking faithfully to the Plan of Separation, "promptly informed them [it] could not be done."[82]

Despite Morris's efforts, a neat division did not take place. The rebuffed St. Louis group submitted a complaint against Morris at the Northern Methodist General Conference of 1848. The protest claimed that the group had been told that, "if we did not join the church South, we could not be Methodists nor have any preachers sent to us" as "there was not provision made for minorities" in the Plan of Separation. The men from St. Louis further protested being "sacrificed upon a Southern altar as a peace offering."[83] Morris later lamented of his travels in 1845, "I accomplished nothing except, perhaps, to involve myself in suspicion. . . . You may reason with a man's judgment, but not with his passions."[84]

In the years after the 1844 schism, both branches published screeds against each other in newspapers and books. Charles Elliott's *History of the Great Secession*, a meticulously compiled, thousand-page case for the sinfulness and illegality of the Methodist Episcopal Church, South, was the most substantial of these. The flourishing religious press carried an increasing number of vitriolic attacks on individuals and groups within the church. Methodists fought this "newspaper war" with particular viciousness. The various *Christian Advocates* attacked each other with relish.[85] Assorted Baptist *Banners* and *Recorders* from various regions also engaged in a war of words, and Presbyterian papers weighed in as well.[86] Editorial positions on the divisions and their aftermath could be even more polarized than the newspaper's readership. Editors commented on every local struggle, be it for possession of property or control of congregants. A Maryland reader remarked that the Baltimore *Christian Advocate* had "done infinite mischief in our city and all though our state."[87]

CONCLUSION

By the middle of the 1840s, the dispute between antislavery and proslavery Methodists and Baptists had reached a breaking point. Abolitionists within the denominations pushed for definitive statements on slavery's sinfulness. Defensive southerners in turn resisted any attempt to condemn slavery or bar clergy from owning slaves. Ultimately, both denominations divided, South from North. The dispute and division that occurred in these churches was a product not just of the growing national debate over slavery. It was also the consequence of the very structure of the denominations themselves. Because they held meetings that drew attendees from both North and South, the churches became one of the first venues in the United States for a direct clash over slavery and abolition.

But sectional division among Methodists and Baptists was more than just an ominous portent of secession, or an early nail in the coffin of the Union. It also shaped the American religious landscape by creating an ecclesiastical border. This border, however, was much easier to define in theory than in practice. Division did not mark the end of disputes over slavery, abolition, and politics within the churches. Instead, the schisms inaugurated a period of intense discord in the border region, where congregations had members with both northern and southern sympathies. A single border congregation might be home to a range of views on slavery and abolition. After the national denominational organizations and societies had fought and fractured, the same fight played out in church after church throughout the broad border region.

The border was home to a large number of evangelicals who viewed themselves as moderates or conservatives—condemning both abolitionists and slaveholders for allowing a political question to divide their denominations. This stance was based on the belief that slavery was a political question—not a problem with moral or theological dimensions. Clergy, they therefore argued, not only could, but should, avoid the topic. From this vantage point, border evangelicals condemned abolitionists and slaveholders equally. They positioned themselves, in contrast, as moderates, as particularly well suited to the role of intermediaries between North and South. In other words, they began to identify more as residents of the border than as residents of the West. Christians of the "Middle States," as one Kentucky Baptist put it, "form a connecting link between the South and the North, and hold a conservative influence over the two extremes."[88]

For border evangelicals, participating in the acrimonious meetings and conventions that led to schism was just the prelude to a period of strife as the process of denominational division met the messy reality of border life. Leaders of the sectionalized national denominations—men like Henry Bascom and Matthew Simpson—fought to bring the region to the South or to keep it affiliated with the North. At the local level, churches fractured as they struggled to divide property, select ministers, and identify with a region. The experience would teach border evangelicals many lessons about the dangers of conflict and would, eventually, shape their responses to the secession crisis.

— 3 —

COMBUSTIBLE MATTER

Conflict on the Border after Division

The 1844 Plan of Separation inaugurated a season of struggle for Reverend Lorenzo Waugh. Born in what is now West Virginia, Waugh became a Methodist preacher and received an appointment in Missouri several years before denominational division.[1] When the Missouri Conference convened for the first time since the schism, its members faced the task that confronted Methodists across the border region: determining "whether they would remain in the Methodist Episcopal Church or unite with the new organization." By Waugh's account, those who wished to "go south" came to the conference "expecting a pressing contest" and used "all the influence and ingenuity they possessed" to "foxily" persuade the conference to vote to join the southern church. "My heart sickens at the tragedy," Waugh concluded.[2]

Although he and his fellow "adhering preachers" had been outvoted, Waugh resolved to remain in Missouri, where he continued to speak out against the Plan of Separation and Southern Methodists. Soon, opponents accused Waugh of abolitionism. The southern-affiliated Missouri Conference tried him *in absentia* and expelled him from the conference for "sowing dissentions." Over the next several years, Waugh attempted to tell his version of events: that the Southern Methodists withdrew in defense of slavery, and that he was no abolitionist. Rather, Waugh insisted, he was an "*anti-ultra* [anti-abolitionist], antislavery *conservative* Methodist." He maintained that many ordinary Methodists in the state shared his sentiments and opposed division.[3]

Late in 1848, Jonathan K. Hawkins, a minister who sided with the southern church, shared with a colleague "some information relative to the Northerns" in Kirksville, Missouri. Hawkins reported that "Waugh has been trying to disaffect our members by telling them we are seceeders. . . . he is selling his pamphlets where he can and I believe in some occasions gives them away." To counteract Waugh, Hawkins called a gathering and "gave publickly a history of his cause since the division and informed them of his expulsion." Despite his efforts, eight congregants in Kirksville elected to join the northern church. Hawkins declared he hated to "dirty my hand" with Waugh, but he feared the consequences of Waugh's work and urged his colleague to visit the circuit to lecture in favor of the southern church. "A little pains and labour on our part now," he noted, "may save us much trouble later."[4] As this case shows, the struggle over sectional affiliation in Missouri grew intensely personal and took place town by town and church by church.

The question of national division may have been decided at the Annual Conference in 1844, but on the border, the act of division resolved little. In fact, it was the prelude to years of conflict over how and where to draw the line between northern and southern churches. In his case, Waugh contended that southern sympathizing clergy had conspired to "deceive the members into the new southern organization."[5] In 1848, he attended the General Conference in Pittsburgh and entreated leaders of the Northern Methodists not to give up on the church in Missouri, "beyond '*the dark line*.'" Waugh worried that the "the extreme measures adopted by our southern brethren to *drive* us off or starve us out are not yet fully known by our brethren at a distance." Waugh sought to make prominent Northern Methodists aware of these "measures."[6] Waugh's case illustrates how local struggles complicated division. He and other members of the northern minority insisted they still had a place in Missouri. They argued that the question of the Missouri Conference's affiliation could only be resolved within the individual societies of the conference, each of which should cast a vote.

During the latter half of the 1840s, following sectional division over slavery, disputes plagued border churches. Unrest was particularly severe in the Methodist Church, but Baptists also battled over territory, property, clergy, and congregational affiliation. The events on the border served as a warning about the dangers of sectionalism to Presbyterians as well. These incidents taught a lesson about the consequences of political conflict. Adversaries located the root cause of their dispute in divergent political positions rather than in theological differences.

Whether individual congregations remained affiliated with northern branches or "went South," the process of division was fraught, and border residents—men like Waugh and his detractors—placed the blame on those viewed as extremists: those who were "ultra" proslavery or, worse, abolitionists.[7] The charge of abolitionism was particularly potent on the border. Whether affiliated with the North or the South, border evangelicals viewed abolitionists as extremists and as a threat to peace and order.[8] The Southern Methodists who wanted Waugh to either join their branch or cease preaching on his circuit accused Waugh of being an abolitionist.

In the process of division, regional identification with the West broke down. This disintegration manifested in various ways. Clergy increasingly identified with the North or the South. They jealously defended their right to evangelize border territory. The regional press joined in the fray. And, in a sign of the degree of division, both sides displayed a willingness to resort to secular arbiters. These highly public altercations spilled out of the confines of the churches and into the public realm. They had the effect of conferring legitimacy on the newly formed southern branches. Ultimately, local conflicts resulted in a firmer division between northern and southern branches on the national level and, in the border region, a greater appreciation for how local disputes could damage congregations and disrupt worship. Lorenzo Waugh's grievances against the Southern Methodists in Missouri illustrate the nature of these post-schism border disputes.

In building his case against the southern Methodists in Missouri, Waugh revealed how conflict and chaos that occurred locally percolated up to the national level. Waugh's experience highlights the three types of local conflict that followed national denominational division. First, evangelicals clashed over territory and affiliation. During the antebellum years, no sectional branch wished to confine its activities to a fixed geographic area, particularly not in the West. Therefore, neither branch conceded that their group was strictly sectional. Waugh, for example, never referred to the MEC as the "northern church." The fact that the West was becoming a border between rival denominations made evangelization of the region all the more tantalizing. At the same time, however, these branches resented missionary incursions from the other side. Waugh disputed southern claims to Missouri, resisting the Southern Methodists who told him he must "quit the state" if he did not join the southern branch.[9]

Territorial disputes also raised the question of congregational affiliation. Members of a single border congregation often disagreed over whether they were southern or northern. Waugh describes the difficulties he faced in "ascertaining who . . . of their free good will wish to join the Methodist Episcopal

Church South and who in the same way wish to remain in the Methodist Episcopal Church."[10] His chief accusation against southern clergy was that they deceived the laity and denied local congregations the opportunity to vote on their affiliation.

Waugh's local disputes highlight a second source of contention: clergy appointments. He noted numerous cases of conflict between ministers and their flocks. Divided congregations also fought bitterly over who should minister to their ranks. Members of the Weston Circuit, for example, refused to "go south" and complained that southern "preachers were forced upon us the next year." In other cases, southern-sympathizing congregants rejected northern-leaning clergy like Waugh. These controversies often drew participants from the community who had no affiliation with the congregation involved.

Waugh also clashed with Southern Methodists over a third point of conflict: "the church's property."[11] Who had a right to church buildings and funds when one denomination became two? All along the border, contests arose over the possession of the institutions of the evangelical West—church buildings, seminaries, newspapers, publishing houses, and other physical property possessed by divided groups. The disputes raised the question of how to evaluate the nature of schism. They could not always be resolved internally and pulled the state into the fray. The cases were often settled in secular courts, which effectively ruled on the legitimacy of denominational branches. These three types of local conflict deepened the sectionalism within American evangelicalism.

CONTESTED TERRITORY

The fundamental question at stake in the first of these types of conflict—territorial disputes—was whether the divided denominations should also divide missionary arenas. Neither side was eager to limit itself and, in any case, doing so would have required an unlikely degree of cooperation. There was no external mandate forcing Southern Baptists, for example, to confine their missions to slave states and Northern Baptists to free states. After all, neither branch had limited its membership to supporters or opponents of slavery. Old School and New School Presbyterians were not restricted to territorial limits, since their division was not a direct response to the slavery controversy. The Methodist division attempted to stipulate geographic boundaries, but even in this case, the Plan of Separation left plenty of room for ambiguity.

The newly divided national bodies all laid claim to the border region. Missionaries in these areas competed for converts. "Everywhere along the border," Northern Methodist Charles Elliott complained in his *History of the Great Secession*, "Southern bishops were sending preachers to minorities and interior societies." Furthermore, he protested, "measures are in progress" to occupy "as much of the free states as can be transferred. . . . The spirit of conquest is now at work."[12] Elliot saw no irony in having written his book in part to prove the legitimacy of Northern Methodist conferences and missions established in slaveholding territory.

Meanwhile, Reverend Milton Jamison of Glasgow, Missouri—his eye on the Iowa border—was eager to see his state firmly in the hands of the Southern Methodists. "I presume you will soon have full sweep over the border lines," he wrote to Jacob Lanius, encouraging him to look beyond Missouri to Iowa, where he could organize missionary societies "connected with the South."[13] Jamison encouraged Lanius to contact families in Iowa who had expressed interest in the southern church.

For their part, from the moment they formed their own branch, Southern Baptists fretted about the missionaries that the northern-funded American and Foreign Bible Society sent below the Mason-Dixon Line. Their activity was "regarded as a direct attempt . . . to divide the South."[14] Even the Presbyterians engaged in territorial struggles—recall the Missouri New School Presbyterian who was "anxious to preoccupy the ground and keep out *Old Schoolism*."[15] A fellow New School Presbyterian wrote of the Old School in Kentucky, "they have wealth, numbers, influence, ambition, jealousy, and energy. . . . they can kill us off, or starve us out."[16]

Congregations on the border joined in the debate, erupting into internal conflict over whether they were northern or southern. When forced to choose one section, congregations splintered. Jonathan Hawkins, Waugh's Southern Methodist rival, remarked, "The people around Tippecanoe [Missouri] . . . have taken their position, in feelings either North or South and they will be hard to move." Now, it seemed, each side "had no idea of being identified" with the other.[17] A Virginia newspaper reported that "a very large portion of the Methodists in southwestern Virginia, ministers as well as laymen, are opposed to the separation" because it would render them Southern Methodists. Congregations in these towns "became sites of violent disruption."[18]

In some cases, churches sought to form a new congregation under the authority of their desired sectional branch. In the Methodist case, these attempts violated the Plan of Separation. For example, in Louisville, which was supposed to receive missionaries only from the southern church, forty members of the Asbury Chapel—reportedly "ultra fanatical in their Northern principles"—quarreled with the southern-leaning portion of the congregation over "the preacher sent by the Louisville Conference." The northern faction "intend[ed] *officially* to repudiate the M.E. Church South," and they requested a new minister "be sent under the Ind[iana] An[nua]l Conf[erence] of the M.E. Church," even though that body was theoretically prohibited from doing so.[19] Even in an area where larger bodies had reached an agreement, therefore, disputes could erupt at the congregational level.

It is hardly surprising that northern or southern evangelicals in divided branches would not consent to restricted missionary fields. For northerners, accepting such boundaries would amount to conceding that theirs was a sectional branch and not the one true church from which southerners had splintered. For southerners, limiting territory would be a concession to northern authority at a time when they sought to prove their equality with—not subordination to—their sectional counterpart. As long as missionaries from both denominational branches served within the region, a neat border could not be drawn. In these missionary conflicts, some border residents sided with the North and others with the South. And some, troubled by the havoc wrought by sectionalization, began to formulate a third position, angling to maintain local unity in the face of division.

CLERGY AND ABOLITIONISM

During the 1840s, border residents freely acknowledged that conflict over slavery lay at the root of their disputes. This point of contention became manifest in a second source of antagonism: selecting and approving clergy in the aftermath of denominational division. Even in communities where very few people owned slaves, residents evaluated ministers by their views of the institution.

In the earliest days of missionary work in the West, residents complained about the ministers sent to frontier outposts. Suspicion of "Eastern" men, "with Eastern habits [that] . . . did not suit the West" persisted into the 1840s and was combined with an increasing animosity toward outsiders suspected of bringing the slavery controversy into the community.[20] As opposition to abolition intensified across the border region, clergy fell under intense scrutiny. The arrival of a new preacher, fresh information about an old preacher brought to light, or even a whispered rumor, might be all that was needed to set off a confrontation.

Between the institution of the Plan of Separation in 1844 and the next General Conference, held in 1848, over thirty Methodist churches and congregations in the border region reported conflicts over property, the ministry, and affiliation. Hardly a meeting passed anywhere in the region that did not erupt in contentious debate. By the time of the 1856 General Conference, several dozen ministers had suffered harassment, threats to family, and been driven out of town. "There is combustible matter here," wrote Methodist Reverend Light from Shelbyville, Missouri. "The Northern preacher from La Grange [has] been here since Saturday preaching and using the most dishonorable devices to distract the church." When Light warned the interloper that he might meet trouble if he stayed, the northerner replied that he would "organize a Northern Church here, if he has to run the risk of martyrdom."[21] Northern-affiliated Methodists in Missouri made similar complaints about southern clergy. Lorenzo Waugh accused them of acting in a "reckless, lawless, and overbearing manner" to drive out Northern Methodists and take control of churches.[22]

An incident in Parkersburg, Virginia, illustrates how the appointment of a minister could become a point of community concern. Situated in what is now West Virginia, the town of Parkersburg lay within slaveholding territory, but in an area where very few residents owned slaves. Until 1844, the town had belonged to the Ohio Annual Conference, which encompassed the southern half of the free state of Ohio, as well as a large portion of western Virginia.[23] Parkersburg lay just on the Virginia side of the Ohio River. After division, many local Methodists felt strongly that they should affiliate with the northern church. Unsurprisingly, western Virginia became a hotbed of border unrest following the Plan of Separation. One historian has even credited the disputes with helping to form the state of West Virginia.[24]

That unrest turned to outright animosity in Parkersburg as a result of the influx of preachers from other states. Once again, the problem stemmed from ambiguity in the Plan of Separation. Parkersburg was located in the Kanawha District where, at a meeting of the district committee, "the vote was unanimous to remain" in the northern church, "with the exception of one member." Northern Methodists took this as a vote for affiliation under the Plan of Separation. In individual congregations however, lay members voted to adhere to the North by much slimmer margins—and some elections were too close to call. Minority or not, many local congregants desired a Southern Methodist preacher, and they appealed to nearby Southern Methodist conferences, which willingly sent ministers.[25] In 1847, a southern Bishop, claiming authority under the Plan of Separation, formed the Southern Methodist Guyandotte District within the bounds of the Northern Methodist Kanawha District. Parkersburg lay in the center of the area claimed by both the Kanawha and the Guyandotte districts.

In 1844, the Parkersburg Methodist Church boasted a congregation of just over two hundred white members.[26] The minister of the congregation, Reverend Arza Brown, favored adherence to the northern branch, and he reported a majority vote of 112 to 89 in favor of affiliation with the North.[27] In response, the northern-affiliated Ohio Conference sent the Reverend John Dillon to Parkersburg. When Dillon arrived, he was met by an indignant crowd that stated, in no uncertain terms, that the town's Methodist congregation did not favor the North and wanted nothing to do with a northern minister. On the Sunday of his arrival, in fact, a Southern Methodist minister already stood at the pulpit.[28] Dillon waited through the sermon and then announced to the congregation that he would preach at three o'clock that afternoon. In response, "It was announced by a Bro. Neal that the pulpit would be closed against him."[29]

Brother Neal and his southern supporters were true to their word. They hastily locked the doors of the church to prevent Dillon from entering. By three o'clock that afternoon, a crowd of curious residents crowded around the Methodist Church—many no doubt seeking novelty more than holy instruction. Those in search of a spectacle were not disappointed. A northern-sympathizing congregant led Dillon to a side door that Neal had neglected to latch. Dillon entered, threw open the front doors, and the northern sympathizers swept into the church. According to a recollection from several years later, "Bro. Dillon preached though ordered out of the house by some who came in and the southern party remained generally insulting. Boxes were rattled in the basement and stones were rolled on the floor to interrupt the services above." The crowds, inside and outside the church, were of roughly equal numbers. After the sermon, the anti-northern group announced a meeting, to be held the following morning at the courthouse.[30] The meeting and its aftermath reveal how a conflict in one congregation could become the business of an entire community.

At this point, the conflict had spilled out of the bounds of the congregation to become a community concern. The next morning saw a "large assembly" of not just the two Methodist factions, but also members of other denominations and "men not members of any church." These latter, according to reports, "joined the Southern party" to "declare that a minister for the North should not stay." These men swiftly appointed a group to visit Dillon and persuade him to leave the town voluntarily. Dillon prevaricated, saying he "was not prepared to say what he would do."

Dillon's response inflamed his opponents, who, later that day, "appointed a committee of *forty*" to force Dillon out of town. If he was still in Parkersburg by the coming Saturday, the committee would "seize him and set across the Ohio River." The committee posted notices around Parkersburg warning Dillon that he must leave or would be made to leave by force. Many of these men were not Methodists; some were even "utterly opposed to Methodism." Dillon's presence—and his purported views on slavery—had become a community concern.

Dillon's defenders, undaunted, gathered to support him, but ultimately Dillon decided to obey the committee's orders to leave Parkersburg. Dillon soon returned, "but when he returned the church was locked against him." He did not hold services there again. Despite receiving threats of a tarring and feathering, he continued to hold services for the Methodist Episcopal Church, first in a private home and later in a new chapel that he and his supporters built.[31]

The Parkersburg case illustrates several features common to local contests over a minister: a larger regional body sent a new minister to Parkersburg; his arrival sparked a confrontation; and he became a symbol around which factions formed. He became a catalyst for conflict beyond the church. Dillon's own views on slavery were less important than what he represented. Northern-affiliated preachers became synonymous with abolitionism, even though few in the region were antislavery (and those who were, only mildly so). Another Methodist minister working in western Virginia warned a colleague that those affiliated with a northern church "are watched and questioned." He went on: "if you do not become half pro-slavery, you are all down as an *Abolitionist*."[32] When he opposed the division of the Methodist Church in Missouri, Lorenzo Waugh was swiftly charged with abolitionism—a charge he vehemently denied.

Southern-affiliated border clergy attempted to steer the border faithful away from the northern church by playing on white-supremacist fears. They argued that abolitionists sought immediate social and political equality for African Americans. This claim was intended to persuade conservative anti-slavery clergy to join the southern branches. A Southern Methodist minister played on racist fears by asserting that his rival, "who goes North and entertains entirely Northern principles," had been heard to state "that a negro has an equal right to vote or have a voice with white people in church matters." The same southern minister accused another northern clergyman of saying "that it is write [*sic*] for a white man to marry a black girl and a black man to marry a white girl." The conflation of abolitionism and interracial sex went to the heart of white-supremacist fears about the consequences of abolition in the border region.[33]

Border congregants evaluated a minister's stance on slavery based on which branch of the denomination he represented. This state of affairs prompted a northern Virginia Methodist, Jesse T. Peck, to sardonically remark that "he had the unspeakable honor of being handled as an uncompromising Abolitionist. Strange enough to me!"[34] Indeed, many northeastern preachers knew, when they were entering border areas, to avoid mentioning slavery for fear of alienating their audience. One New School Presbyterian summed up the situation: "I believe I or any other native Kentuckian might preach or talk with the utmost freedom in reference to the teachings of the gospel in regard to slavery. . . . But it would be hazardous for a minister from another state to do so."[35]

Southern evangelical leaders insisted that northern churches promoted abolition—even as these denominations studiously toed the anti-abolition line to avoid alienating moderates. For their part, northern-affiliated clergy caricatured the southern denominations as single-minded advocates of slavery and schism. Both the northern and the southern arguments held appeal for border evangelicals, most of whom despised abolitionism but were also suspicious of slaveholding elites. For many, it seemed that the only position on slavery that was not schismatic, politicized, nor disruptive was a carefully maintained neutrality. "[A] serious difficulty existed in the conflict between the Northern doctrine that slaveholding is a sin, and the Southern doctrine, that it is not," observed Cincinnati Baptist John Stevens. "How could this difficulty be met?" Stevens answered his own question: "[L]et the subject of slavery entirely alone. . . . act, as nearly as possible, as if there were no such institution in being."[36] Such advice might have seemed reasonable, but it proved hard to follow as conflicts over sectional affiliation time and again became proxy struggles over slavery and abolition.

PROPERTY DISPUTES

Disputes over property show a third way in which the border became sectionalized. Like disputes over territory and clergy, contests over church property had both practical and symbolic dimensions. Neither side wished to give up valuable assets, and securing a church building bolstered claims to legitimacy as well as territory. Of course, congregational disputes had occurred before schism. Protestants were no strangers to internal discord. In these cases, the minority group left and established a new meeting place. In the case of sectional schism, however, members of the divided branches found it increasingly difficult to resolve property disputes internally. This was particularly true for larger properties owned by the denomination as a whole—the institutions of the evangelical West. Cases over this type of property found their way to secular courts. Being parties to a secular suit served to legitimate the new southern branches, designating them as equal to, rather than minority offshoots of, their formerly united denominations. Western identity began to disintegrate in the face of sectionalism and the slavery debates. As Kentucky Presbyterian and abolitionist John Fee put it, "soon the question of parties in Church and State will be pro and anti slavery.[37] New fissures opened up across the region.

The fate of the Western Baptist Theological Institute exemplifies border-state property disputes. The institute had been founded "for the whole West."[38] In the twelve years it took to raise funds for an endowment, however, Baptists of those states lost their unity of purpose. The institution opened its doors in 1845, the same year as the national Baptist schism. Western Baptists continued to avoid discussion of slavery in their general meetings out of practical necessity.

Shortly after the division, however, the Louisville *Baptist Banner and Western Pioneer* published a letter from John Waller of Kentucky, in which he asked the president of the Theological Institute about his views on the sinfulness of slavery. "The very existence of the institute is staked on this issue," Waller insisted.[39] Robert Pattison, the seminary president, declined to reply.[40] Waller, who had initially opposed denominational division, hoped that once again "Northern and Southern Baptists shall be united in love."[41] But he opposed abolitionism, and, in a response typical of border evangelicals, he roundly condemned the board's pronouncement that it would not appoint slaveholding missionaries. The atmosphere surrounding Covington and the institute grew tense as Waller pressed the president, Pattison, for a statement.

Waller and the Kentucky members of the board feared that Pattison and the Ohio trustees viewed slave ownership as a sin—a doctrinal position that would render the institute unappealing to Baptists from slave states. By 1845, the General Association of Kentucky Baptists had already resolved that they could not yet recommend the institute to potential scholars without further assurance that the trustees did not consider slaveholding a sin. None of the Ohioans were abolitionists. They all hailed from, or had lived for a considerable time in, the West, and they held, at most, conservative antislavery views. When pressed, however, they would not deny that slavery was a sin. Ideological stalemates like this one contributed to the aversion to political questions that would define the evangelical theology of border-region moderates.

In the summer of 1847, Kentucky trustee James M. Frost attempted to salvage the institute with a letter published in the *Tennessee Baptist*. "An institution *wholly Northern* cannot live in this community," he wrote. "The moment all Southern influence withdraws from it, nothing in my humble judgment can save it. The community living on the border is even more sensitive than it is in the interior. I assure our brethren of the South, therefore, that they need have no fears whatever of Covington favoring abolitionism." His statement was not controversial in itself, but Frost ended the letter with a provocative call to arms: "Let the South not start another institution which it would take years to endow, but rally 'round Covington, already *well endowed*, and make it such an institution as we need."[42] Frost's letter appealed to his readers on sectional grounds. Although intended to reassure anxious southerners that the institute was not a nest of abolitionism, southerners construed the letter as a call to wrest all control of the institute away from Ohio, and it was reprinted to that end in the South. Northerners, likewise, read the letter as a challenge. The conflict over the Theological Institute was thoroughly sectionalized; the combatants perceived it as a contest between the North and South—and between antislavery and proslavery beliefs.

After James Frost's editorial, Kentucky board members demanded that the institute appoint more trustees from their state. But their demands went unheeded. With the aid of the Kentucky Baptist association, some aggrieved Kentucky board members covertly appealed to a secular source: the Kentucky state legislature, which had granted the original charter. On January 28, 1848, the Kentucky legislature presented the stunned Ohioans on the institute's board with an amendment to the seminary charter that raised the total number of Kentucky board members to twenty-six and stipulated that all future appointees must be Kentucky residents. This effectively gave total control of the institute to the Kentucky Baptists. When the former record keeper refused to hand over the seminary keys, the Kentucky faction, undeterred, broke the bolts on the doors and entered the institute by force.[43]

In turning to the state legislature, the Kentucky board members displayed a willingness to invoke secular arbiters to resolve denominational disputes. They dramatically repudiated the bond that had formerly existed between western Baptist brethren. They also created a test of the separation of church and secular governments. Their readiness to enlist secular assistance was a testament to how deep and irreconcilable intradenominational division had become.

Even as the Kentucky brethren were breaking down doors, Ohioans appealed the decision, fiercely protesting the turn of events. In response, Kentuckians drew on an old tactic for unifying western Protestants: anti-Catholic fearmongering. They claimed that the Ohioans had spent the past year concocting secret plans to sell the institute to Jesuits, "to be abused and desecrated in fostering the 'damnable heresis' of Papism."[44] Kentuckians alleged that Ohioans planned to use proceeds from the sale to rebuild the entire seminary on the Ohio side of the river. For their part, the Kentucky board members claimed that their questions about slavery had simply been intended to ensure that anyone from the border region, including those from slave states, would be comfortable at the seminary. The Ohioans protested that they were in fact protecting the comfort of northwesterners.

Both sides were correct. The institute *had* been planned in 1833 to serve the entire population of the evangelical West, including Missouri, Ohio, Indiana, Illinois, Kentucky, and western Virginia. By the end of the 1840s, however, an institution that acknowledged there was sin in slave ownership would not be hospitable to southwesterners; and an institution that openly proclaimed the moral equality of slaveholders and nonslaveholders would not be hospitable to northwesterners. The constituency and the region that the institute had originally been intended to serve no longer existed. Indeed, by 1845, the vision of the evangelical West had deteriorated under the acrimony of the slavery controversy.

Once sectional lines had been drawn, both parties in the Covington case were past compromise. In conflict over property, disputes found their way out of the confines of the churches and into civil courts. These cases introduced secular arbiters into denominational conflicts. This development was central to the sectionalization of America's major evangelical denominations because it marked the point at which the fractured denominations were willing to violate two imperatives: first, the imperative to keep strict separation between the sacred and the secular, and second, the imperative to avoid the sin of schism. Once these boundaries had been crossed, the intervention of the state—in the form of the courts—legitimized the withdrawing southern branches. When controversy over property could not be resolved in church courts, denominational unity was broken past the point of repair. The post-schism property disputes were not the first church-property disputes to be resolved in secular courts.[45] They were, however, the first to emerge from sectional denominational divisions over slavery.

To turn to secular courts to resolve property disputes, evangelicals had to overcome their discomfort with violating two imperatives. The first of these was the separation of church and state, which was both a constitutional principle American Protestants fiercely guarded and a doctrinal imperative. In the early republic, as Amanda Porterfield describes, church governments became part of the web of American public life. She argues that religious governments were "based on allegiance to a heavenly kingdom suspended above the imperfections" of the secular world. These religious governments "supplanted—and in important respects superseded—local, state, and federal authority." Parallel governments reflected the "doctrine of two kingdoms" that most American Christians employed to organize their understanding of spheres of authority. Church-property suits in the secular courts blurred the lines between these "parallel forms of government."[46]

Evangelical concern for defending churches from incursions by the state stemmed from an American religious ideal with roots as deep as the Puritan conviction that separation served to protect the church. This "evangelical principle of separation," as one historian termed it, rested on the notion that state involvement with religious institutions corrupted the purity of the latter.[47] In his First Epistle to the Corinthians, the apostle Paul chastised Christians for taking their disputes to civil courts: "Dare any of you, having a matter against another, go to law before the unjust, and not before the saints?" Paul reprimanded, "Now therefore there is utterly a fault among you, because ye go to law one with another."[48] But, like the troubled church in Corinth, the border churches appealed to secular courts. In 1853, a Northern Methodist observing a property suit fretted, "I have seen nothing since I have been in the ministry that so perils the character of our preachers."[49]

A second cause of hesitance in appealing to secular courts was reluctance to commit (or appear to commit) the sin of schism. The division of the denomination into two separate branches within one nation expressly violated the biblical imperative for unity of the church. Christ himself had prayed of the churches, "that they might be one; as thou, Father, art in me."[50] One Baptist remarked that he feared "to go to the judgment with the sin of such a schism upon our soul."[51] Resorting to secular courts divided, rather than united, the churches.

The courts also expressed reluctance to rule in these cases. In particular, they resisted determining which of two warring factions constituted the "true church." Reflecting separation of church and state, American courts generally preferred to respect a denomination's own authority to determine church membership.[52] For example, an 1842 Kentucky Supreme Court ruling averred, "the judicial eye cannot penetrate the veil of the church for the forbidden purpose" of determining who was or was not part of a religious group.[53] While litigants saw the cases as hinging on questions of doctrinal purity, courts approached them as property disputes. In truth, there was no way to separate these questions completely, as decisions about who had a right to disputed property had the effect of conferring legitimacy on the winning party. These cases illustrate how lawsuits affected the relationship between the two branches.

Several prominent cases of disputed church property arose during the prewar years. The Methodist Book Concern case is one example that garnered nationwide attention during the 1840s and 1850s. The Book Concerns were combined printing presses, publishing houses, and distribution systems for religious literature. One was located in New York, another in Cincinnati. The New York Concern alone was the single most financially successful denominational publisher of the nineteenth century.[54] It is unsurprising that the concern became the subject of a dispute between Northern and Southern Methodists. The ensuing case illustrates how different conceptions of the relationship between northern and southern branches led to suits in which courts ruled on the nature of that very relationship.

Like so many Methodist disputes, the case originated with the Plan of Separation debacle. The plan, as conceived in 1844, allowed for a division of the proceeds and property of the New York and Western (Cincinnati) concerns. The attempt to manage the division of property without litigation or secular arbiters reflected a desire to keep church and state separate and to avoid the appearance of acrimonious schism. The plan failed to prevent these outcomes, however. When Northern Methodists repudiated the Plan of Separation, they repudiated the division of the Book Concern property as well.[55] This enraged the Southern Methodists, who needed the funds generated by the publishing house to support their fledgling denomination. If the South lost a share of the Book Concern, it would "be left no other alternative to sustain our honesty of purpose," asserted Bishop William Capers.[56] Another Southern Methodist Bishop called the controversy "worse than needless" and hoped the funds could be "divided without litigation."[57]

From the northern perspective, the Methodist Church had not "divided" at all. Rather, "the South separated or seceded," leaving the Methodist Episcopal Church "an undivided body" with no obligation to surrender property. Charles Elliott charged that "the South prize more the recognition of the Methodist Episcopal Church than the money."[58] Elliott pinpointed the greater implications of the case: if the southern church was one half of a church that no longer existed, it deserved half that church's property; if, on the other hand, Northern Methodists constituted the true church from which the South had withdrawn, all property rightfully remained with the North. The legitimacy of the entire denomination was at stake.

The battle quickly wound up on the dockets of the secular courts. In 1849, the U.S. Circuit Court for southern New York was asked to judge whether the Southern Methodist branch constituted a legitimate denomination. The court found in the favor of the Southern Methodists. The following year, the Cincinnati case came before the U.S. Circuit Court for the District of Ohio, which dismissed the bill.[59] The southerners appealed to the U.S. Supreme Court, which decided in the southerners' favor. Justice Samuel Nelson, who had presided over the New York Circuit Court in the New York case, wrote the Supreme Court decision. Nelson concluded, "There is no longer one Methodist Episcopal Church with territorial jurisdiction coextensive with the United States, but there are two churches instead, divided in territorial jurisdiction by a fixed line, each existing by an independent organization, exclusive of the other." In the final settlements, the courts awarded the southern branches over $350,000 in cash, stock, and property from the two concerns. Southern Methodists also received external recognition of their claims to legitimacy and of their understanding of the relationship between the branches. For their part, Northern Methodists viewed the decision as evidence that the courts protected slavery.[60]

Other antebellum property cases originated in local disputes, such as conflict over church edifices. Many of these were likewise resolved in favor of the South. *Gibson v. Armstrong*, the Maysville Church case, was the first involving northern and southern branches disputing the ownership of a building. Problems began in 1845 following Methodist division. Maysville lay on the Kentucky side of the Ohio River and was home to a profoundly divided congregation of 281 white members.[61] An initial vote yielded a majority in favor of remaining with the North. However, shortly thereafter, a significant number of the Maysville Methodists changed their minds.

The cause of this change of heart is not entirely clear. According to northern-sympathizing residents, "With the hue and cry of abolitionist, the agents of the South . . . prevailed on one hundred and nine to join the church South." Southern sympathizers contended that the first vote had excluded some members, and that there had always been a southern majority. No matter who stirred up the trouble, neither side was willing to give up the church building. The case, the first of its kind, ended up in the Kentucky Court of Appeals, where Chief Justice Thomas Marshall, respecting the second vote, found in favor of the southerners. In response, northerners huffed that "the minority who went south, by various stratagems succeeded in wresting the church property out of the hands of the majority."[62]

As in the Book Concern cases, Justice Marshall rejected the northern branch's claim that it still represented the entirety of Methodism in the United States. "The one united Methodist Church," he concluded, "ceased to exist by division into two churches, of distinct territorial jurisdiction." And what of the Methodist Episcopal Church that existed before 1844 and whose name appeared on the deed of the Maysville church? "There is in fact no such church," ruled Marshall. From the perspective of the courts, internal divisions did not weaken the Protestant "moral establishment" or threaten the state, so it made sense to recognize both branches.[63] In later years, the courts would place boundaries on religious liberty, as in the case of Mormons and polygamy. However, this would never be the case for sectionally divided evangelical Protestant denominations, even after the abolition of slavery. Justice Marshall's decision set a precedent for deciding subsequent cases in the favor of the southern branch—and therefore provided legal recognition of Southern Methodist legitimacy.[64] Still, even when courts did not rule in their favor, secular court cases served to validate southern branches by recognizing them as legitimate entities. This was the case when the dispute over the Western Baptist Theological Institute found resolution in the courts.

In 1854, the Supreme Court of Kentucky ruled that the Kentucky legislature's alteration of the institute charter was illegal, but by this time, both parties agreed that they could not work together.[65] Litigation signaled the end of cooperation. To bring the matter to a close, Kentucky and Ohio Baptists settled upon an outside arbiter, Supreme Court Justice John McLean of Ohio. McLean divided the Western Baptist Theological Institute property equally between the two parties.[66]

The stories of the Methodist Book Concern conflict, the Maysville church disputes, and the short-lived Western Baptist Theological Institute illustrate how conflict over property both reflected and contributed to the sectionalization of the region's religious bodies during the decades before the Civil War. The evangelicals of the 1830s and early 1840s shared a vision of the West as the best hope for the conversion of the nation and the expansion of their denominations. But that shared notion of an evangelical West could not hold the region together in the face of controversies over the sinfulness of slave ownership. When national bodies divided into sectional branches, most evangelicals in the far North and deep South threw their allegiance and their property wholeheartedly behind one side or another. But in the southern portion of free states and the northern portion of slave states, individuals and congregations were torn between the two sections. The depth of the division was revealed in their willingness to resort to secular courts for the resolution of property cases. Most of these cases were resolved in favor of the southern branches, who secured their claim to the capital and clout western institutions conferred. But even when they did not win, being heard in court buttressed the southern branches' claims to legitimacy. These cases would later provide raw material for church historians constructing histories of southern denominational distinctiveness and did not rely on either slavery or the Confederacy.

SLAVERY AND A REGION SECTIONALIZED

Sectionalized denominational divisions left the identity of the evangelical West in tatters. By the 1850s, most western evangelicals displayed more concern over their affiliations with the North or the South than with protecting and serving the distinct needs of border Christians. Not every westerner, however, had become entirely sectionalized along a North-South axis.[67] In this climate, many border congregations continued to function by leaving questions of affiliation—not to mention slavery—unresolved. One Missouri Presbyterian congregation would not debate their position on slavery. Discussion "in the pulpit" was "universally regarded inexpedient and impracticable."[68] In 1857, the ecumenical American Home Mission Society endeavored to discontinue funding for missionaries to any congregation that would admit a slaveholder. When asked if he served a proslavery congregation, a Missouri Presbyterian minister was uncertain how to reply: "A man in Missouri might give a different answer to this question from the one that would be given in New York."[69] By this he meant that, to a New Yorker, any congregation that tolerated slave-owning members must be openly proslavery. In Missouri, however, a mix of opinions on slavery could coexist in one congregation—so long as congregants kept those opinions out of church affairs.

Even after sectional division, evangelical denominations consistently placed a premium on growth in the border region. Expansion offered the means for each branch to gain social clout and enlarge its coffers. More importantly, it was a spiritual mandate that could not be ignored. Just as pre-schism evangelicals viewed the West as crucial because of its potential for growth, post-schism evangelicals eyed the border with the same ends in mind.

Each section jealously guarded its right to evangelize and establish churches in the border region while at the same time denouncing the other section for its incursions. This pattern of intersectional strife would last to the end of the nineteenth century. The editor of the Baptist Louisville *Western Recorder* maintained the border south "should not be intruded upon by agents of the Northern Society."[70] A Methodist from Missouri assured a friend that he did not give "any countenance" to the "Northerners in their revolutionary movements upon our territory"[71] At the same time, a Baltimore Methodist wrote to warn a friend that "the South would encroach on our limits."[72] Southern Methodist minister Jesse Boring eloquently expressed his concern about retaining and expanding territory in an 1850 letter to Bishop Robert Paine: "Are we doomed to remain within the small compass of Slaveholding Territory, and is this the last broad Commission of Christ to the ministry limited thus in regard to the ministry of the Church South? Surely not." Boring wrote, "If we as a church are cut off from extension, and the privilege of Contributing to the world's conversion, we must necessarily dwindle and die."[73] Boring anticipated a problem that would arrive sooner than he expected. So long as the southern churches defended the formation of separate branches as necessary to protect slavery, their justification for a separate existence would only last as long as slavery did. By avoiding claims to theological distinctiveness (a necessity to refute charges of schism), the southern churches linked their survival to the survival of slavery.

By the mid-1850s, northern and southern branches' characterizations of their sectional counterparts had become a tool in appealing to border evangelicals. Northern branches characterized the southern church as schismatic, proslavery, and sinful. As Southern Methodist Bishop Capers put it, "the settled policy of the Northern Connection is to hold us up as seceders and glorify themselves as the true and only legitimate Methodist Church."[74] Charles Elliott called the creation of the southern branch "an act of secession" declaring the southern branch "a pro-slavery church."[75] Lorenzo Waugh referenced secession when he argued that Southern Methodist behavior was preposterous and illegal. It was as if hypothetical "southern senators" who, in defense of slavery, went so far as to "*renounce* all *connection* with . . . the United States" and proceeded to "set up a '*new, separate, distinct*, and *independent*' civil organization."[76] Waugh could not have known that, in a little more than ten years, his analogy would no longer seem preposterous.

Meanwhile, the southern churches cast themselves as more morally and theologically pure than their northern counterparts. They characterized the northern branches as hotbeds of abolition and secular politicization—an incendiary allegation. Bishop Matthew Simpson remarked that those who favored uniting with the South "charged ignorance of the Bible in Northern Abolitionists and declared that they did not appeal to the Bible for the justness of their cause but to the writings of Jefferson."[77] In this manner, southerners attempted to align the West with their new denominations by appealing to the strong anti-abolitionist sentiments that pervaded the region. And, indeed, some westerners were persuaded that rising abolitionism in the Northeast was reason enough to join a proslavery church, even if they themselves were not proslavery. "Hitherto the South and West were too divided to unite in any plan of general operations," argued an 1845 editorial in the *Baptist Banner and Western Pioneer*. "But as the Boston Board have withdrawn the veil themselves" by refusing to appoint slaveholders, "the grounds of division are removed."[78] By focusing on securing western allegiance, national denominational branches brought the West's identity as a border to the fore. While the vision of an evangelical West did not entirely disappear, neither did it prove strong enough to overcome the sectionalizing force of the slavery debate.

CONCLUSION

By the mid-1850s, controversy generated by sectional schism and the process of denominational division began to recede. Northern and southern branches grudgingly agreed upon missionary "territory."[79] Individual churches accepted ministers. Cases over church property slowly found resolution in state and federal courts. Many border evangelicals and border-region religious organizations remained within the northern branches of their denominations, reflecting their prioritization of denominational unity over an explicit position on the slavery question. These evangelicals in the border states came to represent a sort of "loyal opposition" within the northern branches of each denomination. Their emphasis on unity over politicization forced denominational leaders from the North to temper their impulse toward adopting an outright antislavery stance for fear of losing brethren in the border states to southern branches.

Likewise, border congregants who aligned with the South provided a conservative check on radical proslavery impulses in the southern churches. The Danville Methodists—who voted to join the South but noted that they "deplore the warmth and indiscretion manifested by some of our Southern brethren"—provide a good example.[80] The Methodist annual conferences in Kentucky and Missouri elected to join the Church South, and for over a decade, voted to prevent the General Conference of the Church South from editing the Discipline (the bylaws and doctrine of the church) to explicitly state that slave owning was not a sin. As long as the northern branches did not become too politicized, most border evangelicals favored adherence to the North over uniting with the southern branches of the church, which had veered alarmingly toward the sin of schism through the formation of their sectional branches. "Has the division restored the harmony and good feeling between the brethren of the North and South?" asked one Baptist, "We think all must say it has not."[81]

Dividing the churches did nothing to halt the rising tide of sectionalism. Rather, it heralded sectional division in the nation as a whole. As disputes generated by schism died down, national politics loomed ever larger. In the 1840s, evangelical denominations clashed over internal conflicts; in the 1850s, the new sectional branches responded to external political controversy. Border churches would be tested anew by the decade of crisis that preceded Civil War. The western border became the site of sectional struggles over the expansion of slavery into the territories. In defense, border evangelicals who remained with northern churches increasingly relied upon their understanding of the doctrine of the spirituality of the church. The doctrine of spirituality prioritized political neutrality in the pulpit over expressions of support for the secular government. Border evangelicals of all three denominations adopted this position and demanded it of the northern branches with which they were affiliated.

— 4 —

MORAL AND POLITICAL THUNDERSTORMS

National Politics and Border Evangelicals

In the 1850s, the sectional conflict that culminated in the Civil War permeated the evangelical churches. On the border, it perpetuated the acrimonious divisions of the 1840s by keeping alive debates over slavery and sin. Within a decade, the same questions that had divided the churches—slavery, westward expansion, local autonomy—strained the unity of the nation itself. Southern evangelicals strengthened their biblical defense of slavery and, as the secession crisis came to a head, defended southern secession as well. Northern denominations, in contrast, found that retaining the loyalty of border clergy and congregants meant forgoing explicit expressions of antislavery sentiment. Once war began, however, northern clergy sprang to the defense of the Union cause. During this period, as sectional political debate dominated civil society, most border evangelicals attempted to maintain political neutrality in a highly politicized era. They responded to the events of the 1850s from a perspective shaped by the denominational divisions of the previous decade.

"When moral principles are the ground of controversy, and when the discussion turns upon the great questions of human rights, then no tongue should be dumb, no press should be silent," wrote Matthew Simpson in response to the Fugitive Slave Act in 1850. At thirty-eight, Simpson had served as president at two Methodist colleges and had spent two years as the editor of the influential Cincinnati *Western Christian Advocate*. He had become a leading light within the church. He had also, in remarkable contrast to his earlier beliefs, become "a vigorous controversialist."[1]

Seven years prior, during his tenure as president of Indiana Asbury, Simpson scrupulously avoided revealing even a hint of his own political views. "My most intimate friend has not heard me express any opinion even as to my own vote," Simpson had avowed in 1843. "I am not active in political life."[2] In 1848, Simpson accepted the editorship of the *Western Christian Advocate* with a pledge to avoid "controversy" and "make the paper strictly a church paper for the defense of the doctrines and polity of Methodism."[3] This nonconfrontational ethos was representative of antebellum border evangelicals. However, the Compromise of 1850—and the passage of the Fugitive Slave Act in particular, impelled Simpson to take a public stand on a political issue. Simpson, always privately antislavery, published an editorial in opposition to the act in his newfound political voice.

The harshest criticism Simpson received for his editorial came not from southerners, but from fellow border Methodists. "[N]ot only *you* will be calumniated, but the whole Methodist Church may be drawn into the whirlpool of politics," an Indiana resident cautioned. This correspondent also warned Simpson that he was at risk of being branded "an Abolitionist."[4] A former student from western Virginia urged Simpson "to leave off the *fugitive slave law from this time henceforth and forever*," arguing that political debate could never make the church "one whit more spiritual."[5] Another reader from the Indiana-Kentucky border urged Simpson to "abide" by the act and allow "*prudence* and a little *time*" to let the controversy come to rest.[6]

Much to the dismay of border moderates, it seemed that prudence and patience had vanished from formerly sober minds in the North and South. Simpson was just one of many evangelicals who publicly engaged with the moral and political debates surrounding slavery and westward expansion. During these years, however, border evangelicals often clung stubbornly to the hope that a careful separation of the moral and the political was possible and that moderation could prevent "alarming agitation."[7]

A DECADE OF SECTIONALIZATION

In the 1850s, the nation as a whole confronted the same problems that divided the Methodist and Baptist churches in the previous decade: maintaining unity in the face of a profound and deepening sectional rift over slavery. Mounting tension over the institution recast the West. Once a unifying focus of nationalistic and millennial dreams, the region became a contested wedge between North and South. The contest over land and slavery in the West strained the ties that had bound the region together.[8]

In 1846, while American soldiers fought in the Mexican War, congressmen anticipated that an American victory would herald the acquisition of vast tracts of new land in the far West.[9] In that year, Representative David Wilmot of Pennsylvania introduced his famous proviso proposing "neither slavery nor involuntary servitude shall ever exist in any part of said territory."[10] The proviso crystallized the growing tension between the sections. It passed in the northern-dominated House and failed in the southern-dominated Senate. In this climate of suspicion and sectional antagonism, Kentucky senator Henry Clay offered a complex set of resolutions designed to satisfy both sections—the Compromise of 1850.[11]

Congressional debates over the compromise lasted six months and also served as a referendum on the value of maintaining the Union. In this forum, two elder statesmen invoked Methodist and Baptist division to plead their case. South Carolina Senator John C. Calhoun offered these denominational splits as cautionary examples of the folly of allowing debate over slavery to divide the nation. Calhoun explained that "the great religious denominations . . . originally embraced the whole Union" and "all these denominations . . . were organized very much upon the principle of our political institutions." As border evangelicals had during sectional division, he compared the national denominational meetings to Congress. "The strong ties which hold each denomination together formed a strong cord to hold the whole Union together; but, as powerful as they were, they have not been able to resist the explosive effect of slavery agitation."[12] Calhoun saw the disintegration of the churches as both an alarming gauge of the state of the union and a powerful warning against attempts to end or limit slavery.

Senator Daniel Webster, Calhoun's colleague from Massachusetts, extended the church analogy in his response. Webster, like Calhoun, saw the division of the church as an ominous sign and a foreboding symbol. But for Webster, the lessons to be drawn from the division were of the danger of inflexibility, of failure to compromise, and of an inability to tolerate the inevitable diversity that arose in a church that spanned "the whole country from Maine to Georgia." Webster explained that he had "read all the proceedings," but still did not think "that there was any real ground" for the Methodist split. Rather, Methodists were divided because "[i]n all such disputes, there will sometimes be men found with whom everything is absolute—absolutely wrong or absolutely right." Such inflexible thinking in the face of deep moral disagreement, Webster contended, had doomed the Methodists, North and South. Webster concluded that divisions such as the one that threatened the

Union could easily be avoided through flexibility and compromise.[13] Calhoun and Webster's exchange served to cement in popular memory the idea that evangelical denominational divisions were at least partly responsible for the disintegration of sectional ties nationwide.[14]

With the passage of the Compromise of 1850, border evangelicals hoped that the sectional crisis had been resolved. "The signs discernable in our political and moral heavens seem to indicate that the slavery question will soon pass away and reveal a bright and benignant firmament," a Kentucky Baptist newspaper optimistically suggested.[15] "On the whole . . . the sentiments of the North towards the South are generally more favorable than they are usually supposed to be," remarked another editorial. "The more frequent interchange of personal Christian intercourse, particularly among ministers, would no doubt contribute to the promotion and perpetuity of that Union."[16] This optimism proved unfounded. As events in Kansas would soon reveal, "more frequent interchange" between northerners and southerners only led to more frequent conflict.

The Compromise of 1850 temporarily saved the Union but ultimately did as much to exacerbate sectionalism as to combat it.[17] Still, moderates who supported the Union above all favored the compromise, including the Fugitive Slave Act. Matthew Simpson's public opposition to the act generated consternation among border ministers who urged him to "abide by the *compromise measures*."[18] Compromise—the moderate solution to intractable sectional difference—had held the nation together through earlier crises. Border evangelicals also knew that, unless respected, compromises could fail spectacularly in populations with mixed political views, particularly when they generated competition, as the Methodist Plan of Separation had done. Nevertheless, border moderates clung to the hope that compromise could spare the Union.[19]

BLEEDING KANSAS

The intensity of sectional animosity came to the fore in the West, during the violent aftermath of the 1854 Kansas-Nebraska Act. The act extended popular sovereignty to the newly organized Kansas and Nebraska territories. Popular sovereignty allowed residents of territories to vote upon whether slavery would be permitted. Proslavery and free-soil advocates competed to rush settlers into the territory—each side hoping to outnumber the other by the time of the territorial election of 1855.[20] In the scramble to settle Kansas, both northerners and southerners aided emigrants in reaching the territory. But election fraud gave the slavery advocates an advantage: Kansas bordered the slave state of Missouri, and Missourians could easily cross the border and stuff the ballot box in favor of slavery in the territory. The contested elections bitterly divided the territory, enthroned competing governments, fostered guerrilla warfare, and cost the lives of over two hundred people.[21]

Local evangelicals found themselves at the center of the "moral and political thunderstorms" of the Kansas controversy.[22] Reverend Thomas Lamar, a Presbyterian minister in Weston, Missouri, noted in 1854 that "the chances for building up a permanent church, where I have been laboring, have very much diminished." He explained that most members of his congregation "expect to move over to Kansas Territory." Lamar had recently learned that "the Proslavery men are making every effort now in Kansas to organize a body of men sufficiently powerful to drive out all the free state men." In addition, he had heard that, at Lawrence, these men were "doing all in their power to arm and fortify for a successful resistance."[23] Iowa senator James Harlan, a devout Methodist, wrote to Matthew Simpson from Washington, D.C., to share his worries that "in less than ninety days there will have commenced a terrible struggle on the soil of Kansas between her *bonafide* citizens and armed marauders from Southern states."[24]

Just as proslavery and antislavery advocates hurried to maximize the number of emigrants to Kansas from their sections, members of northern and southern branches of the evangelical churches fretted about establishing their denominations in the newly opened territory.[25] In 1856, the Southern Baptist Convention "recognized the Territory of Kansas as a desirable field for Missionary operations" and made plans for a mission "to occupy the ground." John Hill Luther was a South Carolina Baptist who relocated to Kansas City, Missouri. From there, he raised funds for the Kansas mission, urging fellow Baptists to send "men and money."[26] Luther tied the interests of the West, territorial expansion, and the protection of southern interests to the establishment of the Southern Baptist denomination in Kansas. The Southern Baptists were not alone in their urgency to settle Kansas. "I find this is an important period with our church in this territory," wrote Northern Methodist Bishop Janes in the spring of 1858. "People are rushing in by the multitudes. Ministers of other denominations are coming in large numbers and with large means. A few months now must determine the relative position of denominations."[27]

Morality and politics were inseparable in the Kansas conflict. John Hill

Luther argued that Southern Baptists in the territory played a dual role. First, he wrote, "as citizens we display a patriotic ardor in establishing our constitutional rights, and protecting our homes and our honest interests." Second, as clergy, they provided "the pure Gospel earnestly preached, and the pastoral relation faithfully sustained." The latter, he argued, were the "mightier forces in forming the sentiments and habits of the people."[28] With so much at stake, settlers were willing to lay down their lives for the future of Kansas. Nicole Etcheson argues that this "blend of morality, constitutional rights, and politics" could not be untangled democratically. She roots much of the local impetus for violent conflict in the seemingly irresolvable "tension between morality and majority rule." Popular sovereignty could not resolve an issue that people on both sides had freighted with such great moral weight.[29]

Popular sovereignty complemented the developing ideas behind the doctrine of spirituality adopted by moderate border-state evangelicals. Advocates of popular sovereignty wished to keep morality separate from politics—they viewed slavery as a political issue only, one that could be resolved at the ballot box, and not at the pulpit. Stephen Douglas, the Illinois senator who was the architect of popular sovereignty, condemned ministers who opposed the Kansas-Nebraska Act on moral grounds as "political preachers."[30] Evangelical border moderates embraced a complementary position—they argued that politics, in this case, abolitionism, should be kept separate from religion. Douglas sought to keep morality out of politics; these clergy angled to keep a moral issue out of religion. "My own course has been, and will continue to be, to avoid entirely the discussion of political questions, in public or in private," a Missouri minister wrote in 1856. As for the "rabid and infuriated advocates of Southern or of Northern rights," who demanded he take a side in the slavery debate: "to comply with the demands of either party would be, in our view, to rend asunder the church of Christ, to desecrate or dissolve the ministry, and, in trying to save the country, or a part of it, to inflict an irreparable injury upon the kingdom and cause of our Lord Jesus Christ."[31] This, in a nutshell, was the moderate argument against "political preaching" on the border.

Like Douglas, moderate border evangelicals defined slavery as a purely political issue and one, therefore, about which clergy had no place expressing opinions. Both shared a common hope: that the nation could continue to exist, and even prosper, half slave and half free. And for both, a valuable prize was at stake. Popular-sovereignty advocates stood to lose the Union, and the moderate evangelicals stood to lose the United States for the Kingdom of God.

Such thinking emerged from the racism that enabled both groups to value national unity above the liberty of enslaved African Americans. Keeping religion out of politics and politics out of religion meant keeping millions enslaved.

Settlers in Kansas maintained no such separation. There, free-soil and proslavery settlers—who had both merged the moral and the political—clashed over the future of the territory. Again, the political conflict affected evangelicals. Thomas Lamar, a minister who lived on the western border of Missouri, informed an eastern correspondent that "the rabid proslavery citizens of the county" had joined together to defend slavery in Kansas." He reported that the "Platte County Defensive Association" had "passed a resolution, affirming 'slavery to be a political and moral good.'"[32]

A close look at another minister's experience in Platte County illustrates how accelerating sectionalization and the "tension between morality and majority rule" affected evangelicals.[33] Frederick Starr, a Presbyterian from Rochester, New York, came to Platte County in 1849. When the territory opened, Starr, a Free Soiler, immediately staked a claim just across the Missouri River from Fort Leavenworth. He did so in the interests of defending the recently repealed Missouri Compromise—which he considered one of "the old time honored and sacred landmarks of our nation"—and also in the interest of owning potentially valuable property within the proposed city of Leavenworth. Starr declared his land "the best site for a city in the whole territory."[34]

While Starr engaged in the usual struggles for congregants with missionaries from other denominations, his chief antagonists were the proslavery leaders of the Platte County Defensive Association. The Defensive Association condemned Starr as "a *Political Priest*" and spread reports that left him "stigmatized as an Abolitionist."[35] The association called Starr before a kangaroo court of proslavery residents and accused him of abolitionism. When directly questioned on his beliefs about slavery, Starr echoed the association's own creed with his reply: "I believe slavery is a political and moral evil." However, he continued, he was no abolitionist. "I say the man who calls me an abolitionist is a worse man and a worse thief than any negro stealer," Starr asserted, condemning "the slanderer who would fain brand innocent men as abolitionists."

"I came to this state," Starr told his fellow citizens, "to bless if possible the souls of both masters and slaves." He clarified that he would never "interfere" with slavery itself.[36] But these assurances that he was not an abolitionist were not enough to clear Starr in the eyes of the Defensive Association. For while he opposed abolitionism, Starr did believe that owning slaves was a sin. In contrast, the association's leader championed slavery as "a blessing to the white race and the negro."[37] Starr represented what Luke Harlow calls "Christian conservative antislavery."[38] As Starr's experience illustrates, this position rapidly became difficult to sustain in the heightened political climate of the 1850s. Late that spring, Starr fled the region under the threat of physical violence.

Starr's predicament made him a minor hero among midwestern free-soil Christians, who described him as a martyr "driven from his post in Kansas as a Christian Missionary . . . at the Bidding and Dictation of the Slave Power."[39] After his ordeal, Starr gave lectures encouraging free-soil northerners to settle in Kansas. At these lectures, Starr declared that he "went to Missouri to preach the Gospel" and that, before he went, "he did not expect to agitate the question of Slavery." Nonetheless, his experience in Kansas convinced Starr that "ministers of the Gospel" should "look after the interests of their flock political as well as religious." Starr was remembered in a modest way as an abolitionist hero, despite his denunciation of abolitionism. Upon the occasion of his death in 1867, a New York state minister delivered a memorial sermon praising Starr for advocating abolition "at the peril of his life and long before public and even Christian sentiment was what it is now." This posthumous judgment drew on Starr's later shift to antislavery "sentiment," but mischaracterized the views Starr had held while living in Kansas. There he had denounced abolitionism.[40]

Starr's experience and his subsequent framing of the story—whether an accurate account of personal transformation or a politically advantageous embellishment—illustrates several characteristics of evangelical religion in the Northwest during the 1850s. Sectional conflict gradually pushed Starr from a policy of noninvolvement to open expression of antislavery sentiment. Likewise, northern denominations gradually grew more antislavery over the course of the decade.[41] Starr's experience on the highly contested Kansas-Missouri border also underscored an emerging reality: only the most unswervingly, exactingly "nonpolitical" ministers could work productively in the border region. Missionaries and evangelicals who did became involved in politics, whether intentionally or not, also served as a powerful lesson about the dangers inherent in political engagement, particularly in the contested border region.

Of course, defining oneself as "nonpolitical" was an inherently political act, no matter how assiduously these clergy insisted it was not. "As for myself, I have kept clear of taking sides either way," wrote another Presbyterian minister from western Missouri. Unlike Starr, he successfully maintained his post during the Kansas debacle. He met with the usual accusations of abolitionism, but the charges did not stick. He owed his success—at least until the war came—to his refusal to champion or condemn either party in the Bleeding Kansas controversy, explaining, "some good men acted *very wrong* who went to K[ansas], from both sections of the country." Furthermore, he blamed members of "'Kansas Aid Societies' both North and South" who interfered from "outside of the territory."[42] Placing blame for local strife on outside agitators from the North and the South and practicing strict neutrality proved an effective strategy, but it also meant feigning that the struggle over slavery was devoid of moral significance. As both northern and southern denominational leaders actively promoted their sections' respective causes in the sectionalized political contests unfolding in the West, border moderates insisted that the slavery issue could somehow be avoided.

Slavery divided political parties just as it had denominations, and the process destroyed the once nationally prominent Whig Party. After the fallout from the Kansas-Nebraska Act, the disintegration of the Whigs was nearly complete. Antislavery northerners could be found in a fractured array of parties. Among their ranks were disaffected northern Democrats; northern Whigs; Temperance Party members; anti-Catholic nativist Know-Nothings; and Free Soilers who opposed the spread of slavery into territories on the grounds that it limited opportunities for white men. In 1854, northerners concerned about the expansion of slavery founded a new party—the Republican Party. It appealed to many in the splintering northern electorate and swiftly rose to dominance in the North.[43]

The newly coalesced Republican Party lost the presidential election of 1856, but that defeat held the promise of future success. It revealed the strength of the northern voting bloc when united in a single party and behind a single candidate. From Missouri, Thomas Horace Cleland observed that a Republican president was "sure to be elected in 1860!" He expressed "great fears of the dissolution of the union—the South will not bear an 'abolishion' president."[44] Cleland's fears were realized four years later. The election of Abraham Lincoln—who was antislavery, if not abolitionist—strained national ties to the breaking point, setting into motion secession and Civil War.

SECTIONAL DENOMINATIONS POLITICIZED

As in the political parties, the division between northern and southern denominational branches deepened in response to the escalating sectional crisis of the 1850s. Once the denominations divided sectionally, members from the opposing sections no longer served as internal checks limiting proslavery advocacy, in the case of the South, or antislavery viewpoints, in the case of the North. Division among American evangelicals also increased in response to—and contributed to—national sectionalism. In all three denominations, southerners and northerners took more outspoken positions on slavery. Presbyterians, for their part, finally faced explicitly sectional division. And Northern Methodists again wrestled with the question of slavery and sin.

In the 1850s, southern ministers honed a biblically based argument defending slavery as a positive good.[45] "No man who calls slavery an evil can honestly defend it," wrote a Southern Baptist in 1860, criticizing the hypocrisy of moderate evangelicals who subscribed to the "necessary evil" defense of slavery. "We defend slavery because of our honest conviction that it is socially, politically, and morally right. This is the only true Southern platform, and it is as scriptural as [it is] Southern."[46] The author's insistence on the positive, biblical morality of slavery reflects the fully articulated proslavery theology of the South.

Meanwhile, in the North, abolitionist evangelicals worked diligently to persuade members of their denominations to adopt strict antislavery positions. However, the presence of border moderates, as well as an ingrained conservatism, curtailed the abolitionists' progress. Mainstream northern evangelicals did not adopt a fully developed antislavery theology during the 1850s as abolitionists had hoped. John McKivigan reminds us that the abundance of scholarly attention to abolitionists in the antebellum churches has obscured the essentially conservative character of those institutions in the nineteenth century: "Despite more than three decades of abolitionist lobbying, few denominations ever accepted the principles of the inherent sinfulness of slaveholding and the equality of the races." Much of the motivation to maintain this conservative stance can be attributed to the desire to appease border moderates.[47]

Most northern evangelicals considered the preservation of the Union a higher priority than the abolition of slavery. This can be attributed to pervasive racism that allowed the emancipation of the enslaved to be cast as a purely political—instead of a moral—issue. Old School Presbyterian Charles Hodge, of Princeton, wrote an address "On the State of the Country" late in 1860. He published it, he explained, in order to prove to "conservative men at the South" that the whole North was not abolitionized, and that the mass of the people were true friends to the constitutional rights of the South. If people like him did not act on behalf of the Union cause, Hodge feared, the country would be "plunged into unknown evils."[48] He did not see the incongruity in giving sectional division a moral valence—calling it evil—while protesting that slavery could only be discussed in political terms. After his paper was published, a reader from Ohio wrote to Hodge to thank him: "you have in these articles, and in your commentaries, expressed the very sentiments of fully nine tenths of the ministers and private members of our Church in all this region and in the whole west and northwest."[49]

Nevertheless, the northern churches did become significantly more antislavery during the 1850s. Once northern churches were separated from the moderating influences of their southern counterparts, the pleas of abolitionists found a more receptive audience. The political events of the decade also increased antislavery sentiment. One example of this increased polarization can be found in the New School Presbyterian sectional schism.

The split between the New and Old School Presbyterians in 1837 allowed the Presbyterian Church to avoid sectional divisions until the eve of the Civil War. Old School Presbyterians resolutely continued to table all concerns related to slavery. The expansive and inclusive New School, less hesitant to take on social and political issues, declared slavery an "evil" from its earliest days and had condemned slavery since 1837. Despite this policy, the predominantly northern New School included a significant number of southern members until 1857. Harold Parker credits this cohesiveness to the experience of expulsion from the Old School and a righteous faith in doctrinal superiority.[50] Before 1857, doctrinal principles acted as a unifying force even in the face of the controversial issue of slavery.

Northerners in the New School gradually became more outspoken critics of slavery over the course of the 1850s. When cases involving the censure of a slaveholding Mississippi minister and a scornful denunciation of Presbyterian slave owners arose at the General Assembly in 1857, Southern New School loyalty began to falter.[51] Southerners complained about frequent condemnations of slavery on the floor of the assembly, and the antislavery majority of the New School responded by expelling the southern presbyteries. Later that year, these six presbyteries met in Washington and constituted themselves as an independent southern branch of the New School Presbyterian Church. Like other sectionalized branches, they declared themselves "a national church."[52]

New School Presbyterians on the border deplored the split. They resented being caught between increasing abolitionist sympathies among northern brethren and rising sectional defensiveness in the South. "Everything like spirituality and vital religion seems to be twice dead and plucked up by the roots," lamented Reverend Mills, a missionary in Kentucky. Mills explained that he and his fellow border New Schoolers would only join the Southern New School if it "*publicly takes the right ground on slavery.*" By "the right ground," he meant a moderate antislavery stance, not a pro-southern, positive defense of the institution. Like many border evangelicals of this era, Mills objected both to northern abolitionist tendencies and to southern proslavery theology. If both branches persisted in their "bad management of the slavery question," Mills proposed, "we will then just remain as an *independent church,*" one that would provide for both sections "a specimen of our own good management."[53]

New School Presbyterians in Missouri expressed similar frustration, feeling that they did not "belong to either the North or the South."[54] A minister from LaGrange described a typical border congregation: "One tenth of the members of this church are slaveholders and about one fourth are members of slaveholding families." The rest of the congregation were "decidedly opposed to the extension of slavery and in favor of gradual emancipation. There are none who hold to ultra antislavery sentiments or who think the practice of slaveholding *itself sinful.*" The minister did not know how his mixed congregation would weather the "political passions . . . on the merits of emancipation" prompted by the New School division.[55]

Increased politicization contributed to rifts among Northern Methodists as well. In 1860, over the protestations of border moderates, the Northern Methodist Episcopal Church approved the "New Chapter" at its General Conference in Buffalo, New York. The New Chapter expressly condemned "buying, selling, or holding of human beings" as "inconsistent" with "that Rule in our Discipline which requires all who desire to continue among us 'to do no harm' and 'to avoid evil of every kind.'"[56] This amounted to calling slavery evil and generated significant protests from border-state Northern Methodists. The passage of the 1860 New Chapter was a full-fledged repudiation of the earlier Northern Methodist position that "mere ownership of slave property . . . constitutes no legal barrier to the election or ordination of ministers."[57] Thus, without actually labeling slaveholding a sin, the antislavery contingent—riding a wave of sectional enthusiasm—passed the most explicit condemnation of the institution ever adopted in the General Conference up to that point. The New Chapter did not prohibit slavery, but it did condemn it and "affectionately admonish all our preachers and people to keep themselves pure from this great evil and seek its extirpation by all lawful and Christian means."[58]

The New Chapter enraged northern-affiliated border Methodists, many of whom were still smarting from the Plan of Separation debacle of the 1840s. The worst conflicts occurred in Maryland, Kentucky, and Missouri. In all three states, sizable groups advocated a complete rupture with the northern branch and union with the South. Observing the situation in 1860, a western Virginia minister declared, "as the matter now stands, the Church in Va. is in great peril."[59] Similar reports emerged from Maryland. "In *our Conf[eren]ce* there is a great aversion to the New Chapter," reported Reverend Hy Slicer of Baltimore.[60]

Concerned border Methodists, particularly those in the Baltimore Conference—which extended into a portion of Virginia—sought to prevent the division.[61] "I can't be a party to the complete degradation of the Baltimore Conference," wrote Elisha P. Phelps from Lewisburg, Virginia. Phelps made an "effort to maintain the unity of the Church," proposing that, to this end, the Baltimore Conference "authorize the publication of the discipline, *omitting* the New Chapter, thus assuring our people and the public that said conference will not recognize said chapter as *law or doctrine* nor circulate it among us."[62] These efforts failed, and the Baltimore Conference divided in the fall of 1860, following a meeting at Staunton, Virginia.[63] "I had many sad hours at Staunton," reported Reverend Ricketts of Washington, D.C., who was "deeply afflicted and mortified" to observe the depth of sectionalization there. Ricketts called the division a "fearful deed" and deplored the "many mournful jeremiads in behalf of *poor, suffering down-trodden oppressed Virginia!*"[64] Ricketts's observations reveal the extent of politicization: the Virginia Methodists in the Baltimore Conference identified the actions of their church with the political cause of their state, and therefore decided to join the Southern Methodists.

Moderate Methodists worried, as did one Maryland minister, that, with the division of the Baltimore Conference, "the whole Border will in the end follow" it south, ultimately threatening "the M.E.C. *north* of Mason's and Dixon's line."[65] Despite these fears, the division in the Baltimore conference was the only realignment caused by the New Chapter. Although outraged over the New Chapter, other border Methodists affiliated with the North retained that connection. This speaks to the strength of their antipathy to southern radicalism. Although greatly angered, most moderates still saw the northern church as the more conservative choice.

For example, a Baltimore Methodist who condemned the New Chapter nevertheless asserted that he desired "to remain in the old church a while longer." Many of his congregants owned slaves, but he insisted that they did not "sanction the traffic in slaves" as the Southern Methodists did. However, he feared that the Northern Methodist Episcopal Church would adopt an even stronger antislavery position in the future. In that case, he told his congregants, "we will have good reason to secede."[66] Northern-affiliated border Methodists were reaching their limit. Still, they remained in the church, and as long as they did so, they prevented the northern churches from becoming as strongly antislavery as the southern churches were proslavery.

Moderates formed a smaller minority in the South, and their influence within the denomination was much weaker than in the North. Concentrated on the border and in the upper South, they had less internal leverage, and their position weakened over the course of the 1850s. By joining the southern branches, they implicitly accepted the argument that slavery was not a sin. Nevertheless, moderate opposition did prevent proslavery alterations to the language on slavery in the Discipline of the Southern Methodist Episcopal Church until 1854, a full ten years after the 1844 schism. And even when they did change the language, Southern Methodists did not go so far as to embrace slavery as a positive good.[67] In fact, it wasn't until 1858 that the Southern General Conference was able to pass the "Alabama Resolution," which expunged the Discipline of the old, equivocal rule on slavery and rendered the denomination adamantly proslavery in word as well as in deed. Delegates from the border and upper South strongly opposed the Alabama Resolution and attempted to block its passage, but to no avail.[68]

EVANGELICALS AND THE COMING OF WAR

Following Abraham Lincoln's election in November of 1860, southern secessionist agitation reached a peak. That December, South Carolina formally left the Union, followed by six other states. And after the Confederate Army fired on Fort Sumter in April of 1861, the upper South states of Tennessee, Arkansas, North Carolina, and Virginia seceded as well.[69] Most northern evangelicals could scarcely resist some comment on the coming of war. Still, even in the midst of war fever, they had to be careful to appease both the moderates and the abolitionists within their respective branches.[70] As for southern evangelicals, they linked the cause of slavery and the preservation of the South to God's divine plan and defended the South with patriotic sermons and addresses.

In an influential and widely read piece, Benjamin Morgan Palmer, an Old School Presbyterian from New Orleans, argued that the South should be independent following Lincoln's election.[71] Likewise, in the Southern Methodist Episcopal Church, William Wightman, of Alabama, depicted the newly formed Confederacy as a divinely sanctioned "new order of things." And in 1863, Bishop George Pierce addressed the Confederate legislature, declaring that the cause of the Confederate government "shall ally us in friendship with heaven and stamp upon all our prosperity the seal of the divine blessing."[72] Baptists evinced no less fervor for the Confederate cause. "I confidently believe that in leading us through this fiery trial, God is preparing a chosen people for a great mission," proclaimed Alabama Baptist Isaac Taylor Tichenor in 1863.[73] Southern clergy used the authority of the pulpit to defend the Confederacy and argue for its divine mandate. This rhetoric, as it turns out, did not die with the Confederacy, but would subsequently be channeled into the preservation of separate southern denominations after the Civil War.

Southern evangelicals had been more politicized than their northern counterparts in the 1850s. However, upon the outbreak of war, most northern clergy patriotically declared their support for the Union cause and expressed a conviction that God favored it. The Methodist General Conference of 1864 called the Union cause the "cause of God and humanity," and Bishop Simpson declared Union victory "the design of Providence."[74] At the 1861 meeting of a Baptist assembly in Brooklyn, attendees resolved, "the National Government deserves loyal adhesion and unstinted support. . . . The Gospel of Christ, then, sanctions true patriotism."[75] As early as 1862, Northern Baptists began to send missionaries into the South, and thousands of Baptists joined the Union Army as chaplains.[76]

At their 1861 General Assembly, northern New School Presbyterians, recently unfettered from the dampening influence of southern moderates, passed a resolution declaring "an undiminished attachment to the great principles of civil and religious freedom, on which our National Government is based." Furthermore, they stated, "there is no blood or treasure too precious to be devoted to the defense and perpetuity of the Government." In addition, the northern New School called for members to be "fervent in prayer for the President of the United States" and declared that the injury done to the Union by the act of secession constituted an "injury . . . done to the kingdom of the Redeemer."[77] The northern New School Assembly enjoyed unanimous patriotism at the outbreak of war because of the 1857 sectional schism. In contrast, the arrival of war found the Old School Presbyterians still united. Secession proved the breaking point for the last remaining national organization within the major evangelical denominations. In 1861, the Old School divided into northern and southern branches.

OLD SCHOOL PRESBYTERIAN SCHISM

In the antebellum Old School, Presbyterians rigorously avoided all political topics, including slavery. This choice reflected both the explosiveness of the issue and the conservative nature of their faith. Faced with the changing role of the church in response to the American political crisis, "the Old School sought to claim a smaller domain but one with more secure boundaries."[78] For a time, this strategy succeeded. With the coming of the Civil War, however, even the Old School could not table political questions.

In May 1861, the Old School convened in Philadelphia. At the convention, Reverend Gardiner Spring of New York suggested that the assembly make "some expression of their devotion to the Union of these States, and their loyalty to the government." This suggestion resulted in the "Spring Resolutions," a document condemning secession and professing "unabated loyalty" to the federal government and the U.S. Constitution.[79]

The resolutions constituted a direct challenge to any minister sympathetic to the southern cause. They also limited options for those who favored a strict separation of the spiritual and the political. The southern and conservative border clergymen in attendance immediately registered a protest. Charles Hodge, of the conservative Princeton Seminary, led the group. Hodge pointed out that the resolutions forced southerners "to choose between allegiance to their State and allegiance to the church."[80] Much to the horror of the conservative Presbyterian leaders, the assembly adopted Dr. Spring's resolutions. The faction that opposed the resolutions consisted primarily of border Presbyterians because southern Old School Presbyterians—the Spring Resolutions' harshest critics—largely did not attend the 1861 General Assembly. Instead, angry Southern Presbyterians withdrew from the North and directed their energies toward forming a southern church.[81] James Lyon observed that the resolutions made "an instantaneous unit of the Southern Churches!"[82] They broke the silence on political topics and formed the perfect excuse for southerners to withdraw. In later years, southerners would use the resolutions as evidence that the southern church was innocent of schism and to justify the continued separation of the Northern and Southern Old School bodies.

To the border moderates who opposed political debate at the General Assembly, it seemed as though madness had seized men on both sides of the controversy. Nonetheless, horror of schism and a commitment to church unity ensured that, despite their misgivings, the border Synods remained with the Northern Old School.[83]

After the disruptive General Assembly of 1861, Southern Presbyterian leaders spent the summer and autumn feverishly organizing their presbyteries and formally withdrawing from the now avowedly pro-Union body. On December 4, the Southern Old School Synods met in Atlanta and constituted themselves as the Presbyterian Church in the Confederate States of America (PCCSA).[84] By the end of 1861, the American Presbyterian Church was thus divided into four branches: the Northern PCUSA New School, the Southern New School (now called the United Synod of the South), the Northern PCUSA Old School, and the newly formed PCCSA.

James Henley Thornwell of South Carolina articulated the grievances and justified the actions of the synods of the PCCSA in his "Address to the Churches of the World," which became the new organization's founding text. Thornwell's address was crafted to ensure that the PCCSA would "not be regarded in any corner of the world as guilty of schism." The southern churches withdrew from the Presbyterian Church of the United States of America, Thornwell explained, precisely because of a desire to avoid political debate, out of which schism could so easily arise. Quite simply, if the two bodies remained united, "the political questions which divide us as citizens, will be obtruded on our Church Courts, and discussed by Christian Ministers with all the acrimony, bitterness and rancor" that these questions historically produced.[85]

Thornwell did not claim, however, that doctrinal differences distinguished the newly formed PCCSA from its parent body, the Old School PCUSA. His justification for division was purely political; as the nation divided, so too should the Presbyterian Church. The claims to uniquely southern doctrinal purity that emerged after the war do not appear in the address. Quite the opposite: "There is no schism," wrote Thornwell of the relationship between Northern and Southern Presbyterians, "churches may be perfectly at one in every principle of faith and order, and yet geographically distinct, and mutually independent."[86] According to Thornwell, the PCCSA simply constituted a new national organization for a new nation. It was an organization that leant explicit support to the Confederate cause.

The melding of causes divine and political occurred more slowly in the North because so many moderates remained within the northern branches. John McKivigan asserts that most churches "complied with the scruples of their conservative element and proclaimed support solely for military efforts to maintain the civil government," retaining a low profile on the slavery question. By 1864, however, nearly every major evangelical group in the North had issued public declarations of support not only for the Union, but for the abolition of slavery as well.[87]

CONCLUSION

During the 1830s and 1840s, both the challenges of evangelizing the West and internal divisions over the sinfulness of slavery preoccupied the Presbyterian, Methodist, and Baptist denominations in the United States. In the 1850s, the debates over slavery that had divided the churches plunged the nation as a whole into discord. The border was the site of many of the major instances of sectional conflict during the decade. Kansas and Nebraska territories lay just west of Missouri, and the violent struggle over slavery in the territories played out on the border. The Ohio River marked the dividing line between freedom and slavery and became the symbol of the controversial Fugitive Slave Act.

Southern evangelicals, who formed their own denominational branches in defense of their belief that slavery was not a sin, became increasingly involved in the positive defense of slavery. They supported the extension of slavery to the territories and denounced abolitionism. At the same time, northern evangelicals gradually grew more supportive of the antislavery position. However, two factors forestalled an outright embrace of a sectionalized political position in northern churches during the 1850s. The first of these was fear of alienating border moderates, who made up a significant minority of the northern branches. The second was a strain of racism that enabled many northerners to cast emancipation as purely political and not moral. Border moderates continued to denounce "political preaching" despite the direct moral implications of the slavery debate and related political topics of the day.

By mid-century, the major evangelical denominations, once the outsiders and upstarts of the Second Great Awakening, were woven into the fabric of civil society. As the nation plunged headlong into war, northern and southern evangelicals enthusiastically followed. On the border, meanwhile, evangelical moderates put their nonpolitical ideals and the doctrine of spirituality to the greatest test—remaining neutral in a civil war. In wartime, denominational organizations and secular authorities would both demand that churches align themselves politically. By the end of the war, the weight of these demands would prove to be almost unbearable, and border evangelicals would begin a transition from a loyal opposition within the northern denominations to independence to eventual affiliation with southern denominations. This process was the product of both the political peculiarities of the border region and the constraints imposed by genuine religious conviction.

— 5 —

WORSHIPPING UNDER THE SHADOW OF THE FLAG

Wartime Conflict and Federal Response

Early in 1863, Union Provost Marshal William S. Fish decreed that the American flag must fly over every congregation gathering in the city of Baltimore. Reverend John Dashiell ignored the order. That Sunday, Dashiell discovered a surprising sight: a flag had been lashed to the exterior of the meeting place, and the window behind it securely locked. Before beginning his service, Dashiell "broke one of the panes of glass and removed the flag." Similar mutual provocations continued for several weeks, until the Methodist congregation resolved to meet elsewhere. But Provost Marshal Fish was not satisfied. Backed by an order from Major General Robert C. Schenck, Fish wrote to Dashiell: "I understand that rather than worship God under the shadow of the American flag, you have . . . chosen some other place for no other purpose than evading this order." He ordered Dashiell to "cause to be conspicuously displayed, in the public building or buildings where you meet tomorrow . . . the American flag."[1]

A trustee of the church sent Fish an assurance that the congregation was not disloyal. Rather, they objected to the display of the flag "upon the ground and reason that they were denied the right to worship God *without* the display of such ensign."[2] But Fish would not be swayed. He ordered the Union cavalry to arrest and imprison Dashiell.

In Kentucky, Stuart Robinson, minister and editor of the Louisville *True Presbyterian,* took note of the incident, clipping an article from the *Baltimore Gazette* and pasting it carefully into one of his scrapbooks. During the Civil War, Robinson recorded many similar cases of clergy arrested, forced to take oaths, and imprisoned. He archived each incident to use as evidence for his claim that the federal government intervened regularly in religious affairs, thus violating "the entire separation of Church and State." Worse yet, he charged, northern Christians happily assisted with this "wanton dalliance of the Protestant Church with the State." In "Ecclesiastico-Military Councils," Robinson alleged, northern churches and federal authorities cooperated to limit freedoms, pervert true religion, and persecute the faithful—all in the name of ensuring loyalty to the Union.[3]

Robinson's concerns reflected the unease of a large number of evangelicals living in the border region during the Civil War years. Border evangelicals had successfully embraced neutrality as a strategy for navigating denominational conflict over slavery in the preceding decades. Many remained, in the words of one Baptist, "determined to take a high neutral stand, knowing no North or South."[4]

But the strategy of neutrality was effective only so long as a balance of power existed between northern and southern churches. The coming of the war and military involvement with churches upset this balance. Military authorities, knowing the strategic importance of securing the border for the Union, enacted measures designed to ensure the emotional loyalty of the people, not just the political loyalty of the state. These included attempts to enforce the patriotism of border evangelicals. Clergy and churches occupied a gray area between public and private that led to unprecedented state involvement with border churches during the war. Because of their presumed local influence, border clergy were subject to mandatory loyalty oaths, coerced patriotism, arrest and detention, forced newspaper closures, and even banishment.

Throughout the war, border clergy nevertheless insisted that preaching could be politically neutral. But Union authorities (and Unionist evangelicals) disagreed; they argued that in the pulpit, just as in politics, neutrality was "treason in effect."[5] The interactions between "neutral" border clergy, federal authorities, and Unionist evangelicals shaped the religious life of evangelical Protestants on the border during the war years. While the Civil War lasted, Unionists—from the church and the military—managed to exert control over moderate and Confederate-sympathizing border clergy. However, the experience strengthened the border commitment to the "spirituality of the church"—the separation of politics and pulpit. Ultimately, close monitoring of border clergy in wartime fostered antagonism that led to postwar discord. Secular involvement was limited to the war years but had long-lasting effects on American religion. The strain of the war years severely eroded the bonds that tied border evangelicals to the northern branches of their denominations.

After the war, the churches of the border region would begin a transition from a loyal opposition within the northern denominations to independence and, eventually, to affiliation with southern denominations.

THE BORDER AND LOYALTY IN THE FIRST YEARS OF WAR

Early in the war, Abraham Lincoln is reported to have remarked, "I hope to have God on my side, but I must have Kentucky."[6] The border region—that area within which members of individual congregations divided over their sectional identity—was also a critical military and political battleground in the contest between the North and the South. The combined white population of the border slave-states alone—Delaware, Maryland, Kentucky, Missouri, and the area that is now West Virginia—totaled 3,408,837. In addition, the southern regions of Ohio, Indiana, and Illinois boasted a white population of 2,629,699. The total white Confederate population numbered 5,094,318. This meant that the border was both vital to Union strategy and a tempting prize for the Confederacy.[7] Lincoln famously wrote, "I think to lose Kentucky is nearly the same as to lose the whole game. Kentucky gone, we cannot hold Missouri, nor, as I think, Maryland. These all against us, and the job on our hands is too large for us. We would as well to consent to separation at once, including the surrender of this capitol."[8]

Maryland, Missouri, and Kentucky each harbored considerable numbers of Confederate sympathizers. All three stayed loyal in the war, but only after internal squabbling left the population divided. Initially, Union authorities tolerated a certain amount of dissent, but this toleration ended after secession movements within the states failed. Stephen Ash has noted that, from the southern perspective, life in occupied Confederate territory changed along with northern war objectives. He argues, "the North moved from a conciliatory and conservative policy to a punitive and radical one."[9] Border residents saw a similar shift occur. Just as deference to moderate demands revealed the high value northern denominations placed on continued loyalty from border churches, early federal concessions showed the importance of border-state loyalty to Lincoln's early war strategy. After the initial crisis of securing the border had passed, the divided loyalties in the region came under federal scrutiny. The Union Army and the federal government kept a watchful eye on the activities of border residents, and much of what they saw raised concern.

Although organized opposition was rare, Republican leaders feared widespread disloyalty in the North, particularly in the Midwest and along the border. Federal authorities investigated claims of treasonous societies, instituted loyalty oaths, and arrested citizens who fell under suspicion.[10] Border residents not openly sympathetic to the Union may have had any of a number of reasons for their stance—a commitment to neutrality, objection to war, opposition to the Republican Party, "western sectionalism," personal or economic ties to the South, racism, or outright allegiance to the Confederate cause.[11] In any case, failure to demonstrate loyalty aroused the suspicions of federal authorities. Neutrality seemed to carry great subversive potential. On the grounds of ensuring loyalty, federal officials interrogated, arrested, and banished many border ministers during the Civil War, and their experiences reveal the limits of enforced patriotism in the region.

Whatever their personal allegiances, clergy who sought to remain publically neutral in the war denounced "political preachers" as agitators. And they used the same language border moderates used during earlier denominational schisms. James Todd, a Louisville Presbyterian, wrote, "my sympathies were and are privately my own and are for the South." However, he thought, of the Union and the Confederacy, "both are wrong."[12] In his journal, a Kentucky Baptist vented his frustrations: "Ah it is a pity that there are so many rebels and traitors among the Baptists in Kentucky . . . endeavoring to overturn this Best government on earth." He did not reserve judgment for secessionists alone, also condemning the "diabolical plans" of "the Radicals and abolitionists." In this conflict, he believed "[b]oth wrong and their sins cry to Heaven." Around the same time, another border Baptist wished that "political agitators could be thrown aside in both sections."[13]

When evangelicals spoke about "politics" and "political questions," however, they usually meant the Union cause and specifically the emancipation of enslaved people. By classifying slavery as primarily political, they abjured moral responsibility for the institution and prioritized their commitment to church unity. Professing political neutrality in the Civil War was a way of avoiding Unionist demands to publically support the federal cause. Whether Unionist or Confederate, proslavery or antislavery, these ministers regarded slavery as a political problem that wrought discord in churches and communities. Sectional denominational division had been a devastating and bewildering experience, and these men were keen to avoid repeating it. Unlike their peers in the far North and deep South, border moderates interacted daily with people who held wildly different positions on slavery and sectional division.

Additionally, their prominent community role opened them to public attack. Under such conditions, spirituality's appeal is easily understood.

Evangelicals in the border states had come to represent a sort of "loyal opposition" within the northern branches of each denomination. Their emphasis on unity over politicization forced denominational leaders from the North to temper their impulse toward an outright embrace of abolitionism. As long as they did so, border evangelicals favored adherence to the North over uniting with the southern branches of the church, which may have committed the sin of schism. This conservatism frustrated northerners who resented the border clergy's devotion to the status quo and refusal to engage in debates over slavery. On the eve of the Civil War, one antislavery Northern Methodist wrote of border residents that they threatened to "involve us in permanent trouble for the sake of temporary triumph—to sacrifice principle and position to gain quiet for a brief space."[14] The war years strained affiliation with the North to the breaking point. Along with federal officials, northern evangelicals placed a new emphasis on political and sectional loyalty within the churches. One conservative Presbyterian who was "anti-slavery" but did not "believe Slavery sin per se," expressed confusion and anger as the possibility of neutrality regarding slavery faded away.[15]

Border evangelicals watched with alarm as the war politicized both the northern and the southern branches of their denominations and as a consequence eliminated their "nonpolitical" middle ground. As historian Emory Bucke notes, "upon the outbreak of war," each church rallied "at once to the cause with which it, in fact, was already identified."[16] The war revived the barely quieted conflicts of the 1840s and further alienated border moderates. Federal authorities exacerbated this tense religious climate by demanding that clergy publically display signs of loyalty to the Union. Nonpolitical clergy in the border region largely resisted this pressure. When federal authorities tested that resistance, their actions had consequences.

MILITARY AND RELIGIOUS LIFE ON THE WARTIME BORDER

Clergy generally encountered federal authority in the form of a provost marshal and his agents. These officers oversaw day-to-day life and enforced martial law in occupied areas. Holding a position created out of wartime necessity, the provost marshals operated in an ad hoc manner. Decisions made by one branch of the office could be overruled by another, even within a single state.

Provost marshals and their subordinates had varied responsibilities. Among other duties, they acted as military police, seized property, arrested the disloyal, regulated interactions between soldiers and civilians, enlisted soldiers, managed escaped slaves, issued travel passes, and administered loyalty tests. It was in this last capacity that the office of the provost marshal could most directly affect the daily practice of religion in border communities.[17]

The war and the years that followed were a period of a singular preoccupation with loyalty in the United States. Harold Hyman writes, "The Civil War was one in which a nation tried to identify loyalty and punish disloyalty on a huge scale." This concern with identifying loyalty was particularly pronounced in the border states. As Hyman notes, not only was it a "geographical border region"; it was also an "intellectual border region" and "an area of confusion, indecision."[18] It is hardly a surprise, then, that Union officers charged with controlling the border instituted oaths and demanded displays of loyalty in an attempt to bring order.[19]

Federal officials perceived disloyal ministers, or those suspected of disloyalty, as particularly dangerous—a threat to the loyalty of the whole population. Secular authorities feared that, by dint of their special status, clergy could avoid capture and imprisonment. In addition, they might use their influence to encourage men and women to sympathize with the Confederacy and keep anti-Union sentiment alive. "There are no charges against me, but that I am a man of influence, and if disposed, could do a great deal of harm?" queried minister Berry Hill Spencer in April of 1863, after three months of banishment from his home state of Missouri. Spencer, a Southern Methodist loyal to the Union, spent the years during and immediately following the Civil War caught between the conflicting demands of his faith and his government. "What reason has anyone to fear that I would use my influence for evil?" Spencer asked the provost marshal of Danville, Missouri.[20] In a protest against special loyalty oaths for ministers in Kentucky, Beriah Magoffin assailed the notion that ministers constituted a particularly dangerous class. Magoffin called the oath "altogether needless" and asserted that ministers and priests are not privileged classes, but simply private citizens."[21] The argument that clergy had as little public influence as any other private citizen became increasingly difficult to sustain in wartime.

If a disloyal minister posed a greater threat to the Union than a disloyal citizen in general, then an avowedly loyal and patriotic minister was a particular asset. Provost marshals did not just expect passive loyalty or individual expressions of patriotism from ministers; they wanted clergy to actively promote the Union cause on the divided border. Federal authorities enforced this behavior by questioning clergy individually and administering loyalty oaths; compelling patriotic displays and prayers in church; arresting clergy charged with disloyalty; and punishing such clergy by removing them from their pulpits, suppressing their publications, putting them in jail, or banishing them from the state. These methods generated indignation among border clergy, who sought to maintain neutrality. Those who came under the scrutiny of Union authorities accused Unionist evangelicals of collaborating with the military to "establish a Religion by the Sword and by the point of the Bayonet" and vowed not to "submit to such an indignity" as to continue to worship in these churches.[22]

However, clergy had little power to resist. The provost marshal could use his authority to adjudicate squabbles within congregations. He could decide in favor of the Union party and use the resources at his command to enforce such decisions, as Henry Keeton of Missouri discovered. Keeton, a layman, spent the antebellum years helping to establish a Southern Methodist congregation near Mexico, Missouri. At the onset of war, Keeton "enrold myself loyal to the Government" and consequently found that Confederate-sympathizing Methodists "severed nearly every tye that I had in the church."[23]

With Keeton in the lead, a small company of loyal Mexico Methodists withdrew and formed their own congregation in 1863. But "they had no place to have preaching so we would have it in our houses and at the Preacher's house." This state of affairs came to the attention of General Clinton Fisk, who ordered Keeton's Unionist faction "to take possession of the church." Fisk clearly hoped to promote loyalty, but Keeton was hesitant. He explained, "I did not want to do that as our brethren would have throne it up to us that the soldiers had to protect us."[24] In the contested small towns of rural Missouri—as elsewhere in the border region—military authorities viewed pro-Union congregations as a great asset and southern-affiliated churches as a liability. Keeton's account reveals how secular authorities willingly involved themselves in church affairs to help strengthen Unionist congregations.

Not all border ministers refused military aid in resolving congregational squabbles over church property. In early 1862, George Morrison, an Old School Presbyterian minister in Lexington, Kentucky, quarreled with his church elders. According to Morrison, a Unionist, the elders sympathized with the Confederacy. Taking advantage of the chaos afforded by a Confederate invasion, a group of disgruntled congregants met covertly and voted to dissolve their relationship with Morrison. They also secured possession of the church keys and records. Despite his distaste for his Confederate congregants, Morrison claimed that he felt obliged to pursue the case and regain control of the church for the "Kingdom of my Lord Jesus Christ, as she is passing through the fiery ordeal of these times."[25]

Morrison's stand on principle locked him in a stalemate with his disaffected congregation, which refused to relinquish the keys and church records. He argued that he could not in good conscience "surrender the secular and spiritual control of this church, and of the loyal people who worship there, into the hands of a disloyal and rebellious faction."[26] His claim that a large portion of his congregants were loyal Unionists is debatable, but Morrison's argument reflects the stance of northern churches during the war. He equated loyalty to the Kingdom of God with loyalty to the Union—which gave him both a divine and a political mandate to keep the church out of the hands of Confederate sympathizers.

In 1864, after repeatedly failing to retrieve the keys and record book, Reverend Morrison availed himself of the aid of the provost marshal, who himself seized the "keys and records" and placed them "in the hands of those to whom they rightfully belonged."[27] Thus, a federal agent intervened and forcibly returned control of the contested property to a Unionist minister. The Synod of Kentucky "disapprobated" Morrison's actions, but Unionists, arguing that the Union cause was also God's, supported Morrison's use of the willing official. The border Presbyterians who claimed political neutrality, however, viewed the case as a violation. Stuart Robinson, the fractious Louisville champion of border spirituality, was "disgusted with Morrison's proceedings in the matter" and condemned the "interference by a Provost Marshal and his squad."[28]

In a similar situation in 1862, Kansas City minister Monson Pugh, a Southern Methodist, reportedly received anonymous threats that led him to vacate his position. Furthermore, two Kansas City residents made statements to the provost marshal, asserting that Pugh was a secessionist. With Pugh away, his Unionist congregants called on military authorities to assist Northern Methodists in taking possession of the building.[29] Likewise, in Independence, Missouri, an officer ordered Southern Methodists to surrender the keys to their church to a known loyal minister after Union occupation of the town in 1862.[30]

The threat of appeal to federal authorities could also be used to resolve local property disputes. Dr. William Plumer was a professor at Western Theological Seminary and pastor of the Central Presbyterian Church in the eastern Pennsylvania town of Allegheny City. In 1862, he ran into trouble with a portion of his congregation for refusing to ask "God's *blessing* upon the Government of our country in its efforts to *suppress the rebellion*."[31] In consequence, a large Unionist faction demanded Plumer's resignation. In a familiar pattern, the congregation divided and reached a stalemate over the property. "He ought to be removed by some authority," a disgruntled Union-sympathizing congregant remarked. "If neither the Church, Presbytery, nor Directors can do it, *let the government do it*."[32] Feuding border residents employed the military presence as a tool in resolving their disputes.

The case of Samuel B. McPheeters—the best-known example of a border clergyman charged with disloyalty—also involved military seizure of a church building. The members of McPheeters's Pine Street Presbyterian Church in St. Louis, like those in the Mount Pleasant Church, were of divided sectional loyalties. McPheeters himself was eventually banished for suspected disloyalty, and the congregation was in such an uproar that General Samuel Curtis "appointed a military commission to control the governance of the Pine Street Church."[33] This commission secured the church for loyal congregants. Again, the federal action rankled border evangelicals. "The Pine Street Church is still 'run' by the military," an aggrieved McPheeters supporter wrote.[34] Instances of military involvement with redistribution of church property occurred sporadically on the border during the early years of the war. These incidents grew more frequent in the final years of war and early in Reconstruction.

When dealing with border clergy, federal officials' primary aim was not to take possession of property, but to secure active loyalty and prosecute disloyalty in individuals. To this end, they employed the oath: a flexible test that could stand alone or form the basis of a more elaborate investigation. A suspect minister might undergo loyalty tests ranging from casual questions about political sympathies to formally imposed oaths.[35] Loyalty oaths forced border ministers of many political persuasions out of their neutrality. A House committee charged with ensuring governmental loyalty during the war determined that disloyal people fell into three classes: those who openly sympathized with the Confederacy; people who were not publically loyal to the federal government; and finally, "those who failed to comply with the loyalty oath requirements."[36] All three categories were considered disloyal and subject to punishment. Under this framework, neutrality in wartime could be tantamount to treason. In Kentucky and Missouri, oaths ruled the day as provost marshals attempted to secure allegiance from a population that was hard to pin down politically. The oaths could be issued on the spot, and military authorities could improvise their specific content.

For example, in 1861, a Union general stopped Jonathan Palmer Finley, a Methodist minister who was privately Unionist, at a blockade in Missouri. The general asked Finley, "Have you taken any part in this rebellion?" Finley avowed that he had not. "On which side are you of this question?" the general pressed. "As a minister of the gospel," Finley answered, "I take no side nor part in political matters! . . . I think a minister should have nothing to do with political questions." The general had a different idea. He told Finley, "you ought to preach union forever."[37] In another case that year, Reverend Sears of Milan, Missouri, claimed that "about one mile from town," three Union soldiers under the command of Major Williams "dashed up, arrested, and detained him about an hour, and until he consented to take an unconstitutional oath, prescribed by themselves, as a condition of release."[38] From Lexington, William Pratt, a Kentucky Unionist affiliated with the Southern Baptist Convention, reported in 1862 that he was not "permitted to pass on the streets without permit from military authorities or to go out of town." Pratt was also detained later that year while traveling to an association meeting.[39]

One oath that aroused tremendous ire among clergy on the border was Special Order 61—the Rosecrans Oath of 1864. It applied to the entire Department of the Missouri and required that everyone who taught "religion and morality to the people" must take an oath of loyalty to the Union to retain the "privilege of assemblage."[40] As usual, responsibility for enforcing the order fell to the provost marshal. Missouri clergy had already submitted to the Convention Oath of 1861. The Rosecrans Oath, however, stipulated that entire religious groups could not gather unless they took the oath as an assurance of political loyalty. This stipulation sparked outrage across a population already weary of oaths and martial law.

The perpetually incensed Stuart Robinson declared the order to be an "odd piece of impertinence" from "a muddy-headed Papist ignorant of the first principles of free Protestantism"—Rosecrans was Catholic—and "a preposterous absurdity." Robinson compared the effect of the order to the repression of Protestants in England under James II, and he called the affair an "outrage upon Christ's free spiritual commonwealth."[41] When the Synod of Missouri met in St. Louis in October 1864, the meeting quickly devolved into a showdown between those who had consented to take the oath and those who had not. With military assistance, the oath takers gained control of the record books and ousted those who would not swear loyalty. The oath takers constituted only a tiny minority of the Synod—fourteen out of a total membership of seventy ministers and well over one hundred lay members.[42]

Rosecrans defended the order as a necessary tool to curb the traitorous gatherings of Missouri's Confederate guerrillas: "If all who claim to meet for religious purposes can do so without question," he reasoned, traitors such as members of Confederate General Sterling Price's army might, "under the garb of religion . . . assemble with impunity and plot treason in our midst." Rosecrans argued that, by requiring an oath for religious gatherings, he was, in reality, protecting the sanctity of religion "from the danger and disgrace of being used as a cloak of malice," and securing its freedom from "the surveillance freely exercised over political meetings."[43] Rosecrans's defense of his actions reflects the heightened suspicion and mistrust in the acutely divided border region, where it seemed reasonable to suspect that Confederate guerrillas and raiders might orchestrate a spurious ecclesiastical meeting in order to plan treasonous activity. Rosecrans did not address the reality that disloyal civilians easily could—and no doubt did—take these oaths falsely. In any case, as the events in the Missouri Synod showed, the oath had the effect of inhibiting religious gatherings, whether people took it or not.

Not all border clergy opposed the Rosecrans Oath. Indeed, those who supported the Union cause and believed that the churches owed full and public support to the federal government considered it a reasonable measure. For outspoken Unionists living among Confederate sympathizers, the oath offered some hope that local churches would fall in line with their views on the proper relationship between clergy and the war. "I cannot, and will not, sit under the preaching of a disloyal man," wrote Joseph Lewis, a Baptist from Glasgow, Missouri. Lewis applauded the Rosecrans Oath as a tool enabling authorities to "'substitute' loyal for disloyal ministers." His only concern was that the law would not apply to Baptists, since they did not often meet in assemblies other than congregational meetings. If the order did not include church meetings, Lewis wondered, "can't you help make it do so?"[44] Lewis's sentiments would have made him a model minister in the eyes of federal administrators in more ways than one. Not only did he highly esteem the power of oath taking to ensure loyalty; he also feared the corrosive effects that preaching by a disloyal minister might have on the community.

Still, responses like Lewis's were relatively rare. Many Christians particularly objected to oath taking because it violated Christ's imperative, "I say unto you, swear not at all."[45] Thus, specific oaths for clergy seemed like persecution. Stuart Robinson likened the administration of oaths to the events preceding the bloody St. Bartholomew's Day Massacre of Huguenots in sixteenth-century France.[46] In addition, many resented the intrusion of oaths on personal liberties. In his protest, Beriah Magoffin reminded the Kentucky House of Representatives, "the matter of *test oaths* is specially odious to every American freeman acquainted with the history of the struggle against tyranny which won our free system."[47] Thus, ministers who wished to avoid oath taking could invoke the Biblical injunction against them, the history of oaths as an instrument of religious persecution, and the patriots of the American Revolution in defense of their refusal.

MONITORING RELIGIOUS PATRIOTISM

Federal officials expected clergy on the border not just to personally profess support for the Union, but also to actively promote Unionism and loyalty within in their churches. A congregation could fall under suspicion of disloyalty if its minister failed to do any of the following: display the Union flag in the church building; explicitly pray for northern victory and the continued health of federal officials; and participate in national days of prayer, fasting, and thanksgiving. A minister who met all of these expectations was seen as a tremendous asset to the Union cause in border communities. Military officials, with the willing aid of loyal ministers, devoted considerable effort to ensuring patriotic church services.

A Union flag hung in houses of worship served as a very visible sign of loyalty and, to Unionist observers, the absence of a flag implied disloyalty. In the 1863 Baltimore case involving a Methodist minister and an American flag, the congregation that did not want to display the flag was targeted by "some person or persons unknown" who surreptitiously hung a flag outside the meeting place each night. The case came to the attention of Provost Marshal William Fish when a Union lieutenant reported having seen Reverend John Dashiell repeatedly remove an unwanted Union flag from his place of worship. Fish took a hard line. Dashiell was arrested and ordered to display "the American flag" at his meeting the following day.[48]

Provost marshals issued orders on the spot to compel displays of loyalty from specific local ministers. Following the battle at Camp Jackson in 1863, the trustees of the Southern Methodist Church in St. Charles received an order from Provost Marshal Benjamin Emmons to "cause the National Flag to be raised over their church in this city without delay."[49] In Ray County, Missouri, Major Thomas Biggers "issued an order that no minister of the gospel should preach who did not carry with him the Union flag." When Reverend John McGlothlin told an officer, "I will recognize no State or military authority to prescribe qualifications for the work of the ministry," the officer arrested McGlothlin. For refusing to take a loyalty oath, carry a flag, and post bond, he was imprisoned for over a month.[50]

Sometimes, Unionist civilians either enforced flag displays themselves or reported noncompliance. As in the case of property transfers, they enlisted military aid to their advantage in resolving a local dispute. James Penn, a Southern Methodist minister, reported that, while preaching in Williamstown, Missouri, in 1863, "flags were brought and placed on and around the pulpit, and a company of armed men sat near to prevent any one from taking them down."[51] Jesse Bird, another Southern Methodist minister, repeatedly discovered Union flags hung over the doors of churches where he worked. Bird refused to enter or preach in these churches. Loyalist locals reported him to the military authorities in St. Joseph. Bird reported that, when he refused to take an oath of loyalty, he was banished from the state.[52]

Union officials also worried about loyalty in meetings of church leadership, such as the Methodist Conferences and the Presbyterian Assemblies. Other border administrators shared General Rosecrans's fear that disloyal religious groups "may assemble with impunity and plot treason in our midst."[53] Stuart Robinson, ever alert to such cases, reported an incident "in a Kentucky Conference" of the Northern Methodist Church during which "a petty Military Satrap sent to the assembly a flag to be saluted; and so far from resisting with dignity the impertinence, one portion of the body, who knew no better, indulged in "Roaring-Ralph-Stackpole" oratory over it, while the more sensible portion quieted their consciences with the argument that it was too small a matter to quarrel about, and submitted to the indignity in silence."[54] In a similar case, a session of the Southern Methodist Church meeting in Westport, Missouri, became the subject of Major Willis Ransom's "Special Order No. 10," which mandated that "the Stars and Stripes be conspicuously displayed in front of the pulpit of the church where said meeting is held."[55]

A plan to raise an American flag over the 1863 meeting of the Northern Old School General Assembly generated stormy conflict before the assembly even convened. The assembly had never displayed a flag in the past. Border-state delegates opposed the flag display twenty-nine to eight, but their protests were overturned and the flag flew over the meeting that spring in Peoria, Illinois.[56] The flag debate highlighted the growing rift between border Presbyterians and the rest of the Northern Old School denomination.

While federal authorities wished to see American flags flying outside all border churches, they placed even more importance on the content of the sermons themselves. Loyal listeners expected sermons to contain prayers for the success of the Union and the observation of all declared fast days, days of prayer, and days of thanksgiving. As religious services were open to the public, tepid or qualified prayers for the Union quickly drew critical attention. The Baltimore minister who announced he could not find anything to be thankful for on a federally ordered day of thanksgiving was castigated in Union newspapers across the nation.

Fast days, days of prayer and humiliation, feast days, and days of thanksgiving were all common features of Christian services in the nineteenth-century United States. On designated days, ministers directed the prayers of the entire congregation toward a particular cause or outcome. Leaders often called for these special days in times of national trial. On fast days, the faithful might be asked to "reverently and submissively supplicate" for God's mercy and "humbly and reverently . . . prostrate themselves before the mercy seat and supplicate that aid and deliverance which God only can afford."[57] If positive events transpired, congregations celebrated and praised the divine on thanksgiving and feast days. Days of prayer could be initiated by a single congregation or by a group of clergy in a community, but frequently, and especially during the harrowing years of the Civil War, orders for fast days and days of thanksgiving came from national and state officials. David Waldstricher argues that these feast and fast days were designed to promote both political and religious unity, expressly linking religion and the state.[58] Meant to engage the entire nation in Christian and patriotic unity, these events became objects of discord on the border.

Union officials monitoring loyalty on the border expected sermons to contain prayers for the success of the Union and the health and welfare of the federal government. From Kansas City, Monson Pugh reported he was "ordered to pray for the President of the United States by name, for the U.S. Congress, and for the success of the Union army."[59] In a similar instance, members of an Episcopalian congregation in Alexandria, Virginia, related that one morning Reverend John Stewart omitted "the prayer for the President." Upon noting the omission, a cavalry captain in attendance "undertook to officiate . . . by reading the Prayer for the President of the United States." The church erupted in chaos as the captain "advanced to the altar where Mr. Stewart was kneeling, still continuing the Litany, and ordered his arrest." The captain informed interceders that the arrest was warranted because "the omission of the prayer revealed [Reverend Stewart] to be 'a rebel and a traitor.'"[60]

The Stewart case illustrates how military authorities considered the refusal to pray for Union success traitorous. But self-described nonpolitical ministers argued that mandatory prayer violated civil liberties and that "political preachers" were the true source of local unrest. An exchange between a federal officer and a slaveholding Methodist minister illustrates these clashing interpretations of loyalty. In Chillicothe, Missouri, Brigadier General Willard Hall told a minister unwilling to pray for Union victory, "You claim to be neutral. A citizen has no right to be neutral when enemies are assailing his government." The minister replied that he would not give "utterance to a political sentiment in the pulpit." Furthermore, he contended, "political preaching has sown the seeds that are bringing forth the death of the nation."[61] General Willard ordered the minister to step down from his position at the church. Stuart Robinson denounced these instances of "the Church as Ceasar's agent for crushing rebellion."[62] Many border clergy simply refused to participate in mandated prayer—they opposed it on principle and argued that bringing national politics into the pulpit only served to create controversy within congregations.

Political conflict within a church would mean the loss of congregants and a divided church. Jonathan Fuller, a Baptist minister in Kansas City, knew that his congregation carefully noted his every action. When he decided not to read aloud an announcement about an anti-Union citizen's defense organization, "considerable remark was made about the omission." On another Sunday his choir leader, "a regular down east Yankee," planned to open the service with the patriotic hymn "My Country, 'Tis of Thee." This placed Fuller in a difficult spot. "It was a delicate question," Fuller wrote, "If the hymn was sung, the Rebels and 'softs' [moderates] generally might regard it as an insult to their sensibilities and withdraw from the congregation. If on the other had I should suppress the piece, the Radicals of the Methodist Church might get hold of it and use it against me." Fuller was spared the conflict "providentially" when the choirmaster arrived late for the opening hymn, allowing Fuller to substitute something less incendiary. Still, he was "looking for an explosion any moment."[63] A month later, Fuller confessed "much anxiety and some dread" about an upcoming fast day: "I am afraid that my congregation may split upon that rock. I fear that even the utmost mildness and Christian charity of my utterance will not save me from offending someone's sensitiveness."[64] Elsewhere in Missouri, Presbyterian minister Jonathan Palmer Finley also struggled with a divided congregation. He did not observe a "day of national humiliation" because, in their "divided condition," his congregants "could not so unite" in praying "to support and encourage the federal gov[ernmen]t."[65] In such an environment, it was difficult to strike a balance that would not upset some party in the church.

Federally enforced loyalty in churches no doubt did increase the number of sermons and prayers given in support of the Union cause. In the long run, however, the tactic garnered a great deal of ill will. Even if the stories of persecution and forced prayer were exaggerated—as many of them doubtless were—secular authorities attempting to "force the conscience at the point of the bayonet" made for an unsavory image.[66] American Christians fiercely guarded the separation of church and state—which was seen to protect religion as much, if not more, than the government.[67] After the war, stories of military interference with worship became a useful tool for advocates of separation from northern churches.

Federal officials did not only monitor messages from the pulpit. They also suppressed newspapers deemed treasonous or insufficiently loyal. In 1864, Major General Stephen Burbridge ordered Stuart Robinson to cease publication of the *True Presbyterian*. The order stipulated that, if Robinson continued to publish, the provost marshal should "seize the press, type and paper . . . and arrest the editor and publishers."[68] In blocking publication of the *True Presbyterian*, the Union Army effectively shut down the primary source of news about other newspapers that met a similar fate. These included the Louisville *Baptist Recorder*, which Burbridge suppressed on the same day as the *True Presbyterian*, and the St. Louis *Christian Advocate*, the northernmost publication associated with the Southern Methodist Church. David McAnally, the *Advocate*'s editor, published a series of articles opposing the war. In spring of 1862, Provost Marshal George Leighton suppressed the *Christian Advocate*, closed the office where it was printed, and imprisoned McAnally.[69] Regional newspapers, once the institutional backbone of the evangelical West, had sectionalized following denominational division. Now they were targeted as mouthpieces of religious and political sectionalism.

No matter how unpopular the suppressing of newspapers became, no method of monitoring clerical loyalty created more animosity than arrests and banishment. Several representative cases illustrate how banishment helped to fuel martyrdom myths about persecuted nonpolitical preachers. Berry Hill Spencer, a Southern Methodist minister and teacher, was ejected from Missouri in 1863. Following the 1844 schism, Spencer, a life-long Missourian, joined the Southern Methodists, but fifteen years later he opposed secession. When the war broke out, Spencer did not hesitate to take required oaths of allegiance to the Union. In 1862, he swore "allegiance to the Government of the United States and the State of Missouri" twice—"before the clerk in both Lincoln and Montgomery counties."[70] Nevertheless, in January of 1863, the provost marshal in Danville ordered Spencer to "leave the state of Missouri."[71] Spencer attempted to appeal his banishment, but to no avail. On January 28, "with a most sad heart," he left Missouri.[72] He settled in Ashby's Mills, Indiana, where, for the next ten months, he devoted himself to ascertaining why he had been banished and endeavoring "to effect a revocation of my order of Banishment."[73]

When he recalled his banishment after the war, Spencer remarked, "we had no trial, either civil or military, nor would they condescend to tell us what were the charges against us." Informal sources suggested to Spencer that he "*was banished because* [he] *was a Southern Methodist Preacher!*"[74] Spencer's contacts in Missouri told him that he had been accused of "encouraging others to go into the rebellion." It appears that personal enemies used Spencer's affiliation with Southern Methodism to impugn his loyalty. Spencer himself came to the conclusion that the charges against him had been trumped up "for *a religious*, and not for *a political* reason." He suspected that local Northern Methodists, with whom he had clashed over administration of the Danville School, had reported him to federal authorities on charges of disloyalty and treason. This put the school entirely under Northern Methodist control.[75]

During his exile in Indiana, Spencer encountered many Methodists in the vicinity of Ashby's Mills who shared his distaste for abolition and "political preaching." Their reluctance to go to church during the war was evidence that introducing political topics could hurt church attendance, as so many border clergy feared it would. Spencer wrote to his wife about "men who have been to hear me preach, who have not been for years" because they disliked hearing a "political harangue instead of the Gospel." In the southern tier of free states, this conservative sentiment could be found in many communities and had divided scores of congregations just like those in Ashby's Mills.[76] Spencer was certain he could "organize a congregation" of such people if he so desired. Doing so would have been dangerous for Spencer, since suspicion dogged him in exile. He once heard a rumor that he was "to be arrested upon the charge of being connected with a secret organization called 'Knights of the Golden Circle,'"[77] a secret society rumored to be active in plots to undermine the Union war effort throughout the Northwest.[78]

In September of 1863, for reasons as opaque as those that prompted the initial banishment, Major General John Schofield permitted Spencer to return to Missouri.[79] Upon his return home, Spencer directed his anger at local Northern Methodists and their treatment of "the persecuted church in Missouri." Spencer refused to take a postwar test oath. He was determined to defend his "*duty of preaching the Gospel without any admixture of human policy*" and to defend the Southern Methodists "though it may cost me a martyr's death!"[80]

No such dramatic fate awaited Spencer, but his story is illustrative. The impromptu banishment, the lack of a trial, and the confused chain of command surrounding the order typify the ad hoc nature of military actions toward civilians in the border. It appears that the charges against Spencer were never formally recorded. In fact, when Spencer inquired with the Danville provost marshal, the officer replied, "I am utterly at loss to comprehend the case."[81] The only existing evidence that Northern Methodist enemies slandered Spencer comes from Spencer's own pen. However, if his adversaries took advantage of military distrust to remove Spencer from control of the Danville School, they would not have been the only clergy to do so during the Civil War. Indeed, it was not uncommon for clergy to use secular means to pursue religious ends. It was particularly easy to impugn members of southern denominations since their affiliation already cast them under a cloud of suspicion.

Finally, the Spencer case illustrates how banishing clergy—an act intended to promote loyalty in the border region—had the unintended consequence of generating antagonism from southern-affiliated evangelicals. His exile only gave Spencer cause to stir up disgruntled "Copperhead Christians" who rejected political preaching from a pulpit in Indiana. In addition, Southern Methodists, both in the border region and in the South, used Spencer's case—and other banishment cases—to condemn the federal government and the northern denominations as hopelessly corrupt. Observing from Kentucky, Southern Methodist Bishop Hubbard Kavanaugh remarked that Spencer's case and others like it had "deeply impressed the people" and contributed to antiwar sentiment throughout the state.[82] Spencer himself had willingly taken several loyalty oaths at the onset of war, but he refused to take another oath after his banishment.

THE MCPHEETERS CASE: THE PERSECUTED IDEAL

The best-known banished clergyman was Samuel B. McPheeters, who became a *cause célèbre* on the border.[83] His case has received extensive attention both from observers at the time and from modern historians. This is largely due to his personal connections and his audience with the president. Despite the many ways in which it was *not* representative, it came to exemplify the criticisms border conservatives aimed at federal interactions with clergy. Samuel McPheeters was born in North Carolina and lived in St. Louis, where he was the minister at the Pine Street Presbyterian Church. McPheeters took oaths of loyalty to the U.S. Constitution and to Missouri early in the war but otherwise attempted to remain scrupulously neutral, presenting himself "not as a friend or advocate of any party or section, but as an ambassador of One whose 'kingdom is not of this world.'"[84] In sum, he attempted to adopt the ideal nonpolitical border stance.

In another action that exemplified the experience of border-state moderates, McPheeters opposed the 1862 Northern Old School Assembly's patriotic resolutions. At that meeting, Unionist Presbyterians clashed with "nonpolitical" advocates of the spirituality of the church. McPheeters openly opposed a pro-Union statement "On the State of the Church and the Country." When confronted about his loyalty, McPheeters asserted, "I deny distinctly and emphatically, the right of any ecclesiastical court to question me concerning my political opinions. It is none of their business." A Unionist retorted, "you are not loyal according to my idea of loyalty."[85] The exchange encapsulates the competing definitions of loyalty among border and northern evangelicals during the Civil War. McPheeters had a negative definition of loyalty characteristic of border clergy: an absence of support for the Confederacy. Breckinridge had a positive definition of loyalty—one that required an active statement of support for the Union. Most military officials in the North adopted this latter definition.

The controversy in the General Assembly had captured the attention of ordinary Presbyterians back home in St. Louis. Members of the Pine Street congregation followed the General Assembly's example and divided into staunch

Unionist and "nonpolitical" parties. McPheeters found himself in a tinderbox of sectional conflict upon his return. Like many other border ministers, he would have known that an incident might at any time ignite the flames of factionalism and destroy the unity of his church.

The disintegration of the Pine Street congregation began with a baptism. McPheeters's political sympathies might have been opaque, but those of his congregant Samuel Robbins could not have been clearer. On June 8, 1862, Robbins brought his son to church and asked McPheeters to christen the boy "Sterling Price," after the Confederate general who had spent the spring raiding the state and attacking Union troops.[86] McPheeters proceeded to christen the child as requested. News of the event spread through the city. Within days, the Unionist faction at Pine Street insisted "no neutral ground" was possible and demanded that McPheeters declare his loyalty to the Union.[87]

McPheeters refused and again defended his position of neutrality. But to no avail—the whole affair spilled out of the confines of Presbyterian institutions and landed in the lap of the Union military authorities in St. Louis. They proved quite willing to become involved in cases of suspected ministerial disloyalty. Provost Marshal Franklin A. Dick, under order from Major General Samuel Curtis, issued "Special Order No. 152," banishing McPheeters from the state. Dick condemned McPheeters for his "unmistakable evidence of sympathy with the rebellion," and for "failing to remove a widespread and increasing impression that he desires the success of the rebel cause." Furthermore, he was known to have "refused to observe" fast days and thanksgivings and, the document alleged, he had "used all the influence of his ministerial character" to prevent his congregation from "manifesting its loyalty" and to exert "an injurious influence, especially on the youth."[88] Dick's order illustrates his fear that disloyal clergy could spread disloyalty in the general population. Unless McPheeters actively displayed patriotism, Dick viewed him as an advocate for the Confederate cause.

McPheeters's banishment order highlights the numerous concerns Union officials had about ambiguously loyal ministers: that their neutrality served as a mask for Confederate sympathies, that they possessed excessive influence over the members of their communities, and that they refused to participate in national prayers and fast days for the success of the Union. General Curtis's order also underscores the high value federal authorities placed on openly loyal ministers: it specifically called for McPheeters to be replaced by "a loyal

Minister of the Gospel." Curtis then authorized a military commission to manage the Pine Street Church.[89]

The events that followed challenge depictions of McPheeters as utterly passive and meek. He immediately traveled to Washington to appeal his case directly to President Lincoln. With the aid of Attorney General Edward Bates, a fellow Presbyterian who sympathized with "neutral" clergy, McPheeters gained an audience with the president. Lincoln was reportedly "perplexed" by the case, but immediately telegraphed General Curtis and commanded him to suspend the order of banishment.[90] On January 2, 1862, Lincoln sent further explanation of his decision. While he admitted, "I believe he does sympathize with the rebels," sympathy alone could not constitute grounds for banishment. Lincoln went on to point out that McPheeters took a loyalty oath and there was no evidence he had violated it. A person could not be exiled merely "upon the suspicion of his secret sympathies." In this letter, Lincoln stated his position on military involvement with churches, which he would repeat verbatim when future cases came to his attention: "The U.S. government must not . . . undertake to run the churches. When an individual, in a church or out of it, becomes dangerous to the public interest, he must be checked; but let the churches, as such take care of themselves."[91]

McPheeters appears in almost every account of religion, loyalty, and civil liberties in the Civil War North. But the problem with allowing the McPheeters case to represent all clergy loyalty cases is that Lincoln's response (the government should not "undertake to run the churches") becomes the last word on the subject.[92] But, in fact, individual decision-making among federal officials on the border remained little affected by the president's remarks. In fact, Union officers on the ground held views that starkly opposed Lincoln's; they continued to fear the potential threat of disloyal clergy and exerted themselves to mitigate that threat.[93] Federal involvement with churches by no means ended with Lincoln's judgment. Neither did support for this involvement from Unionist clergy. McPheeters's own experience after his return from Washington bears this out.

McPheeters spent the rest of his days in St. Louis in a state of limbo. General Curtis and Provost Marshal Dick removed the order of banishment but did not allow McPheeters to preach. The Pine Street Church operated under the military commission, but McPheeters's suspension did nothing to quell controversy within the congregation. The minister's supporters lobbied for his reinstatement with as much vigor as his detractors had shown in demanding his removal. One aggrieved McPheeters supporter referred to the leader of the Unionist faction in his church as "Judas Iscariot" and declared him "as destitute of patriotism as he is of honor." Revealing how federal intervention intended to secure loyalty could unintentionally have the opposite effect, he concluded that the federal government was "fighting against *God* by persecuting a branch of His church."[94]

Over the course of the year, these letters and petitions achieved their desired effect. Curtis lifted the bonds on McPheeters, reinstalling him at Pine Street in January of 1864. Unsurprisingly, his return only served to incite the Unionists in the congregation to resume their previous efforts to remove their pastor. The Unionist response made it clear that no single solution would satisfy the combative Pine Street congregation.[95] The case consequently came before the Old School General Assembly of 1864.

McPheeters's case received several days of deliberation, and many argued in his favor, including some former adversaries. However, the case came before the Presbytery of St. Louis shortly after the "Rosecrans Oath" took effect. Those who refused to take the oath were not seated at the Presbytery meeting; many men who might have been sympathetic to McPheeters's three-year stand for neutrality had missed the meeting precisely because they shared his views. The assembly voted 119–49 in favor of the Unionist faction at Pine Street. Vander Velde writes, "the General Assembly's action revealed that a majority of the Old School Church had come to the position that anything short of a positive declaration of loyalty in the pulpit was justly punishable."[96] McPheeters left St. Louis and lived out the remaining six years of his life in Louisville. His story endured as the centerpiece of the collective memory of unjust persecution of border clergy during the Civil War.

CONCLUSION

Attempts to police ministerial loyalty in the border states sometimes backfired. Clergy wielded considerable influence—both in what they said and what they did not say—but this influence carried with it a general cloak of inviolability. Ministers were not political figures or public personages and, therefore, their arrest on political grounds roused public indignation. The same factors that cast clergy under suspicion—their influence within the community and their frequent professions of neutrality on political issues—also made arrests and banishments tremendously unpopular among the faithful. Stories of these arrests became powerful propaganda against the federal government and the war.

The cases of clergy arrested during the Civil War vividly reveal the limits of enforced loyalty in the North. Much of the northern border strategy was plainly effective—the states remained in the Union despite deeply divided populations. Federal officials used oaths and other tests of patriotism to put an end to "neutrality" among clergy. However, efforts to secure political loyalty had the potential to break down outside the explicitly political realm. After the war, some of these loyalty tactics became part of the evidence used to motivate border-state affiliation with the South—a major component of which was the postwar realignment within border churches.

War reintroduced, on a national scale, the problems churches had faced during denominational schisms. The threats of division, local unrest, and political conflict again descended on the border. But in this instance, the loyalty of border residents—not only to their denominations, but to the nation as a whole—fell under suspicion. As the war progressed, southern denominational affiliation and neutrality both became shorthand for political disloyalty, and could be counted as treason.

Before the Civil War began, most border evangelicals considered the North to be the least schismatic of the two sections. After the experience of wartime, border clergy developed a dissatisfaction with the political actions of the northern churches in the course of the war and an inclination to disassociate from northerners and the federal government. Their discontent inclined border residents to sympathize with southern evangelicals. As the war entered its final years, and northern evangelical patriotism reached a fever pitch, dissatisfaction among moderate border evangelicals also intensified. The conclusion of the Civil War and the advent of northern religious Reconstruction ultimately severed the attenuated bonds between border evangelicals and northern denominations.

— 6 —

ALMOST LIKE FOUNDING AN EMPIRE

Union Victory and Religious Reconstruction

On the evening of March 9, 1864, Reverend Michael Cramer arrived in war-torn Nashville from his home city of Cincinnati. He brought with him a federal commission, along with an ardent devotion to the Union and a single-mindedness of purpose. His object: to assume the pulpit of McKendree Chapel, a former Southern Methodist church, which had been confiscated by the Union Army and was currently serving as a military hospital. The reverend, a Northern Methodist, was convinced that, with his commission in hand, McKendree was his for the taking.

Cramer, appalled by Nashville's eighteen-dollar-a-week hotels, found lodging at the United States Christian Commission headquarters. From there, he went immediately in search of his prize. His first impression of McKendree was inauspicious. It was, he reported, in "a very bad condition." The building would require major repairs, but Cramer was undeterred. He hurried off to find the Union officer to whom he had been directed: General Gordon Granger. It would, he imagined, be a simple matter of presenting Granger with the commission and, in return, accepting formal ownership of the church. Unfortunately, much to Cramer's frustration, General Granger had left town on military business and would not be back in Nashville until the following week. And there was more unwelcome news for Cramer: someone else—a Reverend Samuel Baldwin—had already applied for possession of McKendree. Even worse, Baldwin "had been promised to have it, provided he could establish his loyalty." Baldwin's claim was backed by congregants who had petitioned Andrew Johnson (then serving as military governor of occupied Tennessee), stating, "we each claim to be honestly loyal Citizens of the United States."[1] Cramer reassured himself that Baldwin was "well known as a secession sympathizer although he claims to have taken the oath of allegiance under the Amnesty Proclamation." The Cincinnati native was confident that his own impeccable credentials of loyalty would eclipse his rival's claim. He had, after all, excellent connections, having married Ulysses S. Grant's youngest sister just the year before. But Cramer's troubles in Nashville were only just beginning.[2]

Religious Reconstruction began in the final year of war, as the prospect of Union victory propelled northern evangelical patriotism to a jubilant peak. From 1864 to the end of the 1860s, three groups of evangelicals struggled over loyalty, abolition, and reunion: northerners, southerners, and border moderates. I approach this unsettled half-decade from these three perspectives to show how the last years of war and the first years of peace would shape American religion in the latter half of the nineteenth century. Attempts to redistribute church property and ensure the loyalty of ministers in occupied areas not only impeded sectional reunion, they also did much to alienate border moderates. By the end of the 1860s, border evangelicals identified less with the northern church than they ever had—and they moved to establish independence from northern ecclesiastical affiliation. This occurred most dramatically in the Presbyterian Church, but took place among Methodists and Baptists as well.

NORTHERN CHURCHES RESPOND TO UNION VICTORY

Northern evangelicals viewed the outcome of the war as evidence of God's direct support for the Union.[3] From their perspective, there was no longer any need to suspend discussion of slavery and Christianity; the debate, they reasoned, was resolved and God had struck a clear blow against slavery. "God's just doom has been wreaked on the giant hypocrite," read an 1865 Northern New School Presbyterian resolution.[4] Unlike churches on the border, where, throughout the war, some northern-affiliated ministers had objected to the practice of fast days and prayers for the Union, churches in the North had consistently embraced these practices and found it easy to celebrate both a national and a spiritual victory in 1865.[5] And so it came as a surprise to northerners that many border evangelicals still refused to embrace the Union and the end of slavery. Border residents persisted in their attempts to maintain neutrality, even with Union victory assured. "Nothing is more unsatisfactory and more surprising to the people of the North," declared a Cincinnati editorial, than the fact that "Kentucky refuses to take a stand either for or against the government."[6] Continued claims of border neutrality aroused suspicion and prompted northern church leaders to continue to monitor the political allegiance of their border brethren—a practice that began under federal authorities during the war. Northern church leaders also started to reconstruct religion in the conquered portions of the South and the occupied border through missionary efforts and the redistribution of church property confiscated by the military. These activities, carried out under military protection, exacerbated the frustration and indignation of border Christians.

The triumphalist attitude and actions of northern churches angered border evangelicals who had cultivated the doctrine of spirituality throughout the years before and during the Civil War. Even border residents who privately supported the Union began to pull away from the northern denominations when their postwar actions made it impossible for members to remain while professing neutrality. Northern condemnation of southern evangelicals began with denominational schism, escalated throughout the Civil War, and surged with the Union's double victory over secession and slavery.[7] For example, by the Civil War's "triumphant conclusion," the New School Presbyterian General Assembly was extolling "the power and excellence of our free institutions, when sustained by a virtuous and intelligent people, and the deep malignancy of that spirit of absolutism which has sought to overthrow them."[8] One Northern Baptist suggested that southerners must "repent and do works worthy of repentance" before they could be granted liberty to evangelize again.[9] Reverend Allen, a Nashville Presbyterian, expressed grave doubts about Southern Presbyterian loyalty. "Many within the Southern Church," he stated, are "*hopeless rebels*—that's the trouble and the *only trouble*."[10] These rebel tendencies, Allen argued, must be eliminated. Southern Methodists were "unfit for communion in Christ's Church" unless they would "repent before God and the nation in sackcloth and ashes for their offenses."[11] One historian argues that Unionist Christians saw secession itself as an act of Satan. This mindset would bolster the conviction that Union victory was a great moral triumph.[12]

With victory at hand, it was also easier to condemn the moderates on the border who had embraced neutrality. Northerners accused these moderates of raising "the hobgoblin of political intermeddling," and of persuading their peers not to condemn the South. "God be thanked that the day of compromise with slavery is over," read an editorial in Kentucky's pro-Union *Danville Quarterly Review*, "when weak men and trimmers joined together in crying that the peace of the church must be preserved." The editorial chided fellow Kentucky

Presbyterians for having "tried so long to avoid offending erring brethren that we do not know which side we really occupy." The author threw down the gauntlet for neutrals and moderates: "There are but two parties in our country, that which is for its preservation and that which is for its destruction; and all men must range themselves on the one side or the other."[13] This editorial summed up the feelings of the northern denominations toward the neutrality of border Christians: with northern triumph, God's will had been revealed—remaining neutral meant denying God's righteousness.

Lincoln's assassination, on April 14, 1865, heightened northern consensus, patriotism, and outrage. And, as Stowell notes, it "dramatically changed the attitude of Northern Christians."[14] This shift contributed to northern evangelical demands for a speedy reunion with their southern counterparts. They assumed that reunion would take place on northern terms and result in truly national denominational bodies.

It might seem puzzling that northern evangelicals placed so much confidence in not only securing a speedy postwar reunion with southern branches, but also in retroactively obtaining support for abolition from the border states. These assumptions were premised, in part, on the fact that southern churches, like much of the South, were in shambles by the end of the war. As early as 1863, a Northern Methodist minister in Nashville wrote, "I think the presiding opinion among the Southern Methodists is that their church is disorganized *beyond the hope of recovery*."[15] Another Northern Methodist was confident that the denomination would again "attain the blessing of peace, of oneness."[16] The Home Mission Society (Northern Baptists), who had not sent missionaries to the South since the sectional division of 1845, began once again to fund missions below the Mason-Dixon Line.[17]

Another factor also fueled northern optimism about a forthcoming sectional reunion. This was the prewar insistence, on the part of southerners, that their division was not theological, but purely political. For example, in 1844, Southern Methodist Ignatius Few proclaimed it was slavery alone that made it "best for the interests of all concerned that the Church in the North and South should be distinct."[18] If, as Few suggested, political differences over slavery were the root cause of denominational schism, then it made sense that northerners would imagine that religious reunion would follow on the heels of abolition. This is precisely the view articulated in a Northern Methodist newspaper from 1867: "the abolition of slavery has removed the greatest obstacle to a future union between Northern and Southern Methodists."[19] Similarly, in 1865, one Kentucky Presbyterian affiliated with the northern branch optimistically observed, "The remarkable fact is that the strifes which now agitate our Church root themselves in two issues, both of which are dead. The late rebellion is one—that has ceased; slavery is another—that too is extirpated forever."[20]

Several factors prevented this simple reunion scenario from taking place. First, northern evangelicals refused to curtail missionary activity in the South. Neither northern nor southern denominations had ever conceded that they were sectional. In fact, all three northern denominations had, to some extent, continued to send missionaries into areas that were claimed by the southern churches before and even during the war. Northerners had not abandoned the conviction that their branches represented the true church, and that they were free to evangelize anywhere. Likewise, southern evangelicals insisted that, in principle, they could send missionaries anywhere in the United States, even though they had no funds to do so.[21]

Second, the embrace of emancipation created a shift in power within northern branches late in the war. Border states had acted as a conservative check in the years after denominational schism. Even after southern churches had departed, the presence of border moderates—who embraced "spirituality" and disapproved of explicitly political statements—restrained northern evangelicals from endorsing a direct condemnation of slavery. Union victory, however, shifted the balance of power back toward the more explicitly antislavery members of the northern church. Now that the war was won and slavery was destroyed, there was no longer any need to appease slaveholders or moderates on the border. At the 1864 Old School Presbyterian Assembly in Newark, New Jersey, one attendant noted that, in marked contrast to prewar assemblies, "Intense interest seems to be manifested by the Assembly and community on the subject of slavery." The same observer also noted a "burning zeal" for resolutions denouncing slavery as "the sum of all villainies; the sin of sins." This zeal translated to a suspicion of border moderates who were still attempting neutrality on the subject of slavery. One member of the assembly denounced another "in harshest terms as a pro-slavery man."[22] This shift in attitude angered border moderates and advocates of "spirituality," who found they could no longer curtail political "fanaticism, extravagance, misrepresentation, and excitement" within their denominations.[23]

A preoccupation with testing loyalty constituted a third impediment to swift reunion. Oath taking was anathema to evangelicals—particularly those who embraced neutrality or spirituality. Wartime oaths issued by the military had aroused the ire of many border evangelicals, "stirring up intense feeling . . . and adding fuel to the present bitterness."[24] And yet, in the postwar years, after Union officials had withdrawn from the border, many northern churches began imposing their own loyalty campaigns on oath-weary border residents. For example, Northern Presbyterians demanded that all ministers who had resided in the border region during the war—regardless of the politics they had professed at that time—take an oath of loyalty and swear they had never aided the Confederacy.[25] This demand played a key role in motivating Missouri and Kentucky Presbyterians to withdraw from the Northern Old School General Assembly.

A few northerners did warn against offending conservative allies in the border and the defeated South, but even these circumspect voices anticipated an impending reunion. Reverend Donnan, a member of a northern branch of the Presbyterian Church remarked, of his southern counterparts, "As the victory is ours, and our hopes now realized, we can not only afford to be forbearing, but duty demands it of us. . . . It is certainly no time to torment them with their errors or ill success." Notwithstanding these words of caution, Donnan was confident that North and South "are on the same plain and going the same way and differences will disappear."[26] While Donnan may have been correct about the best way to win over the southern church, his optimism about reunion was misplaced. At any rate, his fellow Presbyterians did not follow his recommendation of humility; northerners, victors in a long and bloody struggle, were in no mood to be gentle and forbearing. For their part, southerners, still stinging from defeat, did not see themselves as being "on the same plain and going the same way" as those in the North.

SOUTHERN CHURCHES AND CONFEDERATE DEFEAT

Before and during the war, most southern evangelicals in all three denominations had insisted that they were not schismatics because their divisions were political, not theological. But after the war, northern evangelicals pushed for reunion on the grounds that war and abolition had swept away these political differences. With both slavery and the Confederacy destroyed, southern evangelical branches scrambled to justify continued independence.

Southern clergy faced the end of the war with less certainty and unity of conviction than they possessed before the conflict started. While some members of the southern denominations argued that reunification would be desirable, the majority asserted that the political demise of an independent South by no means necessitated the ecclesiastical death of the southern churches. "The same reasons that made necessary the existence of the Southern Baptist Convention still exist and make necessary the existence and continuation of the convention," declared one Southern Baptist. "There exists no practical necessity for a union of Northern and Southern Baptists in the Missionary work."[27]

Indeed, southerners explicitly refuted northern claims that, with slavery abolished, nothing stood in the way of reunion. "You say," wrote Southern Methodist Bishops Paine and McTyeire, addressing northern church leaders, that "the great cause which led to the separation from us of both the Wesleyan Methodists of this country and of the Methodist Episcopal Church has passed away." But, they continued, "Slavery was not, in any proper sense, the cause, but the occasion only, of that separation." This message was precisely the opposite of what Southern Methodists like Ignatius Few had claimed in the 1840s. At that time, they had argued that denominational schism was caused by slavery and slavery alone—not by any theological differences. Southern Methodists now insisted that the controversy over slavery had revealed that the two branches of the church fundamentally diverged when it came to "certain principles." One of these was the proper role of the church in politicized controversies.[28]

Likewise, at the 1865 Southern General Assembly, delegates declared their intention to sustain the separate Southern Presbyterian Church. "The reasons for its continuance not only remain as conclusive as at first," the assembly resolved, "but have been exceedingly strengthened by events of public notoriety, occurring each succeeding year." Among these "events of public notoriety," southerners counted "political preaching" and the exultant—some called it vindictive—tone of the northern churches.[29]

Although they were determined to remain separate from northern churches after Confederate defeat, southern evangelical leaders were uncertain about how to achieve this end. Building robust membership rolls and gathering financial resources were vitally important, but the demoralized and impoverished populace of the postwar South could not provide these essentials. Therefore evangelical membership constituted a desirable prize for the southern denominations.

Southern Presbyterians as well as Methodists considered changing their names in order to increase their appeal among border constituents, providing a measure of how much they desired affiliation with the border.[30] When the Presbyterian Church in the Confederate States of America met in December 1865, it faced a pressing need for a new designation. Frederick Ross pragmatically proposed the name "Presbyterian Church, South," and declared, "we are not going to unite with the Church North; let them, if they wish, unite with us." Others rejected the name, though, on the grounds that it may appear "spiteful, or offensive, or sectional." William H. Mitchell, no doubt thinking of the border, believed "South" might impose a "barrier between us and any with whom it may one day be our lot to stand side by side." When it came to a vote, the assembly selected "The Presbyterian Church in the United States" by an overwhelming majority.[31]

Southern Methodists held their first postwar General Conference in New Orleans in 1866. The previous year, Bishop Hubbard Kavanaugh had reported "a general desire on the *border everywhere* that the word 'South' should be removed from our church designation."[32] Spurred by such reports, many delegates "recommended a change in our name and style that left off the word 'South' in deference to those who were embarrassed by it."[33] After extensive deliberation, a majority of delegates in attendance selected "The Methodist Church" as a non-sectional alternative that might appeal to the border. The decision then went to the annual conferences for approval. Border conferences that belonged to the Southern Methodist Church expressed a greater preference for the name than conferences in any other area. "The vote of the Missouri conference favoring the change of the name of our denomination from Methodist Episcopal Church, South to Methodist Episcopal Church was greater than anticipated," delegates reported.[34] However, since southern conferences far outnumbered border conferences, the new name was ultimately rejected in favor of the old, sectional name.[35]

The debate over the use of "South" in Presbyterian and Methodist denominational names reveals much about the immediate postwar condition of southern and border churches. On the one hand, the willingness of southern denominations to consider removing "South" from their names in hopes of promoting growth speaks to their poverty immediately after the war. On the other hand, the debates over new names also sent a clear signal that these branches had no intention of reuniting with their northern counterparts. If they had, no new name would have been needed. Finally, these debates show an eagerness to court border moderates. Southern churches recognized that border evangelicals might dislike belonging to a church with a sectional—and thus political—name. This rhetorical deference to border spirituality and neutrality shows that, in the late 1860s, southern evangelicals placed their border counterparts—even those who already belonged to a southern church—in a unique category. Border evangelicals were clearly not southern—otherwise southern denominations would not have worried about changing their names. Neither, however, were they northern—otherwise they would have embraced the celebrations of Union victory.

BORDER CHURCHES AND THE END OF WAR

Many border evangelicals spent the antebellum and war years refining a doctrine of nonpolitical spirituality, arguing that state involvement with religious institutions corrupted the purity of the latter.[36] During the politically charged first half of the nineteenth century, the argument that religion and politics should be kept separate was popular along the border. As long as the northern branches did not become too politicized, these "neutral" border evangelicals preferred to remain affiliated with the North, rather than join their southern counterparts, who they believed had veered alarmingly toward the sin of schism. But theirs was a tenuous loyalty. So long as northern branches wished to retain the allegiance of their border brethren, they had to suspend debate over the compatibility of slavery and Christianity.[37] This was increasingly difficult in the latter half of the war as more and more northerners accepted and even embraced the reality that a Union victory would spell the end of slavery.

The celebrations, proclamations, and jubilation that emerged from northern pulpits, as well as the scrutiny aimed at ministers who had not openly supported the Union, offended many in the border, especially those who had sought to maintain a position of political neutrality and doctrinal spirituality. In 1864, a Bowling Green Presbyterian explained, "We want preachers of the gospel, not politicians, nor preachers of politics." Men who come to preach in the border region, he believed, "ought to be men of common sense who know how and when to conciliate." The church could not heal from its wartime ordeals if preachers "thrust questions about the war and rebellion in the faces of those who hear them." In other words, he sought ministers who would not celebrate Union victory. This, he argued, would be the only way to effect any sort of reunion. He noted that a local Presbyterian church had "gone through the war, thus far, and in this way, with eminent success." He concluded, "If we can accomplish anything at all in the way of reuniting our Church, or enlarging it, it must be done in this manner."[38]

No matter which side border residents supported and to which church they belonged, they evinced a more muted response to Union victory than did their northern counterparts. They also reacted negatively to northern patriotism and the linking of the Union with God's will. "The end of the war should have brought peace in the largest and best sense of the term," argued the editor of the *Missouri Baptist Journal*, "but the conflict continues. Many Eastern pulpits are as fierce today in denunciation of the South as ever." The editor continued, "the spirit of exultation, national pride, sectional superiority, and bitterness toward the Christians of other sections, is higher than ever before."[39] Border evangelicals abhorred the "strong political force in the Religious sentiment of the East." Kentucky Presbyterian Stuart Robinson remarked, "By our superior moderation [we] put ourselves clearly in the right."[40]

These evangelical responses to Union victory reflect a broader trend in the way that border residents regarded the Union cause during the last years of the war. The tipping point was the arrival of the Emancipation Proclamation, which signaled that enslaved people would be freed in the event of a Union victory. While most northern Unionists embraced, or at least accepted the inevitability of, emancipation, white Unionists along the border responded to the proclamation with outrage and indignation. Border Unionism was conservative at its root. As Aaron Astor argues, most white Kentuckians and Missourians fought for the Union, but they did so because they felt it would best protect the white-supremacist social order associated with slavery. With the Emancipation Proclamation, and the subsequent enlistment of black troops, border interests and Union war objectives began to part ways. This set the stage for the border's postwar political realignment.[41] The Union Army was a consistent presence in the border as these dramatic changes took place. Indeed, secular authorities were deeply involved in the first stages of religious Reconstruction.

SECULAR INVOLVEMENT IN RELIGIOUS RECONSTRUCTION

Like political and social Reconstruction, religious Reconstruction commenced before the war ended. Even as battles raged elsewhere, northern evangelicals carried out missionary work in cities under Union control.[42] In these efforts, the Union ended up aiding Unionist evangelicals in obtaining church buildings. The buildings were available because the army often commandeered churches in occupied territory to use as temporary headquarters, hospitals, and offices.[43] This practice explains why Michael Cramer located a former Southern Methodist church that had been used as a military hospital.

Cramer had come to Nashville under the authority of Bishop Matthew Simpson, who, in turn, had been designated by Secretary of War Edwin Stanton as one of the religious leaders in charge of redistributing Methodist Church property confiscated by the Union Army. This federally sanctioned effort coincided with a late-war resurgence in northern missionary activity in the border and upper South regions. Unionists like Cramer saw impending Union victory as nothing less than the resolution of the sectional conflict that had divided the major denominations twenty years earlier. From his home in Cincinnati, Cramer had witnessed the consequences of division over slavery within the churches. He headed south to Nashville with the expectation that the Emancipation Proclamation and Union military success would soon bring that painful chapter of Methodist history to a close.[44]

This was the context within which a Northern Methodist preacher from Cincinnati was granted federal sanction to enter Nashville and set up a pulpit in a formerly southern-affiliated church. To understand how things reached this point, consider the position of Union officers, stationed in the border and upper South at the end of the war. With church buildings no longer needed for military operations, the Union Army faced the question of what to do with those buildings they had commandeered—particularly those that belonged to southern-affiliated congregations.

Union officials did not confiscate churches with the sole intention of turning them over to loyal clergy, but they were intensely suspicious of southern-affiliated ministers and congregations.[45] As a result, when federal troops withdrew, they hesitated to return church keys to congregations suspected of disloyalty. One obvious solution was transferring the property to loyal clergy. Military leaders accepted this approach but did so cautiously. Most recognized the questionable constitutionality of military interference with churches, even in a time of war. Furthermore, despite mistrusting southern-affiliated clergy, squabbles over chapels were low on the military's list of priorities.

Because northern branches of evangelical denominations had proven their loyalty to the federal government, it made sense for the army to turn unneeded churches over to ministers from these denominations. Military need and the desires of northern denominations complemented each other perfectly and each gained from the arrangement. "The state is held for the government," wrote a Missouri missionary from Kansas City. "I propose to hold this place by military occupation (by the aid of the home guard) for the *Gospel*."[46]

Members of northern churches, confident that reunion would be forthcoming and eager to have the chance to establish themselves south of the Mason-Dixon Line, pressed to receive churches from the military. They were assisted by federal orders that explicitly authorized and facilitated the transfer of church property from military control to northern clergy. The most prominent of these was the Stanton-Ames Order. Signed by Secretary of War Edwin Stanton late in 1863, it authorized military authorities to entrust churches to Edward Ames, a Northern Methodist Bishop of unimpeachable loyalty.[47] On November 30, 1863, the War Department ordered: "All houses of worship belonging to the Methodist Episcopal Church South in which a loyal minister . . . does not now officiate, are placed at the disposal of the Right Rev. Bishop Ames." The order directed "commanding officers . . . to report houses of worship of this description" and to "furnish Bishop Ames every facility and assistance . . . in placing loyal ministers in possession of these houses."[48] Michael Cramer held his commission under this order.

Orders granting churches to loyal leaders of other denominations soon followed. In January of 1865, the War Department granted the Northern Baptist American Home Bishop Society "full and formal authority . . . to take possession of every abandoned Baptist meeting house within the insurrectionary districts, and every other Baptist Church edifice in the hands of the Confederates.[49] In March of the same year, generals received commands to "give aid, countenance and support" to Northern Presbyterian ministers in possessing disloyal churches.[50]

Once a northern minister gained control of church property, however, he often struggled to retain it. This was particularly true if the local population preferred southern denominations. Disputes over church buildings introduced another point of tension for border-state evangelicals and added further impetus to their slow movement away from affiliation with the northern denominations. In Nashville, Michael Cramer experienced this first-hand.

Cramer was the type of person who, having set upon a goal, pursued it with single-minded zeal. He could not tolerate the prospect of a week-long wait for the return to Nashville of his contact, General Granger. He wanted to start building a flock of Northern Methodists at McKendree Chapel without delay, so he decided to take up his case with Major General George Thomas. "I saw him and telegraphed," Cramer wrote, but to no avail. Frustrated, and hearing that his Southern Methodist rival, Baldwin, also "made vigorous efforts at Gen. Granger's Headquarters to secure McKendree Church," Cramer turned to his brother-in-law, Ulysses S. Grant. "I was compelled to apply to Gen. Grant before his departure from Nashville. He at once issued an order to turn it over to me, and to have it repaired at Government expenses," Cramer happily reported.[51]

Cramer's relief at securing McKendree ahead of his rival soon faded. Repairs proceeded slowly owing to a lumber shortage. And, much to Cramer's chagrin, Baldwin was not easily discouraged. "The Southern preachers and bishops are determined to outgeneral us," Cramer reported. "They intend to take the Oath of Allegiance and petition the President of the U.S. to restore their churches." Cramer was determined to meet them at every step. "If they petition him . . . I intend to get up another petition."[52] While waiting, Cramer looked over other properties in the area with an acquisitive eye. "You gave no direction with reference to the Tulip Street M.E. Church in Edgefield," Cramer wrote to Simpson. "Shall I have the church turned over to me or shall I leave it for the present?"[53] Several days later, he reported, "I have been informed there is a fine church in Clarksville. . . . what shall I do concerning it? Shall I go and inspect the ecclesiastical affairs there?"[54]

To Cramer's surprise, Southern Methodists were not the only ones opposed to his work in Tennessee. He reported paying a visit to a member of the northern church in Edgefield who, as it turned out, was "not in favor of having 'Northern' preachers appointed there."[55] In other words, the Edgefield congregant was critical of the Nashville operation even though he belonged to a northern church. He condemned his denomination's entanglement with secular authorities and disapproved of northern religious Reconstruction measures. Many on the border shared this perspective. In May 1864, as Southern Methodists advanced their plans to regain control of McKendree Chapel, Cramer worried: "we are losing ground by not having the church in operation."[56]

It was with great relief that, on June 12, 1864, Michael Cramer preached his first sermon in the repaired McKendree Chapel. Cramer had secured promises of protection from General Joseph Webster, and he finally felt assured that Baldwin's efforts had been fruitless: "He cannot molest me any longer. Our enterprise here is now resting on a solid foundation."[57]

The Union Army was not the only secular authority monitoring churches and ministers during the early years of Reconstruction. Following the example set by wartime military loyalty oaths, the Missouri Constitutional Convention of 1865 included a "Test Oath" in the new constitution. Radical Republicans in Missouri worried about maintaining control of the state after the war. The new constitution required voters to swear they had neither endorsed the Confederacy nor provided "aid, comfort, countenance or support to persons engaged in any such hostility." The oath left thirty-five thousand to fifty-thousand residents—"a quarter to a third of the voting population"—unable to vote. This ensured that Republicans would remain in power so long as it was in effect.[58]

The constitution stipulated that ministers must take the Test Oath before preaching or practicing. It stated that "any bishop, priest, minister, elder, or other clergyman of any religious sect or denomination" who did not comply would be subject to a fine of not less than five hundred dollars and six months imprisonment.[59] The requirement particularly incensed the clergy because it mandated oath taking, which was proscribed for Christians, and because it forced a political position upon border moderates. Even in the highly politicized war years, many border clergy had managed to avoid making their political sentiments public. In fact, maintaining neutrality—even well after neutrality had failed as a political strategy—became a point of pride as well as a coping mechanism. One Missouri minister described how clergy attempted "to keep their churches together by riding the fence or concealing their opinions." As the war dragged on, however, he predicted that these congregations must eventually "go to pieces" as external pressures made "riding the fence" increasingly difficult.[60] It was impossible, after the passage of the Test Oath, to live in Missouri, work as a minister, and maintain political neutrality regarding the Civil War. Paradoxically, the oath meant that it was easier to be a neutral minister in Missouri during the war than after its conclusion.

The Test Oath generated a powerful response, both from within the state and without, and further provoked the border evangelicals who already felt that they had been under attack during the war. "Every man who takes the oath [in order] to preach Christ's gospel is helping to subordinate the prerogatives of God to the Authority of men," a Missouri Baptist wrote.[61] Another Missouri minister complained, "The test oath prescribes a civil condition prerequisite to spiritual obedience to Christ. In whatever aspect we view the operation of this test oath, we find in it an assumption by the state, of authority in religious concernments."[62]

Sometimes, local pressure to comply with the oath accompanied attempts to seize church property. When John Godby, a Methodist, "preached and married people without taking the oath," he "was indicted and the sheriff sent to arrest" him. While Godby evaded arrest, a Catholic priest and a Baptist preacher in his community both served time in prison. During a sermon one Sunday, Godby recalled, "a Northern Methodist preacher arose in the congregation and said: 'I will preach here next Sunday if I live,'" but Godby's congregants and the church trustees opposed the radical constitution and rebuked the interloper.[63]

Preachers working in Missouri after the war were often caught between the demands of a powerful Union minority and those of a neutral or southern-sympathizing faction in their congregations. In describing the sort of man who was wanted to work in Missouri, Presbyterian minister James A. Paige wrote, "He should be emphatically loyal, for the ruling party sentiment is what is here distinguished as 'Radical.'" But, Paige continued, "as a minister he should keep his party politics in abeyance" because a number of congregants did not concur with the Radical program.[64]

Missouri evangelicals resented not only the impositions of the state government, but also the northern evangelicals, who were complicit in those offenses. "Let it be remembered that the religious persecution in Missouri, so far from exciting the sympathy of eastern Baptists in behalf of our churches and ministers, meets generally with their approval," observed one editorial. "The freedmen of the South furnish material *ad infinitum* for letter writers," he continued, "but the persecuted churches of Missouri are regarded as outside barbarians."[65] Having been forced out of neutrality, these frustrated border ministers now felt like victims of persecution. And while enforcement of the oaths was relatively lax (only about thirty-six ministers were indicted out of the hundreds who refused to take the oath), the arrests that did occur united nonpolitical Missouri clergy and heightened their dissatisfaction with the North.[66]

Secular involvement in religious Reconstruction in occupied cities and on the border—and the northern branches' willingness to embrace that involvement—angered and alienated many evangelicals in the region and became a factor in pushing border residents from affiliation with northern churches toward independence, or further reinforced their affiliation with the South.

UNWELCOME MISSIONARIES

While border and southern evangelicals frowned upon northern triumphalism, and chafed at secular involvement, they considered the surge in northern evangelization of the South and the border the most galling development of the final years of war and the first years of peace. From the northern perspective, white southerners were failing to provide for themselves, let alone the spiritual needs of their former slaves. Northern Baptist Daniel B. Purinton expected to hear, from the South, "a true Macedonian bleating for spiritual food as shall make your ears tingle, your hearts bleed, and your hands give."[67] This anticipated need inspired northern church leaders to send missionaries into the defeated states. Northerners saw a chance to establish themselves in communities where southern denominations had made exclusive territorial claims for the past several decades. "The Methodist Episcopal Church," wrote New Yorker James Mitchell, has "resolved to recover the ground wrenched from her by the great secession [of 1844]."[68] From Mississippi, James Lynch, an African American Northern Methodist serving as a missionary to freedpeople, concurred: "Now is the time to plant our church in every county of the state."[69]

Since 1844, Southern Methodists had greatly outnumbered Northern Methodists on the border, particularly in Missouri and Kentucky. However, many of these border Southern Methodists were notably moderate compared to their brethren in the South. At the outbreak of war, every Southern Methodist conference on the border, save Maryland, passed resolutions in support of the federal government. Conferences in Kentucky, Missouri, Delaware, and western Virginia all explicitly supported the Union. In western Virginia, Northern Methodists outnumbered Southern, and Maryland was evenly divided, although the Southern Methodist faction was more strongly pro-southern than elsewhere on the border.[70]

In this favorable climate, Northern Methodists made gains in the border region for the first time since 1844. Kentucky Methodists considered joining the northern church, and in 1864, the Kentucky Conference of the Methodist Episcopal Church, South, again declared loyalty to the Union.[71] In 1863, when Secretary of War Edwin Stanton granted Northern Methodists the use of Southern Methodist churches in the border and South, northern Methodists began in earnest to extend their influence. For a brief moment, it appeared that northern Methodism might spread across the nation and again become the national denomination its members longed for it to be. The Holston Conference, organized in eastern Tennessee and West Virginia, was one great success for Northern Methodists.

"Parson" William Brownlow, an outspoken Tennessee Unionist, editor, and Methodist minister initiated the process of establishing the Holston Conference in 1864.[72] Eastern Tennessee had never been home to a large slave-owning population, and support for the Confederacy was weak in the region.[73] In addition, missionaries there could call on the protection of the Union Army under the Stanton-Ames Order. The work was encouraging. "The Union people of East Tenn[essee] . . . are utterly disgusted with the Church South," reported Joseph Jones in the summer of 1864.[74] In June of 1865, in a high-water mark for Northern Methodism in the South, the Holston Annual Conference held its first meeting under the guidance of Bishop Davis Clark.[75]

Bishop Clark served in many capacities during religious Reconstruction. He also worked to establish black Northern Methodist congregations in the South. No northern evangelical could ignore the potential harvest of souls belonging to the formerly enslaved. In 1866, the church gave Clark access to nearly thirty-two thousand dollars to "use in the South." He allotted twelve thousand out of this sum "to aid in establishing a Col[ored] Ch[urch] and school in Memphis" and in twelve other southern towns.

Even though black southerners swiftly began to develop their own religious organizations, northerners believed that the freed slaves of the South were deficient in religious leadership and practices. A Methodist described work on the border as "quite like missionary work among the heathen."[76] Northerners argued that, both in slavery and in freedom, white southerners denied black people access to religious instruction. This meant that freedpeople were doubly imperiled: first, by their own ignorance, and second by a lack of white assistance. When it came to former slaves, Presbyterian Samuel C. Alexander lamented, southerners "would far more willingly build prisons and penitentiaries for them than assist in building churches and schoolhouses." However, he also believed black southerners to be unfit to provide for their own religious instruction, calling black ministers "extremely ignorant and, often immoral." The only solution, as Alexander saw it, was mission work "through the Northern Church."[77]

Southern evangelicals resented northern incursions and particularly northern evangelizing among freed slaves, but they had scant resources and ambivalent feelings about taking on the task themselves. In addition, freedpeople, faced with the prospect of joining denominational branches that had supported the Confederacy, felt a healthy ambivalence of their own. Before black southerners began to form their own independent denominations during Reconstruction, northern evangelicals enjoyed a brief window for mission work, largely without competition.[78]

The northern missionary impulse was not limited to former slaves. The border region also became the object of northern missionary efforts. It especially rankled neutral border evangelicals when northerners questioned their loyalty. As Matthew Cramer's suspicion of Samuel Baldwin illustrates, even publicly taking a loyalty oath was not always enough to dismiss fears that self-styled neutral moderates were not "loyal at heart."[79] In response, border evangelicals became increasingly antagonistic toward northerners who mingled politics and religion. One Presbyterian explained that the border "did not wish to join the Southern General Assembly," but as for northern policies of religious Reconstruction: "we will not be partakers of your folly or of your evil . . . until you cease to meddle with affairs that are secular."[80] Stuart Robinson claimed that "ten times as many" moderate evangelicals "have been suppressed and banished from the loyal states of Missouri and Kentucky alone" than Baptist missionaries abroad have been suppressed by "intolerant cruel" Turkish autocrats.[81] Caroline Moss, an active Missouri Baptist, also complained of "the brethren of the North" who "come into our field of labour when they are so much needed in other points."[82] Moss herself had opposed secession and favored the Union in the war, but she did not welcome northern missionaries.

Missions to the South vividly illustrate the northern evangelical conviction that northern branches were *national* branches, expansive in their geographic reach. Thus, even after secular authorities had ceased to be involved with churches in the South, northern evangelicals linked their missions to the federal cause. Union victory and emancipation, according to a New York Methodist, were the "grand conclusions" of "the logic of humanity, the logic of Christianity, and the logic of events." Northern evangelicals assumed it was their Christian duty to build upon the principles of that "grand conclusion" through missions to the South.[83]

RECONSTRUCTING FROM WITHIN: POSTWAR PRESBYTERIAN RUPTURE

Northern churches did not rely solely on military assistance to begin religious Reconstruction. Many of the efforts to eliminate neutrality or anti-Union sentiments took place within denominations—particularly in the Presbyterian Church, but also in the Methodist Church, and, to some extent, the Baptist Church. Tests, conditions, and property confiscation engineered by one's own denomination were even more infuriating to border moderates than oaths or tests imposed by secular authorities. The most notable of these loyalty tests were the Reconstruction Resolutions imposed by the northern branch of the Old School Presbyterian Church upon Presbyterians in the border states. Unlike the Methodists, the major border Presbyterian and Baptist organizations remained affiliated with their northern branches throughout the Civil War, acting as a conservative check on those denominations. However, with Union victory assured, northern evangelicals felt free to impose loyalty tests as part of religious Reconstruction. The process by which border Presbyterians withdrew from the Northern Presbyterian Church offers a dramatic example of how Reconstruction in the churches prompted areas affiliated primarily with northern denominations to withdraw their fellowship from the North.

As the Civil War drew to a close, the Old School Presbyterians patriotically condemned the "malignant and wicked" actions of the formerly seceded states and expected a speedy reunion following victory and the abolition of slavery. The 1865 Old School General Assembly drafted resolutions that at once stipulated the conditions under which Southern Presbyterians could reunite and enumerated their manifold errors, including endeavoring "to conserve and perpetuate the system of slavery." The resolutions did not equivocate. They called secession and slavery "a great crime, both against our national government and against God."[84]

The Reconstruction Resolutions, as the document came to be called, laid claim to the property of any church where at least one congregant remained in the northern branch. They also called for a loyalty test to be applied to ministers "from any Presbytery or other ecclesiastical body in the Southern States"—including Kentucky, Maryland, and Missouri. The test required southern ministers to take an oath that he had not "in any way, directly or indirectly," supported the Confederacy and that he did not believe slavery to be "a Divine institution."[85]

The Reconstruction Resolutions effectively branded as disloyal the border-state Old School Presbyterians who had managed to maintain their neutrality through the war. Delegates from Maryland, Tennessee, Missouri, and Kentucky, who had remained with the Northern Assembly out of loyalty and a conviction of the sinfulness of schism, registered an angry protest. They argued that the resolutions would no longer allow them to maintain neutrality.[86] The resolutions were the last straw for residents of a region that had stayed loyal despite—not because of—northern patriotism. Samuel R. Wilson, a Kentucky conservative, defended border neutrality: "We who stand here between the North and South . . . It is in the cause of Unity; it is in the cause of peace upon the foundations of the truth in Jesus, that we have endeavored to act." Pointing out that federal authorities no longer policed border ministers, Wilson continued, "Caesar is satisfied, Oh! Brethren, are you not satisfied?"[87]

Dissenting border-state delegates, led by the Presbytery of Louisville, offered an alternative, reconciliationist proposal for reincorporating the Southern Synods. They suggested removing the assertion about the sinfulness of slavery and secession, instead approaching southerners "in the spirit of meekness and love."[88] Border delegates particularly condemned the oaths as useless and offensive. Northerners rejected this alternate proposal and pressed on with their original plan.

Southern Presbyterians belonged to a separate denomination and were, of course, under no obligation to take the oaths. In effect, the tests only applied to the border Presbyterians who remained in the northern church. And they were incensed. That autumn, Samuel Wilson led the Presbytery of Louisville in drafting a "Declaration and Testimony" against the seemingly anti-southern and political Reconstruction Resolutions.[89] The declaration charged that, instead of a return to antebellum neutrality on contentious political matters—specifically slavery—the Old School had allowed politics to become entwined with the church to an unconscionable degree and unfairly punished secession—and border-state Presbyterians. The church's "erroneous and heretical doctrines and practices" tended to obliterate all the lines of separation between the "civil and ecclesiastical powers" and would "keep up strife and alienation among brethren."[90]

One hundred nineteen border ministers and elders signed their names to the Declaration and Testimony. In response, the Old School Assembly dissolved the Presbytery of Louisville and several other offending presbyteries, and denounced the paper as "an act of rebellion."[91] In 1867, the General Assembly elected to expel the Synods of Kentucky and Missouri. Any signer who wished to be readmitted would have to take yet another loyalty oath, denouncing the declaration.[92] Oaths of this sort drove the Declaration and Testimony men to draft the controversial document in the first place, so few recanted, and the Synods of Kentucky and Missouri withdrew and constituted themselves as independent bodies. By the late 1860s, most of those who would have opposed the assembly's actions had withdrawn or been exscinded. As the Old School shed its doctrinally conservative southern and border members, it grew steadily closer, theologically and demographically, to the New School Assembly.

The Declaration and Testimony wrought its harshest divisions at the congregational level in areas that were not distinctly southern or northern—namely Kentucky, Missouri, and Maryland. Congregations divided, once again sparking disputes over affiliation and church property. In one prominent example of such a dispute, two groups sought control of the Walnut Street Church in Louisville, Kentucky. One group consisted of Declaration and Testimony men who had withdrawn from the General Assembly, and the other still belonged to (and was recognized by) the Northern Old School. The case turned on which group was the legitimate Walnut Street congregation—raising that old question of whether secular courts could distinguish between original denominations and splintered factions. The U.S. Circuit Court heard the case and, in 1868, found in favor of the northern-affiliated body, ruling that "the members of said church only, who recognize and adhere to the Presbyterian Church in the United States of America [Northern Church] . . . compose the true Third, or Walnut-street, Presbyterian church."[93] The property cases of the 1840s, as well as wartime conflicts, had paved the way for such intervention by outside, secular arbiters.

The aggrieved Declaration and Testimony faction appealed the case, and the state court overturned it, declaring that the General Assembly party had violated the Presbyterian Constitution. But repeated northern appeals brought the case before the Supreme Court, which, in 1871, ruled again in favor of the General Assembly party and against the Declaration and Testimony men. Unlike in cases dealing with Mormonism, the courts declined to rule on the legitimacy of each party's religion, calling the dispute "purely ecclesiastical" and outside of the jurisdiction of civil courts.[94] A majority of six found that secular courts should defer to "the highest tribunal" within the church organization—in this case, the General Assembly.[95] Under this ruling, the General Assembly's decision in the case overrode the protests of the Declaration and Testimony party and the upstart Synod of Kentucky.

The outcome of the Walnut Street case and others like it angered Southern Presbyterians and fueled their conviction that the Northern Church was little more than a puppet of the federal government.[96] The ruling had the effect of unifying the southern party in opposition to the northern branch. Southerners also resented that the Northern General Assembly allocated funds to cover legal fees for the party it supported. This was true: in 1869, the Old School voted to give five thousand dollars in support of the northern party in a border-state property dispute.[97] To the impoverished Southern Assembly, this spending stung like salt in a wound.[98]

Presbyterians in the border states lived through yet another local process of church sectionalization during Reconstruction.[99] Once again, these churches divided by slim margins. For the residents of Kentucky, Tennessee, Missouri, and Maryland, divisions in the border synods were life-changing and revealed that sectionalism had not faded. A northern Presbyterian in Nashville remarked that he had "hoped that when the war was over that Union men in the South would live here more pleasantly. . . . Things here, however, are more unpleasant than I have ever seen them."[100]

The experience of Jonathan Palmer Finley, a conservative Old School minister in Missouri, captures the strains of Presbyterian life on the border in the wake of the Declaration and Testimony controversy. During the war, Finley's congregations split into factions, but he never publicly revealed his political leanings, even when challenged at a Union roadblock. Only in his diary did he record his "ardent and unswerving attachment to the Union." When federal troops demanded a loyalty oath of all ministers, Finley reluctantly complied, although he did not "believe the State has the moral right to require such an oath." Finley was shrewd enough to understand that the end of war would not signal the end of conflict in Missouri. "Soon those not in sympathy with our government will organize separate churches and Presbyteries—dividing our already weak churches," he predicted.[101]

Finley considered the following year the most pivotal of his life. In September 1866, twelve of the twenty-two ministers and elders in the Presbytery of Palmyra, for which he served as clerk, "put their names to the Declaration and Testimony." Finley adamantly opposed the document and refused to record the signers' names as legitimate members of the presbytery. Enraged, the Declaration and Testimony men elected to remove Finley from his office. He refused to resign. Instead, he snatched the presbytery's records and left the building, with eight of his supporters, effectively sundering the Presbytery of Palmyra. He remembered the meeting as "the most marked day in my life."[102]

Afterward, Finley found it very difficult to live and work in Missouri. Former friends refused to worship with him, accusing Finley of the "sin of subordination and schism." Finley could only find comfort in his faith. The church institutions in which he had been raised, and to which he had devoted his life, were teetering on the brink of disintegration. Only a month after the collapse of his own presbytery, the Synod of Missouri also divided into two parties over the Declaration and Testimony. The following spring, the General Assembly expelled the Synods of Kentucky and Missouri.[103]

Finley's account of the tumultuous 1860s illustrates the personal turmoil and general disarray that accompanied the process of sectionalization in the border states. By early 1867, Finley had transitioned from an apolitical Old School Presbyterian to a Unionist Assembly Party man. Try as he might to avoid it, Jonathan Palmer Finley became entangled in the process of postwar sectional and doctrinal differentiation. In autumn of 1866, Finley sadly noticed this sectionalization of doctrine: "I find also that all who were strongly Southern in their feelings stand aloof altogether from those of us who adhere to the Assembly."[104] With the benefit of hindsight, this outcome seems unsurprising; but for Finley, it was a painful realization.

BORDER BACKLASH AND THE SPIRITUALITY OF THE CHURCH

The period immediately following the Civil War saw the greatest challenges to border neutrality and the spirituality of the church; it also saw the fullest articulation of those ideals. Once Union victory had been assured, there was no longer any need to appease border moderates. When the war ended, evangelicals who had attempted to remain neutral before and during the war could no longer sustain their neutrality as northerners in all three denominations undertook religious Reconstruction with zeal. The Presbyterian Reconstruction Resolutions most dramatically challenged neutrality among border Presbyterians, but Baptist and Methodists underwent similar conflicts.

Dissension over mission territory tested border Baptist commitment to sectional neutrality. Northern Baptists began sending missionaries into the South after the war, despite protests from the Southern Baptist Convention. When the Northern Society refused to stop evangelizing below the Mason-Dixon Line, the Southern Baptists began to forge an alliance with church leaders in the border. In 1865, the Southern Convention asked Baptist associations in the border for assurances that they would refuse to cooperate with northern missionaries.[105]

In response, northerners pressured Kentucky and Missouri Baptists to drop their connections with the Southern Convention. This request angered border-state Baptists, who prided themselves on their denomination's nonhierarchical structure. "Coercion in religious matters cannot be successfully carried out against Baptists," Caroline Moss of Missouri wrote. "We meet any attempt [by] our Northern Brethren to compel us to relinquish our connection with the Southern Board with the solemn affirmation—'We are Free—the son of god hath made us free.'"[106] Pressure from the North only prompted Moss to identify more closely with the Southern Convention. Her reaction was shared by Missouri Baptists more broadly. This was a group that had attempted to avoid identifying with a sectional organization. The Missouri General Association stated that it wished to operate "irrespective of party or politics, throughout the state."[107] Missouri Baptists maintained connections with both bodies and "never denied fellowship and membership to 'Northern' or 'Southern' Baptists."[108] But partisan forces from the North pushed them closer than ever toward identifying solely with their southern brethren.

The demands of the Northern Society, and its expectations of loyalty and patriotism, also alienated Kentucky Baptists. In 1865, a minister observed, "the Kentucky Baptists . . . are more intensely Southern today than any other state in the limits of the Convention."[109] In spite of—and in part, because of—pressure from the North, the General Baptist associations in both Kentucky and Missouri voted to maintain connection with the Southern Convention.[110] These border Baptists explained their defiance of northern demands in the language of spirituality. "What temperance Christian," asked a correspondent to the *Missouri Baptist Journal*, "could endure . . . the dregs of whiskey, or froth of beer, in his water or coffee? Such is the incongruity of politics with religious matters."[111]

Northern missionary ventures into the South and the border region yielded similar discontent among Methodists. Although a majority had joined the southern church, a great many border Methodists remained affiliated with the North during the antebellum and war years. However, this affiliation was strained by the events of the war and further attenuated when the Northern Methodist General Conference invested two hundred thousand dollars to establish a "Church Extension Society." The society was intended to promote Northern Methodism in the South. Missionary James Lynch was an advocate of the Extension Society and accused the southern church of attempting to "hinder progress and teach sectionalism." Lynch described his work with freedpeople in the South as "almost like founding an empire."[112] The lavish spending irritated Southern Methodists, who were struggling to raise funds. "Northern Methodism has its foothold in the southern states," a southerner groused, "by the outlay of money; and when the money stops the work will stop."[113]

Maintaining robust congregations, however, was even more critical to the survival of the Northern Methodist Episcopal Church in the South and border region than raising funds. When the military departed and local support was weak, northern efforts in the border and the South stalled. Michael Cramer, the tireless northern minister who took over McKendree Chapel in Nashville, discovered for himself how reliant he was on outside support. In June 1864, shortly after Cramer's first sermon in the chapel, his rival, Samuel Baldwin, reemerged. Enlisting support from politicians and from General Lovell Rousseau, Baldwin petitioned Bishop Simpson to restore the church to his control. "I am a 'loyal man' and hold my appointment from a 'loyal bishop,'" Baldwin protested. "I am fully satisfied," he warned, that the "effect of my being displaced or dispossessed . . . will be injurious to the Union cause."[114] Baldwin also traveled to meet with other disgruntled and dispossessed Methodist clergy in Louisville during the spring of 1864. The convention sent a petition to Washington, D.C., demanding the return of church property under military control. Later in the year, the McKendree Chapel trustees petitioned Andrew Johnson, then military governor of Tennessee, for return of the building, insisting that they were "honestly loyal citizens of the United States."[115]

As Baldwin marshaled support for his case, Cramer went on the offensive. He enlisted seven friends to sign a letter to Matthew Simpson, attesting that Baldwin's "Convention was unmistakably disloyal in its character," and that its purpose was to overturn the Stanton-Ames Order.[116] Although they captured attention, petitions and threats did less for Baldwin's cause than did the end of the war. In 1864, Cramer's congregation consisted of 415 Union soldiers.[117] When the war ended, the military departed from Nashville, taking with it Cramer's source of protection and his entire congregation. By this time, Andrew Johnson had assumed the presidency, and he sided with Baldwin. Without a congregation and secular support, it was difficult for Cramer to maintain control. By August 1865, Cramer was dismissed from the pulpit, and Baldwin was once again in possession of the keys to McKendree Chapel.[118] He hailed Johnson as "God's chosen minister of mercy." In fact, the congregation went so far as to offer up a political prayer: that Johnson "might long live, the prosperous president of the nation."[119]

This outcome, if not the prayer, doubtless pleased Louisville's Stuart Robinson, perhaps the most colorful and outspoken border proponent of spirituality. A conservative Old School Presbyterian, he had remained with the North in 1861. Robinson's frank, caustic, single-minded publication, the Louisville *True Presbyterian,* became the most prominent mouthpiece of border spirituality. Robinson and his paper represent an extreme example of the border response to the sectionalization and political language that dominated the late and postwar years.[120]

Each week, the newspaper ran articles on a set of recurring themes: the importance of the separation of church and state; the folly of Northern Presbyterians who embraced and endorsed the Union and emancipation; and the corrupted purity of the true church, which only lived on in isolated corners of the border region. Robinson titled his paper the *True Presbyterian* because the phrase was "expressive of the idea, that one peculiar and distinctive feature of Presbyterianism as a Church Government, consists in that separation of the secular and spiritual order which this paper advocates against the un-Presbyterian tendencies of the times."[121] Although he was a member of the northern branch of the Presbyterian Church, Robinson directed most of his hostility towards his own branch and displayed increasing sympathy for the Southern Presbyterians, referring to them as "true Christians in the legitimate gospel work of circulating God's word."[122]

Articles in the *True Presbyterian* chart the increasing alienation of border Presbyterians from the North during the war and after religious Reconstruction began. Border Presbyterians began to align themselves with, or at least defend and sympathize with, the South and southern churches—even those of other denominations. Through the paper, Robinson relentlessly promoted the idea of the spirituality of the church. He aggressively attacked the northern churches and their support for the Union, calling the North "the great hotbed of effete, putrid, and fermenting Puritan infidelism."[123] In the last years of the war, and as Reconstruction began, federal involvement with churches and triumphant northern patriotism provoked Robinson into penning a near-constant stream of vitriolic articles. He complained about federal actions and criticized at the doctrinal shortcomings of his northern-affiliated brethren. Robinson deplored "the wanton dalliance of the Protestant Church with the State, on the one hand, and the assumption of authority over church by the state, on the other."[124]

While he claimed he "never published or commented upon political or military news," Robinson's paper drew the ire of federal authorities.[125] When he heard a rumor that his arrest was imminent, Robinson fled to Canada, where he continued to edit the *True Presbyterian* for distribution in Louisville. However, in November of 1864, Major General Stephen Burbridge gave an order to have the paper suppressed. Robinson suspended publication, waited out the war in Toronto, and returned to Louisville in 1866. He was just in time to take part in the withdrawal of the Synod of Kentucky from the Northern Assembly, following the Declaration and Testimony controversy.

Robinson's threatened arrest, along with the suppression of his newspaper, seemed to confirm the worst suspicions of his readers. Union authorities had unwittingly lent credence to Robinson's accusations about the "Ecclesiastico-Military Councils" of the northern secular leaders and the "pestiferous dogmas" of evangelicals in the North.[126] At the same time, the withdrawal of the Kentucky Synod from the General Assembly seemed proof to northerners that Kentucky Presbyterians—previously such staunch supporters of church unity—were nothing more than "weak men." In the words of one reader, the demands for compromise and neutrality by his Kentucky brethren amounted to making the church "join hands with the state for doing evil, while the world is deceived as to her secret purpose by violent protestations of desire to keep free from Political intermeddling."[127] Stuart Robinson's experience reveals how evangelicals on the border attempted to navigate the Civil War by maintaining neutrality and the spirituality of the church. By the end of the war, pressure from both the federal government and northern churches eliminated the possibility of neutrality as a strategy.

Northern evangelicals, who supported the Union; Southern evangelicals, who supported the Confederacy and slavery; and "neutral" border clergy all entered the period of Reconstruction with mutually incompatible expectations. And despite northern hopes for reunion, religious Reconstruction only escalated the distrust and resentment that these groups felt toward one another. An 1868 exchange in the New York *Methodist Quarterly Review* poignantly captured this dynamic. It began with the journal's October 1868 issue, which featured a favorable review of a pamphlet by Thomas Pearne, a staunch Northern Methodist who worked in educational missions to freedpeople in Nashville. Pearne's pamphlet contended that Southern Methodists had supported both slavery and secession. Pearne also argued that Northern Methodists would soon dominate the South, and he refuted charges that the Methodist Episcopal Church was a "sectional, an abolition, a political, a negro-equality Church." None of this sat well with Thomas Osgood Summers, a prominent Southern Methodist, who served as the editor of the Nashville *Christian Advocate*. Summers was quite familiar with Pearne, and he was outraged to see him praised in the pages of the *Methodist Quarterly Review*. This exchange took place in the late 1860s—well after the Union Army had washed its hands entirely of Methodist churches in Nashville. Yet the tensions between northern and southern clergy in that city continued to simmer.

Summers penned an indignant letter to the *Methodist Quarterly Review*, denouncing Pearne as a despicable "carpet-bagger" who was not to be trusted, and urging the "otherwise magnificent Quarterly" to cease publishing material about the ongoing strife between Northern and Southern Methodists.[128] Daniel Whedon, editor of the review, relished the challenge. Summers, he responded, might believe that Southern Methodists were "entitled to exclude all outsiders from entering without their permission," but Whedon and the Northern Methodists did not. Whedon accused the Southern Methodists of clinging to the remnants of slavery and sectionalism. He was certain of the future of both the United States and American Methodism. "We are to be," he asserted, "a continent-wide republic. . . . Our own noble Church," he continued, "will spread abroad her evangelizing power, covering the entire national area, and knowing no limits to her missionary enterprise."[129]

Whedon's assessment would prove hopelessly wide of the mark. But his views reflected those of northern evangelical clergy in the postwar years. Whedon counseled Summers and his fellow Southern Methodists to "exorcize his soul of every last remnant of that spirit" of slavery and "narrow sectionalisms." Northern Methodists directed this effort to "exorcize" sectionalism not just toward Southern Methodists, but also toward members of their own branch who might not be aboard the national "car of destiny" that led away from slavery and secession. Passengers aboard this train "to fortune" must embrace the consequences of Union victory. Neutrality had no place on board.[130]

From Cincinnati, the editor of the *Western Christian Advocate* viewed this sectional acrimony with dismay. "As we have said before," the author writes, "we do not believe that the discussion of the old issues, which died with slavery, can be productive of good." During Reconstruction, the Cincinnati paper continued to deplore rehearsals of "unpleasant history" and suggested "talk of the common heritage of the saints" instead.[131] The editor still held out hope for compromise and reunion. As these articles illustrate, antebellum and wartime controversies continued to enflame tempers and shape allegiances even after war had ended.

CONCLUSION

The end of the war brought changes for all four groups concerned with border churches: federal officials, northern evangelicals, southern evangelicals, neutral border evangelicals. For its part, the Union Army began withdrawing from occupied cities and turned over confiscated churches to Unionist ministers. As the Union prepared to end its brief foray into monitoring loyalty in the churches, northern evangelical denominations grew increasingly invested in ensuring the loyalty of their members.

War had ended slavery and the Confederacy. However, it in no way spelled the end of evangelical concerns about these issues. Northern evangelicals celebrated Union victory and the abolition of slavery, and they expected their neutral and moderate brethren in the border to do so as well. They accepted no excuse for continuing to profess neutrality in the aftermath of a war that had been resolved in favor of the Union. They anticipated that southern branches of the major denominations would soon reunite, and do so on northern terms.

Southern evangelicals might have accepted the reality of military defeat, but they did not view this defeat as a cue to reunite with their northern counterparts. In contrast to northern expectations, Confederate defeat galvanized southern evangelicals to defend their independent denominations; they insisted that there was something more than slavery and the Confederacy keeping the northern and southern branches from reuniting.

Border evangelicals—some affiliated with northern churches and others with southern denominations—found that, in the last years of the war, they stood on shifting ground. The argument against mingling religion and politics, and in favor of neutrality, had ever diminishing traction with northerners as it became clear that the Union would win the war. At the same time, border Unionism was waning. The abolition of slavery and the enlistment of black soldiers helped turn many of the conservative Unionists of the border into belated Confederates.

In truth, the border withdrawal from affiliation with the northern churches represented continuity, not a break, with the priorities and prewar trends of border evangelicals. In keeping with their responses to previous social and political turmoil, they tried to minimize conflict, resisting demands for partisan allegiance or abrupt change, and, as they had done in the past, they directed their sympathies toward the group that they perceived as least radical. In the prewar years, affiliation with the South required an act of explicit division from the northern branch and a positive affirmation that slavery was not a sin. However, as the patriotism of northern churches escalated, southern churches downplayed the role of politics in their creation and existence. This shift began to make the northern denominations appear more radical than the South. Where southerners had once appeared to be overzealous schismatics, that charge was now directed at the jubilantly patriotic northern branches that embraced federal involvement in reconstructing churches.

By insisting on determining the loyalty of border members after the end of the war, northern church leaders intended to foster a shared sense of identity and promote denominational unity. But they ended up deepening the rifts that had developed since the schisms of the antebellum years. The conflicts of the late and postwar years alienated conservative border evangelicals from the northern branches. And the absence of these conservative border voices narrowed the spectrum of opinion, promoting the view that North-South reunion was desirable, attainable, and would take place on northern terms. The Declaration and Testimony protests, Robinson's newspaper, and the border trend toward dissatisfaction with the actions of the northern church all point to this postwar shift in affiliation. Armed with claims to a spiritually pure religion, border evangelicals turned away from the northern denominational branches. Set apart from the mingling of religion and politics they had observed in both branches of their churches before, during, and after the war, border evangelicals claimed to value purity above sectionalism.

Much to the disappointment of border moderates, the end of the war did not signal an end to political engagement in the northern churches. Border moderates, who had clung so long to neutrality, realized that, far from ending what they saw as the politicized church, the conclusion of the war only increased northern evangelical identification with the Union cause and the federal government. The one place where politics seemed to disappear from the pulpit was in the southern denominations. Northern and southern branches had each warmly supported the Union or Confederate cause. But when the war ended, so, too, did the Confederacy. Without a government to pray for, affairs of state disappeared from southern sermons. Estranged border evangelicals, so long opposed to division, at last separated themselves from the North.

— 7 —

A FIRE IN THE FRONT AND A FIRE IN THE REAR

Border Realignment and the Failure of Reunion

William Bell, a Baptist pastor in Saline County, Missouri, wanted nothing to do with "the so-called Missouri Baptist Convention." In the spring of 1867, members of the convention invited Bell and other Baptist leaders to a meeting intended to unite Missouri Baptists. Bell published his refusal in the *Missouri Baptist Journal*, cautioning readers about the dangers of forming a connection with the "National Baptists" of Missouri, a northern "faction," he argued, "whose crowning virtue is fanaticism." Bell dismissed the new convention's goals in racialized terms, asserting that any union would constitute "amalgamation" and produce "a new-born mongrel."[1] Connecting with northern Baptists, Bell implied, was akin to violating the tenets of white supremacy.

Bell suspected that this new convention planned "to supplant and destroy the General Association" and that, despite their claims to friendship, it would ultimately insist upon the General Association's "withdrawal from the 'Southern Baptist Convention.'"[2] His fears were not entirely unfounded. After the Civil War, the Missouri Baptists who had supported the Union and the Test Oath began to worry that most Baptists in the state identified more with the Southern Baptist Convention than with the northern American Baptist Home Mission Society. In 1865, a group of anxious Baptists Unionists sent out a call for "the loyal Baptist churches throughout the state of Missouri" to join together and form a new association—the Missouri Baptist State Convention.[3] The new organization also reached out to the Missouri Baptist General Association even though the latter group had vehemently protested the state's new constitution and the especially the Test Oath, calling it "plainly averse to the teachings of the New Testament."[4]

While many Baptists in the state still wished to affiliate with both the American Baptist Home Mission Society and the Southern Baptist Convention, William Bell (and the *Missouri Baptist Journal*) clearly favored alliance with the southern organization alone. In the same issue in which Bell cautioned against union with "National Baptists," editor John Hill Luther urged Missouri Baptists to attend the upcoming Southern Baptist Convention meeting in Memphis. In this "degenerate age," he argued, the Southern Baptist Convention was "unseduced by politics." A strong delegation from Missouri, he continued, would not only "cheer the hearts of the Atlantic brethren," it would also concretely aid the South, "for they are in want of means, and Missouri has the means to sustain" them. In addition, Luther explained, the Missourians could explain "the peculiar character of the oppression" they suffered at the hands of "Eastern Baptists" with "their persistent and unnatural purpose to supplant our preachers and change our connections." With Unionist Baptists organizing within the state, and northern missionaries entering from without, Luther wrote, "We have had a fire in the front and a fire in the rear."[5]

The conversation about sectional identity, politics, and religion that took place in the pages of the *Missouri Baptist Journal* offers a glimpse of how border evangelicals increasingly aligned with the southern branches of their denominations after Union victory. Just like William Bell, many border evangelicals balked at the arrival of northern missionaries and the imposition of loyalty oaths. Like Luther, they rejected calls to publically support Unionists, insisting "the social and political world was never designed to furnish direct motives to God's people."[6] Border evangelicals insisted that they cast aside northern affiliation because those branches had gone too far in mixing religion and politics—especially in supporting abolition. When they turned from the North, they increasingly embraced affiliation with their southern brethren. In doing so, they ignored the extent to which the Confederacy had "furnished motives" during the war years. They also provided much-needed resources to the churches of the former Confederacy.

The realignment of border churches benefited southern denominations, which struggled to defend their continued independence. Southern evangelicals had overtly supported slavery and the Confederacy, which undermined their claims to spirituality and a nonpolitical church. However, many border evangelicals had refused to publicly support either side during the war. When border churches joined southern branches, they brought with them this history of neutrality. The southern churches found border history useful in justifying continued independence, and they adopted it as their own. This realignment helps explain the strength and endurance of the southern evangelical denominations.

THE POLITICS OF RECONSTRUCTION AND BORDER REALIGNMENT

Like the churches, border states as a whole underwent a process of political and cultural realignment. Because none of the states on the border had seceded from the Union and joined the Confederacy, they were not subject to congressional Reconstruction. As slave states, however, Kentucky, Missouri, and Maryland, as well as diminutive Delaware and the newly formed state of West Virginia, all experienced the abolition of slavery. The political trajectory differed in each state, but by 1870, all were under conservative control. Thus, even the slave states that had never left the Union experienced "Redemption"—the rise to power of anti-radical white-supremacist conservative coalitions. The new political leadership of these states gained control through creating an alliance between conservative Unionists, Democrats, and former Confederate sympathizers.[7]

In Kentucky, the conservative Unionists who had seen the state through the war only grudgingly accepted emancipation. Kentucky did not abolish slavery until required to do so by the Thirteenth Amendment in 1865.[8] By 1867, Kentucky Democrats were able to control the state legislature even without the support of their conservative Union allies. "We have but five Union men here and but one Radical and they are all afraid to open their mouths," a Baptist from north-central Kentucky reported. Although he anticipated "troublous times" at the 1867 elections, this Baptist could not "think but the desperate wickedness of the North will be rebuked in some way."[9] He shared a feeling that had grown throughout the state during the war: that through the abolition of slavery, the North was unjustly antagonizing Kentucky, which had not seceded from the Union. Kentuckians had expected a return to "the Union as it was" when the war was over, and the abolition of slavery made this impossible. Conservative Democrats' swift ascent to power reflected white Kentuckians' rejection of the war's outcome. Kentucky, in the famous words of Dunning school historian and Confederate apologist E. Merton Coulter, "waited until after the war was over to secede from the Union." Coulter described the 1867 state legislature as "Confederate Democratic."[10] Recently, several historians have revisited white Kentucky's turn to the South after the Civil War, connecting it with outrage and a sense of betrayal over the abolition of slavery, and the rise of white supremacist politics.[11]

If Kentuckians "joined the Confederacy" after the war was over, Missourians remained internally divided over their sectional identity. As evidenced by the passage of the 1865 constitution and the application of the Test Oath, the state boasted a stronger Republican Party than did Kentucky, and was home to large, dedicated enclaves of Unionists. German immigrants and other urbanites were a powerful bulwark of Unionism in St. Louis and supplied a solid base of support for the Republicans.[12] The constant raids and guerrilla warfare that plagued the southwestern portion of Missouri also produced a steadfast Unionist contingent. Missouri Radicals—with the aid of the new constitution laws that disfranchised those who had been disloyal to the Union—controlled the state until 1870. The elections of 1870 brought more moderate Liberal Republicans into power—and these Liberal Republicans enfranchised former Confederates. In the middle of the decade, Missouri Democrats, bolstered by re-enfranchised Confederate sympathizers, took control of the state and remained in power for the rest of the century.[13]

The Supreme Court helped weaken radical power in the state. In *Cummings v. Missouri* (1867), the court ruled in favor of a Catholic priest who had been arrested and fined for violation of the 1865 Missouri Constitution. Cummings was charged with "teaching and preaching . . . without having first taken the oath prescribed by the Constitution of the State." The court found the Test Oath unconstitutional, striking a victory for conservatives and Democrats who had abstained from taking the oath.[14] In 1870, when Northern Methodist Matthew Simpson was touring the state, he remarked, "Here in Missouri the Southern spirit is still fierce."[15]

For its part, Maryland also quickly passed into Democratic control. While Unionists briefly gained power and created a new constitution that abolished slavery in 1864, many slaves were swiftly returned to unfree labor conditions as apprentices.[16] By 1867, Democrats, led by former slaveholders, again took command.

White residents of the border states emerged from Reconstruction feeling as if they had been punished despite remaining loyal to the Union. These perceived punishments included the imposition of martial law, suffrage restrictions, and loyalty tests. Most of all, many border residents resented that the war had shifted from a war to preserve the Union—a conservative aim of which border residents approved—to a war to abolish slavery and remake society by extending civil rights to African Americans. Border conservatives desired a return to the prewar status quo: they found the new aims of the Radical Republicans appalling.[17]

Confederate apologists of the Dunning school, like Coulter, viewed white border grievances as legitimate. To accept his claim, however, would be to argue that neutrality was truly possible during the Civil War. Border residents resented that their claim to political neutrality had not been taken at face value. However, their imagined alternatives to emancipation were not only manifestly unfeasible, they also undercut Union war aims, helped perpetuate slavery, and therefore strengthened the Confederacy. Border residents could only claim neutrality as long as the war lasted. Confederate defeat made neutrality impossible.[18]

Politically, white residents of border states followed a conservative path of least change, which finally brought them smack into unpleasant reality: despite staying in the Union, they were forced to abolish slavery. As Aaron Astor has shown, the abolition of slavery upended conservative Unionism in the border region, prompting a turn toward political affiliation with the South. In the face of emancipation, conservative Unionists, feeling themselves like victims, embraced the racist politics of white supremacy.[19]

Shifting loyalties among border evangelicals followed patterns similar to political realignment on the border. Many ministers managed to avoid making any public statement of political affiliation until they were forced to do so. While they could not escape secular Reconstruction and the abolition of slavery, they did have an alternative within the churches. They could choose not to "reconstruct" by joining the southern branches of their denominations. Southern churches still existed, after all, even if the Confederacy did not. It was in this climate that Missouri Baptist William Bell referred obliquely to threats to the racial hierarchy originating in the North: he argued that affiliation with the northern mission boards amounted to "amalgamation" that would result in "mongrel" offspring.[20] In Bell's formulation, affiliation with the North was akin to interracial sex—it violated the social order and threatened white supremacy. And so, armed with claims to a spiritually and racially pure religion, border evangelicals turned away from the northern denominational branches.

The federal government, loyal state governments, new constitutional amendments, and federal troops all enforced political Reconstruction. But no authority existed to compel obedience to religious Reconstruction. No external power could mandate that churches reunite. With the end of war, the contest between the sectional branches in each church again became a private affair. Now evangelicals had only their superior moral claims, doctrinal purity, and theological soundness with which to appeal to potential members. The war had left the southern churches poor, but moral authority did not require wealth. As they recouped from the Confederate defeat, southern evangelicals formulated a justification for the independence and superiority of southern denominational branches. At the same time, border evangelicals came to identify more strongly with the southern churches after the Civil War. Because of differences in denominational structure, this religious realignment occurred in different ways for Presbyterians, Methodists, and Baptists.

Border Presbyterians Turn South

Of the three denominations, border realignment in the Presbyterian Church was the most dramatic. Between 1870 and 1874, the Presbyterians completed a process of consolidation into sectionally and theologically distinct bodies, beginning with the merger of Northern Old and New Schools. As conservative members of the Old School PCUSA left the General Assembly, that body became more liberal and expansive, growing closer to the New School in doctrine. The departure of conservative members also removed checks on the assembly's activity. While some members argued that New School beliefs conflicted with Old School doctrine, reunion nevertheless went forward.[21]

In 1869, both northern branches signed the terms of the union, declaring that "the reunion shall be effected on the doctrinal and ecclesiastical basis of our common Standards."[22] The united Northern Old and New schools met in one General Assembly for the first time in May 1870 amid great fanfare and celebration. The merger consolidated practitioners of the doctrinal inclusiveness associated with the New School into one northern body. Adherents to what had been Old School doctrine thus could be found almost exclusively within the province of the independent border synods and the Southern Assembly. Thus the assemblies completed the process of aligning sectional and theological divisions, and these divisions began to reinforce and perpetuate each other.

After the reunion in the North, the Southern Assembly made much of the point that it alone carried on the Old School tradition. An 1870 report rejected an invitation to consider joining the united northern organization, expressing disapproval of the reunion because it constituted "a total surrender of all the great testimonies of the Church" of which Southern Presbyterians were now "the sole surviving heirs."[23] The sharply reproving tone of the report was intended to speak to another audience as well: border Presbyterians.

The southern report appealed to Missouri and defended Kentucky against the northern church. The year before, the Kentucky Synod had joined the southern church. The southern report contended that the Kentucky Synod had been "violently and unconstitutionally expelled" from the Northern Old School Assembly. The report characterized expulsion as "outlawry against what is now an important and constituent part of our own body."[24] The Southern Presbyterians had adopted the cause of the border synods as their own, considering the wrongs perpetrated against the border Presbyterians as wrongs against themselves.

After the uproar over the Declaration and Testimony, the Southern Church had repeatedly offered support and invited organic union with the exscinded Synods of Kentucky and Missouri. It praised the synods for "contending substantially for the grand principles which have ever been the rallying cry of our Presbyterian ancestry."[25] Initially, the independent Synod of Kentucky asserted a commitment to neutrality that reflected the border tradition of conceiving of their synod as a peacemaker between two errant bodies. "This synod stands in position for work of mediation between the Church of the North and of the South," it resolved in 1866. The synod affirmed its position as an intermediary, expressing "full sympathy with a large body of Conservative Ministers and people in the Northern Assembly . . . and on the other hand, its sympathy with, and readiness to assist to the utmost of its ability, the brethren of the Southern churches." In this declaration, the newly independent synod summarized the position held by border-state ministers before and during the war: that they were a doctrinally faithful minority who stood apart from the North and the South "on the basis of those ancient conservative principles of Presbyterianism."[26]

The Kentucky Synod's declaration contained, however, hints that their independent position would not be long-lived. The resolution was particularly solicitous about Southern Presbyterians, making the case that they were "not schismatical."[27] For their part, southerners followed the events in Kentucky with interest, hoping that the synod would join their branch. In 1867, the Southern General Assembly expressed "deep sympathy with our brethren in

Kentucky in the troubles through which they have been passing." In addition, the Southern Assembly assured Kentucky of a "cordial welcome" if it united with the South.[28] In 1869, the majority of the Kentucky Synod voted to adhere to the South. Southern Presbyterians indicated their warm welcome by electing the irascible Stuart Robinson as moderator of the 1869 General Assembly and holding the 1870 assembly in Louisville, birthplace of the Declaration and Testimony.[29]

Missouri Presbyterians also grew closer to the South. In protest of the Rosecrans Oath, 90 percent of Missouri's Old School Presbyterians declined to meet in 1864, The remaining "rump Synod" was therefore deeply Unionist and passed numerous patriotic measures in 1864. When the Missouri Synod reconvened in its entirety in October of 1865, it members voted to nullify the patriotic resolutions, declaring them "null and void and of no binding force."[30] The synod also reissued statements opposing prayers in favor of the Union.

The Northern General Assembly of 1866 declared the actions of the Missouri Synod "an act of insubordination to the authority of the Church" and demanded that it "reconsider and reverse" its course.[31] Instead, it withdrew and became independent. As in Kentucky, the Missouri Synod grew stronger between 1866 and 1878. The Independent Missouri Synod joined the Southern Presbyterians in 1874, and the Southern Presbyterians immediately adopted the Missouri Synod's cause as its own, just as it had done with Kentucky. In an 1874 response to one of many northern reunion overtures, Southern Presbyterians referred "to the full and lucid testimony of the Synod of Kentucky, and the Synod of Missouri" as "the solemn utterances of our own Church." The report also described earlier treatment of the Missouri Synod as "abusive and slanderous charges made against our ministers and Church."[32] The Southern Assembly responded to union with the Missouri Synod by electing to hold the following year's General Assembly in St. Louis.[33]

With the lines of division between North and South firmly drawn, realignment had the effect of concentrating conservative, Old School–style Presbyterians in the South and more liberal, New School Presbyterians in the North. When the Synods of Kentucky and Missouri entered into organic union with the southern church, they elected to join the body with which they had the most theological and political affinity—finalizing the alignment of the northern church with New School–style theology and the southern church with the Old School style.

Border Methodists and Baptists Affirm Southernness

In contrast to the Presbyterians in the region, a majority of border Methodists had joined the southern church after the 1844 division. Because the Plan of Separation had never produced a geographic dividing line, the border remained home to a mixture of Northern and Southern Methodists. Northern Methodists saw Reconstruction as an opportunity to expand their presence in the region. Northern Methodist property transfer, military aid, and mission work during the war years and the early years of Reconstruction would prove the high tide of Northern Methodism in the border. Afterward, Southern Methodists reasserted their claim over the region.

In 1864, Methodist delegates from Kentucky, Tennessee, and Missouri protested against the seizure of churches under the Stanton-Ames Order. This helped to unite conservative border Methodists. After the war, sympathetic northerners and border moderates also protested northern demands for southern contrition.[34] In 1865, a group of Southern Methodists in Missouri, fearing reunion with the North, issued the "Palmyra Manifesto," a declaration of their determination to preserve the southern church despite Confederate defeat and the abolition of slavery. Southern Methodists responded to this manifesto enthusiastically.[35]

The Baptist Church's nonhierarchical structure meant that each congregation and local association could independently decide whether to associate with northern or southern denominational organizations (or with both). No higher authority could prevent dual allegiances—and the state associations continued to contribute to both the Southern Baptist Convention and the American Baptist Home Mission Society (North).[36] At the end of the Civil War, Northern Baptists pressured Missouri and Kentucky brethren to sever their ties with the Southern Baptist Convention, but Baptists in both states refused.

In 1865, border Baptists received a similar call from the Baptist associations that belonged to the Southern Baptist Convention. The Virginia Baptist Association, in response to northern evangelization in the South, requested that border Baptist associations "decline any cooperation or fellowship with any of the missionaries, ministers, or agents of the American Baptist Home Mission Society."[37] All of the southern state associations agreed with this proposal, but Kentucky and Missouri Baptists again asserted their rights to remain affiliated with both the northern and the southern organizations.[38]

Nevertheless, Missouri and Kentucky Baptists grew ever more distinct from northern organizations and increasingly identified with the Southern Baptist Convention. In contrast to the Presbyterian case, Baptist realignment on the border took place through a slow process, not a single act. The Kentucky Baptist Association in particular developed strong ties to the Southern Baptist Convention and was central to the revitalization of the SBC after the Civil War. The first postwar meeting of the SBC was held in Russellville, Kentucky, at the invitation of the local association.[39]

In Missouri, the process of realignment occurred more haltingly. The state's Baptists remained divided after the war and, although a majority continued to donate to the Southern Baptist Convention, many also contributed to the northern American Baptist Home Mission Society. The ABHMS's interest in evangelizing Missouri exacerbated the conflict. In 1866, the ABHMS issued a statement of concern for "the permanence of [Northern] Baptist institutions in the state of Missouri."[40] Southern Baptists also evinced a conviction that the state of Missouri "belonged" to them. "The South should certainly occupy the same footing in the Missouri church as the North do," Caroline Moss wrote to her sister, "Missouri of *right* belongs to the South."[41] Caught between two sectional claims, Missouri Baptists continued to contribute to both the SBC and the ABHMS.[42] Nevertheless, by the late 1860s, many Missouri Baptists wished to see their brethren affiliate only with the SBC and to strategically direct their support to the southern organization. In the *Missouri Baptist Journal*, William Bell and John Hill Luther argued that, if the state limited its giving to the South, "Missouri has the means to sustain" the southern missionary boards.[43]

Over the course of the late 1870s and 1880s, as the Southern Baptist Convention gained strength and funds, Missouri members demanded with increasing firmness that the state association contribute only to the SBC and not to the ABHMS. This conflict led to mounting unrest among Missouri Baptists. The Missouri Baptist Association finally resolved the issue in 1888 by attempting neutrality. It ordered both organizations to cease sending missionaries to the state entirely.[44] A trend toward a southern affiliation had already been established, however. By the late nineteenth century, most Missouri Baptists affiliated with the Southern Convention. Unlike Kentucky, which quickly transitioned into full membership with the SBC, Missouri retained its independence until 1919, when members finally voted to affiliate exclusively with the Southern Baptist Convention.[45] Thus, Baptists in Kentucky, and, through a slower process, those in Missouri, became solely affiliated with the Southern Baptist Convention. This process of accelerating postwar sectionalization and the elimination of dual affiliation contrasts with narratives of steady white reconciliation in the post–Civil War United States.

BORDER HISTORY AND SOUTHERN DENOMINATIONS

As border evangelicals became part of the southern churches, their history also became part of southern evangelical history. Southern churches had the chance to adopt border history at an opportune moment, as their antebellum record inconveniently conflicted with their postwar goals. Southern Methodists, for example, had to defend separate sectional branches after the abolition of slavery, when their own denomination had previously insisted that only "the naked fact of a difference of opinion about slavery and abolition" had divided the churches before the war.[46] Neither northern nor southern evangelicals eschewed political involvement during the sectional crisis and the Civil War, and southerners had repeatedly contended that slavery was not a sin. A union with border churches lent plausibility to the postwar claim that southern churches were unique in that they "uphold the ancient testimony for the spirituality of the church."[47]

Alliance with the border benefited southern churches in three ways. First, border states brought much-needed membership and funds to struggling southern denominations. In 1867, the Kentucky Synod reported that, in addition to providing $3,000 in support for ministers in the state, it had also contributed $3,000 to the Southern Assembly's fund for sustaining preachers, $250 to individual southern congregations, and another $5,000, as well as donations of food and clothing for impoverished southern families.[48] The Southern Baptist Convention in particular was insolvent after the Civil War and did not have the resources to secure a site for their 1865 meeting. Fortunately, "Bethel Association in Kentucky, led by her strong ministry and wealthy laymen, came to the rescue," and the Kentucky General Association offered to host the SBC.[49] Border Baptists knew their support was needed. John Hill Luther reminded readers, "The Boards [of the SBC] will look for a large delegation from Missouri. Well they may, for they are in want of means and Missouri has the means to sustain."[50]

Affiliation with the border also conferred nonpecuniary benefits on southern churches. A second advantage of securing border membership was that it allowed southerners to credibly claim a nonpolitical history of spirituality. When border evangelicals became southern evangelicals, their history became southern history as well. Southerners claimed that "a pure, nonpolitical, unsecular Christianity" distinguished them from their northern counterparts and made reunion impossible.[51] Border history proved well suited to the job of bolstering such claims, such as when Southern Presbyterians referred to the Kentucky Synod as "members of our body" in their 1870 resolution condemning the outcome of the Declaration and Testimony controversy.[52] In rejecting reunion overtures from the North, Southern Presbyterians bemoaned the "fierce and cruel spirit" manifested by the North against Presbyterians in Kentucky and Missouri during the war and the "harsh and cruel measures" employed against the signers of the Declaration and Testimony when the war had ended.[53] Five years later, again rebuffing a conciliatory northern offer, Southern Presbyterians cited "the oppressive manner in which the Synods of Kentucky and Missouri, together with their Presbyteries and members, were dealt with." They explained that they were "entitled to mention this, as these Synods thus dealt with are now constituent parts of the Southern church."[54]

Southern Methodists also found border history useful. Although a majority of Methodists in the region identified with the southern branch before and during the war, they had insisted that living on the border set them apart. After the war, they became more southern.[55] In *Martyrdom in Missouri*, his two-volume catalog of ministers who encountered conflict with religious and secular authorities, William Leftwich took pains to identify his subjects with the South.[56] He did so even though many of the harassed ministers had belonged to northern churches during the war. By adopting border churches into southern denominations, southerners inherited a history of political neutrality and spirituality that reinforced the postwar image they wished to project. The theology of the spirituality of the church was particularly appealing to postwar southern evangelicals—and it bolstered the claims southern churches had used to defend their position since before the war.

Finally, border affiliation helped attenuate southern churches' association with the defense of slavery. Southern evangelicals seeking continued postwar independence had to refute northerners who argued that "the abolition of slavery has removed the greatest obstacle to a future union."[57] Reunion-seeking northerners could point to numerous instances when southern evangelicals had cited slavery as the sole cause of division. Northern Presbyterians did just that in 1870 when they argued that "*the Southern Church had changed its ground upon the subject of Slavery.*"[58] Adopting the cause of the Declaration and Testimony synods, which had divided from the northern church after the abolition of slavery, helped Southern Presbyterians downplay their historical connection to the defense of the institution. "Those Declaration men, who were so outraged in the unconstitutional proceedings, have found a refuge and a home in our body," explained a Southern Presbyterian rejection of reunion. "By the incorporation of their statement of principles in our official records, we have given our endorsement to the same." These principles, stemming from "the Lord's testimony that His kingdom is not of this world," seemed far removed from the concrete realities of slavery and abolition.[59]

"Slavery was '*beyond the control of all ecclesiastical bodies,*'" William Leftwich reminded readers. Since the eighteenth century, the Methodist Church had deemed it "safe, scriptural, and prudent" for the church to "let it alone." Thus, postwar southerners reasoned, it was not the threat to slavery, but the violation of the Methodist Constitution that drove southerners from the church. Leftwich invoked the American Revolution without irony: "It was not the three cents a pound upon tea that caused the American revolution of 1776, but the right to tax tea to that amount involved the right to make every man in the British colonies a slave." Leftwich continued, "the right to depose Bishop Andrew implied the right to depose every man from the ministry who differed from the numerical majority upon any political question whatever."[60] Southern evangelicals joined in a general late-nineteenth-century recasting of sectionalism and the Civil War that aimed to downplay or eliminate slavery as a cause of the conflict.[61]

RENEWAL OF THE SOUTHERN CHURCHES

By the late 1860s, southern churches began to regroup and assert an independent identity after the staggering losses of the Civil War.[62] Most white southern evangelicals insisted on maintaining separate denominations on an equal footing with northern branches. Affiliation of border evangelicals helped realize this ambition, as did the favorable resolution of property cases and the formation of independent black churches. These latter developments weakened northern justifications for missions to the South. While the resurgence unfolded somewhat differently in each denomination, some themes remained common across all three. First, the churches asserted their equal standing with their northern counterparts in the nation and the world. Second, they insisted on their exclusive jurisdiction over churches in southern states—but no longer over northern states—and demanded that northern churches respect these exclusive claims to evangelize in the South. Finally, these denominations insisted on their own historical and present legitimacy, and in so doing, they argued that they had separated not over slavery, but because they were theologically distinct from northern churches.

At the end of the war, southern evangelical denominations faced poverty and disorganization. Some discouraged leaders even suggested reunion. "I am now for unifying the whole people," wrote one Alabama Baptist in 1865. "The *North* has *so much* more enterprise and efficiency in their machinery and Christian labor, it will be hard for us to compete with them." Spaulding betrayed his intense sectional loyalties however, when he admitted he "would be loath to give it up. . . . If the brethren determine to go forward, I will do all I can to aid."[63] Just as they were for Spaulding, thoughts of abandoning independent southern denominations proved fleeting among evangelicals across the region. Daniel Stowell credits local southern ministers' unflagging work among the general population with preserving southern denominations.[64] However, the religious leadership and institutions of the South were also crucial to the rebirth. These leaders devised the arguments for southern distinctiveness and against reunion that could be marshaled in defense of the southern church—"an institution of the country, a traditional inheritance from our fathers"—before "the church and the world."[65] They argued that retaining separate institutions would ultimately strengthen their churches.[66]

Presbyterians and Methodists, thanks to their denominational structures and a stronger preexisting leadership hierarchy, were the first to recover and mount a defense against northern claims upon the South. The 1865 Southern Presbyterian General Assembly anticipated a challenge and considered the question of what was to be done "when a minister or agent of the Old School General Assembly (North) presents himself among us, with a request to labor in our churches, or occupy one of our vacant houses of worship." The assembly adopted a report stipulating that such men would not be welcome and concluding "that our ministers and churches be, and hereby are warned against all ministers, or other agents, who may come among us to sow the seeds of division and strife in our congregations."[67]

Northern missionaries who entered the South following the war found a similar attitude among Southern Methodists; one missionary observed, "though conquered, they are as bitter, proud, and arrogant as ever."[68] Southern Methodists maintained that, while the Confederacy may have been defeated, the church and her institutions certainly had not been. At the 1866 Southern Methodist General Conference, delegates resolved that the meeting "challenged and revived the confidence of the people and sounded the keynote of the quadrennium for renewed activity and lofty endeavor."[69] The press united in urging southerners to maintain a separate Methodist Church. "We cannot abandon or compromise the principles of action upon which we proceed to a separate organization in the South," a Virginia editor reminded readers.[70]

The leaders of the Southern Baptist Convention found they had to work with great diligence to preserve their organization. Some Southern Baptist state associations, in need of missionary aid, continued to affiliate with the Northern Baptist societies after the war.[71] However, by the 1880s, a push to preserve the sectional Southern Baptist identity—and the SBC itself—coalesced around a group of Baptist leaders with Confederate veteran Isaac Taylor Tichenor at the helm. Northern Baptists who established missions in the South "were invading the territory of the Southern Baptist Convention," Edwin T. Winkler warned. Winkler argued that "a revival of interest in Home Missions must take place among the nine hundred thousand white Baptists of the South."[72] These Southern Baptist leaders recognized the value of preserving institutional autonomy and fought, with great success, to convince state associations to affiliate with the SBC only. When asked about cooperating with Northern Baptists, the SBC's corresponding secretary, William McIntosh, replied, "I cannot see how such a cooperation can be otherwise than hurtful. . . . If they give you their money, it will be upon the condition that you give them yours. And if our Southern churches give their funds to others than their own agencies, how are those agencies to be sustained? . . . the result I fear will be the dissociation of the S[outhern] B[aptist] Convention."[73] McIntosh wanted Southern Baptists' money to stay within southern institutions. By the end of the decade, the SBC had regained its strength and financial solvency.

As they had in the antebellum years, property disputes that reached secular courts had the effect of strengthening southern branches, no matter their outcome. When they were resolved in favor of the southern parties, these lingering property cases from the antebellum and war years of course strengthened southern branches. However, even when they remained unresolved or rulings favored the northern parties, the mere fact of the disputes—and the loss of property—galvanized southern resolve. Southern evangelical sectionalists, in their arguments in defense of separate churches, used the cases as evidence of the iniquity of northern branches. One powerful weapon was the charge that northerners had illegally seized southern property. A good number of these cases concerned churches in the border region. Southern Presbyterian William Brown stated, "The amount of property in dispute, or liable to it, has been estimated at not less than $2,000,000." He explained, "most of the trouble in this matter is in the states of Missouri, Kentucky, and Tennessee."[74] Southern Methodist bishops rejecting reunion overtures in 1869 reminded northerners that "missionaries and agents" sent south had "been very prejudicial." Specifically, "their course in taking possession of some of our houses of worship has inflicted both grief and loss on us . . . being not only a breach of charity, but an invasion of the plainest rights of property."[75]

White southerners also believed that northern missionaries had "stolen" the black southern evangelical population. Initially, white southerners expected freedpeople to join their churches. They also feared that, if southerners did not evangelize the freedpeople, then northerners would do so, using missions as a means to extend their reach into the South. "Into whose hands," he asked, will the freedpeople "fall if we cast them off? . . . the North has declared that the colored population of the South is missionary ground; which belongs peculiarly to them."[76] Following abolition, black southerners largely settled such disputes by withdrawing from segregated, white-run churches and forming denominations and congregations of their own.[77]

White evangelicals, North and South, expressed surprise when black evangelicals formed their own independent churches. "The colored people, generally, still continue in alienation from us," a report of the Southern Presbyterian General Assembly noted in 1868; their absence from white churches was already an established pattern just three years after abolition.[78] "Our colored people have petitioned the Church, to be set apart, as a separate church," wrote Basil Manly in 1865. He realized the departure was an inevitability although, like most white evangelicals, he shared the paternalistic view that they were "not prepared for the responsibility."[79] At the General Assembly of 1874, Southern Presbyterians acknowledged that "the coloured people . . . have clearly and fully separated themselves from us."[80] Grudgingly accepting that black evangelicals had formed their own churches, white southerners largely ceased to organize ministries to their black brethren.

Nonetheless, northern white evangelicals continued to organize missions to southern freedpeople. These missions helped them retain a foothold in the South. "The money needed to provide school-houses, and support for the teachers for the freedmen, to supply pastors . . . the South did not have," a Northern Methodist newspaper explained. The needs of black evangelicals provided a "justification of the presence of the Methodist Episcopal Church, by organization as well as by more agencies, in the Southern States."[81] Baptists shared a similar vision of their southern work: "The Philanthropists of the North, with no personal, political or other selfish interest in the matter, have already contributed since the war, for the education and uplifting of the Negroes of the South, nearly a million dollars a year."[82] Of course the churches in reality did have "interest in the matter," as missions justified their presence in the South.

When black southern evangelicals formed their own churches, northern denominations lost their primary reason for funding southern missions. The remarkable success of independent southern black churches—not to mention the more tepid growth of black churches sponsored by northern evangelicals and the decidedly weak black churches run by southern denominations—sent a clear message. Black southern evangelicals wished to build and control their own churches. The creation of independent black churches gave white southern evangelicals a rationale for reducing funding for missions to freedpeople and directing those resources toward defending their separate southern branches. White southerners also argued that the growth of independent black churches meant that northern evangelicals were not needed or welcome anywhere south of the Mason-Dixon Line.[83]

NORTHERN REUNION OVERTURES

Northern evangelicals continued their attempts to institute a reunion with southern branches throughout the postwar decades. During the immediate postwar years, northern churches had anticipated a swift reunion on northern terms. However, by the 1870s, shifting loyalties on the border, steadily decreasing support from secular authorities, and increased southern denominational strength led northern churches to recognize that an immediate reunion on northern terms would not be forthcoming. "Those who sympathized with the South," remarked a contributor to the northern *Methodist Quarterly Review*, "regard our presence there as a breach of Christian courtesy."[84] Southern denominations successfully resisted northern missionaries and reunion overtures under the guidance of intensely sectional postwar leaders.

By 1870, northerners could no longer count on federal assistance to support their missionary projects in the South, particularly on the border. President Andrew Johnson overturned the Stanton-Ames Order in all states that had remained loyal during the war and limited its application elsewhere. This ended the practice of transferring church buildings belonging to southern-affiliated congregations to northern missionaries.[85] Johnson was sympathetic to southern evangelicals petitioning for property and personally intervened on their behalf to return confiscated churches. Attempts to plant northern-affiliated congregations in buildings belonging to southern-affiliated denominations—the most overt practice of the early phase of religious Reconstruction—could not survive without the support of federal authorities.

Occupied churches not only lost federal support—they also lost their audience. Union troops and freedpeople were most likely to attend these churches, but neither group proved a viable foundation upon which to build lasting congregations.[86] As Reverend Cramer's experience revealed, large congregations interested in hearing a northern preacher could not be sustained in peacetime. Another missionary in Chattanooga reported that he preached to "not more than 30 persons, half of these colored and some soldiers—not a white member, I think." Despite conducting a popular Sabbath school for freedpeople and sometimes attracting congregations of over a hundred black Methodists, this minister evaluated his success in terms of reaching white southern Christians. Building a white southern congregation would, he believed, help move the denomination toward reunion. He complained that "the [white] people here will not attend 'till Military are out of here." Until then, he suggested, the Northern Methodists should expect nobody "except Colored and soldiers"—not the audience he had aspired toward.[87]

The hoped-for white congregations never materialized in occupied churches. Instead, local white residents demanded the return of church buildings. An 1874 letter from a Southern Methodist in Staunton, Virginia, reveals how quickly and completely most of the property transfers failed. A Virginia Methodist described a suit in which Northern Methodists attempted to retain control of a "church edifice" in Stanton. "*One man only* is set forth in the suit as the party claiming to be the M.E. Church [North]. . . . the M.E. Church South is there represented by 400 members."[88] In Independence, Missouri, following Johnson's reversal of the Stanton-Ames Order, Southern Methodist trustees demanded the return of their church building and were initially rebuffed. In response, thirty Southern Methodist women occupied the pews "with their knitting and sewing" and refused to leave until they were arrested, to much local outrage.[89] Arresting white women, unsurprisingly, proved an ineffective strategy. It galvanized local resistance to Northern Methodist possession of the building. After the release of the protesting women, the church was soon returned to Southern Methodist hands. Without white congregants, northern missions to the South and border failed.

Northern evangelicals did not give up hope for reunification as a single national organization. Even as border evangelicals, like their political counterparts, grew increasingly identified with the South alone, northern branches continued to define themselves as national branches with a right to evangelize anywhere in the nation. The northern *Methodist Quarterly Review* printed several articles in the 1870s offering a "justification of the presence of the Methodist Episcopal Church, by organization as well as by mere agencies, in Southern States."[90] Northerners argued that a northern victory clearly indicated God's desire for a unified America, and a unified nation must be home to unified churches.

When southerners rebuffed northern proposals for immediate postwar reunion, northerners altered their strategy. They began to adopt a more conciliatory tone toward southern churches. They followed established channels for proposing reunion and spoke of it as something to be worked toward, not as a unilateral decision for northerners to make—even if it was "a Christian duty."[91] One Northern Methodist overture proposed a gradualist approach: "leaving *organic union* as a question *of the future,* let us make the union of our hearts the question of today."[92] More tempered proposals, such as this one, multiplied in the late 1860s and early 1870s.

Evangelical denominations promoted organic union through the exchange of reunion overtures, which consisted of formally drafted proposals, approved by one religious body and sent to another, proposing that the two bodies were sufficiently similar to join as one. Such overtures had preceded the reunion of Old and New School Presbyterians in the North. Sending overtures represented a concession to the South: these documents, often accompanied by a respectful delegation, argued for reunion on the grounds that the southerners were on equal footing with their northern counterparts. Overtures invited engagement in negotiation in order to reach mutually agreeable terms.

In one such meeting, a group of Northern Methodist bishops, following a decision made at the General Conference, met with bishops from the South in 1869.[93] "Our venerable Mother Church, the Methodist Episcopal, has a powerful hand, but a liberal heart," one Northern Methodist publication boasted in reference to the 1869 meeting; "to all the lesser Methodisms she extends her genial invitation to become, with her, one family." As for the southerners, however, they rejected these more conciliatory reunion offers as well. The southerners "firmly and frankly state the feelings that still exist as a result of the terrible past." Still confident reunion was forthcoming, the author argued that Southern Methodists were simply experiencing a transient "feeling of distrust" that would soon dissipate, after which southerners would join with northerners and "by a true Christian policy, attain a wise reunion."[94] Another northern editor, writing from Cincinnati, disagreed, arguing that Southern Methodists evinced nothing but "haughtiness and bitterness." The writer warned that, as a border resident, he did not expect southerners to display "a ready acquiescence in any suggestions from our church."[95] His predictions proved to be correct. Southern Methodists rejected the 1869 meeting and overture as a "notorious commission."[96]

Northern Presbyterians also attempted to arrange such a meeting. In 1868, the Northern Old School Assembly issued a resolution recognizing "the Southern Presbyterian Church, formerly in connection with this body, as a distinct and separate ecclesiastical organization."[97] This concession paved the way for overtures made in 1869, proposing reunion on the grounds that Northern and Southern Presbyterians held "the same ancient symbols of faith, the same forms of government, and of worship."[98] This reunion overture was met with an even more forceful southern rejection than that of Northern Methodists.

Southern Presbyterians enumerated the various offenses of the northern church at length. These included: entering into unspiritual entanglements with the federal government; slandering the Southern Presbyterians by charging them with supporting the Confederacy and being schismatic; and compromising religious principles by uniting with the New School. In addition, southerners protested how northerners had treated the Declaration and Testimony border synods. Finally, Southern Presbyterians argued, to give up their separate institutions would be to give up their sectional independence. "We would be blind not to perceive the tendency to imperialism in the [northern] Church as well as in the State," the Southern Presbyterians declared. Therefore, "*Our Fifth and Final Objection* to the proposed re-union with the Northern Church; which is *the utter ruin of our Presbyterian Cause at the South, that must inevitably ensue.*"[99]

CONCLUSION

A religious realignment took place in the final quarter of the nineteenth century. Border evangelicals in all three denominations increasingly affiliated with southern denominations. The withdrawal of border evangelicals from northern churches represented continuity with, not a departure from, prewar priorities. Border evangelicals sought to minimize conflict and resisted demands for political affiliation within their denominations. Clinging to an ultimately unsustainable belief that the abolition of slavery was purely political, border evangelicals sought out the section perceived as least radical. Even after abolition, views on slavery remained a touchstone. As northern churches demanded Unionism and denunciation of slavery, southern churches downplayed the role of politics in the memory of their own creation. Southern denominations offered the closest approximation of a return to the prewar status quo—one that did not threaten white supremacy. In contrast, northern denominations appeared more radical than their southern counterparts and were therefore less appealing to border evangelicals.

During the process of realignment, the majority of border evangelicals became affiliated with southern denominations, and southern churches formulated their justification for remaining divided even after the impediment of slavery had been abolished. This justification involved reshaping the memory of how the churches themselves had behaved during the war. Thus was born the trope that northern evangelicals crassly introduced politics into the wartime pulpit while southern churches remained piously aloof from political disputes. Memory of southern evangelical behavior before and during the Civil War was largely borrowed from the history of the border evangelical churches, many of which joined the South only after the war was over.

— 8 —

AN APPEAL TO THE FUTURE

Memory of War and Failure of Reunion

"How like the burnished gold from the crucible does our beloved church shine as she stands victorious and manifestly vindicated!" boasted Charles Elliott. Now in retirement, Elliott had seen the Methodist Church through its antebellum division, through the sectional crisis, and through the Civil War. In 1844, he had written what he hoped would be the definitive history of the antebellum schism—one that would vindicate Northern Methodists. Now, in 1868, he had just published *South-Western Methodism*, in which he endeavored to record for posterity evidence that the Northern Methodist Church was the true church, that southerners had perverted religion to serve the Slave Power, and that the Methodist Church would reunite once more on northern terms.[1]

Elliott argued that "Northern philanthropy and Christian enterprise" first carried Methodism into Missouri, but that "by special entreaties, with prophetic maledictions in the background," many of the Missouri faithful were "seduced into the Southern Methodist Church." Still, a loyal core resisted: "No tinge of pro-slaveryism or disloyalty adhered to them." Thanks to the "heroic suffering and labor" of these loyal Methodists, "to the South-West the future is full of hope and promise."[2]

Elliott's version of the past and his vision of the future were answered with a challenge. In 1870, interested readers could also peruse William Leftwich's two-volume *Martyrdom in Missouri*, "an account of some of those horrible outrages perpetrated on Christian ministers in Missouri." In Leftwich's tales of persecution, however, the true victims in Missouri were the southern and politically neutral Methodists. The persecutors were the members of the "Northern Methodist Connection." Leftwich assured his readers that southerners were among the first settlers in Missouri and that, after the division of 1844, "the whole state had decided . . . positively to adhere South." Thus, according to Leftwich, it was not Southern Methodists who led the people of Missouri astray, but rather Northern Methodists, who endeavored to "beguile unstable souls" by falsely claiming to be the "'Old Church' and 'Old Methodism.'"[3]

Elliott and Leftwich belonged to a wave of evangelicals who sought to shape the public perception of sectional denominational branches after the Civil War. Both used polemical histories of border states as means to this end. Elliott aimed to indict Southern Methodism, defend Northern Methodism, and present a compelling argument for sectional reunion. For his part, Leftwich used the events in Missouri as proof of the political corruption of the northern church, southern spiritual purity, and the impossibility of reunion due to the profound differences between Methodists of the North and South.

In the 1870s and 1880s, the experience of border Christians during the Civil War appeared time and again in polemical histories. In these histories, southerners downplayed their defense of slavery before the war while northerners exaggerated their antebellum opposition to slavery. In addition to making general claims about their histories, northern and southern branches specifically used the history of their denominations in the contested border region to reshape the narrative of their origins and difference. The border experience was rich with the raw materials necessary to craft moving tales of martyred innocents, religious persecution at the hands of church and state, and heroic efforts to preserve "the purity of the gospel."[4] Such material could be found to support or condemn either branch of the church, as demonstrated by Elliott and Leftwich's histories.

Leftwich professed to entertain "gloomy anxieties for the future" of Southern Methodism at the dawn of the 1870s, but he need not have fretted. His interpretation of Missouri's religious history became standard fare as evangelicals in Missouri and other border states transferred their loyalties to southern evangelical denominations. As the southern churches gained the membership of border evangelicals, they also gained a claim to their history—"the horrible chapter of blood and murder which the state of Missouri has given to the history of religious martyrdom."[5] This history helped the southern churches successfully reject overtures of reunion with the North. It helped compel northern branches of each denomination to agree to fraternal relations, agreements that recognized southern distinctiveness, legitimacy, and equality. These agreements allowed southern churches to remain separate into the twentieth century and beyond.

Before any agreements could be reached, however, northern and southern evangelicals had to fight one more battle—this time over the history and meaning of their division. In this war of words, southerners employed their full defense of independence and successfully paved the way for accords that secured the future of their denominations.

CONTEST FOR THE HISTORICAL RECORD

As members of each denomination accepted that intradenominational conflict would not end with the war—or even with Reconstruction—a new genre began to appear in religious newspapers and books: the polemical history. "A new generation has arisen which needs the rehearsal of this great conflict," one Methodist explained.[6] Southern evangelical writers feared that "as time moves on and the older members pass away" the reasons for distinct northern and southern denominations would be forgotten. Perhaps, as Caroline Moss of Missouri worried, southern religion would become "permeated with Northern sentiment."[7] Northern Evangelicals, in turn, feared that southerners would so demonize northerners that the rising generation of southern leaders, raised on a "one-sided, south-sided history," would be in a state of "perpetual quarreling and re-quarreling and re-re-quarreling" and would therefore never agree to reunion or even fraternal relations with the North.[8]

As it became increasingly apparent that swift reunion would not sweep the antagonism of the antebellum schisms and the Civil War under the rug, evangelicals in both sections also saw publications as a chance to establish a record of their sections' role in the conflict. Evangelical historians—perhaps better termed as polemicists—created "an appeal to the future against the past" through narratives that were unfailingly offered as strictly factual accounts.[9] Southern books and articles focused on generating and disseminating a version of the section's history that cast denominational division as a matter of doctrinal difference, not a defense of slavery. Adopting the border-state ideal, these narratives presented southern denominations as having been nonpolitical and "spiritual" before and during the war. Northerners also sought to create a flattering history of their role in the sectional conflict.

In these revisionist narratives, mainstream northern evangelicals are cast as heroic, persecuted abolitionists. Both sides drew on mid-century border conflict as evidence for their arguments.

These volumes, most produced in the last three decades of the century, are a religious counterexample to reconciliationist literature of the late-nineteenth-century United States.[10] While sentimental authors romanticized the Civil War and smoothed away sectional differences, northern and southern evangelical historians rehearsed grievances from fifty-year-old sectional divisions as well as recent wartime wrongs. Evangelical polemicists, North and South, wrote with the goal of furthering specific sectional objectives.

Southern evangelical historical polemics aimed to persuade their readers of four things. First, they insisted that the antebellum divisions had not been about slavery; rather that real doctrinal differences had already divided the churches and the slavery issue merely provoked an inevitable division. Recall the Southern Methodist bishops who had, in 1869, insisted, "Slavery was not, in any proper sense, the cause, but the occasion only of that separation."[11] A Southern Baptist editor in Kentucky insisted that "the same reasons that made necessary the existence of the Southern Baptist Convention still exist."[12] The swiftness with which southern evangelicals rejected slavery's role in their withdrawal from the national denominations parallels a similarly swift reconsideration of the relationship between slavery and secession in the South as a whole.

Southern publications also argued that their churches had never been politicized during the war—unlike the northern church, which had fallen under "the seductive influence of political power." Northerners had "ascended by the devil's ladder to 'thrones of power,' and played such tricks during the continuance of their brief authority as made the angels weep!"[13] In contrast, the southern church "governed her course simply by the word of God during these years of strife."[14] A Southern Presbyterian pamphlet stated that "the Southern Assembly had never, in any form, entangled itself with the state. . . . on the contrary, it declares that it separated from the Northern church in order to escape these political complications."[15] A Southern Baptist declared reunion impossible because Northern Baptist presses were filled "with issues foreign to the nature of spiritual religion . . . conditions abhorrent to the taste and conscience of Southern Christians." The problem, he contended, was that the Northern Baptist press was "a political press and its readers demand that the recognition of political questions be made a part of the ethics and theory of the current faith."[16]

Southerners made a third important claim about their history: that they were the true heirs of their denomination's religious tradition and not schismatics. As such, they argued, southerners were deserving of, at minimum, equal standing with northerners. "The Methodist Episcopal Church, South," argued Edward Myers, was "no offspring of schism or secession, but entitled to a place in the sisterhood of churches of equal legitimacy with her twin sister, the Methodist Episcopal Church."[17] Southern Presbyterians, also outraged by the Old and New school reunion in the North, used that development as evidence that the Southern Presbyterians were the true inheritors of denominational tradition. One southern observer called the reunited northerners "the New Church," leaving Southern Presbyterians as the "surviving heirs of the failing testimonies of our church."[18] The Southern Presbyterian Church was "walking in the good old paths trod by our fathers," while "Northern Presbyterianism is virtually New School, Abolition, Radical Presbyterianism," concluded on editorial.[19] While accused of "unwarranted schism," another Southern Presbyterian argued, it was in truth the northern church that had strayed: "so intense is the loyalty to Caesar—so feeble is the loyalty to Christ!" Southerners viewed themselves as "faithful witnesses to uphold the ancient testimony for the spirituality of the Church."[20]

Fourth, southerners insisted they had suffered unwarranted persecution at the hands of northerners, particularly in the border region. This persecution included the antebellum conflicts that caused southerners to withdraw and form their own denominations as well as the subsequent property cases, local violence, and forced cooperation with federal authorities. The Southern Presbyterians had been "treated as the anaconda treats its victim," claimed an editorial in the *Southern Presbyterian Review*.[21] "The facts prove beyond the possibility of a question that the Southern Baptist Convention is being supplanted in its own domain," Edwin T. Winkler complained. "Northern Baptists were invading the territory" of the Southern Baptist Convention, a circumstance that was "lowering our manhood and sacrificing our self-respect."[22] In the face of calls for reunion and mutual forgiveness, Southern Methodist Bishop Enoch Marvin refused, calling forgiveness "The maudlin sentiment that would daub over the great public crimes committed by the highest dignitaries of the Northern Methodist Church and their representatives in the South and along the border." Marvin declared that "the stench of these recent atrocities is so strong in the nostrils of the people" that forgetting would be impossible.[23]

Most of the southern polemics produced after 1870 made use of border evangelical experience in two ways: first, as part of a southern evangelical history of persecution at the hands of northerners, called "partisan fanatics," and second, as evidence of the moral and doctrinal purity of their branches.[24] The Southern Presbyterian author of the pamphlet on the 1870 northern reunion overture, for instance, devoted three chapters to "*the flagrant violations of the Constitution, in the Assembly's treatment of the signers of the Declaration and Testimony*," even though the drafters of that document had not belonged to the Southern Presbyterian Church at the time of the controversy and those in Missouri still did not.[25] Southern Baptist Edwin T. Winkler, who had complained that northerners violated the "territory of the Southern Baptist Convention," included in that "domain" "every one of the border States," all of which were "occupied by the Home Mission Society [Northern Baptists]."[26] Winkler ignored the fact that state associations were free to affiliate with multiple missionary organizations and that, particularly in Missouri, border-state associations elected to remain auxiliary to the society through the end of the nineteenth century.

Southern Methodists also eagerly seized on border experiences to extol the moral purity of their church. The 1870s saw the publication of a series of books dedicated to proving the innocence of Southern Methodists, their doctrinal purity, and their victimhood at the hands of northerners. William Leftwich's two-part polemic, *Martyrdom in Missouri*, published in 1870, marshaled and presented every report of the persecution of Methodist ministers in that state at the hands of their northern brethren. Even though many of the cases depicted the tribulations of Missouri's politically neutral Methodists, Leftwich grouped these figures with Southern Methodists, making border history part of southern history. All who fell victim to "partisan fanatics in the Church" and "politico-religious fanatics in the country" were cast as spiritual kin to Southern Methodists.[27] This served to increase the plausibility of claims that Southern Methodists had been "striving manfully and humbly to allay the bitterness of strife . . . by wise and godly counsels of peace and quietness."[28]

Two other publications protesting Southern Methodist innocence swiftly followed. One was Albert H. Redford's 1876 *History of the Organization of the Methodist Episcopal Church, South*, which was written out of concern that, "since the division of the Methodist Episcopal Church in the United States, a new generation has come upon the scene, who are not familiar with the circumstances that led to the separation." Redford instructed this younger generation that, in 1844, "the measure contemplated was not schism, but separation for their mutual convenience and prosperity" and that it was not a defense of slavery, but an opposition to northern meddling with "state policy and civil law" that inspired southerners to withdraw.[29] Edward Myers's *The Disruption of the Methodist Episcopal Church* appeared in 1875 on the eve of fraternal relations. Myers's "Appeal to the Future Against the Past" also contended that slavery did not divide the church. Instead, Myers blamed northern repudiation of the Plan of Separation. He likewise cast the border as southern and warned that Northern Methodists planned to "disintegrate and absorb Southern Methodism."[30]

Northern evangelicals, in pursuit of denominational reunion, also entered into the postwar contest to put flattering histories into print. Each of the southern polemics either prompted or responded to a Northern Methodist polemic of equal vehemence. As in the South, Methodists led the way, but Presbyterians and Baptists also joined the scramble to put the "truth" in print. These texts likewise emphasized four major themes. First, northern polemics asserted that southern evangelicals had perverted religion to defend slavery while northerners had attacked the institution. One Northern Methodist, in response to Myers, condemned "the action of Southern Methodism in crushing down our churchly antislavery legislation, in forcing upon us a slave-holding bishop, in forming a Southern Church and then trying to extend that church over the entire North" as "a part of the same great diabolic conspiracy." He went on: "Southern Methodism has, in her place, played second fiddle to the music of the slave-power" and displayed a "dogged adherence to the putrid corpse of dead slavery."[31]

Northerners felt as free to rewrite their history as had the southerners, especially when it came to abolitionism in the North. "The original platform of our American Methodism was pure and absolute abolition," asserted Daniel Whedon, who celebrated Northern Methodists as "heroic maintainers of truth, freedom, and eternal justice."[32] While this might have been true of Methodist abolitionists, Whedon neglected to mention that these "heroic" abolitionists had been driven from the church in the 1830s and denounced by mainstream Northern Methodism. "Responsibility for first drawing the line between Baptists, North and South," lay with Southern Baptists who defended slavery, argued a northern editorial.[33] In 1876, a Northern Presbyterian wrote of Southern Presbyterians, "the institution around which they are made largely to revolve is the system of negro slavery." Meanwhile, the author suggested that northerners condemned slavery and "set forth the duty of seeking its universal extinction."[34]

Second, northerners insisted that the southern branches were politicized during the war, specifically that they supported secession and the Confederacy. "These eloquent ministers of Christ, who have urged so strenuously, as a distinguishing characteristic of the Southern Church, that God and Caesar should be kept wholly apart," Robert Stanton wrote, "were so early in the field in open advocacy of secession, in the pulpit, upon the platform, and in the public journals."[35] A Northern Methodist asserted, "it is not possible for the people of the North to comprehend the measure" of Southern Methodist "pro-slaveryism, Confederate sympathy, or sectional prejudice." Furthermore, Fuller argued, "The annual Conferences formally and repeatedly indorsed the Confederacy in the most explicit and emphatic manner."[36]

Third, northerners sought to show that they had suffered at the hands of southerners before the war. In *South-Western Methodism*, Charles Elliott chronicled incidents of persecution from the 1844 schism through the Civil War, in Missouri and surrounding states. He aimed to prove that "to be a member of the Methodist Episcopal Church in these regions . . . was the greatest crime known by the pro-slavery men of the Southwest." Northern Methodists in Missouri suffered greatly, Elliott argued, even up to the present day: "Their persons are assaulted, their religious services are interfered with, notices threatening violence are sent to them . . . at the instigation, connivance, and approval of members and ministers of the Methodist Episcopal Church, South."[37] According to Northern Presbyterian Robert Stanton, "loyal people were pursued with a bitter persecution" during a Civil War the southern churches bore a responsibility for.[38]

Finally, northern evangelicals, at least until the establishment of fraternal relations, insisted that their branches were the true, original churches and that southern churches were splinter groups at best and, at worst, schismatic. "A Short Catechism of the American Baptist Home Mission Society" contended that the ABHMS was "the parent Society from which the Southern Convention separated in 1845."[39] Methodists followed a similar line of reasoning. "The formation of the Methodist Episcopal Church South, being an illegal withdrawal from a legal jurisdiction, was, and is, a SECESSION," wrote a Northern Methodist.[40] Another article contended, "They *chose to withdraw*, and construct a new organization. . . . Our Church, 'the Old Church,' went on in the regular line of its uninterrupted history."[41]

During the 1870s and 1880s, partly through producing and reading such texts, southern evangelical churches refined an argument for regional religious independence that successfully protected autonomous southern denominations. In their defense, southern evangelicals insisted that, within the international community of their denominations, they were organizations on equal footing with the northern branches. They also argued that they had exclusive claim over evangelization, particularly of white people, in the southern portion of the country. Finally, they defended their distinct theological traditions—allegedly predating the Civil War and not rooted in the defense of slavery—as the reason for remaining separate sectional branches. In supporting this argument, southerners relied on the history and experiences of border-state evangelicals.

FRATERNAL RELATIONS: FORMALIZING DIVISION

Northern evangelicals coupled their polemical histories with regular calls for reunion. Time and again, southerners rejected reunion proposals in favor of establishing fraternal relations. This was the term used to describe the relationship between two branches of the same denomination located in different countries. The branches recognized each other as legitimate, but also as separate. By accepting only fraternal relations, rather than reunion, with the northern branches of each church, southern evangelicals clearly indicated that they would only enter a relationship with northern churches on equal footing. During the antebellum years, southern evangelicals had insisted they were also national denominational organizations with the right to evangelize anywhere. By the postwar years, however, these claims had narrowed. The southern branches of each church claimed no territory outside of the South, but they defended that territory fiercely against interlopers from the North. As southerners perfected their defense of independence, northerners continued to seek rapprochement—still hoping for reunion but willing to accept fraternal relations as a first step toward that end.

During the last quarter of the nineteenth century, all three major evangelical denominations formally established fraternal relations, meaning that the northern and southern branches of each denomination met and, with varying degrees of formality, recognized the legitimacy and equal standing of the southern branches. Methodists established fraternal relations at the Cape May Commission of 1876; Presbyterians accomplished the same end through an exchange of proposals in 1882; and Baptists devised a Comity Agreement at a meeting in Fortress Monroe, Virginia, in 1894.

The atmosphere of seeming cooperation between northern and southern churches coincided with the general post-Reconstruction spirit of reconciliation and reunion, but ultimately fraternal relations agreements led to more firmly established divisions between evangelicals in the two sections. Literature on sectional reconciliation highlights selective forgetting and a shared emphasis on reunion based on the common wartime experiences of white soldiers. Nina Silber argues that "forgetfulness, not memory, appears to be the dominant theme in the reunion culture," and David Blight contends that forgetting all aspects of the war other than the common bonds of soldiers on both sides characterized the reconciliation period.[42] Late-nineteenth-century developments in mainstream evangelical religion reveal a different process—one grounded in formally negotiating, recognizing, and institutionalizing sectional differences. Southern evangelicals insisted on their fundamental differences from their northern counterparts. Hostilities between the sections could only cease when northerners respected these differences.

The narrative of Reconstruction in the churches provides a reminder of the complexity of sectional relationships in post–Civil War America. The late-nineteenth-century feelings of patriotism and common cause described in recent scholarship coexisted with deep sectional differences, including the segregation and violence of the Jim Crow South.[43] They also included an agreement that southern evangelical denominations, formed on the basis of the biblical defense of slavery, constituted theologically distinct denominational branches. Because these churches had adopted the border-state policy of neutrality, they did not feel an imperative to alter the injustices of the social conditions that surrounded them. Southern churches, after the defeat of the Confederacy, were "not of this world" and, therefore, also not a part of worldly "political" disputes.

At first blush, these agreements might appear to represent a move toward organic union, an end long desired in the northern churches. Indeed, northerners hoped that a fraternal agreement would prove the first step toward formal reunion. However, southerners approached the agreements from a different perspective. They viewed them as recognition from the North that the southern branches were legitimate entities. Southern Methodists and Presbyterians even required that their northern counterparts retract statements issued earlier in the century challenging the legitimacy and purity of southern denominations. Establishing fraternal relations for southerners, then, was seen as a means of achieving a greater degree of denominational security. The southern view of fraternal relations triumphed. Ultimately, the agreements gave strength to the South and ended northern attempts to bring about organic union. Rather than hastening reunion, fraternal relations eliminated the possibility of reunion for the foreseeable future.

Methodists

The Methodists were the first of the three denominations to establish fraternal relations. This was in part because of the strength and swiftness of the southern rejection of postwar proposals for organic union. Northern and Southern Methodists had honed their grievances toward each other during the bitter Plan of Separation controversy. At the close of war, Southern Methodists had actively defended their denomination and sparred with the North for over twenty years. Southerners were well prepared to reject organic union on northern terms, and northerners seemed to recognize how entrenched the southern grievances—compounded by recent Confederate defeat—had become. "Much bitterness has been engendered" among Methodists in the South, one northerner reported.[44] Another Northern Methodist (ironically, in an article rehashing the 1844 schism) derided Southern Methodists for their inability to let go of quarter-century-old grudges. The story of the 1844 division, he reported, has been "narrated, repeated, and argued elaborately but one-sidedly, in various forms before the popular mind." As for northerners, "our people and our ministry have taken little interest in the long-past matter," he disingenuously concluded. Forgetting past conflict, of course, aided the northern objective of reunion on northern terms. In contrast, taking "the pains thoroughly to instruct" the younger generation of Southern Methodists "in order that a due spirit of separation may be maintained and the danger of re-union peremptorily prevented" served the southern end of preserving separate sectional denominations.[45]

Southern Methodists would not modify their conditions for establishing a relationship with their northern counterparts. Southerners wanted northerners to recognize their branch of the church as an equal and to respect territorial limits. Southern Methodists at the 1870 General Conference explained that the northern church "must abandon her three hundred thousand members in the Southern States, with all her churches and other institutions, confess the sin of her intrusion, limit herself north of Mason and Dixon's line." If these conditions were met, the Church South would "graciously listen to and consider her petition for an exchange of ecclesiastical courtesies."[46] In the face of this entrenched resistance, Northern Methodists quickly shifted from reunion overtures to proposals for establishing fraternal relations.

In 1872, the Northern Methodist General Conference approved a proposal of fraternal relations to be sent to the Southern Conference.[47] The proposal was to be brought by a delegation—Northern Methodists had not sent such a delegation south since 1848. A letter of instruction from Bishop Edmund Janes to one of the delegates reveals that the northerners saw fraternal relations as a step on the path to organic union. Janes cautioned the delegate to "only propose fraternal relations, not organic union. . . . the latter will come in due time." He also advised the delegate to brush up on the history of the churches and "be prepared to meet any references that may be made to past events" or to "our going into the South."[48]

The Southern General Conference received the delegation and their proposal for fraternal relations two years later at their 1874 meeting in Louisville. While reaffirming that they would not consent to organic union, the Southern Methodists did agree to a convention on fraternal relations. Delegates from the North and South met in Cape May, New Jersey, in August 1876.[49] The delegates to the Cape May Peace Commission reached an agreement and established fraternal relations.

The Cape May Commission's success can be attributed both to northern willingness to accept fraternal relations and to the unwaveringly united front presented by the southern delegates. While northerners clung to the hope that fraternal relations might prove a stepping stone to further union, southerners viewed the Cape May Commission as a way to resolve nagging territorial issues such as border property claims and northern missions. To ensure that these goals were met, the southerners agreed in advance on minimum terms that must be granted before establishing fraternal relations. Foremost was recognition that the southern church was a "co-equal section of the original Methodist Episcopal Church." Second, the southern church's property claims were to be respected.[50] The implications of these conditions were clear: northerners must recognize the southern church as a complete equal, meaning that *neither* branch constituted the original church and that this original church had split equally into two parts, not that the southerners had splintered off. In addition, the southerners wanted property disputes resolved in their favor and northern property claims in the South withdrawn.

Northern Methodists met each of the southern demands. On the first day, the commission adopted a declaration stating, "Each of the said churches is a legitimate Branch of Episcopal Methodism in the United States."[51] The delegates at the Cape May Commission also established a procedure for the adjudication of property conflicts in church courts, a development sorely needed since the 1844 Plan of Separation.[52]

The property resolution also favored Southern Methodists. The general rule devised was that either branch could "remain in possession" of church property unless a larger group from the other branch laid claim to it.[53] This rule applied to Northern Methodist congregations in former slave states that met in churches that had been transferred to northern authority during the war. Since the commission also recognized Southern Methodists as equally historically legitimate, a minority of northerners could no longer claim property on the grounds that the represented the only true Methodist Episcopal Church in the United States.

In the wake of the Cape May Commission, most of the simmering tension between Northern and Southern Methodists subsided. In the North, particularly New England, Methodists complained that the agreement "conceded too much" to the South, particularly in allowing that the Southern Methodists constituted an equal branch of the church.[54] Most northern complaints came from the congregations that lost their property in the adjudications at Cape May.[55] A Tennessee Northern Methodist complained that the property cases had been solved "all on one side [and] at our expense."[56] MEC missionaries working in the South also felt that their authority in that region had been compromised. In response to curtailed missions in the South, one editorial protested, "we are Americans, and have a right every-where in our free America."[57]

After 1876, Northern Methodist travelers to the South received a much warmer welcome. "The preachers of the Church South seem to be earnestly disposed to fraternity," reported a Northern Methodist who visited Georgia after the Cape May Commission.[58] Reverend Mitchell, a visitor in 1880, also reported that Southern Methodists "manifest a becoming spirit of hospitality," which he contrasted favorably to the chilly reception he had received on former visits. Mitchell knew that "the great question of the future" would be organic union—and imagined that his warm reception in

Georgia indicated such a reunion would soon take place.[59] Mitchell and other sanguine northerners misread the cues. Southerners could welcome northern counterparts as guests precisely because northerners no longer posed a threat to southern authority. Fraternal relations did not prove, as northerners hoped, a stepping-stone to reunion. Rather, the agreements authorized the Southern Methodist Church to exist on an equal plane with the Northern, securing its claim to independence. Reunion between Northern and Southern Methodists did not take place until 1939.[60]

Presbyterians

With little fanfare, the two branches of the Presbyterian Church established fraternal relations in 1882. On the morning of May 9, the Southern Committee of Foreign Correspondence submitted a report stating that "after the most careful consideration" they recommended the adoption of a brief statement, to be sent immediately to the northern church. This statement explained "that while receding from no principle, we do hereby declare our regret for and withdrawal of all expressions of our Assembly which may be regarded as reflecting upon, or offensive to, the General Assembly of the Presbyterian Church in the United States of America."[61] The northern church accepted this tepid overture, adding that, in doing so, it "receded from no principle."[62] Presbyterians made plans to exchange delegates at the following year's assemblies and closed the issue. After over a decade of impassioned debate and failed fraternal overtures, this anticlimactic establishment of fraternal relations demands explanation.

Fraternal relations in the Presbyterian Church occurred as a new generation of Presbyterian leaders rose to power. Both sides had come to feel a measure of security in their differences. Only one of the men assembled in Atlanta in May of 1882 had also attended the fateful 1861 assembly, and only twenty-two of the seventy-four delegates had been ordained in the church before the war.[63] The agreement to an exchange of delegates passed almost without opposition on the floor of the Southern Assembly but garnered considerable protest from the remaining older members of the Presbyterian leadership. The aging Benjamin Morgan Palmer, not himself in attendance, declared the action of the Atlanta Assembly a "lasting injury" that would in due time necessitate organic union. He feared "we must as certainly crumble into the Northern Church at last, as a bank of sand is washed away by the constant action of water."[64] Robert Lewis Dabney, also absent, was shocked to hear of "this surrender of doctrinal purity." He feared it would lead to "*unity of doctrinal and ecclesiastical principles.*"[65] Both now in their seventies, Palmer and Dabney voiced the fears of men who had lived through the war and fought for recognition of a separate Southern Church.

The new generation of denominational leaders realized that an exchange of delegates secured, rather than threatened, the independence of their assembly. By exchanging delegates, each body recognized the other's legitimacy. The northern church subsequently curtailed much of its missionary activity and expenditures in the South, opening the field to the work of southern evangelists. In addition, both assemblies also began to settle remaining property disputes outside of civil courts.[66] In 1882, each assembly gave the other leave to continue missionary work, unhindered, in its own section.

When delegates from the North attended their first Southern Assembly in 1883, they greeted their host body with short, courteous speeches. A delegate from New York echoed the sentiments of his fellow travelers when he declared, "we come to you on equal terms. We meet as Churches and as gentlemen." The description of the event in the *Southern Presbyterian Review* assured readers, no doubt alert for signs to the contrary, that "there was no tendency in the northern church to the union of the two Assemblies; but only a desire for friendly, efficient cooperation." As if to prove that the new relations in no way threatened their independence, the Southern Assembly reminded attendees that "the divergence between the two Churches" constituted "'*an insuperable obstacle*' to organic union" and that the "*question of organic union is not to be entertained as a subject before the church.*"[67] Sectional division remained ingrained in American Presbyterianism.

Baptists

Northern and Southern Baptists did not peaceably settle their relationship until the 1894 Fortress Monroe Comity Agreement.[68] Baptists took so long to reach comity for two reasons. One was the decentralized structure of Baptist organization, which made it difficult to rally unity. The second, in part caused by the first, was the extreme poverty of the Southern Baptist Convention in the wake of war.[69] The Southern Baptists experienced a longer period of uncertainty about their future following the Civil War than their Methodist and Presbyterian counterparts. During this period, Northern Baptists, under the American Baptist Home Mission Society, continued to send missionaries to the South, particularly to educate black southerners.

Unlike those of Methodists and Presbyterians, the Baptists' major sectional institutions were not structurally equivalent. The Southern Baptist Convention was a unified, central body with authority over constituent organizations. The SBC had its own Home Mission Board, which was analogous to the Northern Society. In contrast, Northern Baptist authority still rested, at least theoretically, at the congregational level. Congregations as well as state and regional groups voluntarily associated with the American Baptist Home Mission Society, which collected funds and organized mission and publication projects. The Mission Society had been chartered in 1832, before sectional division, for the purpose of "promoting the preaching of the Gospel in North America."[70] Nevertheless, the society did not directly compete with the Southern Baptist Convention. Rather, it entered into auxiliary relationships with Southern Baptist congregations, providing funds, ministers, publications, and schools.[71] Southerners were angered by this intrusion, but also sorely needed the resources from the ABHMS.

From 1864 to 1888, the Northern Society had sought organic union with the Southern Baptist Convention, but the proposals were always swiftly rejected.[72] However, conflicts in the 1880s over missions to Missouri and the Indian Territory finally impressed on both the Northern Society and the Southern Convention the need for a formal agreement.[73] In 1894, the convention proposed "that the time has come" for southerners to take over more of the work of educating and evangelizing "among the colored people of the South."[74] Implicit in this suggestion was the idea that consequently, northerners—whose primary reason for staying in the South was evangelizing black Baptists—would withdraw their southern missions. This proposal led to the 1894 meeting at Fortress Monroe, Virginia. The meeting took place during a decade many historians consider the peak of white Civil War reconciliation and reunion sentiment.[75] However, while it might have appeared at first glance to promote union, the Baptist meeting also served to clarify and cement sectional difference.

As with Methodists and Presbyterians earlier in the century, Northern and Southern Baptists came to their meeting with differing expectations. Like their Methodist and Presbyterian counterparts before them, southerners hoped that the agreement would result in the formal recognition of the legitimacy of the southern organization. Southern Baptists particularly desired this recognition because it would augment their authority in the eyes of southern state associations as well as the North. Southerners also wanted the society to respect the convention's territorial claims over the former slave states. Northern Baptists agreed to the meeting because, like Northern Methodists and Presbyterians, they hoped that the comity agreement would prove the first step toward organic union. The convention's offer to take over much of the labor and costs of the mission to black southerners also came at an opportune moment. In 1894, the society felt the financial pinch of the economic depression while an influx of white immigrants in the North seemed to cry out for missionary attention.[76]

The meeting at Fortress Monroe resulted in three agreements. First, the Southern Baptist Convention was granted a local advisory committee "at each point where a school controlled by the American Baptist Home Mission Society is or shall be located." This gave Southern Baptists oversight of the northern operations among black southerners. While northerners would continue to fund the schools, the southern advisory committees controlled their operations and could "recommend . . . any changes in the conduct, or in the teaching forces." In exchange, southerners would cease attempts to subvert the schools and encourage local children to attend. Second, the Joint Committee agreed that the two associations would "cooperate in the mission work among the colored people of the South." This meant an end to missionaries competing against each other within communities.

Finally, the committee laid the groundwork for a plan to resolve the contested issue of territory. The question of territorial limits had been the chief point of contention between the two groups since 1862, when the American Baptist Home Mission Society resumed missions in the South. To resolve this, the committee proposed "that in the prosecution of their work already begun on contiguous fields, or on the same field, that all antagonisms be avoided. . . . we further recommend to those bodies and their agents in opening new work to direct their efforts to localities not occupied by the other."[77] This vague injunction against conflict formed the basis for informal, yet respected, territorial fields for each group. Over the next decade, a boundary line took shape. It "stretched south of Delaware, Pennsylvania, West Virginia, Ohio, Indiana and Oklahoma, and divided Illinois and Missouri."[78]

Ultimately, the plan set forth at Fortress Monroe eliminated the worst conflicts over mission work among Baptists in the United States. As with similar agreements made by Methodists and Baptists, it also favored the southern objectives. For the Southern Baptist Convention, the agreement represented "the first formal recognition by the Society of the territorial unity of the South, and the Convention as its voice."[79] Southerners were "gratified at the hearty approval given the agreement reached by the Joint Committee," since that agreement conferred recognition and legitimacy upon Southern Baptists.[80] "How much this all means no man can tell," Henry Lyman Morehouse of the ABHMS mused. Still, he remained hopeful that "It will bring our brethren, white and black, into closer fraternal relations. . . . Indeed, this is but the beginning of a process."[81] This was a vain hope. The Southern Baptists had a clearer view of the future at Fortress Monroe. Over the next six decades, the Northern and Southern Baptists would grow more sectionalized and more distinct. In 1907, Northern Baptists adopted the convention model and named themselves the Northern Baptist Convention.[82] While Southern Baptists can now be found in all corners of the United States, no reunion has occurred.

CONCLUSION

The postwar interactions between northern and southern evangelicals provide an arresting counterpoint to the narrative of postwar reconciliation. The story is often told as one of initial animosity followed by a steady post-Reconstruction economic and emotional reunion that neared completion by the end of the nineteenth century. This account of reunion minimizes the instances in which southern nationalism successfully lived on. Not all myths produced in the last quarter of the nineteenth century served to help smooth over conflicts between the North and the South: some served to perpetuate division.

Following the brief years of northern religious Reconstruction, southern evangelicals successfully resisted pressure to reunite—an act that would have helped satisfy the biblical imperative for Christian unity. Reinforced by border evangelicals, who joined them in the postwar years, southern denominations used border history to defend denominational independence. They defended this independence as necessary to fulfill another theological imperative: maintaining the purity of the church. The relative valuations of these imperatives reflect the priorities of each region in the postwar decades.

Over the first half of the nineteenth century, the upstart evangelical denominations that swept the nation during the Second Great Awakening had grown into respectable mainstream churches. Their institutions had become central features of civil society. When the sectional crisis and Civil War threw mid-century America into disarray, the evangelical churches were too large, too powerful, and too enmeshed in daily life to avoid involvement as well. Only along the border, where the demand for day-to-day cooperation overshadowed the demand for response to the national crisis, did evangelicals attempt to adopt political neutrality and an otherworldly focus that eschewed political involvement—and a refusal to accept the moral dimensions of the slavery question. With the defeat of the Confederacy and the implementation of Reconstruction, southern evangelicals again became outsiders—this time to northern culture—and adopted nonpolitical border spirituality as their own heritage.

Not all myths produced after the Civil War helped smooth over conflicts between the North and the South: some served to sustain sectional division. Polemical histories were key to a lasting divide in American religion. One Southern Methodist historian explained: "the Church, South, . . . seeks to uphold its own legitimacy, and to maintain the honor of 'the fathers' and the honorableness of its origin, and to transmit an unsullied name to those who come after."[83] Writing slavery out of their origin story allowed southern evangelicals, for a century and more after the abolition of slavery itself, to successfully perpetuate denominational branches formed to defend that very institution.

CONCLUSION

THE RIGHT AS GOD GIVES US TO SEE THE RIGHT

"With malice toward none; with charity for all; with firmness in the right as God gives us to see the right, let us strive on to finish the work we are in; to bind up the nation's wounds." So Abraham Lincoln charged the nation in his 1865 Second Inaugural Address. As he faced the challenge of Reconstruction, Lincoln referenced the divisive potential of religious conflict. In this war, he observed, both sides "read the same Bible, and pray to the same God, and each invokes His aid against the other."[1]

In acknowledging that both northerners and southerners claimed God's support for their side, Lincoln was drawing attention to the deeply divergent interpretations of the Civil War that existed in the two regions. Lincoln argued that God "gives to both North and South this terrible war." Therefore, each side should accept blame, bury their antagonism, and reunite to rebuild the nation. His call for "malice toward none" reflects the depth of enmity that existed between the sections. Malice, of course, also persisted between the northern and southern branches of the major evangelical Protestant churches in the United States. Sectionalized religious responses to the end of war suggested that reunion in the churches would not come swiftly. Northerners demanded loyalty to the Union and prompt denominational reunion. Southerners rejected calls to celebrate the reunited nation and assumed their denominations would remain separate. Along the border, evangelicals hoped that the end of the war would mean the end of politics in the pulpit.

The Civil War in the churches began well before 1861, with the division in the major evangelical denominations, and it lasted well beyond Union victory, Reconstruction, and Redemption. C. Vann Woodward observed that "the rupture between the North and the South had come earliest in the great Protestant sects, and there it was the slowest to heal." This was because, he argued, "the Southern churches became for a time centers of resistance to the invasion of Northern culture."[2] The enduring rift in the major evangelical denominations has largely been ignored in explanations of the failures of Reconstruction and the limitations of reunion. But the southern churches remained demonstrable strongholds of southern exceptionalism.

The story of division in the churches serves as a reminder that reunion did not occur evenly and equally across all facets of civil society. Northerners and southerners may have reunited and experienced reconciliation in some areas, but in others, sectional difference and sectionalism persisted. This was particularly true of the churches. They did not reunite after the war; instead, they institutionalized sectional division.

The narrative of the evangelical churches after the Civil War intersects with two historiographic schools. One is the study of the myth of the Lost Cause that took root in the postwar South; and the other is the study of reconciliation and reunion between the North and the South. Polemical denominational histories demonstrate that postwar southerners dedicated a great deal of energy to constructing a history that legitimated the Confederate cause and glorified southern culture and virtue.[3] Evangelicals played an important role not just in shaping the Lost Cause narrative in southern civil religion, but also in developing their own, internal, denomination-specific myths of causes lost and won. These latter myths would persist even as reconciliation occurred elsewhere in southern society. The Methodist conflicts over the Plan of Separation, Southern Baptist grievances about postwar northern missionaries, and the memories of the wrongs done to the Declaration and Testimony synods in the Presbyterian Church all became fodder for this mythology. The persecution of border evangelicals and the response of border moderates became key components in constructing an account of nonpolitical southern churches that predated the Civil War.

Unlike scholars who examine the myth of the Lost Cause, historians of postwar reunion focus on the national process through which the North and the South reunited: by agreeing on an acceptable version of the past, usually at the expense of civil rights and social justice.[4] Like studies of Lost Cause mythology, however, reunion studies also emphasize the retelling of the past and shaping of public memory of the Civil War. Continued division in the major evangelical churches stands in marked contrast to the sort of national reunion that occurred though milestones of reconciliation, such as veterans' gatherings, tourism, the Spanish-American War, and the election of Woodrow

Wilson. Reunion could only occur because so much sectionalism still existed. The post-Reconstruction decades might look different if we viewed late-nineteenth-century reunion events as secular analogues of fraternal relations and comity agreements in the evangelical churches during the same period. These agreements did not so much hasten real reunion as prolong the process; they served to curtail overt sectional antagonism while protecting and acknowledging sectional difference.

By the end of the nineteenth century, border evangelicals were no longer central to narratives of denominational difference. However, their stories served as the justification for separate sectional faiths after the Civil War. They became part of the history of the southern branches, and, therefore, part of a frequently rehearsed catalog of wartime Yankee abuses. This was an ironic turn, given that it was the border evangelicals themselves who first opposed division over slavery and prioritized the preservation of denominational unity. In their opposition to division and conflict within the church, border evangelicals embraced a theology of spirituality and political neutrality. "I thank God that I am not responsible for the state of things existing," wrote Elisha Phelps after the Methodist Baltimore Conference lay meeting late in 1860. Both the conference, and the nation itself, threatened to divide. Despite his own "effort to maintain the unity of the church," Phelps feared "the politicians in church and state" would drive the conference apart.[5] A border Baptist was "determined to take a high neutral stand, knowing no North or South."[6] A Missouri Presbyterian remarked, "It can hardly be said that we belong to either the North or the South."[7] Border-state evangelicals clung to the hope that political neutrality and spirituality could prevent the division of God's kingdom in the United States.

Ultimately, these strategies proved ineffective. Remaining neutral in the debates over slavery and secession meant valuing church unity over the freedom of millions of enslaved African Americans. Still, it is not difficult to understand the appeal of neutrality in the face of divisive moral and political conflicts. Border moderates were profoundly disturbed to see debates over slavery and secession break up their churches and denominational institutions. As a result, they came to view the debates—instead of slavery itself—as the most pressing problem their churches faced. In the polarized landscape of the mid-nineteenth century, political arguments could generate explosive conflict. Within this context, attempting to remain neutral was not only appealing—it also acquired a patina of virtue. Thus, moderate white border clergy convinced themselves of their moral superiority to those who engaged in partisan debates. They could not see that the ability to dismiss the slavery debate as a purely political matter was a privilege not available to everyone. (African Americans, for example, had no such luxury.) In fact, as parties on both sides pressured them to declare their loyalties and the possibility of remaining neutral dwindled and disappeared, neutral evangelicals began to perceive themselves as victims.

When the war was over, neutrality about slavery was no longer an option in the northern churches. Border evangelicals who had once affiliated with the North, and who had hoped to return to a pre-emancipation status quo, felt persecuted by their denominations. This sense of persecution led them away from the northern churches. They began to affiliate, instead, with southern churches, which continued to defend slavery even after it had been abolished. Thus, attempts to remain neutral regarding slavery ultimately led to membership in proslavery denominations

This attempt by moderates to remain neutral in the face of moral disputes reverberates in present-day conflicts. It reveals why many people turn to moderation or neutrality as a strategy in the face of intensely charged conflicts. And it offers an explanation for why people who attempt to remain neutral come to feel that they occupy the moral high ground. This is the logic that led many Americans to advise a "go slow" approach in response to demands for equality during the civil rights movement. This reasoning likewise found voice in proponents of "color blindness," rather than affirmative action, as a solution to structural racism in the late twentieth century. Indeed, it is the logic of those who responded to the Black Lives Matter movement of the early twenty-first century with the blithe rebuttal, "All Lives Matter." These responses are available only to those who are not, themselves, victims of segregation and racism. Such responses might seem like solutions, but they only ease the discomfort that privileged observers feel. They do nothing to redress underlying problems. As a consequence, when "neutral" parties are called to task for abetting racism and segregation, they themselves feel persecuted. This, then, is the problem of neutrality in the face of a moral crisis: neutrality cannot be neutral.

The nation's three largest evangelical denominations—Baptists, Methodists, and Presbyterians—experienced spectacular growth in the early nineteenth century. All three channeled their growth into the development of institutions across the West. Expansion into the West, however, also threatened the unity of national evangelical denominations. In the 1840s, controversies over the sinfulness of slavery divided Methodists and Baptists into separate sectional denominational branches. Later, Presbyterians followed suit with their own denominational division in the lead-up to the secession crisis. On the border and in the West, many evangelicals were more committed to preserving denominational unity than they were to defending or attacking slavery. For these border moderates, the fallout from prewar schisms that roiled their congregations served to reinforce the value of treating slavery as a political—not a moral—issue, and then banishing political topics from the pulpit.

When the Civil War broke out, these border evangelicals eschewed the patriotic sermons, flag displays, and national days of prayer that characterized both northern and southern churches. Border evangelicals attempted to be nonpolitical in the pulpit and professed neutrality in the political conflict. Northern evangelical patriotism and loyalty tests, as well as secular pressure to swear loyalty to the Union from the army and state governments, made neutrality nearly impossible—and often criminal—for border ministers. For a few years, federal authorities became intimately involved in monitoring and enforcing loyalty among border clergy. They also redistributed church property to demonstrably loyal ministers and congregations. And the ensuing lawsuits brought questions about the legitimacy of divided churches into secular courts.

Toward the end of the Civil War and into the first years of Reconstruction, federal authorities and northern church leaders grew increasingly hostile to border moderates and their claims of political neutrality. Northern opposition to neutrality contributed to border evangelical grievances. At the same time, southern denominations, which had formed before the Civil War because of northern arguments that slavery was sinful, now sought to maintain independence after the abolition of slavery. Southerners needed to create an argument to defend their denominational distinctiveness in the face of northern pressure to reunite on northern terms. For their part, border evangelicals, angered and alienated by northern religious Reconstruction, gradually joined southern branches. They brought with them both financial resources and a history that provided a compelling argument for denominational distinctiveness: the spirituality of the church. Southerners embraced this history as their own when they welcomed border churches into their denominations. Ironically, the failed border strategy for preventing denominational division became a key ingredient for perpetuating sectional denominational branches after the Civil War.

Northern and southern evangelicals entered into fraternal relations and comity agreements with differing expectations. Northerners, while abandoning hopes for immediate reunion, expected that the increased communication would hasten the day when the two branches would again become one. Southerners, in contrast, entered the agreements with the intention of resisting all pressure for reunion. In the decades that followed these agreements, the southern vision of fraternal relations triumphed. As southern branches built up their strength and independence, and black southern evangelicals formed independent churches, northern branches abandoned their national ambitions and resigned themselves to sectionalism. Reunion would not take place until well into the twentieth century.

The Methodist Episcopal churches, North and South, as well as the Methodist Protestant Church, formally united as the Methodist Church at the 1939 "Uniting Conference" in Kansas City. In order to accomplish this reunion, Methodists, over the protests of black delegates, agreed on a Plan of Union that completely segregated the church, both in the North and the South. While white Methodist annual conferences were organized geographically, black Methodists subsequently met in a single conference that encompassed all congregations, regardless of location. The new Methodist Church—now the largest Protestant church in the nation—"was racially segregated to its core."[8] This was the price of national reunion in the Jim Crow era.

It would be another four and a half decades before Presbyterians achieved their own national reunion. The process began in 1951, as the PCUSA, PCUS, and several other large national Presbyterian organizations entered into negotiations to reach an agreement on union. The PCUS (Southern Church) ultimately withdrew from the deal, but the other participants formed the United Presbyterian Church—the largest American Presbyterian branch—in 1958. More than a century had passed since sectional division in the Presbyterian Church. It was not until June 10, 1983, that the United Presbyterian Church, descendent of the PCUSA, merged with the PCUS to form the Presbyterian Church (USA). Five years later, denominational leaders consolidated their New York and Georgia headquarters into a single location in Louisville, Kentucky.[9]

While twentieth-century Methodists and Presbyterians found ways to turn two sectionalized branches back into a single national organization, Baptists transformed their sectional branches into two separate national denominations, both of which still thrive today. Northern Baptists began the twentieth century with a historic act: the creation of the Northern Baptist Convention.

Following the model of the SBC, the NBC consolidated its varied boards and societies into one single organization and explicitly acknowledged the sectional nature of the church. The Northern Baptists were the largest Baptist body in the United States when the NBC was established; but in the decades that followed, they lost ground to the spectacularly successful Southern Baptist Convention.[10]

Over the course of the twentieth century, Southern Baptists continued to assert their denominational independence and distinct identity. By 1950, Southern Baptist membership was five times larger than that of their northern counterparts.[11] Northern and Southern Baptist rivalry soon resurfaced. Southerners declared they would no longer accept territorial limits and began expansion into the North. In response, the NBC changed its name to the American Baptist Convention.[12] This change did little to stem the Southern Baptist tide; over the next fifty years, the SBC rejected its own territorial limitations and expanded throughout the United States and the world. Today, the descendant branches of Northern and Southern Baptists are each national denominations, and reunion seems as unlikely as ever.

Many historians argue that a gradual process of reconciliation between the North and the South occurred during the decades after the Civil War. Within the religious sphere, however, this was not the case. When evangelical churches first divided, their members asserted it was over a single point of disagreement: slavery. In all other respects, they claimed, they remained the same. Twenty years and a Civil War later, slavery no longer existed. Nevertheless, the sectional rift in the churches had not only persisted, it had actually grown more pronounced. Once politics, morality, and theology became aligned, they powerfully reinforced one another and perpetuated sectionalism. The nation was once more a single political entity, but its largest evangelical denominations remained divided. In his Second Inaugural Address, Abraham Lincoln called upon Americans to meet the challenges of Reconstruction "with firmness in the right as God gives us to see the right." Evangelicals, North, South, and on the border acted with firmness, but they did not share a common vision of what constituted "the right."

NOTES

INTRODUCTION

1. Robert L. Stanton, *The Church and the Rebellion: A Consideration of the Rebellion Against the Government of the United States; and the Agency of the Church, North and South in Relation Thereto* (New York: Derby and Miller, 1864), vi, 562.

2. Mark Noll, *The Civil War as a Theological Crisis* (Chapel Hill: University of North Carolina Press, 2006), 9–11. See also George Rable, *God's Almost Chosen Peoples: A Religious History of the American Civil War* (Chapel Hill: University of North Carolina Press, 2010), 5.

3. Mark Noll, *America's God: From Jonathan Edwards to Abraham Lincoln* (New York: Oxford University Press, 2002), 166; Richard Carwardine, *Evangelicals and Politics in Antebellum America* (Knoxville: University of Tennessee Press, 1997), 5.

4. Noll, *America's God,* 5, 499. See also Carwardine, *Evangelicals and Politics,* 2, 43–44. For similar arguments, see Curtis D. Johnson, *Redeeming America: Evangelicals and the Road to Civil War* (Chicago: Ivan R. Dee, 1993), and Mitchell Snay, *Gospel of Disunion: Religion and Separatism in the Antebellum South* (Cambridge, U.K.: Oxford University Press, 1993). David Sehat introduces the idea of a Protestant "moral establishment" that dominated antebellum American culture. See Sehat, *The Myth of American Religious Freedom* (New York: Oxford University Press, 2011), 51–69.

5. Johnson, *Redeeming America,* 4–7. Noll, *America's God,* 5, 564–65.

6. Snay, *Gospel of Disunion*; C. C. Goen, *Broken Churches, Broken Nation: Denominational Schisms and the Coming of the American Civil War* (Macon, Ga.: Mercer University Press, 1985); also Carwardine, *Evangelicals and Politics.*

7. See Lacy Ford, *Deliver Us from Evil: The Slavery Question in the Old* South (New York: Oxford University Press, 2009); John Patrick Daly, *When Slavery Was Called Freedom: Evangelicalism, Proslavery, and the Causes of the Civil War* (Lexington: University Press of Kentucky, 2002); and Charles F. Irons, *The Origins of Proslavery Christianity: White and Black Evangelicals in Colonial and Antebellum Virginia* (Chapel Hill: University of North Carolina Press, 2008). Anne Loveland argues that antebellum southern churches did not develop a political defense of slavery in *Southern Evangelicals and the Social Order, 1800–1860* (Baton Rouge: Louisiana State University Press, 1980). For the influence of Christian abolitionists, see John McKivigan, *The War against Proslavery Religion: Abolitionism and the Northern Churches, 1830–1865* (Ithaca, N.Y.: Cornell University Press, 1984), 161–201.

8. For a perspective that spans the middle decades of the nineteenth century, see Ernest Lee Tuveson, *Redeemer Nation: The Idea of America's Millennial Role* (Chicago: University of Chicago Press, 1968); Robert T. Handy, *A Christian America: Protestant Hopes and Historical Realities* (New York: Oxford University Press, 1971); and Nicole Guétin, *Religious Ideology in American Politics: A History* (Jefferson, N.C.: McFarland & Co., 2009). For religion's role in the war and Reconstruction, see Rable, *God's Almost Chosen Peoples*; Harry Stout, *Upon the Altar of the Nation: A Moral History of the Civil* War (New York: Viking, 2006); David Goldfield, *America Aflame: How the Civil War Created a Nation* (New York: Bloomsbury Press,

2011); Randall Miller et al., *Religion and the American Civil War* (New York: Oxford University Press, 1998); Sean A. Scott, *A Visitation of God: Northern Civilians Interpret the Civil War* (New York: Oxford University Press, 2011); Luke E. Harlow, *Religion, Race, and the Making of Confederate Kentucky, 1830–1880* (New York: Cambridge University Press, 2014). For the postwar period, see Edward Blum, *Reforging the White Republic: Race, Religion, and American Nationalism, 1865–1898* (Baton Rouge: Louisiana State University Press, 2005); and Edward J. Blum and W. Scott Poole, eds., *Vale of Tears: New Essays on Religion and Reconstruction* (Macon, Ga.: Mercer University Press, 2005).

9. In *Civil War as a Theological Crisis* and *America's God,* Mark Noll argues that the slavery debates instigated a theological crisis over biblical interpretation. See also E. Brooks Holifield, *Theology in America: Christian Thought from the Age of the Puritans to the Civil War* (New Haven, Conn.: Yale University Press, 2003); Molly Oshatz, *Slavery and Sin: The Fight against Slavery and the Rise of Liberal Protestantism* (New York: Oxford University Press, 2011). See also Jack P. Maddex, "From Theocracy to Spirituality: The Southern Presbyterian Reversal on Church and State," *Journal of Presbyterian History* 54 (1976): 438–57. Harlow's *Religion, Race, and the Making of Confederate Kentucky* addresses theological responses to slavery and war. For a study of conservative theology in a border state, see Preston Graham Jr., *A Kingdom Not of This World: Stuart Robinson's Struggle to Distinguish the Sacred from the Secular during the Civil War* (Macon, Ga.: Mercer University Press, 2002). For a recent overview of the politics of the Civil War and religion, see Timothy Wesley, *The Politics of Faith during the Civil War* (Baton Rouge: Louisiana State University Press, 2013). Daniel Stowell's *Rebuilding Zion: The Religious Reconstruction of the South, 1863–1877* (New York: Oxford University Press, 1998) investigates how the churches rebuilt after the Civil War. Several scholars have examined how Reconstruction affected individual denominations. See Ralph E. Morrow, *Northern Methodism and Reconstruction* (East Lansing: Michigan State University Press, 1956); Paul Harvey, *Redeeming the South: Religious Cultures and Racial Identities among Southern Baptists, 1865–1925* (Chapel Hill: University of North Carolina Press, 1997). See Michael Williams Sr., *Isaac Taylor Tichenor: The Creation of a Baptist New South* (Tuscaloosa: University of Alabama Press, 2005), for an account of the rebuilding of the Southern Baptist Convention.

10. For example, see John Nelson Norwood, *The Schism in the Methodist Episcopal Church, 1844: A Study of Slavery and Ecclesiastical Politics* (Alfred, N.Y.: Alfred Press, 1923); E. Luther Copeland, *The Southern Baptist Convention and the Judgment of History: The Taint of an Original Sin* (New York: University Press of America, 1995); Robert Andrew Baker, "Relations Between Northern and Southern Baptists," PhD diss., Yale University, 1948; and Lewis G. Vander Velde, *The Presbyterian Churches and the Federal Union, 1861–1869* (Cambridge, U.K.: Oxford University Press, 1932).

11. Laurie Maffly-Kipp, "The Burdens of Church History," *Church History* 82 (2013): 355.

12. Amanda Porterfield, *Conceived in Doubt: Religion and Politics in the New American Nation* (Chicago: University of Chicago Press, 2012).

13. George Fredrickson, "The Coming of the Lord: The Northern Protestant Clergy and the Civil War Crisis," in Miller et al., *Religion and the American Civil War,* 111–12. Bridget Ford argues that Protestant denominations formed one of the "bonds of union" that first held together and then divided border residents during the sectional crisis; see Ford, *Bonds of Union: Religion, Race, and Politics in a Civil War Borderland* (Chapel Hill: University of North

Carolina Press, 2016). Elesha J. Coffman illustrates how a religious publication created institutional networks; see Coffman, *The Christian Century: The Rise of the Protestant Mainline* (New York: Oxford University Press, 2013). For a twentieth-century example of the sometimes hidden power of institutions and the networks they create, see Kate Bowler, *Blessed: A History of the American Prosperity Gospel* (New York: Oxford University Press, 2013).

14. Jonathan Palmer Finley Diaries, September 1, 1866, Presbyterian Historical Society.

15. Nicole Etcheson, *The Emerging Northwest: Upland Southerners and the Political Culture of the Old Northwest, 1787–1861* (Bloomington: Indiana University Press, 1996). See also Kim M. Gruenwald, *River of Enterprise: The Commercial Origins of Regional Identity in the Ohio Valley, 1790–1850* (Bloomington: Indiana University Press, 2002); and Adam Arenson, *The Great Heart of the Republic: St. Louis and the Cultural Civil War* (Cambridge, Mass.: Harvard University Press, 2011). For an evangelical perspective on the meaning of the West, see Jon Gjerde and S. Deborah Kang, *Catholicism and the Shaping of Nineteenth-Century America* (New York: Cambridge University Press, 2012), 96–137.

16. Recent scholarship supersedes older works like Edward Conrad Smith, *The Borderland in the Civil War* (1927; rpt. Freeport, N.Y.: Books for Libraries Press, 1969); and Richard O. Curry, ed., *Radicalism, Racism, and Party Realignment: The Border States During Reconstruction* (Baltimore: Johns Hopkins University Press, 1969). For scholarship on slavery and the border, see Diane Mutti Burke, *On Slavery's Border: Missouri's Small Slaveholding Households, 1815–1865* (Athens: University of Georgia Press, 2010); Stanley Harrold, *Border War: Fighting over Slavery before the Civil War* (Chapel Hill: University of North Carolina Press, 2010); and Matthew Salafia, *Slavery's Borderland: Freedom and Bondage along the Ohio River* (Philadelphia: University of Pennsylvania Press, 2013). For scholarship on the border states during the Civil War, see Christopher Phillips, *The Civil War in the Border South* (Santa Barbara, Calif.: Praeger, 2013) and *The Rivers Ran Backward: The Civil War and the Remaking of the American Middle Border* (New York: Oxford University Press, 2016); William C. Harris, *Lincoln and the Border States: Preserving the Union* (Lawrence: University Press of Kansas, 2011); Aaron Astor, *Rebels on the Border: Civil War, Emancipation, and the Reconstruction of Kentucky and Missouri* (Baton Rouge: Louisiana State University Press, 2012); Jeremy Neely, *The Border Between Them: Violence and Reconciliation on the Kansas-Missouri Line* (Columbia: University of Missouri Press, 2011), and a recent book of essays, Jonathan Earle and Diane Mutti Burke, eds., *Bleeding Kansas, Bleeding Missouri: The Long Civil War on the Border* (Lawrence: University Press of Kansas, 2013).

17. Countless historians have approached the Civil War from the national level. Some examples on the subject of religion and the war include Edward Blum, *Reforging the White Republic*; Harry Stout, *Upon the Altar of the Nation*; Rable, *God's Almost Chosen Peoples*; and Noll, *Civil War as a Theological Crisis*.

18. For Maryland, see Barbara Jeanne Fields, *Slavery and Freedom on the Middle Ground: Maryland during the Nineteenth Century* (New Haven, Conn.: Yale University Press, 1985). On Missouri, see Arenson, *Great Heart of the Republic*; Burke, *On Slavery's Border*; Dennis Boman, *Lincoln and Citizens' Rights in Civil War Missouri* (Baton Rouge: Louisiana State University Press, 2011); and Mark Geiger, *Financial Fraud and Guerrilla Violence in Missouri's Civil War, 1861–1865* (New Haven, Conn.: Yale University Press, 2010). Marcus McArthur has written several pieces on clergy and loyalty in Missouri; see his "Treason in the Pulpit: The

Problem of Apolitical Preaching in Civil War Missouri" *Journal of Church and State* 54 (2011): 545–66; "Sent into a Land of Strangers: The Banishment of the Reverend Berry Hill Spencer," *Missouri Historical Review* 106 (2011): 14–31; and "'There Can Be No Neutral Ground': Samuel B. McPheeters and the Collision of Church and State in St. Louis, 1860–1864," *Journal of Presbyterian History* 89 (2011): 16–26. See also Lucas Volkman, "Houses Divided: Evangelical Schisms, Society, and Law and the Crisis of the Union in Missouri, 1837–1876," PhD diss., University of Missouri, Columbia, 2012. Recent works on Kentucky include Harlow, *Religion, Race, and the Making of Confederate Kentucky*; Patrick Lewis, *For Slavery and Union: Benjamin Buckner and Kentucky Loyalties in the Civil War* (Lexington: University Press of Kentucky, 2015); James Finck, *Divided Loyalties: Kentucky's Struggle for Armed Neutrality in the Civil* War (El Dorado Hills, Calif.: Savas Beatie, 2012); Jacob Lee, "All Men of Decency Ought to Quit the Army: Benjamin F. Buckner, Manhood and Proslavery Unionism in Kentucky," *Register of the Kentucky Historical Society* 107 (2009): 513–50; and "Unionism, Emancipation, and the Origins of Kentucky's Confederate Identity," *Register of the Kentucky Historical Society* 111 (2013): 199–233; Anne Marshall, *Creating a Confederate Kentucky: The Lost Cause and Civil War Memory in a Border State* (Chapel Hill: University of North Carolina Press, 2010).

19. For antebellum violence, see Earle and Burke, eds., *Bleeding Kansas, Bleeding Missouri*; Nicole Etcheson, *Bleeding Kansas: Contested Liberty in the Civil Was Era* (Lawrence: University Press of Kansas, 2004); and Gunja SenGupta, *For God and Mammon: Evangelicals and Entrepreneurs, Masters and Slaves in Territorial Kansas, 1854–1860* (Athens: University of Georgia Press, 1996). See also Michael Fellman, *Inside War: The Guerrilla Conflict in Missouri During the American Civil War* (New York: Oxford University Press, 1989), and Daniel Sutherland, *A Savage Conflict: The Decisive Role of Guerrillas in the American Civil War* (Chapel Hill: University of North Carolina Press, 2009).

20. Porterfield, *Conceived in Doubt*, 113–15.

21. Robert W. Zeuner, "The Appeal to Caesar: A History of the Methodist Church Property Case of 1849," *Methodist History* 8 (1969): 3–16; Lucas Volkman, "Houses Divided," and "Church Property Disputes, Religious Freedom, and the Ordeal of African Methodists in Antebellum St. Louis," *Journal of Law and Religion* 83: 117–19. Legal scholars have considered the problem of church property cases; see "Judicial Intervention in Disputes Over the Use of Church Property," *Harvard Law Review* 75 (1962): 1142–86; Troy Harris, "Neutral Principles of the Law and Church Property in the United States." *Journal of Church and State* 30 (1988): 515–31; Louis Weeks and James C. Hickey, "'Implied Trust' for Connectional Churches: 'Watson v. Jones' Revisited," *Journal of Presbyterian History* 54 (1976): 459–70. The decision in the Walnut Street Church case (*Watson v. Jones* 80 U.S. [13 Wall.] 679 [1871]) stated that courts should not evaluate the legitimacy of a denominational branch, but in reality, there was no way to decide church-property cases in secular courts without conferring some legitimacy on the party that won the case. American courts proved much less reluctant to evaluate the authenticity of religion outside of the Protestant mainstream. For Mormons, see Sarah Barringer Gordon, *The Mormon Question: Polygamy and Constitutional Conflict in Nineteenth Century America* (Chapel Hill: University of North Carolina Press, 2002). For Native American religion, see Tisa Wenger, *We Have a Religion: The 1920s Pueblo Indian Dance Controversy and American Religious Freedom* (Chapel Hill: University of North Carolina Press, 2009).

22. Wesley, *Politics of Faith*, 60–92; Boman, *Lincoln and Citizens' Rights*. For a general discussion of loyalty from the secular perspective, see William A. Blair, *With Malice toward Some: Treason and Loyalty in the Civil War Era* (Chapel Hill: University of North Carolina Press, 2014), and Mark E. Neely Jr., *The Fate of Liberty: Abraham Lincoln and Civil Liberties* (New York: Oxford University Press, 1991); Mark Grimsley, *The Hard Hand of War: Union Military Policy toward Southern Civilians, 1861–1865* (New York: Cambridge University Press, 1997). For the border in particular, see Christopher Phillips, "Federal Occupation and the Politics of Loyalty in Western Border Slave States," in Earle and Burke, eds., *Bleeding Kansas, Bleeding Missouri*, 131–50; and Phillips, *Civil War in the Border South*. See also Matthew Stanley, "'Purely Military Matters': John A. McClernand and Civil Liberties in Cairo, Illinois, in 1861," *Ohio Valley History* 8 (2008): 23–41. Clergy suspected of disloyalty often came into contact with provost marshals, who oversaw civilian life in areas of the border under military control. See Blair, *With Malice toward Some*, 100–127; Stephen Ash, *When the Yankees Came: Conflict and Chaos in the Occupied South, 1861–1865* (Chapel Hill: University of North Carolina Press, 1995). For an account of the workings of a provost marshal's office in an occupied city, see Louis Gerteis, *Civil War St. Louis* (Lawrence: University Press of Kansas, 2001). For loyalty trials in northern churches, see Byron C. Andreason, "As Good a Right to Pray: Copperhead Christians on the Civil War Homefront," PhD diss., University of Illinois at Urbana–Champagne, 1998.

23. Charles Regan Wilson, *Baptized in Blood: The Religion of the Lost Cause, 1865–1920* (Athens: University of Georgia Press, 1980); Gains M. Foster, *Ghosts of the Confederacy: Defeat, the Lost Cause, and the Emergence of the New South, 1865–1913* (New York: Oxford University Press, 1987); Rollin G. Osterweis, *The Myth of the Lost Cause, 1865–1900* (Hamden, Conn.: Archer Books, 1973); and David Goldfield, *Still Fighting the Civil War: The American South and Southern History* (Baton Rouge: Louisiana State University Press, 2002). For a border-state approach, see Marshall, *Creating a Confederate Kentucky*, and Astor, *Rebels on the Border*.

24. David Blight, *Race and Reunion: The Civil War in American Memory* (Cambridge, Mass.: Harvard University Press, 2001), 5. Nina Silber makes a similar argument in *Romance of Reunion: Northerners and the South, 1865–1900* (Chapel Hill: University of North Carolina Press, 1993), 4. See also Alice Fahs and Joan Waugh, eds., *The Memory of the Civil War in American Culture* (Chapel Hill: University of North Carolina Press, 2004). For a religious perspective, see Blum, *Reforging the White Republic*.

25. Caroline Janney challenges the notion of shared forgetting in *Remembering the Civil War: Reunion and the Limits of Reconciliation* (Chapel Hill: University of North Carolina Press, 2013). John Neff locates resistance to reconciliation in practices surrounding memorialization in *Honoring the Civil War Dead: Commemoration and the Problem of Reconciliation* (Lawrence: University Press of Kansas, 2005).

26. In contrast, the Protestant Episcopal Church in the Confederate States of America formed after secession and reunited with Northern Episcopalians just months after the fall of the Confederacy. Most congregationally governed denominations, such as the Disciples of Christ, did not have strong enough national ties to experience a schism in the Civil War era.

27. William E. Montgomery, *Under Their Own Vine and Fig Tree: The African-American*

Church in the South, 1865–1900 (Baton Rouge: Louisiana State University Press, 1993). See also Katherine Dvorak, *African-American Exodus: The Segregation of the Southern Churches* (Brooklyn, N.Y.: Carlson Pub., 1991). Paul Harvey and Daniel Stowell also describe this phenomenon. See Harvey, *Redeeming the South,* 45–76; 107–36; Stowell, *Rebuilding Zion,* 65–99. For a discussion of black church leaders in wartime, see Wesley, *Politics of Faith,* 168–93.

28. Most scholarship on this period of revivals recognizes this. See Nancy Cott, "Young Women in the Second Great Awakening in New England," *Feminist Studies* 3 (1975): 15–29; Mary Ryan, "A Women's Awakening: Evangelical Religion and the Families of Utica, New York, 1800–1840," *American Quarterly* 30 (1978): 602–23.

29. Ann Braude, "Women's History *Is* American Religious History," in Thomas Tweed, ed., *Retelling U.S. Religious History* (Berkeley: University of California Press, 1997), 91.

30. "Religious Intelligence," St. Louis *Christian Advocate,* June 20, 1866.

31. See David Paul Nord, *Faith in Reading: Religious Publishing and the Birth of Mass Media in America* (New York: Oxford University Press, 2004).

32. This is not to say that believers themselves viewed these denominational structures as analogous. Evangelicals consistently emphasized their differences.

33. In 1837, the Presbyterian Church in the United States of America (PCUSA) divided into Old School and New School branches. When the New School divided in 1857, the southern branch became the United Synod of the Presbyterian Church in the United States of America (USPCUSA). Following the 1861 division of the Old School, southerners formed the Presbyterian Church of the Confederate States of America (PCCSA). That year, the USPCUSA became the United Synod of the South (USS) and, in 1864, the USS merged with the PCCSA, retaining the latter name. Following Confederate defeat, the PCCSA became the Presbyterian Church in the United States (PCUS), the name it retained into the late twentieth century. Northern Old and New Schools merged in 1870, again becoming the Presbyterian Church in the United States of America (PCUSA). After the Methodist Episcopal Church (MEC) divided in 1844, the southern branch became the Methodist Episcopal Church, South (MECS), a name it retained until reunion in 1939. Reflecting its claim to be the original Methodist Church, the northern branch continued to use the title "Methodist Episcopal Church" until the twentieth-century merger, at which point both branches reverted to the original name. In the interest of clarity, I have taken the most liberties with the names of Baptist organizations. Before the formation of the Southern Baptist Convention (SBC) in 1845, there was no national Baptist body—individual congregations maintained authority. In order to fund and organize missionary activities, Baptists organized regional associations and societies. The American Baptist Home Mission Society (ABHMS) was founded in 1832 and served as a national agency for organizing and funding domestic missions. With the formation of the SBC, the ABHMS became a de facto northern organization. However, it was not a parallel structure to the SBC, which had its own, separate, Home Mission apparatus. Northern Baptists did not organize along the convention model until 1907, when the Northern Baptist Convention was formed. However, Baptists retained a strong sectional identity for most of the nineteenth century, and I therefore use the terms "Southern Baptists" and "Northern Baptists" to refer to evangelicals who donated primarily to the domestic missionary projects of the SBC (southern) or the ABHMS (essentially northern).

34. Matt. 12:25.

35. Don Fehrenbacher, ed., *Abraham Lincoln: Speeches and Writings, 1832–1858* (New York: Library of America, 1989), 426.

36. Stanton, *Church and the Rebellion*, vii.

CHAPTER ONE

1. Thomas Morris, "An Appeal," Cincinnati *Western Christian Advocate*, May 9, 1834.

2. Stephen Aron, *American Confluence: The Missouri Frontier from Borderland to Border State* (Bloomington: Indiana University Press, 2006), situates the history of the area around the confluence of the Ohio, Missouri, and Mississippi rivers within the context of frontier historiography. See also Stephen Aron, *How the West Was Lost: The Transformation of Kentucky from Daniel Boone to Henry Clay* (Baltimore: Johns Hopkins University Press, 1999). For an approach built around the Ohio River's role as a demarcation between freedom and slavery (and the ambiguity of that boundary), see Salafia, *Slavery's Borderland*. For an economic interpretation, see Gruenwald, *River of Enterprise*. See also Etcheson, *Emerging Midwest*. John Craig Hammond argues that the state was weak in the West, which allowed slavery to flourish despite the antislavery intent of the Northwest Ordinance. See Hammond, *Slavery, Freedom, and Expansion in the Early American West* (Charlottesville: University of Virginia Press, 2007). In contrast, William Bergman argues that the state was a powerful force in developing the western economy. See Bergman, *The American National State and the Early West* (New York: Cambridge University Press, 2012).

3. Salafia, *Slavery's Borderland*, 118. For factors that unified the region, see also Ford, *Bonds of Union*, and Phillips, *Rivers Ran Backward*, 23–76. In contrast, Stanley Harrold emphasizes that the Ohio River "separated distinct societies" (*Border War*, 7).

4. Etcheson, *Emerging Midwest*, 2–10; Gruenwald, *River of Enterprise*, 137; Aron, *American Confluence*, 158–59. Sean Wilentz, "Society, Politics, and the Market Revolution, 1815–1845," in Eric Foner, ed., *The New American History* (Philadelphia: Temple University Press, 1990), 51–71. See also Charles Sellers, *The Market Revolution: Jacksonian America, 1815–1846* (New York: Oxford University Press, 1994), and Michael A. Morrison, *Slavery and the American West: The Eclipse of Manifest Destiny and the Coming of the Civil War* (Chapel Hill: University of North Carolina Press, 1997), 39–65.

5. Etcheson, *Emerging Midwest*, 10.

6. Salafia, *Slavery's Borderland*, 215. For an extensive discussion of western politics and regionalism in the antebellum period, see Phillips, *Rivers Ran Backward*, 15–116. See also Hammond, *Slavery, Freedom, and Expansion*, 7; Gruenwald, *River of Enterprise*, 81, 106–11; Etcheson, *Emerging Midwest*, 27, 42. See also David Waldstreicher, *In the Midst of Perpetual Fetes: The Making of American Nationalism, 1776–1820* (Chapel Hill: University of North Carolina Press, 1997), 269–93. On competition with the East, see Arenson, *Great Heart of the Republic*, 2–3.

7. Etcheson, *Emerging Midwest*, 83; Salafia, *Slavery's Borderland*, 43–55; Aron, *American Confluence*, 179–80; and Hammond, *Slavery, Freedom, and Expansion*, 75.

8. James Rollins to My Dear Son, November 14, 1858, in Christopher Phillips, "The

Crime Against Missouri: Slavery, Kansas, and the Cant of Southernness in the Border West," *Civil War History* 48 (2002): 64.

9. Carwardine, *Evangelicals and Politics*, 1.

10. James H. Moorhead, "Between Progress and Apocalypse: A Reassessment of Millennialism in American Religious Thought, 1800–1880," *Journal of American History* 71 (1984): 531. Johnson, *Redeeming America*, 4–7. Noll, *America's God*, 5, 564–65.

11. Nathan Hatch, "The Puzzle of American Methodism," *Church History* 63 (1994): 187, 178. See also Paul Johnson, *A Shopkeeper's Millennium: Society and Revivals in Rochester, New York, 1815–1837* (New York: Hill and Wang, 1978); Mary Ryan, *Cradle of the Middle Class: The Family in Oneida County, New York, 1790–1865* (New York: Cambridge University Press, 1981); and John Wigger, *Taking Heaven by Storm: Methodism and the Rise of Popular Christianity in America* (New York: Oxford University Press, 1998). For the transformation of theology in the early republic, see Noll, *America's God*, 223–364.

12. Matthews, "The Second Great Awakening as an Organizing Process, 1780–1830: An Hypothesis." *American Quarterly* 21 (1969): 37, 39–40. See also Wigger, *Taking Heaven by Storm*, 190.

13. Hatch, "Puzzle of American Methodism," 3, 178–79.

14. For more on the circuit rider, see Nathan Hatch, *The Democratization of American Christianity* (New Haven, Conn.: Yale University Press, 1989), 81–93; and Wigger, *Taking Heaven by Storm*, 48–79. For the challenges of evangelizing the rural West, see Bridget Ford, "Beyond Cane Ridge: The 'Great Western Revivals' in Louisville and Cincinnati, 1828–1845," *Ohio Valley History* 8 (2008): 17–37.

15. Emory S. Bucke, ed., *The History of American Methodism* (New York: Abingdon Press, 1964), vol. 2: 165; Norwood, *Schism in the Methodist Episcopal Church*, map following 225.

16. Matthew Simpson Diary, April 29, 1852, Matthew Simpson Papers, Library of Congress, Manuscript Division.

17. Theda Skocpol, Marshall Ganz, and Ziad Munson, "A Nation of Organizers: The Institutional Origins of Civic Voluntarism," *American Political Science Review* 94 (2000): 527–46.

18. Baker, "Relations Between Northern and Southern Baptists," 9, 10–12.

19. "General Association of Baptists in Kentucky," October 18, 1845 (Georgetown), *Minutes of the Kentucky Baptist Anniversaries* (Louisville, Ky.: Geo. R. Montsarrat's Steam Power Press, 1845), 14–15.

20. Baker, "Relations Between Northern and Southern Baptists," 12–14. See also Matthews, "Second Great Awakening as an Organizing Process," 37–38.

21. Baker, "Relations Between Northern and Southern Baptists," 15–17. See also Williams, *Isaac Taylor Tichenor*, 2.

22. Lefferts A. Loetscher, *A Brief History of the Presbyterians*, 3rd ed. (Philadelphia: Westminster Press, 1978), 61; Elizabeth Adams, "Divided Church, Divided Nation: The Presbyterian Schism, 1837–1838," *Historian* 54 (1992): 686; Goen, *Broken Churches, Broken Nation*, 49.

23. James Lyon, "General Assembly at Augusta," *Southern Presbyterian Review* 14 (1862): 621.

24. *Minutes of the General Assembly of the Presbyterian Church in the United States of America* [New School] (New York: Presbyterian Publication Committee, 1862), vol. 13: 261.

25. Noll, *America's God*, 293–329.

26. John L. O'Sullivan, "Annexation," *New York Democratic Review*, 1845, in Guétin, *Religious Ideology in American Politics*, 7. See also Morrison, *Slavery and the American West*, 13–38.

27. Louisville *Baptist Banner and Western Pioneer*, June 13, 1844.

28. Society for the Promotion of Collegiate and Theological Education at the West, *First Annual Report* [1843?], in James Findlay, "The SPCTEW and Western Colleges: Religion and Higher Education in Mid–Nineteenth Century America," *History of Education Quarterly* 17 (1977): 34.

29. In contrast, premillennialists believed Christ would arrive before his thousand-year reign and therefore expected material improvement only after Christ's return (Moorhead, "Between Progress and Apocalypse," 532).

30. See Handy, *Christian America*, 27–64; Tuveson, *Redeemer Nation*; Klaus J. Hansen, "The Millennium, the West, and Race in the Antebellum American Mind," *Western Historical Quarterly* 3 (1972): 373–90.

31. The most comprehensive and insightful discussion of antebellum hopes and fears about the West is in Gjerde and Kang, *Catholicism and the Shaping of Nineteenth-Century America*, 96–137.

32. Lyman Beecher, *A Plea for the West* (Cincinnati: Truman and Smith, 1835), 11–12, 56, 65–66. See also Robert Dunner, "A Plea for a *Protestant* American Dream: Lyman Beecher's *A Plea for the West*," *Old Northwest* 16 (1992): 189–97. See also Gjerde and Kang, *Catholicism and the Shaping of Nineteenth-Century America*, 96–137.

33. Gjerde and Kang, *Catholicism and the Shaping of Nineteenth-Century America*, 115–21. R. Laurence Moore, *Religious Outsiders and the Making of Americans* (New York: Oxford University Press, 1986), 25–47.

34. John 17:21; Neander Woods, "Our Redeemer's Prayer for Christian Unity," in *Southern Presbyterian Pulpit: A Collection of Sermons* (Richmond, Va.: Presbyterian Committee of Publication, 1896), 128.

35. "Christian Union," *Baptist Banner and Western Pioneer*, January 16, 1840.

36. For more on America's religious marketplace, see Roger Finke and Rodney Stark, *The Churching of America, 1776–1990: Winners and Losers in our Religious Economy* (New Brunswick, N.J.: Rutgers University Press, 1992).

37. J. M. Wilson to Charles Hodge, October 22, 1845, Charles Hodge Papers, Princeton University, Rare Books and Manuscripts Library.

38. George Brenhoke to Artemas Bullard, December 29, 1841, Artemas Bullard Papers, Presbyterian Historical Society.

39. "The West," Louisville *Baptist Banner and Western Pioneer*, June 8, 1843.

40. George Callanhan, "Annals of Methodism in the West," Cincinnati *Western Christian Advocate*, December 27, 1839.

41. "The East and the West," Louisville *Baptist Banner and Western Pioneer*, June 9, 1842. See also Sam Haselby, *The Origins of American Religious Nationalism* (New York: Oxford University Press, 2015).

42. George Callanhan, "Annals of Methodism in the West," Cincinnati *Western Christian Advocate*, December 27, 1837. Keith Harper, "Downwind from the New England Rat: John

Taylor, Organized Missions, and the Regionalization of Religious Identity on the American Frontier," *Ohio Valley History* 9 (2009): 25–42.

43. W. C. Busch, ""Baptist Convention: The General Convention of Western Baptists: Ministerial Support," *Baptist Banner and Western Pioneer*, June 11, 1840.

44. Robert [Stam] to Peter Goodman Rea, February 16, 1843, Peter Goodman Rea Papers, Western Historical Manuscript Collection, University of Missouri, Columbia.

45. John Waller, "The Editor Rambles," Louisville *Baptist Banner and Western Pioneer*, May 28, 1840.

46. Theodore Agnew, "Methodism on the Frontier," in Bucke, ed., *History of American Methodism* 1: 543.

47. For more on the power of institutions, see Fredrickson, "Coming of the Lord," 111–12. For studies of institutional network building in other periods, see Coffman, *Christian Century*, and Bowler, *Blessed*.

48. Hatch, *Democratization of American Christianity*, 126. See also Nord, *Faith in Reading*, 27–40. For the idea of "regional print cultures," see Barton Price, "*The Central Christian Advocate* and the Quest for a Heartland Identity in American Methodism, 1852–1900," *Methodist History* 50 (2012): 196.

49. *Methodist Magazine*, January 1823, quoted in Hatch, *Democratization of American Christianity*, 125.

50. "An Appeal to the Preachers of the Methodist Episcopal Church," Cincinnati *Western Christian Advocate*, May 9, 1834.

51. Hatch, *Democratization of American Christianity*, 126.

52. William Hunter to Matthew Simpson, April 30, 1847, Matthew Simpson Papers, Library of Congress, Manuscript Division.

53. Hatch, *Democratization of American Christianity*, 141–44.

54. P. F. Phelps to Charles Hodge, June 2, 1836, Charles Hodge Papers, Princeton University, Rare Books and Manuscripts Library.

55. Hatch, *Democratization of American Christianity*, 126.

56. Nord, "Religious Reading and Readers in Antebellum America," *Journal of the Early Republic* 15 (1995): 244; Hatch, *Democratization of American Christianity*, 142. See also Nord, *Faith in Reading*, 89–111.

57. William Cannon, "Education, Publication, Benevolent Work, and Missions," in Bucke, ed., *History of American Methodism* 1: 571.

58. Ibid., 579.

59. Candy Gunther Brown, *The Word in the World: Evangelical Writing, Publishing, and Reading in America* (Chapel Hill: University of North Carolina Press, 2004), 53.

60. "Cincinnati Book Concern," Cincinnati *Western Christian Advocate*, July 15, 1836.

61. Brown, *Word in the World*, 46–65. For more on the financial aspects of such publishing operations, see Nord, *Faith in Reading*, 41–59.

62. James Finley, *Sketches of Western Methodism* (Cincinnati: Methodist Book Concern, 1857), 298; "General Book Concern," Cincinnati *Western Christian Advocate*, June 6, 1834.

63. Editorial, Cincinnati *Western Christian Advocate*, October 23, 1835.

64. Joel R. Lyle to Joel K. Lyle, 8 November 1846, Lyle Family Papers, University of Kentucky.

65. Richard Bushman, *Refinement of America: Persons, Houses, Cities* (New York: Vintage Books, 1992), 313–52. See also Finke and Stark, *Churching of America*; David Hempton, *Methodism: Empire of the Spirit* (New Haven, Conn.: Yale University Press, 2005), 178–201.

66. Lucien W. Berry to Mathew Simpson, November 15, 1845, Mathew Simpson Papers, Library of Congress, Manuscript Division.

67. William McKee Dunn, *Early History of Hanover College* (Madison, Ind.: Courier Co., 1883), 11. Kenneth H. Wheeler, "Higher Education in the Antebellum Ohio Valley: Slavery, Sectionalism, and the Erosion of Regional Identity," *Ohio Valley History* 8 (Spring 2008): 5–8. William Warren Sweet, *Methodism in American History* (New York: Methodist Book Concern, 1933), 208, 212.

68. John Stevens, *Brief Historical Sketch of the Western Baptist Theological Institute* (Cincinnati: Queen City Press, 1850), vol. 2: 4. See also Wheeler, "Higher Education in the Antebellum Ohio Valley," 12–15; and Richard Clossman, "Antebellum Dream of a St. Louis Baptist Minister—'But We Are Now Two Parties,'" *American Baptist Quarterly* 22 (2003): 33–51.

69. Stevens, *Brief Historical Sketch of the Western Baptist Theological Institute*, 8.

70. Ibid., 3.

71. Ibid.

72. Board of Trustees of the Western Baptist Theological Institute, "Reply to 'Brief Historical Sketch of the Western Baptist Theological Institute,' In Covington, Kentucky" (1850), 10.

73. Randall Balmer and John R. Fitzmier, *The Presbyterians* (Westport, Conn.: Greenwood Press, 1993), 46–47.

74. James Moorhead, "The 'Restless Spirit of Radicalism': Old School Fears and the Schism of 1837," *Journal of Presbyterian History* 78 (2000): 31.

75. *Minutes of the General Assembly of the Presbyterian Church in the Confederate States of America* (Augusta, Ga.: Steam Power Press Chronicle and Sentinel, 1863), 261. Woods, "Our Redeemer's Prayer for Christian Unity," 128.

76. Harold M. Parker Jr., *The United Synod of the South: The Southern New School Presbyterian Church* (New York: Greenwood Press, 1988), 73.

77. Moorhead, "Restless Spirit of Radicalism," 19–33. See also Hatch, *Democratization of American Christianity*, 196. Balmer and Fitzmier, *Presbyterians*, 48.

78. Carwardine, *Evangelicals and Politics*, 118.

79. F. R. Gray to Artemas Bullard, January 14, 1841, Artemas Bullard Papers, Presbyterian Historical Society.

80. John Blotchford to Artemas Bullard, April 15, 1841, Artemas Bullard Papers, Presbyterian Historical Society.

81. F. R. Gray to Artemas Bullard, January 14 and March 7, 1841, Artemas Bullard Papers, Presbyterian Historical Society.

82. Moorhead, "Restless Spirit of Radicalism," 29. Leonard Richards argues that the same array of fears motivated anti-abolition mobs during this decade as well. See Richards, *"Gentlemen of Property and Standing": Anti-Abolition Mobs in Jacksonian America* (New York: Oxford University Press, 1970).

83. Breckinridge, quoted in Moorhead, "Restless Spirit of Radicalism," 30.

84. Moorhead, "Restless Spirit of Radicalism," 28.

85. J. L. Frary to Artemas Bullard, August 10, 1838, Artemas Bullard Papers, Presbyterian Historical Society.

86. Etcheson, *Emerging Midwest*, 108–10; Gruenwald, *River of Enterprise*, 142. For antislavery, see Gordon Finnie, "The Antislavery Movement in the Upper South Before 1840," *Journal of Southern History* 35 (1969): 319–42. While Finnie uncovers numerous antislavery activists, most supported gradual emancipation coupled with colonization. See also Harlow, *Religion, Race, and the Making of Confederate Kentucky*, 16–44.

87. Finnie, "Antislavery Movement in the Upper South," 342. See also Salafia, *Slavery's Borderland*, 185–214.

88. For a discussion of the gradual emancipation debates in Kentucky and Missouri, see Smith, *Borderland in the Civil War*, 29–33. For more on Kentucky, see Salafia, *Slavery's Borderland*, 51. For the cotton boom, see Ira Berlin, *Generations of Captivity: A History of African-American Slaves* (Cambridge, Mass.: Harvard University Press, 2003), 161–244; and Adam Rothman, *Slave Country: American Expansion and the Origins of the Deep South* (Cambridge, Mass.: Harvard University Press, 2005).

89. Astor, *Rebels on the Border*, 15–32. For a refutation of the "mildness" argument, see Burke, *On Slavery's Border*. Matthew Salafia argues that the proximity to free labor in the border region actually reinforced the system of slavery and further inscribed racism and white supremacy on both sides of the Ohio River. See Salafia, *Slavery's Borderland*, 118, 162–64. See also Hammond, *Slavery, Freedom, and Expansion*, 6.

90. Ellen Eslinger, "The Evolution of Racial Politics in Early Ohio," in Andrew Cayton and Stewart Hobbs, eds., *The Center of a Great Empire: The Ohio Country in the Early American Republic* (Athens: Ohio University Press, 2005), 86–87. Gruenwald, *River of Enterprise*, 142. See also Richard Lyle Power, *Planting Corn Belt Culture: The Impress of the Upland Southerner and Yankee in the Old Northwest* (Indianapolis: Indiana Historical Society, 1953); and Eric Foner, *Free Soil, Free Labor, Free Men: The Ideology of the Republican Party Before the Civil War* (New York: Oxford University Press, 1995), 57, 286.

91. Ira Berlin, *Many Thousands Gone: The First Two Centuries of Slavery in North America* (Cambridge, Mass.: Harvard University Press, 1998), 228–55.

92. Etcheson, *Emerging Midwest*, 110.

93. Harlow, *Religion, Race, and the Making of Confederate Kentucky*, 45–75. Harlow describes a "unity" between conservative antislavery clergy and proslavery clergy (56).

94. LaRoy Sunderland to Matthew Simpson, June 29, 1836, Matthew Simpson Papers, Library of Congress, Manuscript Collection.

95. "Free-Will Baptists," *Baptist Banner and Western Pioneer*, December 26, 1839.

96. Matthew Simpson (uncle) to Matthew Simpson, September 2, 1841, Matthew Simpson Papers, Library of Congress, Manuscript Division.

97. J. M. Sturtevant to Artemas Bullard, November 30, 1837, Artemas Bullard Papers, Presbyterian Historical Society.

98. William Hunter to Matthew Simpson, 10 March 1838, Matthew Simpson Papers, Library of Congress, Manuscript Division.

99. For the efforts of northern evangelical abolitionists to persuade their denominations to condemn slavery as a sin, see McKivigan, *War against Proslavery Religion*.

100. Bucke, ed., *History of American Methodism* 2: 11–47.

101. Monica Najar, "'Meddling With Emancipation': Baptists, Authority, and the Rift over Slavery in the Upper South," *Journal of the Early Republic* 25 (2005): 157–86.

102. Quoted in Ronald Cedric White, *A. Lincoln: A Biography* (New York: Random House, 2009), 18.

CHAPTER TWO

1. Bucke, ed., *History of American Methodism* 2: 88.

2. Ibid., 89.

3. Henry Bascom to William Wightman, March 11, 1845, Methodist Leaders Collection, Manuscripts and Rare Books Library (hereafter MARBL), Emory University.

4. Henry B. Bascom, *Methodism and Slavery: With Other Matters in Controversy between the North and the South* (Frankfurt, Ky.: Hodges, Todd, and Pruett, 1845), 5–8.

5. Matthew Simpson, May 2–7, 1845, "Journal Commencing March 20th 1844," Matthew Simpson Papers, Library of Congress, Manuscript Division.

6. George Walker, "The Convention of Kentucky Baptists Held at Shelbyville," *Louisville Baptist Banner and Western Pioneer*, June 29, 1845.

7. Matthew Salafia locates the roots of this tendency in "a regional counternarrative that emphasized a tradition of compromise and accommodation" (*Slavery's Borderland*, 215). See also Peter Agnew, "'Methodists, to the Rescue!': Thomas Emerson Bond and Separation from the Methodist Episcopal Church, 1840–1848," *Methodist History* 27 (1989): 133–50; Jennifer L. Weber, *Copperheads: The Rise and Fall of Lincoln's Opponents in the North* (New York: Oxford University Press, 2006), 7, 67; and John R. McKivigan, "The Battle for the Border State Soul: The Slavery Debate in the Churches of the Border Region," *Ohio Valley History* 12 (2012): 48–71.

8. Proslavery Southerners also employed this argument. See Lewis Purifoy, "The Southern Methodist Church and the Proslavery Argument," *Journal of Southern History* 32 (1966): 325–41, and R. Drew Smith, "Slavery, Secession, and Southern Protestant Shifts on the Authority of the State," *Journal of Church and State* 36 (1994): 261–76.

9. Bucke, ed., *History of American Methodism* 2: 13–14, and *Journal of the General Conference of the Methodist Episcopal Church*, 1808.

10. Orange Scott, "Address to the General Conference of the Methodist Episcopal Church by the Rev. O. Scott," 1836. In Bucke, ed., *History of American Methodism* 2: 30.

11. Sweet, *Methodism in American History*, 244.

12. Charles Elliott, *History of the Great Secession from the Methodist Episcopal Church* (Cincinnati: Swormstedt & Poe, 1855), 160.

13. Agnew, "Methodists, to the Rescue!" 139; John McKivigan, "The American Baptist Free Mission Society: Abolitionist Reaction to the 1845 Baptist Schism," *Foundations* 21 (1978): 342.

14. Elliott, *History of the Great Secession*, 230.

15. James Flay to John McClintock, March 1, 1842, John McClintock Papers, MARBL, Emory University.

16. Agnew, "Methodists, to the Rescue!" 133–50.

17. Bucke, ed., *History of American Methodism* 2: 32.

18. James Flay to John McClintock, March 1, 1842, John McClintock Papers, MARBL, Emory University. See also Harlow, *Religion, Race, and the Making of Confederate Kentucky*, 106.

19. Bucke, ed., *History of American Methodism* 2: 39–47. See also Ira Ford McLeister and Roy Stephenson Nicholson, *History of the Wesleyan Methodist Church of America* (Marian, Ind.: Wesleyan Methodist Publishing Association, 1959).

20. Bucke, ed., *History of American Methodism* 2: 84.

21. The case became a central feature of Southern Methodist mythology. Although Andrew was a lifelong slave owner, standard accounts of the 1844 schism cast Andrew as a victim of circumstance who was made an unwilling master through marriage. See Mark Auslander, *The Accidental Slaveowner: Revisiting a Myth of Race and Finding an American Family* (Athens: University of Georgia Press, 2011). See also Elliott, *History of the Great Secession*, 295.

22. Sweet, *Methodism in American History*; Auslander, *Accidental Slaveowner*, 67–97.

23. Carwardine, *Evangelicals and Politics*, 167; Norwood, *Schism in the Methodist Episcopal Church*, 94.

24. John McClintock to Robert Emory, May 16, 1844, John McClintock Papers, MARBL, Emory University.

25. John McClintock to Robert Emory, November 23, 1848, John McClintock Papers, MARBL, Emory University. McClintock, who remained a Northern Methodist and supported the Union in the Civil War, nonetheless contended that slaveholders should be allowed membership in the church. See McClintock's "Slavery" series, published in the *Christian Advocate and Journal* in 1847.

26. "That Old 'Plan,'" Cincinnati *Western Christian Advocate*, June 9, 1869.

27. Sweet, *Methodism in American History*, 250. See also Bucke, ed., *History of American Methodism* 2: 62, and Elliott, *History of the Great Secession*, chap. 23.

28. See Elliott, *History of the Great Secession*, 564; also Bucke, ed., *History of American Methodism* 2: 150.

29. Thomas Asbury Morris to Joshua Soule, July 30, 1845, Joshua Soule Papers, MARBL, Emory University.

30. Elliott, *History of the Great Secession*, 543. See also Norwood, *Schism in the Methodist Episcopal Church*, 102–25.

31. J. K. Hawkins to Jacob Lanius, June 15, 1848, Jacob Lanius Correspondence, Central Methodist Archives.

32. This figure is based on cases reported in newspapers and other published sources. Doubtless the actual numbers are much higher. It is safe to say that Plan of Separation occupied the minds of Northern and Southern Methodists for over a decade. Baptists and Presbyterians experienced conflict in similar numbers.

33. Albert Henry Redford, *The History of Methodism in Kentucky* (Nashville: Southern Methodist Publishing House, 1870), vol. 4: 288.

34. Bucke, ed., *History of American Methodism* 2: 162; Elliott, *History of the Great Secession*, 585–87, 594.

35. Norwood, *Schism in the Methodist Episcopal Church*, 138; Charles Elliott and Leroy

Vernon, *South-Western Methodism: A History of the M.E. Church in the Southwest, from 1844–1864* (Cincinnati: Poe and Hitchcock, 1868), 24; J. T. Peck to Matthew Simpson, September 4, 1844, Matthew Simpson Papers, Library of Congress, Manuscript Division.

36. Basil Manly Jr. to Basil Manly Sr., March 28, 1845, Manly Family Papers, Southern Baptist Historical Library and Archives. See also McKivigan, "The American Baptist Free Mission Society," 240–355.

37. Basil Manly Sr. to Basil Manly Jr., November 27, 1844, Manly Family Papers, Southern Baptist Historical Library and Archives.

38. Stevens, *Brief Historical Sketch of the Western Baptist Theological Institute*, 33.

39. Benjamin Franklin Riley, *A History of the Baptists in the Southern States East of the Mississippi* (Philadelphia: American Baptist Publication Society, 1898), 207.

40. I use the phrase "Northern Baptists" for the sake of clarity. Northern Baptists did not, at this point, have their own convention analogous to the newly formed Southern Baptist Convention.

41. "Taking Sides," Louisville *Baptist Banner and Western Pioneer*, May 22, 1845.

42. Basil Manly Jr. to Basil Manly Sr., April 22, 1845, Manly Family Papers, Southern Baptist Historical Library and Archives.

43. "Report of the Board," October 3, 1848, *Minutes of the General Association of Baptists in Kentucky*, Southern Baptist Historical Library and Archives.

44. See Goen, *Broken Churches, Broken Nation*, and Snay, *Gospel of Disunion*.

45. George Walker, "The Convention of Kentucky Baptists Held at Shelbyville," *Louisville Baptist Banner and Western Pioneer*, June 29, 1845.

46. Carwardine, *Evangelicals and Politics*, 167.

47. J. L. Frary to Artemas Bullard, August 10, 1838, Artemas Bullard Papers, Presbyterian Historical Society.

48. Parker, *United Synod of the South*, 113.

49. A. C. Dickerson to Milton Badger, May 8, 1846; John G. Fee, et al. to Milton Badger, June 27, 1848, both in American Home Mission Society Papers, Library of Congress, Manuscript Division. See also Harlow, *Religion, Race, and the Making of Confederate Kentucky*, 67–70.

50. F. Howe to Artemas Bullard, October 28, 1840; E. A. to Artemas Bullard, October 28, 1840; F. R. Gray to Artemas Bullard, January 30, 1848, Artemas Bullard Papers, Presbyterian Historical Society.

51. Salafia, *Slavery's Borderland*, 241.

52. [J. Hill] to Artemas Bullard, December 8, 1846, Artemas Bullard Papers, Presbyterian Historical Society. See also McKivigan, *War against Proslavery Religion*, 50–55.

53. "Abolitionism—Treason," *Louisville Baptist Banner and Western Pioneer*, December 24, 1846; Crawford Mission Springfield District Quarterly Reports, July 26, 1844, Central Methodist Archives; John Hunt to John McClintock, May 20, 1847, John McClintock Papers, MARBL, Emory University; John G. Fee to Misters Badger and Hall, April 1, 1846, American Home Mission Society Papers, Library of Congress, Manuscript Division.

54. John Waller, "More Southern Benevolent Organizations," *Western Baptist Review* 1 (1845): 12. "The State of the Churches North and South," Louisville *Baptist Banner and West-*

ern Pioneer, October 29, 1846. For more on "conservative antislavery," see Harlow, *Religion, Race, and the Making of Confederate Kentucky*, 45–75.

55. Woods, "Our Redeemer's Prayer for Christian Unity," 128. The biblical reference is to John 17:21.

56. John 18:36

57. William Buck, "The South and the A.&F. Bible Society," Louisville *Baptist Banner and Western Pioneer*, October 29, 1846.

58. William Capers to Bishops Soule and Paine, September 21, 1847. Methodist Leaders Miscellany, MARBL, Emory University.

59. "The Southern Baptist Convention," Louisville *Baptist Banner and Western Pioneer*, June 12, 1845. See also Purifoy, "Southern Methodist Church and the Proslavery Argument," 325–26; Smith, "Slavery, Secession, and Southern Protestants on the Authority of the State," and Walter B. Shurden and Lori Redwine Varnadoe, "The Origins of the Southern Baptist Convention: A Historiographical Study," *Baptist History and Heritage* 37 (2002), 74–75.

60. Daly, *When Slavery Was Called Freedom*, 57–72. Harlow, *Religion, Race, and the Making of Confederate Kentucky*, 56.

61. J. W. Sawyer in Baker, "Relations Between Northern and Southern Baptists," 91.

62. New York *Emancipator*, June 24, 1846, in Baker, "Relations Between Northern and Southern Baptists," 91–92.

63. "North and South," Louisville *Baptist Banner and Western Pioneer*, April 10, 1845.

64. "Baptist Board of Foreign Missions—Slavery—No Division," ibid.

65. Ibid.

66. *Minutes of the Kentucky Baptist Anniversaries, General Association of Baptists in Kentucky*, October 20, 1845, Southern Baptist Historical Society Library and Archives.

67. "The Southern Convention," Louisville *Baptist Banner and Western Pioneer*, March 19, 1846.

68. John Waller, "More Southern Benevolent Organizations, *Western Baptist Review* 1 (1845).

69. "Christian Index—Southern Rights—Bible Views," *Western Baptist Review* 2 (1846).

70. "Annual Report of the Board of Managers," Board of the Kentucky and Foreign Bible Society, General Association of Baptists in Kentucky, October 8, 1845, Southern Baptist Historical Society Library and Archives.

71. John Henderson Spencer, *A History of Kentucky Baptists* (Cincinnati: J. R. Baumer, 1885), vol. 1: 692. See also "Our Relation to the Southern Baptist Convention," Louisville *Western Recorder*, April 18, 1855.

72. Bucke, ed., *History of American Methodism* 2: 99–101.

73. Elliott, *History of the Great Secession*, 510–17.

74. J. T. Peck to Matthew Simpson, September 4, 1844, Matthew Simpson Papers, Manuscript Division, Library of Congress.

75. Thomas E. Bond to Matthew Simpson, August 24, 1844, Matthew Simpson Papers, Manuscript Division, Library of Congress.

76. J. P. Durbin to Matthew Simpson. August 1844, Matthew Simpson Papers, Library of Congress, Manuscript Division.

77. Henry Bascom to William Wightman, August 25, 1844, Methodist Leaders Collection, MARBL, Emory University.

78. John F. Marlay, *The Life of the Reverend Thomas A. Morris, D.D.* (Cincinnati: Hitchcock and Walden, 1875), 207.

79. Horace M. Du Bose, *Life of Joshua Soule* (Nashville: Publishing House of the M.E. Church, South, 1911), 9, 237–38.

80. Thomas Morris to Joshua Soule, July 30, 1845, Joshua Soule Papers, MARBL, Emory University.

81. Ibid.

82. Thomas Morris to Joshua Soule, September 29, 1845, Joshua Soule Papers, MARBL, Emory University.

83. Marlay, *Life of the Reverend Thomas A. Morris*, 230–31.

84. Ibid., 221.

85. Agnew, "Methodists, to the Rescue!" 141; Carwardine, *Evangelicals and Politics*, 164. See also Bucke, ed., *History of American Methodism* 2: 126.

86. Carwardine, *Evangelicals and Politics*, 169.

87. John Hunt to Professor McClintock, May 20, 1847, John McClintock Papers, MARBL, Emory University.

88. "The Damage—Can it be Counteracted? How?" Louisville *Baptist Banner and Western Pioneer*, July 10, 1845.

CHAPTER THREE

1. Lorenzo Waugh, *Autobiography of Lorenzo Waugh* (Oakland, Calif.: Pacific Press, 1883).

2. Lorenzo Waugh, *A Candid Statement of the Course Pursued by the Preachers of the Methodist Episcopal Church South, in Trying to Establish Their New Organization in Missouri* (Cincinnati: J. A. & U. P. James, 1848), 8–9.

3. Waugh, *Candid Statement*, 9, 19, 49.

4. Jonathan K. Hawkins to Jacob Lanius, December 11, 1848, Jacob Lanius Correspondence, Central Methodist Archives.

5. Waugh, *Candid Statement*, 55.

6. Lorenzo Waugh to Matthew Simpson, May 10, 1848, Matthew Simpson Papers, Library of Congress, Manuscript Division.

7. Waugh, *Candid Statement*, 49.

8. See Harlow, *Religion, Race, and the Making of Confederate Kentucky*, 99–113.

9. Waugh, *Candid Statement*, 54, 61.

10. Ibid., 43.

11. Ibid., 61, 55, 59.

12. Elliott, *History of the Great Secession*, 577, 584.

13. M. Jamison to Jacob Lanius, April 29, 1848, Jacob Lanius Correspondence, Central Methodist Archives.

14. William C. Buck to William H. Wyckoff, *Louisville Baptist Banner and Western Pioneer*, August 13, 1846.

15. E. A. Carson to Artemas Bullard, December 11, 1841, Artemas Bullard Papers, Presbyterian Historical Society.

16. F. R. Gray to Artemas Bullard, April 22, 1852, Artemas Bullard Papers, Presbyterian Historical Society.

17. J. K. Hawkins to Jacob Lanius, June 5, 1848, typescript, Jacob Lanius Correspondence, Central Methodist Archives.

18. Elliott, *History of the Great Secession*, 537.

19. Thomas M. Eddy to Matthew Simpson, April 28, 1849, Matthew Simpson Papers, Library of Congress, Manuscript Division.

20. Robert Stam to Peter Goodman Rea, February 16, 1843, Peter Goodman Rea Papers, Western Historical Manuscript Collection, University of Missouri, Columbia. For anti-abolition, see Harrold, *Border War*, 116–37.

21. I. A. Light to Jacob Lanius, January 15, 1850, Jacob Lanius Correspondence, Central Methodist Archives.

22. Waugh, *Candid Statement*, 58.

23. See "Map of the Annual Conferences of the Methodist Episcopal Church as They Were May 1, 1844," in Norwood, *Schism in the Methodist Episcopal Church*, endpaper.

24. Norwood, *Schism in the Methodist Episcopal Church*, 137.

25. Elliott, *History of the Great Secession*, 591, 592.

26. Norwood, *Schism in the Methodist Episcopal Church*, 136.

27. Elliott, *History of the Great Secession*, 592.

28. The southern preacher was either organically produced by the people of Parkersburg (southern account) or hastily sent in from elsewhere by a southern Bishop (northern account.)

29. Matthew Simpson Diary, December 26, 1852, Matthew Simpson Papers, Library of Congress, Manuscript Division.

30. Ibid., December 26–29, 1852.

31. Ibid.

32. M. S. Vaughn to Matthew Simpson, April 14, 1856, Matthew Simpson Papers, Library of Congress, Manuscript Division. See also Norwood, *Schism in the Methodist Episcopal Church*, 135–37; Waugh, *Candid Statement*, 49.

33. Waugh, *Candid Statement*, 40. On conservative antislavery, see Harlow, *Religion, Race, and the Making of Confederate Kentucky*, 76–106. See also David B. Chesebrough, *Clergy Dissent in the Old South, 1830–1865* (Carbondale: Southern Illinois University Press, 1996), 30–49.

34. J. T. Peck to Matthew Simpson, September 4, 1844, Matthew Simpson Papers, Library of Congress, Manuscript Division.

35. B. Mills to Milton Badger, February 8, 1853, American Home Mission Society Papers, Library of Congress, Manuscript Division.

36. Stevens, *Brief Historical Sketch of the Western Baptist Theological Institute*, 62.

37. John G. Fee to Milton Badger, July 3, 1845, American Home Mission Society Papers, Library of Congress, Manuscript Division.

38. Stevens, *Brief Historical Sketch of the Western Baptist Theological Institute*, 8.

39. Ibid., 8, 38. See also Wheeler, "Higher Education in the Antebellum Ohio Valley," 1–22.

40. W. C. James, "A History of the Western Baptist Theological Institute," *Publications of the Kentucky Baptist Historical Society* 1 (1905): 63.

41. "More Southern Benevolent Organizations," *Western Baptist Review* 1 (1845).

42. Stevens, *Brief Historical Sketch of the Western Baptist Theological Institute*, 56.

43. Ibid., 96.

44. "The Western Baptist Theological Institute," *Western Baptist Review* 3 (1848): 419, 421–22.

45. For earlier cases in the border region, see Jeffrey Thomas Perry, "'Courts of Conscience': Local Law, the Baptists, and Church Schism in Kentucky, 1780–1840," *Church History* 84 (2015): 124–58.

46. Porterfield, *Conceived in Doubt*, 113–15.

47. Mark DeWolfe Howe, *The Garden and the Wilderness: Religion and Government in American Constitutional History* (Chicago: University of Chicago Press, 1965), 11. See also Philip Hamburger, *Separation of Church and State* (Cambridge, Mass.: Harvard University Press, 2002), 11, 486–87.

48. 1 Corinthians 6:1–8.

49. H. J. Pease to Matthew Simpson, June 1, 1853, Matthew Simpson Papers, Library of Congress, Manuscript Division.

50. Woods, "Our Redeemer's Prayer for Christian Unity," 128. The reference is to John 17:21.

51. John Waller, "More Southern Benevolent Organizations, *Western Baptist Review* 1 (1845).

52. "Judicial Intervention in Disputes Over the Use of Church Property," 1142–86; Harris, "Neutral Principles of the Law and Church Property in the United States," 515–31. See also Volkman, "Church Property Disputes," 117–19.

53. *Shannon v. Frost*, 42 Ky. (3 B Mon.) 253, 258 (1842).

54. Brown, *Word in the World*, 53; Cannon, "Education" in Bucke, ed., *History of American Methodism* 1: 579.

55. Zeuner, "Appeal to Caesar," 3–16.

56. William Capers to Joshua Soule and Robert Paine, September 21, 1847, Methodist Leaders Miscellany, MARBL, Emory University.

57. Thomas Morris to Joshua Soule, July 30, 1845, Joshua Soule Papers, MARBL, Emory University.

58. Elliott, *History of the Great Secession*, 597–605.

59. Norwood, *Schism in the Methodist Episcopal Church*, 163–64. The New York case was *Bascom v. Lane*, 2 F. Cas. 994 (1851); the Western Concern cases were *Smith v. Swormstedt*, 22 F. Cas. 663 (1852) and 57 U.S. 288 (1853).

60. *Smith v. Swormstedt*, 57 U.S. 288 (1853). See also Norwood, *Schism in the Methodist Episcopal Church*, 169–74.

61. Norwood, *Schism in the Methodist Episcopal Church*, 141.

62. Elliott, *History of the Great Secession*, 592–93; William M. Leftwich, *Martyrdom in Missouri* (St. Louis, Mo.: S.W. Book & Pub. Co., 1870), vol. 1: 181.

63. Sehat, *Myth of American Religious Freedom*, 5; 168–69. For more on Mormons and the courts, see Gordon, *Mormon Question*.

64. *Gibson et al. v. Armstrong*, 46 Ky. 481; 1847 Ky. LEXIS 63; 7B. Mon. 481. See also Norwood, *Schism in the Methodist Episcopal Church*, 143–46. Norwood notes three other, very similar, cases.

65. *Sage, etc. v. Dillard, etc.*, 53 KY340 (1854).

66. William Ellis, *A History of Education in Kentucky* (Lexington: University Press of Kentucky, 2011), 52.

67. "More Southern Benevolent Organizations," *Western Baptist Review* 1 (1845).

68. W. W. Whipple to the Secretaries of the American Home Mission Society, June 12, 1857, American Home Mission Society Papers, Library of Congress, Manuscript Division.

69. J. Hill to D. B. Coe, March 10, 1857, American Home Mission Society Papers, Library of Congress, Manuscript Division.

70. "The Bible Union and the South," *Western Recorder*, March 30, 1853.

71. J. K. Hawkins to Jacob Lanius, June 5, 1848, typescript, Jacob Lanius Correspondence, Central Methodist Archives.

72. John McClintock to Stephen Olin, April 1, 1848, John McClintock Papers, MARBL, Emory University.

73. [Jesse] Boring to Bishop Paine, August 15, 1850, Methodist Leaders Miscellany, MARBL, Emory University.

74. Bishop Capers to Bishops Soule and Paine, September 21, 1847, Methodist Leaders Collection, MARBL, Emory University.

75. Elliott, *History of the Great Secession*, 376, 823.

76. Waugh, *Candid Statement*, 59.

77. Matthew Simpson Diary, May 8, 1845, Matthew Simpson Papers, Library of Congress, Manuscript Division.

78. Louisville *Baptist Banner and Western Pioneer*, June 5, 1845.

79. Baker, "Relations Between Northern and Southern Baptists," 93–95.

80. James C. Anderson, Danville Circuit Quarterly Report, August 19, 1844, Central Methodist Archives. See Norwood, *Schism in the Methodist Episcopal Church*, 100–101.

81. "North and South—The Controversy, How is it Perpetuated?" Louisville *Baptist Banner and Western Pioneer*, March 26, 1846.

CHAPTER FOUR

1. Matthew Simpson, quoted in George R. Crooks, *The Life of Bishop Matthew Simpson of the Methodist Episcopal Church* (New York: Harper & Brothers, 1890), 266, 268.

2. Matthew Simpson to James [Shyker], July 3, 1843, Matthew Simpson Papers, Library of Congress, Manuscript Division.

3. Matthew Simpson, quoted in Crooks, *Life of Matthew Simpson*, 257.

4. David McDonald to Matthew Simpson, January 9, 1851, Matthew Simpson Papers, Library of Congress, Manuscript Division.

5. G. Battells to Mathew Simpson, December 29, 1851, Matthew Simpson Papers, Library of Congress, Manuscript Division.

6. William M. Daily to Matthew Simpson, December 5, 1850, Matthew Simpson Papers, Library of Congress, Manuscript Division.

7. Ibid.

8. Etcheson, *Emerging Midwest*, 109–39. See also Kristin K. Epps, "Before the Border War: Slavery and the Settlement of the Western Frontier, 1825–1845," in Earle and Burke, eds., *Bleeding Kansas, Bleeding Missouri*, 29–46. For a discussion of how the fugitive slave issue divided the region, see Harrold, *Border War*, 138–207. In contrast to Stanley, Matthew Salafia and Bridget Ford emphasize the ways in which the border remained unified during the sectional crisis. See Salafia, *Slavery's Borderland*, and Ford, *Bonds of Union*.

9. For a narrative of the coming of the war from the western perspective, see Morrison, *Slavery and the American West*. For a general political narrative, see David Potter, *The Impending Crisis* (New York: Harper and Row, 1976), and James McPherson, *Battle Cry of Freedom: The Civil War Era* (New York: Oxford University Press, 1988), as well as Elizabeth Varon, *Disunion! The Coming of the American Civil War, 1789–1859* (Chapel Hill: University of North Carolina Press, 2011).

10. Quoted in Morrison, *Slavery and the American West*, 41.

11. Potter, *Impending Crisis*, 90–120. See also Morrison, *Slavery and the American West*, 96–126.

12. "Church Topics in Congress," Louisville *Baptist Banner and Western Pioneer*, July 10, 1850.

13. Ibid.

14. Some historians have also made this case. See Goen, *Broken Churches, Broken Nation*, and Snay, *Gospel of Disunion*.

15. "The Slavery Agitation," Louisville *Western Recorder*, July 30, 1851.

16. "Feeling of the North towards the South," Louisville *Baptist Banner & Western Pioneer*, October 20, 1850.

17. Harrold, *Border War*, 138–58. Wesley, *Politics of Faith*, 17.

18. William M. Daily to Matthew Simpson, December 5, 1850.

19. See Salafia, *Slavery's Borderland*, 228.

20. Morrison, *Slavery and the American West*, 120–23. See also Etcheson, *Bleeding Kansas*. See also SenGupta, *For God and Mammon*.

21. Potter, *Impending Crisis*, 207–24.

22. E. R. Ames to Matthew Simpson, June 24, 1854, Matthew Simpson Papers, Library of Congress, Manuscript Division.

23. Thomas Lamar to Milton Badger, August 28, 1854, American Home Mission Society Papers, Missouri, Library of Congress, Manuscript Division.

24. James Harlan to Matthew Simpson, February 11, 1856, Matthew Simpson Papers, Library of Congress, Manuscript Division.

25. SenGupta, *For God and Mammon*, 41–78. For more on sectionalized ecclesiastical competition in Kansas, see Carwardine, *Evangelicals and Politics*, 245–48; Bucke, ed., *History of American Methodism* 2: 428–33.

26. J. H. Luther to James P. Boyce, January 15, 1857, James P. Boyce Papers, Southern Baptist Theological Seminary Archives. See also Robert S. Duncan, *A History of the Baptists in Missouri* (St. Louis, Mo.: Scammell and Co., 1882), 791.

27. E. Janes to Matthew Simpson, April 12, 1858, Matthew Simpson Papers, Library of Congress, Manuscript Division.

28. J. H. Luther to James P. Boyce, January 15, 1857, James P. Boyce Papers, Southern Baptist Theological Seminary Archives.

29. Nicole Etcheson, "The Great Principle of Self-Government: Popular Sovereignty and Bleeding Kansas," *Kansas History* 27 (2004): 25–29; Etcheson, *Bleeding Kansas*, 6–8; Wesley, *Politics of Faith*, 19; William Warren Sweet, "Some Religious Aspects of the Kansas Struggle," *Journal of Religion* 7 (1927): 578–95.

30. Etcheson, *Bleeding Kansas*, 17–18.

31. W. W. Whipple to "The Rev. Secretaries," September 16, 1856, American Home Mission Society Papers, Missouri, Library of Congress, Manuscript Division.

32. Thomas Lamar to Milton Badger, August 28, 1854, American Home Mission Society Papers, Missouri, Library of Congress, Manuscript Division.

33. Etcheson, *Bleeding Kansas*, 7.

34. Frederick Starr Jr. to "Dear Father," August 1, 1854, Frederick Starr Jr. Papers, Western Historical Manuscript Collection, University of Missouri, Columbia.

35. Frederick Starr Jr. to "My Dear Father," March 19, 1855; Frederick Starr Jr. to "Dear Father and All," October 30, 1854, Frederick Starr Jr. Papers, Western Historical Manuscript Collection, University of Missouri, Columbia.

36. Frederick Starr Jr. to "Dear Father," February 22, 1855, Frederick Starr Jr. Papers, Western Historical Manuscript Collection, University of Missouri, Columbia.

37. Benjamin Stringfellow, quoted in Etcheson, *Bleeding Kansas*, 33. Harlow, *Religion, Race and the Making of Confederate Kentucky*, 76. See also Harrold, *Border War*, 96–97.

38. Harlow, *Religion, Race, and the Making of Confederate Kentucky*, 76.

39. "PUBLIC MEETING!" notice, June 4, 1855, Frederick Starr Jr. Papers, Western Historical Manuscript Collection, University of Missouri, Columbia.

40. "Kansas and Missouri: Mr. Starr's Third Lecture," [New York *Tribune*, 1855], clipping, Frederick Starr Jr. Papers, Western Historical Manuscript Collection, University of Missouri, Columbia. David Magie, *Memorial Sermon of the Late Frederick Starr, Jr.* (Rochester, N.Y., 1867), 15. Frederick Starr Jr. to "Dear Father," February 22, 1855, Frederick Starr Jr. Papers, Western Historical Manuscript Collection, University of Missouri, Columbia.

41. Wesley, *Politics of Faith*, 8–31.

42. J. N. Banks to D. P. Noyes, December 4, 1856, American Home Mission Society Papers–Missouri, Library of Congress, Manuscript Division.

43. See Foner, *Free Soil, Free Labor, Free Men*.

44. Thomas Horace Cleland, "Memorandum Book," November 4, 1856, Thomas Horace Cleland Papers, Filson Historical Society.

45. See Daly, *When Slavery Was Called Freedom*, 111–36. Daly argues that southern clergy played a significant role in creating southern nationalism in the 1850s. See also Snay, *Gospel of Disunion*, 151–209, and Eugene Genovese, *The Slaveholders' Dilemma: Freedom and Progress in Southern Conservative Thought, 1820–1860* (Columbia: University of South Carolina Press, 1992). See also Noll, *Civil War as a Theological Crisis*.

46. "The Baptists on Slavery," Louisville *Western Recorder*, March 3, 1860, reprinted from the *Southwestern Baptist*.

47. McKivigan, *War against Proslavery Religion*, 161–201. Timothy Wesley argues that northern clergy were more politicized and antislavery than McKivigan asserts (*Politics of Faith*, 17–20).

48. Charles Hodge to Henry A. Boardman, December 16, 1860, Charles Hodge Papers, Princeton University, Rare Books and Manuscripts Library.

49. Frederick Brown to Charles Hodge, January 17, 1861, Charles Hodge Papers, Princeton University, Rare Books and Manuscripts Library. See also James J. Gigantino II, "'The Whole North is Not Abolitionized': Slavery's Slow Death in New Jersey, 1830–1860," *Journal of the Early Republic* 34 (2014): 411–37.

50. Parker, *United Synod of the South*, 113.

51. Ibid., 140–42.

52. "Address of Protest [1857]," appendix to Parker, *United Synod of the South*, 309.

53. B. Mills to D. B. Coe, November 5, 1957, American Home Mission Society Papers—Kentucky, Library of Congress, Manuscript Division.

54. W. W. Whipple to "the Rev. Secries. of the A.H.M.S.," September 1857, American Home Mission Society Papers—Missouri, Library of Congress, Manuscript Division.

55. W. W. Whipple to "the Secretaries of the A.H.M.S.," June 12, 1857, American Home Mission Society Papers—Missouri, Library of Congress, Manuscript Division.

56. Quoted in Bucke, ed., *History of American Methodism* 2: 209.

57. *Journal of the General Conference of the Methodist Episcopal Church*, 1840, quoted in Bucke, ed., *History of American Methodism* 2: 21.

58. Ibid., 1860, quoted in Bucke, ed., *History of American Methodism* 2: 209.

59. G. [Battelle] to Matthew Simpson, September 6, 1860, Matthew Simpson Papers, Library of Congress, Manuscript Division. See also Richard Duncan, "Maryland Methodists and the Civil War," *Maryland Historical Magazine* 59 (1964): 351–59.

60. Hy Slicer to Matthew Simpson, November 13, 1860, Matthew Simpson Papers, Library of Congress, Manuscript Division.

61. Bucke, ed., *History of American Methodism* 2: 210.

62. E. P. Phelps to Matthew Simpson, December 19, 1860, Matthew Simpson Papers, Library of Congress, Manuscript Division.

63. Bucke, ed., *History of American Methodism* 2: 210.

64. R. Ricketts to Matthew Simpson, April 17, 1861, Matthew Simpson Papers, Library of Congress, Manuscript Division.

65. J. Lanahan to Matthew Simpson, March 1861, Matthew Simpson Papers, Library of Congress, Manuscript Division.

66. E. P. Phelps to Matthew Simpson, August 23, 1860, Matthew Simpson Papers, Library of Congress, Manuscript Division.

67. Norwood, *Schism in the Methodist Episcopal Church*, 100–101.

68. Bucke, ed., *History of American Methodism* 2: 204–5.

69. McPherson, *Battle Cry of Freedom*, 234–307.

70. Scott, *Visitation of God*, 14–21. McKivigan, *War against Proslavery Religion*, 183–201.

71. Daly, *When Slavery Was Called Freedom*, 131.

72. William Wightman and George Pierce, in Bucke, ed., *History of American Methodism* 2: 230, 234.

73. Isaac T. Tichenor's "Fast Day Sermon," in Williams, *Isaac Taylor Tichenor*, 45.

74. Bucke, ed., *History of American Methodism* 2: 215; 219.

75. Chester Forrester Dunham, *The Attitude of the Northern Clergy Toward the South, 1860–1865* (Toledo, Ohio: Gray Co., 1942), 118.

76. Baker, "Relations Between Northern and Southern Baptists," 166; Dunham, *Attitude of the Northern Clergy Toward the South*, 68.

77. Reprinted in Vander Velde, *Presbyterian Churches and the Federal Union*, 344–45.

78. Moorhead, "Restless Spirit of Radicalism," 31.

79. Gardiner Spring, quoted in Thomas Carey Johnson, "A History of the Southern Presbyterian Church," in *A History of the Methodist Church, South, the United Presbyterian Church, the Cumberland Presbyterian Church, and the Presbyterian Church, South in the United States* (New York, 1894), vol. 11: 326, 327–28. Harlow, *Religion, Race, and the Making of Confederate Kentucky*, 144–47.

80. Charles Hodge, quoted in Johnson, "History of the Southern Presbyterian Church," vol. 9: 329.

81. Adger, "General Assembly of 1861," 297.

82. James Lyon, "The General Assembly of the Presbyterian Church in the Confederate States of America," *Southern Presbyterian Review* 14 (1862): 619.

83. Will Gilliam Jr., "Robert J. Breckinridge: Kentucky Unionist," *Register of the Kentucky Historical Society* 69 (1971): 362–85.

84. Thomas Carey Johnson, *The Life and Letters of Benjamin Morgan Palmer* (1906; reprint, Edinburgh, Scotland: Banner of Truth Trust, 1987), 246.

85. PCCSA (South), *Minutes*, 1861, 5.

86. Ibid., 54.

87. McKivigan, *War against Proslavery Religion*, 185. See also Scott, *Visitation of God*, 161.

CHAPTER FIVE

1. John M. Buck, "Freedom of Religion in Baltimore—The Interference of the Military with Church Worship—Tart Correspondence with General Schenck by the Recording Steward" [*Baltimore Gazette* February 1863], Scrapbook 1, Stuart Robinson Papers, Filson Historical Society.

2. Ibid.

3. Stuart Robinson, "Church and State," Louisville *True Presbyterian*, July 24, 1862; Robinson, "Indications of Public Opinion in the Church," Louisville *True Presbyterian*, May 12, 1864; Robinson, "War in the Ecclesiastico-Military Councils of the Administration," Louisville *True Presbyterian*, March 17, 1864.

4. "Juntus," "New York Correspondence," *Western Recorder*, February 4, 1860.

5. Abraham Lincoln, "Message to Congress in Special Session," July 4, 1861, in Fehrenbacher, ed., *Abraham Lincoln: Speeches and Writings*, 252. Christopher Phillips argues that Confederate officials also "regarded neutrality as disloyalty" (*Rivers Ran Backward*, 13).

6. William Gienapp, "Abraham Lincoln and the Border States," *Journal of the Abraham Lincoln Association* 13 (1992): 13–46.

7. Statistics from 1860 Census, in W. M. Brewer, "Lincoln and the Border States," *Journal of Negro History* 34 (1949): 46–72. See also Harris, *Lincoln and the Border States*, 2–8,

8. Abraham Lincoln to Orville Browning, September 22, 1861, in Gienapp, "Abraham Lincoln and the Border States," 15.

9. Ash, *When the Yankees Came*, x. For an overview of border-state politics in the Civil War, see Harris, *Lincoln and the Border States*, 42–158. For Missouri and Kentucky, see Astor, *Rebels on the Border*, 75–93. For Maryland, see Harris, *Lincoln and the Border States*, 42–79, and Neely, *Fate of Liberty*, 4. In Missouri, early violence polarized Unionists and secessionists, setting the stage for a protracted guerrilla war. See Harris, *Lincoln and the Border States*, 119–58; Gerteis, *Civil War St. Louis*, 5. For more on guerrilla warfare in Missouri, see Fellman, *Inside War*. Kentucky positioned itself as neutral in 1861, but a Confederate foray into the state finally prompted Union occupation in September of 1861, and Kentucky declared for the Union. See Harris, *Lincoln and the Border States*, 80–118; Thomas C. Mackey, "Not a Pariah, but a Keystone: Kentucky and Secession," in Kent T. Dollar, Larry H. Whiteaker, and W. Calvin Dickinson, eds., *Sister States, Enemy States: The Civil War in Kentucky and Tennessee* (Lexington: University Press of Kentucky, 2009), 33.

10. Blair, *With Malice toward Some*, 201–33. Scholars agree that the existence of treason, particularly in the North, was wildly exaggerated. See Frank L. Klement, *Dark Lanterns: Secret Political Societies, Conspiracies, and Treason Trials in the Civil War* (Baton Rouge: Louisiana State University Press, 1984), and Weber, *Copperheads*. See also Neely, *Fate of Liberty*, 26; and Andreason, "As Good a Right to Pray."

11. Weber, *Copperheads*, 27. For a general discussion of clergy and loyalty, see Wesley, *Politics of Faith*, 43–92.

12. James Todd to Miss Mary Wallace, May 14, 1862, Edmund T. Halsey Papers, Filson Historical Society. For the variety of ways in which clergy positioned themselves in relationship to Civil War politics, see Wesley, *Politics of Faith*, 93–121. For the political views of "proslavery Unionists" in Kentucky, see Harlow, *Religion, Race, and the Making of Confederate Kentucky*, 108–33.

13. Samuel Haycraft Journal, September 27, 1863, Transcribed Journal of Samuel Haycraft Jr., Filson Historical Society. W. H. Green to Charles Manly, January 24, 1861, Manly Family Papers, Southern Baptist Historical Library and Archives.

14. R. Ricketts to Matthew Simpson, March 19, 1861, Matthew Simpson Papers, Library of Congress, Manuscript Division.

15. Edwin Carter to Charles Hodge, January 29, 1861, Charles Hodge Papers, Princeton University, Rare Books and Manuscripts Library.

16. Bucke, ed., *History of American Methodism* 2: 207.

17. Blair, *With Malice toward Some*, 11–127; Ash, *When the Yankees Came*, 83–90. See also Phillips, *Civil War in the Border South*, 31–39; Neely, *Fate of Liberty*, 39; Harold Melvin Hyman, *Era of the Oath: Northern Loyalty Tests During the Civil War and Reconstruction* (Philadelphia: University of Pennsylvania Press, 1954), 13–14.

18. Hyman, *Era of the Oath*, introduction, 4, 2. William Blair argues that the preoccupation with loyalty extended into the Reconstruction era (*With Malice toward Some*, 234–67).

19. For the secular politics of loyalty on the border, see Christopher Phillips, "'A Question of Power Not One of Law': Federal Occupation and the Politics of Loyalty in the Western Border Slave States during the American Civil War," in Earle and Burke, eds., *Bleeding Kansas, Bleeding Missouri*, 131–50.

20. Berry Hill Spencer to A. G. Stewart, April 22, 1863, Berry Hill Spencer Correspondence, Missouri Historical Society.

21. Beriah Magoffin, "Open Letter to the Kentucky House of Representatives," March 8, 1862, clipping, Stuart Robinson Scrapbook 1, Stuart Robinson Papers, Filson Historical Society.

22. J. W. Hoover to Matthew Simpson, April 22, 1864, Matthew Simpson Papers, Library of Congress, Manuscript Division.

23. Henry R. Keeton memoir, manuscript, January 28, 1880, Western Historical Manuscript Collection, University of Missouri, Columbia.

24. Ibid.

25. "Disloyalty in the Church: The Mount Pleasant Church Case in and out of the Church Courts," *Danville Quarterly Review*, March 1864, 128.

26. Ibid., 142.

27. Ibid., 144.

28. "The Case of Mr. Morrison and his Provost Marshal before the Assembly," Louisville *True Presbyterian*, June 2, 1864.

29. Leftwich, *Martyrdom in Missouri* 1: 184–92. Southern Methodists regained possession after the war. Leftwich compiled his volume in defense of southern churches from newspaper clippings and personal letters. See chapter 8 of the current volume for further discussion. Statement of William F. Sexson, January 28, 1863, and Statement of George W. Neville, January 29, 1863, Missouri Union Provost Marshal Papers, 1861–66, Missouri Digital Heritage, s1.sos.mo.gov/records/archives/archivesdb/provost/.

30. "Religious Intelligence," St. Louis *Christian Advocate*, June 20, 1866.

31. Quoted in Vander Velde, *Presbyterian Churches and the Federal Union*, 296.

32. "Allegheny City Presbytery and Rev. Dr. Plumer," Louisville *True Presbyterian*, July 24, 1862. See also Vander Velde, *Presbyterian Churches and the Federal Union*, 298–300.

33. Gerteis, *Civil War St. Louis*, 184. See also George M. Apperson, "Presbyterians and Radical Republicans: President Lincoln, Dr. McPheeters, and the Civil War in Missouri," *American Presbyterians* 73 (1995): 239–50.

34. N. Ramney to "Hon. Chs. Gibson assistant Adjt. Genl. U.S.," February 24, 1863, Charles Gibson Papers, Missouri Historical Society.

35. See Blair, *With Malice toward Some*; Phillips, *Civil War in the Border South*, 37–40; Hyman, *Era of the Oath*, 36; 13–14. See also Neely, *Fate of Liberty*, 39.

36. The House committee was known as the Potter Committee. Blair, *With Malice toward Some*, 50–51. Hyman, *Era of the Oath*, 5.

37. Jonathan Palmer Finley Diaries, December 25, 1861, Presbyterian Historical Society.

38. Leftwich, *Martyrdom in Missouri* 2: 129.

39. William M. Pratt Diary, vols. 2 and 3, William M. Pratt Papers, University of Kentucky, Special Collections, Manuscripts.

40. U.S. War Department, *Official Records of the Union and Confederate Armies*, ser. 1, vol. 34, chap. 46: 348–50.

41. "Gen. Rosecrans and the Protestant Church Courts Under Surveillance of a Military Papist," Louisville *Free Presbyterian*, March 31, 1864.

42. See Vander Velde, *Presbyterian Churches and the Federal Union*, 215–16; Milan Kedro,

"The Civil War's Effect upon an Urban Church: The St. Louis Presbytery under Martial Law," *Missouri Historical Society Bulletin* 27 (1971): 187–88.

43. General William Rosecrans in Vander Velde, *Presbyterian Churches and the Federal Union*, 214.

44. Joseph A. Lewis to Jonathan B. Fuller, March 13, 1864, Jonathan B. Fuller Papers, Western Historical Manuscript Collection, University of Missouri, Kansas City.

45. Matt. 5:34. See also James 5:12, "But above all things, my brethren, swear not."

46. "The Test Oath Just Two Hundred Years Ago," Louisville *True Presbyterian*, April 24, 1862.

47. Beriah Magoffin, "Open Letter to the Kentucky House of Representatives," March 8, 1862, clipping, Stuart Robinson Scrapbook 1, Stuart Robinson Papers, Filson Historical Society.

48. John M. Buck, "Freedom of Religion in Baltimore—The Interference of the Military with Church Worship—Tart Correspondence with General Schenck by the Recording Steward," [Baltimore *Gazette*, February 1863.] Scrapbook 1, Stuart Robinson Papers, Filson Historical Society.

49. Reproduced in Leftwich, *Martyrdom in Missouri* 1: 339.

50. Leftwich, *Martyrdom in Missouri* 1: 290–91.

51. Ibid., 293.

52. Ibid., 309–10.

53. General William Rosecrans in Vander Velde, *Presbyterian Churches and the Federal Union*, 214.

54. "Gen. Rosecrans and the Protestant Church Courts Under Surveillance of a Military Papist," Louisville *Free Presbyterian*, March 31, 1864. Ralph Stackpole was a fictional type known for making boasting, hyperbolic, and ignorant speeches. See Liz Hutter, "Ho for Salt River!" *Common Place* 7 (2007), www.common-place.org/vol-07/no-3/hutter/.

55. Reproduced in Leftwich, *Martyrdom in Missouri* 1: 337–38.

56. Vander Velde, *Presbyterian Churches and the Federal Union*, 120–24.

57. Andrew Monroe, "Fasting and Prayer," St. Louis *Christian Advocate*, June 13, 1861.

58. Waldstreicher, *In the Midst of Perpetual Fetes*, 22, 145–48; Richard J. Janet, "Prayer and Politics: General Fasts in the Early American Republic," *Mid-America* 67 (1985): 97–107.

59. In Leftwich, *Martyrdom in Missouri* 1: 336.

60. "The Alexandria Arrest," reprint of "Alexandria Virginia Episcopalians to Abraham Lincoln," *Daily Enquirer*, clipping, February 19, 1862, Stuart Robinson Papers, Filson Historical Society. See also John A. Marshall, *American Bastille: A History of the Arbitrary Arrests and Imprisonment of American Citizens in the Northern and Border States, On Account of Their Political Opinions, During the Late Civil War* (Philadelphia: T. W. Hartley & Co., 1884), 92–96.

61. Quoted in Leftwich, *Martyrdom in Missouri* 1: 382, 385.

62. "The 'Presbyterian' and the Ninety-Six Southern Ministers' Appeal for Peace," Louisville *True Presbyterian*, July 30, 1863.

63. Jonathan B. Fuller to "Dear Father," June 20, 1864, Jonathan B. Fuller Papers, Western Historical Manuscript Collection, University of Missouri, Kansas City.

64. Ibid., July 18, 1864.

65. Jonathan Palmer Finley Diaries, July 1, 1861, Presbyterian Historical Society.

66. Leftwich, *Martyrdom in Missouri* 1: 126.

67. Sehat, *Myth of American Religious Freedom,* 13–50; Howe, *Garden and the Wilderness,* 11. Hamburger, *Separation of Church and State,* 486–87.

68. In Graham, *Kingdom Not of This World,* 58.

69. Ibid., 57. Marshall, *American Bastille,* 487–500. See also Gerteis, *Civil War St. Louis,* 179–80.

70. Berry Hill Spencer, Oath of Allegiance, Lincoln County, Missouri; Berry Hill Spencer to "My dear Wife," February 5, 1863, Berry Hill Spencer Correspondence, Missouri Historical Society. See also McArthur, "Sent into a Land of Strangers," 14–31.

71. General Merrill to "Provost Marshal or commanding officer," January 13, 1863, Berry Hill Spencer Correspondence, Missouri Historical Society.

72. Berry Hill Spencer Account Book, Berry Hill Spencer Correspondence, Missouri Historical Society.

73. Berry Hill Spencer to Carrie Spencer, February 5, 1863, Berry Hill Spencer Correspondence, Missouri Historical Society.

74. Leftwich, *Martyrdom in Missouri* 1: 397.

75. Berry Hill Spencer to Carrie Spencer, March 7, 1863, Berry Hill Spencer Correspondence, Missouri Historical Society.

76. Berry Hill Spencer to Carrie Spencer, July 10, 1863, Berry Hill Spencer Correspondence, Missouri Historical Society. Andreason, "As Good a Right to Pray." See also Byron C. Andreason, "Proscribed Preachers, New Churches: Civil Wars in the Illinois Protestant Churches During the Civil War," *Civil War History* 44 (1998): 194–211, and Byron C. Andreason, "Civil War Church Trials: Repressing Dissent on the Northern Home Front," in *An Uncommon Time: The Civil War and the Northern Home Front*, ed. Paul A. Cimbala and Randall M. Miller (New York: Fordham University Press, 2002), 214–42.

77. Berry Hill Spencer to Carrie Spencer, March 21, 1863, Berry Hill Spencer Correspondence, Missouri Historical Society.

78. See Klement, *Dark Lanterns.* See also Weber, *Copperheads.*

79. "Special Order No. 97," September 16, 1863, Berry Hill Spencer Correspondence, Missouri Historical Society.

80. Statement of Beliefs, [1865], Berry Hill Spencer Correspondence, Missouri Historical Society.

81. Quoted in Leftwich, *Martyrdom in Missouri* 1: 403.

82. Hubbard Kavanaugh to Berry Hill Spencer, February 27, 1863, Berry Hill Spencer Correspondence, Missouri Historical Society.

83. Several historians have written detailed accounts of the McPheeters saga, although most uncritically condemn Union actions in the case. My account draws from these sources as well as from primary material. See Vander Velde, *Presbyterian Churches and the Federal Union,* 305–24. See also Apperson, "Presbyterians and Radical Republicans," 239–50, and Graham, *Kingdom Not of This World,* 64–89. An updated overview can be found in Gerteis, *Civil War St. Louis,* 182–86.

84. Quoted in Graham, *Kingdom Not of This World,* 72.

85. "North Missouri," "The General Assembly—Drs. Breckinridge and Robinson—The

Memorial from Missouri—The Three St. Louis Pastors—The Deliverance on Loyalty," Louisville *True Presbyterian*, July 3, 1862.

86. Apperson, "Presbyterians and Radical Republicans," 246.

87. Quoted in Graham, *Kingdom Not of This World*, 75.

88. The entire order is printed in "State vs. Church," Louisville *True Presbyterian*, February 26, 1863.

89. "State vs. Church," Louisville *True Presbyterian*, February 26, 1863. Gerteis, *Civil War St. Louis*, 184.

90. Vander Velde, *Presbyterian Churches and the Federal Union*, 313–14. Gerteis, *Civil War St. Louis*, 1, 77.

91. Abraham Lincoln to Samuel R. Curtis, January 2, 1863, Fehrenbacher, ed., *Abraham Lincoln: Speeches and Writings*, 426–27.

92. For an example, see Apperson, "Presbyterians and Radical Republicans," 239–50. See also Rable, *God's Almost Chosen Peoples*, 321–22, and Stout, *Upon the Altar of the Nation*, 388.

93. Recently William Blair has recognized that "subordinates completely ignored the president's guidelines for church affairs" (*With Malice toward Some*, 142).

94. N. Ramney to Charles Gibson, February 24, 1863, Charles Gibson Papers, Missouri Historical Society.

95. Vander Velde, *Presbyterian Churches and the Federal Union*, 316–19.

96. Ibid., 323.

CHAPTER SIX

1. The United States Christian Commission (USCC) was a voluntary, nongovernmental soldier's aid society that provided religious and material support to Union soldiers. See Drew Gilpin Faust, *This Republic of Suffering: Death and the American Civil War* (New York: Vintage Books, 2009), 107–11. McKendree Church Trustees to Andrew Johnson, December 31, 1864, in LeRoy P. Graf, ed., *The Papers of Andrew Johnson, Volume 7, 1864–1865* (Knoxville: University of Tennessee Press, 1986), 369–70.

2. M. J. Cramer to Matthew Simpson, March 11, 1864, Matthew Simpson Papers, Library of Congress, Manuscript Division. A brief biography of Cramer can be found in *Christian Work Illustrated Family Newsletter*, February 3, 1898, 171.

3. Stowell, *Rebuilding Zion*, 49. See also Moorhead, *American Apocalypse*; George C. Rable, *God's Almost Chosen Peoples*, 370–87. Scott, *Visitation of God*; Stout, *Upon the Altar of the Nation*.

4. *Minutes of the General Assembly of the Presbyterian Church in the United States of America* [New School] (New York: Presbyterian Publication Committee, 1865), vol. 14: 39.

5. See Stowell, *Rebuilding Zion*, 49–64. See also Blum, *Reforging the White Republic*, 40.

6. Stuart Robinson, "The Guillotine Prepared for Kentucky," Louisville *True Presbyterian*, April 14, 1864.

7. Rable, *God's Almost Chosen Peoples*, 374–76; Stowell, *Rebuilding Zion*, 49–64. See also Blum, *Reforging the White Republic*, 20–86.

8. *Minutes of the General Assembly of the Presbyterian Church in the United States of America* [New School] (New York: Presbyterian Publication Committee, 1865), vol. 14: 37.

9. J. M. Pendleton, Home Mission Society Annual Report, 1865, in Baker, "Relations Between Northern and Southern Baptists," 103.

10. R. H. Allen to A. T. McGill, November 7, 1865, Alexander Taggart McGill Papers, Presbyterian Historical Society.

11. Quoted in Morrow, *Northern Methodism and Reconstruction*, 69.

12. Edward Blum, "'The First Secessionist Was Satan': Secession and the Religious Politics of Evil in Civil War America," *Civil War History* 60 (2014): 234–69.

13. "Slavery in the Church Courts," *Danville Quarterly Review*, December 1864, 516.

14. Stowell, *Rebuilding Zion*, 53.

15. S. Reed to Matthew Simpson, November 23, 1863, Matthew Simpson Papers, Library of Congress, Manuscript Division.

16. "Spirit of the Southern Methodist Press," *Methodist Quarterly Review*, January 1866, 124.

17. Baker, "Relations Between Northern and Southern Baptists," 99–106.

18. Ignatius Few to William Wightman, June 29, 1844, Methodist Leaders Miscellany, MARBL, Emory University.

19. "Union," *Missouri Baptist Journal*, February 18, 1867. The quoted section was drawn from an article in the *Missouri Methodist*.

20. "An Able Speech: Rev. Dr. Humphrey's Address," Louisville *Daily Courier*, July 13, 1866.

21. "Neglect of the Sanctuary," *Missouri Baptist Journal*, January 15, 1866. See also Stowell, *Rebuilding Zion*, 100–113.

22. "Jottings from the Assembly," Louisville *True Presbyterian*, June 2, 1864.

23. "A Letter from the General Assembly," Louisville *True Presbyterian*, June 2, 1864.

24. Beriah Magoffin, "Open Letter to the Kentucky House of Representatives," March 8, 1862, Scrapbook 1, Stuart Robinson Papers, Filson Historical Society.

25. PCUSA (Old School, North), *Minutes*, 1865, 560.

26. A. M. Donnan to A. T. McGill, May 16, 1865, Alexander Taggert McGill Papers, Presbyterian Historical Society.

27. "Union of Churches North and South," *Baptist Monthly* 1 (1865): 129–37. See also Stowell, *Rebuilding Zion*, 40; Rable, *God's Almost Chosen Peoples*, and Wilson, *Baptized in Blood*.

28. R. Paine and H. N. McTyeire, "To the Bishops of the Methodist Episcopal Church," Cincinnati *Western Christian Advocate*, May 19, 1869.

29. PCUS (South), *Minutes*, 1865, 384.

30. Stowell, *Rebuilding Zion*, 106.

31. "The General Assembly of 1865," *Southern Presbyterian Review*, March 1866, 77, 76, 78.

32. H. H. Kavanaugh to Joshua Soule, May 24, 1865, Joshua Soule Papers, MARBL, Emory University.

33. Geo. F. Pierce, H. N. McTyeire, C. M. Lee, and J. E. Evans, "To the Conferences of the Meth. Prot. Church," May 11, 1867, Methodist Leaders Miscellany, MARBL, Emory University.

34. "Change of Name," *Missouri Baptist Journal*, October 8, 1866.

35. Stowell, *Rebuilding Zion*, 106.

36. Hamburger, *Separation of Church and State,* 486–87. See also Howe, *Garden and the Wilderness,* 11. See also Sehat, *Myth of American Religious Freedom,* 31–50.

37. Baker, "Relations Between Northern and Southern Baptists," 91–92.

38. "The Presbyterian's Correspondent in South-Western Kentucky," Louisville *True Presbyterian,* March 31, 1864.

39. "Spiritual Ruin," *Missouri Baptist Journal,* February 19, 1866.

40. Stuart Robinson, "To The Presbyterian People of Kentucky," pamphlet [1865], Filson Historical Society.

41. Astor, *Rebels on the Border,* 4. See also Lee, "Unionism, Emancipation, and the Origins of Kentucky's Confederate Identity," 199–233; Jacob Lee, "'Between Two Fires': Cassius M. Clay, Slavery, and Antislavery in the Kentucky Borderlands," *Ohio Valley History* 6 (2006): 50–70; Marshall, *Creating a Confederate Kentucky.*

42. Eric Foner, *Reconstruction: America's Unfinished Revolution, 1863–1877* (New York: Harper and Row, 1988), 37. See also Willie Lee Rose, *Rehearsal for Reconstruction: The Port Royal Experiment* (Indianapolis, Ind.: Bobbs-Merrill, 1964), and LaWanda Cox, *Lincoln and Black Freedom* (Columbia: University of South Carolina Press, 1981).

43. For more on church confiscation, see Ash, *When the Yankees Came,* 89–90.

44. Michael J. Cramer to Matthew Simpson, April 22, 1864, Matthew Simpson Papers, Library of Congress, Manuscript Division.

45. Wesley, *Politics of Faith,* 64–82; 142–47. See also Blair, *With Malice toward Some,* 141–43; and Ash, *When the Yankees Came,* 89.

46. Edwin Harlow to Milton Badger, July 1, 1865, American Home Mission Society Papers, Library of Congress, Manuscript Division.

47. Bucke, ed., *History of American Methodism* 2: 249.

48. U.S. War Department, *Official Records of the Union and Confederate Armies,* ser. 1, vol. 34, chap. 36: 311.

49. Baker, "Relations Between Northern and Southern Baptists," 95.

50. Vander Velde, *Presbyterian Churches and the Federal Union,* 459.

51. Michael Cramer to Matthew Simpson, March 19, 1864, Matthew Simpson Papers, Library of Congress, Manuscript Division.

52. Ibid., April 22, 1864.

53. Ibid., April 2, 1864.

54. Ibid., April 6, 1864.

55. Ibid., March 18, 1864.

56. Ibid., May 3, 1864.

57. Ibid., June 20, 1864. Graf, ed., *Papers of Andrew Johnson* 7: 369–70; 8: 72, 605.

58. Martha Kohl, "Enforcing a Vision of Community: The Role of the Test Oath in Missouri's Reconstruction," *Civil War History* 40 (1994): 292. See also Blair, *With Malice toward Some,* 271–72.

59. Thomas Barclay, "The Test Oath for the Clergy in Missouri," *Missouri Historical Review* 18 (1924): 346.

60. [Jonas Reston] to Milton Badger, October 6, 1863, American Home Mission Society Papers, Library of Congress, Manuscript Division.

61. Caroline Moss to "Sister Theo," April 18, 1865, Caroline O. P. Moss Diary, Partee Center, William Jewell College.

62. Vindex, "The True Position," reprinted in *Missouri Baptist Journal*, May 21, 1866.

63. John E. Godby, draft of unpublished autobiography, "Godby's Light and Shadows," c. 1880, Central Methodist Biography File, Central Methodist Archives.

64. J. A. Paige to A. T. McGill, May 10, 1866, Alexander T. McGill Papers, Presbyterian Historical Society.

65. "A Record," *Missouri Baptist Journal*, May 21, 1866.

66. Barclay, "Test Oath for the Clergy in Missouri," 365.

67. D. B. Purinton, "American Home Mission Society Annual Report," 1863, quoted in Baker, "Relations Between Northern and Southern Baptists," 281. Stowell, *Rebuilding Zion*, 55–58. See also Baker, "Relations Between Northern and Southern Baptists," 99–121, and Morrow, *Northern Methodism and Reconstruction*, 96–105.

68. James Mitchell to Matthew Simpson, July 15, 1867, Matthew Simpson Papers, Library of Congress, Manuscript Division.

69. James Lynch to Matthew Simpson, December 3, 1868, Matthew Simpson Papers, Library of Congress, Manuscript Division.

70. Sweet, *Methodism in American History*, 279, 310. In 1861, there was a total of 11,000 Northern Methodists in Kentucky and Missouri. See Morrow, *Northern Methodism and Reconstruction*, 29.

71. Bucke, ed., *History of American Methodism* 2: 261.

72. Ibid., 250.

73. Morrow, *Northern Methodism and Reconstruction*, 42.

74. Joseph Jones to Matthew Simpson, July 22, 1864, Matthew Simpson Papers, Library of Congress, Manuscript Division..

75. Morrow, *Northern Methodism and Reconstruction*, 43.

76. S. Colman to Matthew Simpson, February 1, 1864, Matthew Simpson Papers, Library of Congress, Manuscript Division.

77. S. C. Alexander to Charles Hodge, August 29, 1866, Charles Hodge Papers, Princeton University, Rare Books and Manuscripts Library. See also Joe M. Richardson, *Christian Reconstruction: The American Missionary Association and Southern Blacks, 1861–1890* (Athens: University of Georgia Press, 1986); Blum, *Reforging the White Republic*, 51–86; and Judkin Browning, "'Bringing Light to Our Land . . . When She Was Dark as Night': Northerners, Freedpeople, and Education during Military Occupation in North Carolina, 1862–1865," *American Nineteenth Century History* 9 (2008): 1–17.

78. For more on the formation of independent black denominations in the postwar South, see Montgomery, *Under Their Own Vine and Fig Tree*. See also Blum, *Reforging the White Republic*, and Harvey, *Redeeming the South*.

79. Michael J. Cramer to Matthew Simpson, March 18, 1864, Matthew Simpson Papers, Library of Congress, Manuscript Division.

80. "S——. S——.," "A New Conspiracy, Ecclesiastical," Louisville *True Presbyterian*, September 15, 1864.

81. "The American Board of Missions: Its Patriotism, Protest, and Pronunciamento," Louisville *True Presbyterian*, November 10, 1864.

82. Caroline Moss to William C. Ligon, July 14, 1865, Caroline O. P. Moss Diary, Partee Center, William Jewell College.

83. "Periodicals," *Methodist Quarterly Review,* January 1869, 156.

84. PCUSA (Old School, North), *Minutes,* 1865, 560.

85. Ibid., 560, 563.

86. Harold Parker, "The Synod of Kentucky: From Old School Assembly to the Southern Church," *Journal of Presbyterian History* 41 (1963): 20.

87. Samuel R. Wilson, *Reply to the Attack of the Rev. R. J. Breckinridge, D.D., LL.D. upon the Louisville Presbytery* (Louisville, Ky.: Hanna and Duncan, 1865), 51–52, Western Historical Manuscript Collection, University of Missouri, Columbia.

88. PCUSA (Old School, North), *Minutes,* 1867, 566–84.

89. Parker, "Synod of Kentucky," 20.

90. *Minutes of the General Assembly of the Presbyterian Church in the United States of America* [Old School] (Philadelphia: Presbyterian Board of Publication 1866), vol. 18: 34–36. *A Memorable Historical Document: Its Antecedents and Its Outcome: The Declaration and Testimony,* 1867, Presbyterian Historical Society.

91. *Minutes of the General Assembly of the Presbyterian Church in the United States of America* [Old School] (Philadelphia: Presbyterian Board of Publication 1866), vol. 18: 39. Presbyter, *Reunion Overture of the Northern General Assembly to the Southern Presbyterian Church, Considered: or the Records of the Northern O.S. Assembly, from A.D. 1861 to 1869, Reviewed* (Jackson, Miss.: Clarion Steam Printing Establishment, 1870), 39.

92. *Minutes of the General Assembly of the Presbyterian Church in the United States of America* [Old School] (Philadelphia: Presbyterian Board of Publication, 1867), vol. 18: 336–33.

93. *Third or Walnut Street Presbyterian Church, Louisville, KY: Jurisdiction of Federal and State Courts—Civil vs. Ecclesiastical Courts—Rights on Church Property, &c.: Fulton* et al., *Plaintiffs against Farley* et al., *Defendants Louisville Chancery Court. Opinion of Special Chancellor A. Barnett, Member of the Louisville Bar, October 1869* (Louisville, Ky.: Courier-Journal Job Department, 1869), 6.

94. *Watson v. Jones* 80 U.S. (13 Wall.) 679 (1871). See Harris, "Neutral Principles of the Law and Church Property in the United States," 515–31; Weeks and Hickey, "'Implied Trust' for Connectional Churches," 459–70. For cases when courts did evaluate the legitimacy of religion in the late nineteenth century, see Gordon, *Mormon Question.* Americans were less hesitant to evaluate the legitimacy of non-Christian religion. See Wenger, *We Have a Religion.*

95. *Third or Walnut Street Presbyterian Church, Louisville, KY: Jurisdiction of Federal and State Courts—Civil vs. Ecclesiastical Courts—Rights on Church Property, &c.,* 7.

96. "Walnut Street Church Decision in the United States Supreme Court," *Southern Presbyterian Review* 29 (1878): 4.

97. *Minutes of the General Assembly of the Presbyterian Church in the United States of America* [Old School] (Philadelphia: Presbyterian Board of Publication, 1869), vol. 18: 958.

98. *Minutes of the General Assembly of the Presbyterian Church in the United States of America,* New Series [North] (New York: Presbyterian Board of Publication, 1875), 637.

99. For more on changing politics in the border states, see Foner, *Reconstruction,* 421–23. See also Astor, *Rebels on the Border,* 146–242.

100. "Jonathan Palmer Finley Diaries," November 27, 1866, Presbyterian Historical Society. Alfred Nevin, ed., *Encyclopedia of the Presbyterian Church in the United States of America, Including the Northern and Southern Assemblies* (Philadelphia: Presbyterian Encyclopedia Publishing Co., 1884), 25.

101. R. H. Allen to A. T. McGill, May 11, 1862; July [?], 1864; June 19, 1864, Alexander Taggart McGill Papers, Presbyterian Historical Society.

102. Ibid., September 1, 1866.

103. Ibid., September 16, 23, 29, 1866; October 8–16, 1866; April 4, 1867.

104. Ibid., September 16, 1866.

105. Baker, "Relations Between Northern and Southern Baptists," 99–103.

106. Caroline Moss to William C. Ligon, 14 July 1865, Caroline O. P. Moss Diary, Partee Center, William Jewell College.

107. Missouri General Association, 1866 statement, in Duncan, *History of the Baptists in Missouri*, 352.

108. Duncan, *History of the Baptists in Missouri*, 354.

109. Samuel Henderson to Basil Manly, June 8, 1866, Manly Family Papers, Southern Baptist Historical Society and Archives.

110. Baker, "Relations Between Northern and Southern Baptists," 102.

111. "A. S.," "Politics and Religion," *Missouri Baptist Journal*, December 23, 1867.

112. James Lynch to Matthew Simpson, December 3, 1868, Matthew Simpson Papers, Library of Congress, Manuscript Division. For more on the Church Extension Society, see Morrow, *Northern Methodism and Reconstruction*, 32, 50–52.

113. Nashville *Advocate*, September 3, 1870, quoted in Morrow, *Northern Methodism and Reconstruction*, 53.

114. Samuel D. Baldwin to Matthew Simpson, April 21, 1864, Matthew Simpson Papers, Library of Congress, Manuscript Division.

115. McKendree Church Trustees to Andrew Johnson, December 31, 1864, in Graf, ed., *Papers of Andrew Johnson* 7: 369.

116. Matthew Cramer et al. to Matthew Simpson, April 27, 1864, Matthew Simpson Papers, Library of Congress, Manuscript Division.

117. W. K. Norris to Matthew Simpson, 1864, Matthew Simpson Papers, Library of Congress, Manuscript Division.

118. A. A. Gee to Matthew Simpson, August 22, 1865, Matthew Simpson Papers, Library of Congress, Manuscript Division.

119. Samuel D. Baldwin to Andrew Johnson, October 13, 1865, Paul H. Bergeron, ed., *The Papers of Andrew Johnson, Volume 9, September 1865–January 1866* (Knoxville: University of Tennessee Press, 1991), 234–35.

120. The most comprehensive account of Robinson's life and doctrine is Graham, *Kingdom Not of this World*. For a more nuanced critique, see Harlow, *Religion, Race, and the Making of Confederate Kentucky*, 134–56.

121. "Prefatory—Position of the Church in Kentucky—Our Idea No Novelty with Us," Louisville *True Presbyterian*, April 3, 1862.

122. "The Ingratitude of Rev. Dr. Hoge and the South, and the Magnanimity of the Bible Society," Louisville *True Presbyterian*, July 30, 1863.

123. "Rapid Progress of the Northern Infidel Negrophilism to Utter and Shameless Depravity," Louisville *True Presbyterian*, April 14, 1864.

124. "Indications of Public Opinion in the Church," Louisville *True Presbyterian*, May 12, 1864.

125. Stuart Robinson, *The Press in the Federal States and Federal Despotism in Kentucky*, quoted in Graham, *Kingdom Not of This World*, 58.

126. "War in the Ecclesiastico-Military Councils of the Administration," Louisville *True Presbyterian*, March 17, 1864.

127. "Slavery in the Church Courts, *Danville Quarterly Review*, December 1864.

128. "Periodicals," *Methodist Quarterly Review*, January 1869, 153. The contents of Pearne's pamphlet, *An Address on the Two Churches, or The Methodist Episcopal Church and the Methodist Episcopal Church, South*, was originally delivered at a Knoxville, Tennessee, church in 1867. "Pamphlets," *Methodist Quarterly Review*, October 1868, 634.

129. "Periodicals," *Methodist Quarterly Review*, January 1869, 154–55.

130. Ibid., 155.

131. "That Old 'Plan,'" Cincinnati *Western Christian Advocate*, June 9, 1869; Jeremiah H. Bayliss, "The Two Methodisms," Cincinnati *Western Christian Advocate*, June 24, 1874.

CHAPTER SEVEN

1. William M. Bell, "Bible Baptists versus National Baptists," Palmyra *Missouri Baptist Journal*, April 22, 1867. For more information on Bell and other Missouri Baptists, see William Pope Yeaman, *A History of the Missouri Baptist General Association* (Columbia, Mo.: Press of E. W. Stephens, 1899).

2. William M. Bell, "Bible Baptists versus National Baptists," Palmyra *Missouri Baptist Journal*, April 22, 1867.

3. Yeaman, *History of the Missouri Baptist General Association*, 133.

4. Ibid., 127.

5. John Hill Luther, "The Southern Convention," Palmyra *Missouri Baptist Journal*, April 22, 1867.

6. Ibid.

7. Foner, *Reconstruction*, 37–43, 421. For Reconstruction in the border states, see Curry, ed., *Radicalism, Racism, and Party Realignment*. For Kentucky, see Marshall, *Creating a Confederate Kentucky*, 9–54, and Aaron Astor, "The Crouching Lion's Fate: Slave Politics and Conservative Unionism in Kentucky," *Register of the Kentucky Historical Society* 110 (2012): 293–326. See also J. Michael Rhyne, "Rehearsal for Redemption: The Politics of Post-Emancipation Violence in Kentucky's Bluegrass Region, 1865–1867," PhD diss., University of Cincinnati, 2006. For Kentucky and Missouri, see Astor, *Rebels on the Border*, 146–207. For Maryland, see Fields, *Slavery and Freedom on the Middle Ground*, 131–66.

8. Ross A. Webb, "Kentucky: Pariah Among the Elect," in Curry, ed., *Radicalism, Racism, and Party Realignment*, 117. Although Kentucky did have a Republican Union Party, it never gained power in the state.

9. S. E. Ustick to T. W. Ustick, July 30, 1866, Thomas Watt Ustick Papers, Western Historical Manuscript Collection, University of Missouri, Columbia.

10. E. Merton Coulter, *Civil War and Readjustment in Kentucky* (Chapel Hill: University

of North Carolina Press, 1926), 439, 304. Dunning school historians of Reconstruction, writing in the early twentieth century, were highly critical of the Republican program and Republican-led state governments in the South. In an interpretation used to justify Jim Crow laws, historians held that extending civil rights and suffrage to African Americans had been a mistake and that Congressional Reconstruction was misguided, corrupt, and unjust to white southerners. See Eric Foner, "Reconstruction Revisited," *Reviews in American History* 10 (1982): 82–100.

11. Marshall, *Creating a Confederate Kentucky*; Astor, *Rebels on the Border.*

12. Foner, *Reconstruction*, 41; Gerteis, *Civil War Saint Louis*, 97–98. Walter D. Kampenhofer, "Missouri Germans and the Cause of Union and Freedom," *Missouri Historical Review* 106 (2012): 115–36.

13. William E. Parrish, "Reconstruction Politics in Missouri, 1865–1870," in Curry, ed., *Radicalism, Racism, and Party Realignment*, 35–36.

14. *Cummings v. Missouri*, 71 US 277, 1866 U.S. LEXIS 885, 7 (1867).

15. Matthew Simpson to Ellen Simpson, October 2, 1870, Matthew Simpson Papers, Library of Congress, Manuscript Division.

16. Fields, *Slavery and Freedom on the Middle Ground*, 139.

17. Astor, *Rebels on the Border*, 94–120.

18. Harlow, *Religion, Race, and the Making of Confederate Kentucky*, 157–85.

19. Astor, *Rebels on the Border*, 94–120.

20. William M. Bell, "Bible Baptists versus National Baptists," Palmyra *Missouri Baptist Journal*, April 22, 1867.

21. PCUSA (Old School, North), *Minutes*, 1868, 659. See Harlow, *Religion, Race, and the Making of a Confederate Kentucky*, 201–7.

22. PCUSA (Old School, North), *Minutes*, 1869, 914.

23. PCUS (South), *Minutes*, 1870, 529–30.

24. Ibid., 530.

25. Ibid., 144–45.

26. *Minutes of the Synod of Kentucky* (Independent), 1866, quoted in Vander Velde, *Presbyterian Churches and the Federal Union*, 265.

27. Ibid.

28. PCUS (South), *Minutes*, 1867, 144.

29. Parker, "Synod of Kentucky," 30.

30. Quoted in Vander Velde, *Presbyterian Churches and the Federal Union*, 271.

31. Ibid.

32. PCUS (South), *Minutes*, 1874, 505–6. While still independent, the Kentucky Synod organized the Presbytery of Central Ohio, which was made up of Ohio Presbyterians opposed to the northern union between Old and New School Presbyterians. Always small, the Presbytery of Ohio disintegrated in 1878, making the Ohio River the northern border of Southern Presbyterianism (Parker, "Synod of Kentucky," 32).

33. PCUS (South), *Minutes*, 1874, 483.

34. Morrow, *Northern Methodism and Reconstruction*, 36–37; 67–68.

35. Bucke, ed., *History of American Methodism* 2: 267–68.

36. Baker, "Relations Between Northern and Southern Baptists," 28–42, 156–83.

37. *American Annual Cyclopedia and Register of Important Events of the Year 1865* (New York: Appleton and Co., 1869), vol. 5: 106.

38. Yeaman, *History of the Missouri Baptist General Association,* 133–59. See also Baker, "Relations Between Northern and Southern Baptists," 102.

39. Frank Masters, *A History of Baptists in Kentucky* (Louisville: Kentucky Baptist Historical Society, 1953), 353.

40. *Baptist Home Missions in North America* (New York: Baptist Home Mission Rooms, 1883), 425.

41. Caroline Moss to "Dear Sister Chary," February 5, 1877, Caroline O. P. Moss Diary, Partee Center, William Jewell College.

42. Baker, "Relations Between Northern and Southern Baptists," 179.

43. John Hill Luther, "The Southern Convention," Palmyra *Missouri Baptist Journal,* April 22, 1867.

44. Ibid.

45. Baker, "Relations Between Northern and Southern Baptists," 215–16.

46. William Capers to Bishops Soule and Paine, September 21, 1847, Methodist Leaders Miscellany, MARBL, Emory University.

47. Presbyter, *Reunion Overture of the Northern General Assembly to the Southern Presbyterian Church,* 14.

48. Parker, "Synod of Kentucky," 31.

49. Masters, *History of the Baptists in Kentucky,* 1953.

50. "The Southern Convention," *Missouri Baptist Journal,* April 22, 1867.

51. Leftwich, *Martyrdom in Missouri* 1: 140. See Maddex, "From Theocracy to Spirituality," 438–57.

52. PCUS (South), *Minutes,* 1870, 530.

53. Presbyter, *Reunion Overture of the Northern General Assembly to the Southern Presbyterian Church,* 32, 40.

54. *Correspondence Between the Conference Committees of the Presbyterian General Assemblies (North and South)* (St. Louis, Mo.: Democratic Lithographing and Printing Co., 1875), 10.

55. See Harlow, *Religion, Race, and the Making of Confederate Kentucky,* 220; Astor, "Crouching Lion's Fate," 324–26; Salafia, *Slavery's Borderland,* 228; 249–50. Christopher Phillips argues that the states of this region were "more divided at the end of the war than at its beginning" (*Rivers Ran Backward,* 318).

56. Leftwich, *Martyrdom in Missouri* 2: 373, 364.

57. "Union," Palmyra *Missouri Baptist Journal,* February 18, 1867.

58. Presbyter, *Reunion Overture of the Northern General Assembly to the Southern Presbyterian Church,* 61.

59. Ibid., 49.

60. Leftwich, *Martyrdom in Missouri* 1: 62–66.

61. Blight, *Race and Reunion,* 383.

62. The best overview of the postwar southern evangelical recovery is Stowell, *Rebuilding Zion.* For an interpretation that emphasizes reunion over sectional differences, see Blum,

Reforging the White Republic, 146–208. For the Methodist story, see Morrow, *Northern Methodism and Reconstruction*. Michael Williams's biography, *Isaac Taylor Tichenor*, describes the rebuilding of the Southern Baptist Convention. See also Harvey, *Redeeming the South*, 17–76.

63. A. T. Spaulding to John Broadus, September 17, 1865, John A. Broadus Papers, Southern Baptist Theological Seminary Archives.

64. Stowell, *Rebuilding Zion*, 102.

65. *Correspondence Between the Conference Committees of the Presbyterian General Assemblies*, 17–18.

66. Maffly-Kipp, "Burdens of Church History."

67. PCUS (South), *Minutes*, 1865, 359.

68. *Central Advocate*, September 13, 1865, quoted in Morrow, *Northern Methodism and Reconstruction*, 97.

69. Quoted in Stowell, *Rebuilding Zion*, 106.

70. *Episcopal Methodist*, November 15, 1865, quoted in "The Spirit of the Southern Methodist Press," *Methodist Quarterly Review* 18 (January 1866): 128. See also Blum, *Reforging the White Republic*, 34–37.

71. Baker, "Relations Between Northern and Southern Baptists," 170–74; Williams, *Isaac Taylor Tichenor*, 146–66.

72. E. T. Winkler, "Home Missions at the South," *Baptist Home Mission Monthly* 4 (October 1882): 274.

73. William McIntosh to J. W. Bozeman, May 23, 1882, Home Mission Board Executive Office Files, Southern Baptist Historical Library and Archives.

74. *Correspondence Between the Conference Committees of the Presbyterian General Assemblies*, 15.

75. Bishops McTyeire and Paine, "To the Bishops of the Methodist Episcopal Church," in A. H. Redford, *History of the Organization of the Methodist Episcopal Church, South* (Nashville: Southern Methodist Publishing House, 1871), 635.

76. "The Freedmen," Palmyra *Missouri Baptist Journal*, May 21, 1866.

77. Eric Foner, *Reconstruction*, 88–94. See also Montgomery, *Under Their Own Vine and Fig Tree*, and Dvorak, *African-American Exodus*. Paul Harvey and Daniel Stowell also describe this phenomenon. See Harvey, *Redeeming the South*, 45–76; 107–36; Stowell, *Rebuilding Zion*, 65–99.

78. PCUS (South), *Minutes*, 1868, 398.

79. Basil Manly Sr. to Jane Smith, November 16, 1865, Manly Collection of Manuscripts, Southern Baptist Historical Library and Archives.

80. PCUS (South), *Minutes*, 1874, 592.

81. "The Methodist Episcopal Church in the Southern States," *Methodist Quarterly* 24 (January 1872): 105–6.

82. T. J. Morgan, "Our Southern Work," *Baptist Home Mission Monthly* 16 (May 1894): 152.

83. See Blum, *Reforging the White Republic*.

84. "Our Work at the South, *Methodist Quarterly Review*, January 1874.

85. See E. R. Ames to Matthew Simpson, January 2, 1866, Matthew Simpson Papers, Library of Congress, Manuscript Division. Bucke, ed., *History of American Methodism* 2: 269.

86. Weber, *Copperheads*, 2.

87. C. Holman to Matthew Simpson, February 1, 1864, Matthew Simpson Papers, Library of Congress, Manuscript Division.

88. John S. Martin to Matthew Simpson, September 28, 1874, Matthew Simpson Papers, Library of Congress, Manuscript Division.

89. "Religious Intelligence," St. Louis *Christian Advocate,* June 20, 1866.

90. "The Methodist Episcopal Church in the Southern States," *Methodist Quarterly Review* 24 (January 1872).

91. "Our Work at the South," *Methodist Quarterly Review* 26 (January 1874).

92. Reverend Fowler, quoted in Edward Myers, *The Disruption of the Methodist Episcopal Church, 1844–1846* (Nashville: A. H. Redford, 1875), 202.

93. Bucke, ed., *History of American Methodism* 2: 300.

94. "The Episcopal Correspondence on Church Reunion," *Methodist Quarterly Review,* July 1869.

95. "Methodist Union Again," Cincinnati *Western Christian Advocate,* June 9, 1869.

96. "The Southern General Conference," *Methodist Quarterly Review,* July 1870.

97. PCUSA (Old School, North), *Minutes,* 1869, 925.

98. Johnson, "History of the Southern Presbyterian Church," 462.

99. Presbyter, *Reunion Overture of the Northern General Assembly to the Southern Presbyterian Church,* 82–85.

CHAPTER EIGHT

1. Elliott and Vernon, *South-Western Methodism,* 468.

2. Ibid., preface; 20, 457, 455, 468–69.

3. Leftwich, *Martyrdom in Missouri* 1: 3–14, 87, 89.

4. Ibid., 4, 14.

5. Ibid., vol. 2: 28.

6. "History, Biography & Topography," *Methodist Quarterly Review* 33 (1881): 582.

7. Caroline Moss to A. H. Tupper, January 17, 1876, Caroline O. P. Moss Diary, Partee Center, William Jewell College.

8. "Quarterly Book Table," *Methodist Quarterly Review* 28 (1876): 171.

9. Myers, *Disruption of the Methodist Episcopal Church*; "Morehouse Co-operation: The Conference at Fortress Monroe," *Baptist Home Mission Monthly* 10 (October 1894): 407.

10. For examples of reconciliationist literature, see Blight, *Race and Reunion,* 210–45. See also Silber, *Romance of Reunion,* 39–60.

11. R. Paine and H. N. McTyeire, "To the Bishops of the Methodist Episcopal Church," Cincinnati *Western Christian Advocate,* May 19, 1869.

12. "Union of Churches North & South," *Baptist Monthly* 5 (November 1865): 130.

13. T. O. Summers, "Introduction," in Leftwich, *Martyrdom in Missouri* 1: 12.

14. James H. Brookes, "Introduction," in Leftwich, *Martyrdom in Missouri* 2: 16.

15. Presbyter, *Reunion Overture of the Northern General Assembly to the Southern Presbyterian Church,* 55.

16. "Baptists North & South," Palmyra *Missouri Baptist Journal,* September 2, 1867.

17. Myers, *Disruption of the Methodist Episcopal Church,* 9.

18. "The New Church," *Southern Presbyterian Review* 21 (October 1870): 568.

19. "Our Church—Its Condition, Wants, and Prospects," *Southern Presbyterian Review* 22 (1871): 125.

20. Presbyter, *Reunion Overture of the Northern General Assembly to the Southern Presbyterian Church,* 14.

21. "Unification," *Southern Presbyterian Review* 22 (October 1869): 476.

22. E. T. Winkler, "Home Missions at the South," *Baptist Home Mission Monthly* 4 (1882): 275.

23. E. M. Marvin, "Prefatory Note," in Leftwich, *Martyrdom in Missouri* 1: 6–7.

24. Leftwich, *Martyrdom in Missouri* 2: 26–27.

25. Presbyter, *Reunion Overture of the Northern General Assembly to the Southern Presbyterian Church,* 35.

26. E. T. Winkler, "Home Missions at the South," *Baptist Home Mission Monthly* 4 (1882): 274.

27. Leftwich, *Martyrdom in Missouri* 2: 26–27.

28. Ibid., vol. 1: 150.

29. Redford, *History of the Organization of the Methodist Episcopal Church, South,* vi, 373, 438–39.

30. Myers, *Disruption of the Methodist Episcopal Church,* 40, 185–87.

31. "Review Two," *Methodist Quarterly Review* 28 (1876): 382–83.

32. D. D. Whedon, "Introduction," in Erasmus Q. Fuller, *An Appeal to the Records: A Vindication of the Methodist Episcopal Church* (Cincinnati: Hitchcock and Walden, 1876), 9. While it is true that eighteenth-century Methodists opposed slavery, by the nineteenth century, northerners actively opposed statements condemning slavery.

33. "Not Sectional, Not Northern," *Baptist Home Mission Monthly* 6 (September 1884): 225.

34. Robert L. Stanton, "The Ecclesiastical Disruption of 1861," *Presbyterian Quarterly and Princeton Review* 4 (April 1876): 339, 376.

35. Ibid., 333.

36. Fuller, *Appeal to the Records,* 373, 274–75.

37. Elliott and Vernon, *South-Western Methodism,* preface, 254.

38. Stanton, *Church and the Rebellion,* 26.

39. Thomas Morgan, "A Short Catechism (Revised and Enlarged) of the American Baptist Home Mission Society," *Baptist Home Mission Monthly* 17 (January 1895): 8.

40. "Did the 'Church South' Secede?" *Methodist Quarterly Review* 22 (1870): 263.

41. "History, Biography, and Topography," *Methodist Quarterly Review* 27 (1875): 167.

42.Silber, *Romance of Reunion,* 4; Blight, *Race and Reunion,* 5. Edward Blum, in *Reforging the White Republic,* argues that Christian white supremacy smoothed over sectionalism.

43. Several historians have challenged the narrative of steady postwar reconciliation by emphasizing areas in which northerners and southerners did not reunite. John Neff argues that a study of commemoration practices reveals a "persistence of animosity" (*Honoring the Civil War Dead,* 5). More recently, Caroline Janney has argued that Union veterans did not accept reconciliationist narratives (*Remembering the Civil War,* 9). Anne Marshall also describes how memories of the war could be used to perpetuate division in a border state (*Creating a Confederate Kentucky*).

44. "Church Property Questions in the South," *Methodist Quarterly Review,* October 1871.

45. "History, Biography, Topography," *Methodist Quarterly Review*, January 1875.

46. "The Southern General Conference," *Methodist Quarterly Review*, July 1870.

47. See Morrow, *Northern Methodism and Reconstruction*, 83–91. See also Bucke, ed., *History of American Methodism* 2: 299–303, 664–71.

48. Bishop Janes to C. H. Fowler, quotes in Bucke, ed., *History of American Methodism* 2: 663.

49. Bucke, ed., *History of American Methodism* 2: 302, 664.

50. Quoted in Bucke, ed., *History of American Methodism* 2: 665.

51. Ibid., 667.

52. Morrow, *Northern Methodism and Reconstruction*, 87.

53. Quoted in Bucke, ed., *History of American Methodism* 2: 669.

54. Ibid., 670

55. Morrow, *Northern Methodism and Reconstruction*, 89–90.

56. *Southwestern Advocate*, November 22, 1876, quoted in Morrow, *Northern Methodism and Reconstruction*, 90.

57. "Our Southern Field," *Methodist Quarterly Review*, April 1878.

58. L. Scott to Matthew Simpson, November 30, 1876, Matthew Simpson Papers, Library of Congress, Manuscript Division.

59. J. Mitchell to Matthew Simpson, January 16, 1880, Matthew Simpson Papers, Library of Congress, Manuscript Division.

60. For more on the 1939 reunion, see Morris L. Davis, *The Methodist Unification: Christianity and the Politics of Race in the Jim Crow Era* (New York: New York University Press, 2008).

61. PCUS (South), *Minutes*, 1882, 531.

62. R. W. Alexander, *A Digest of the Acts and Proceedings of the General Assembly of the Presbyterian Church in the United States* (Richmond, Va.: Presbyterian Committee of Publication, 1888), 494.

63. John T. Ames, "The Establishment of Fraternal Relations Between the Presbyterian Churches, U.S., and U.S.A.," PhD diss., Duke University, 1970, 32.

64. Johnson, *Life and Letters of Benjamin Morgan Palmer*, 455–57.

65. Thomas Cary Johnson, *The Life and Letters of Robert Lewis Dabney* (Richmond, Va.: Presbyterian Committee of Publication, 1903), 373–74.

66. PCUSA (North), *Minutes, New Series*, 1884, 68–69.

67. J. W. Flinn, "The General Assembly of 1883," *Southern Presbyterian Review* 34 (1883): 789, 812.

68. Accounts of the Fortress Monroe meeting and Comity Agreement can be found in Baker, "Relations Between Northern and Southern Baptists," 184–92. See also Williams, *Isaac Taylor Tichenor*, 181, 188–91, and Copeland, *Southern Baptist Convention and the Judgment of History*, 53–57.

69. Joe W. Burton, *Road to Recovery: Southern Baptist Renewal Following the Civil War* (Nashville: Boardman Press, 1977), 21–35.

70. Copeland, *Southern Baptist Convention and the Judgment of History*, 51.

71. Ibid., 54.

72. Baker, "Relations Between Northern and Southern Baptists," 184.

73. Williams, *Isaac Taylor Tichenor*, 188.

74. Baker, "Relations Between Northern and Southern Baptists," 190.

75. Silber, *Romance of Reunion*, 159–98; Blight, *Race and Reunion*, 351–54; Blum, *Reforging the White Republic*, 236.

76. Williams, *Isaac Taylor Tichenor*, 188.

77. "Proceedings of Joint Conference," *Baptist Home Mission Monthly* 16 (October 1894): 405.

78. Copeland, *Southern Baptist Convention and the Judgment of History*, 55–56. This agreement lasted into the 1950s, after which Southern Baptists, ironically, began to expand into the rest of the nation, abandoning geographic limits, although retaining the "southern" moniker.

79. Baker, "Relations Between Northern and Southern Baptists," 192.

80. Isaac T. Tichenor to T. J. Morgan, September 29, 1894, Frost Papers, Southern Baptist Historical Library and Archives.

81. H. L. Morehouse, "Co-operation Accomplished," *Baptist Home Mission Monthly* 18 (1896): 884.

82. The Northern Baptist Convention again changed its name to the American Baptist Convention in 1950, as Northern and Southern Baptist rivalry again emerged and southerners declared an end to territorial limitations and expanded into the North. In 1972, the American Baptist Convention became the American Baptist Churches in the United States of America (ABC/USA). See Copeland, *Southern Baptist Convention and the Judgment of History*, 49–51, 57–60.

83. Myers, *Disruption of the Methodist Episcopal Church*, 213–14.

CONCLUSION

1. Fehrenbacher, ed., *Abraham Lincoln: Speeches and Writings*, 687.

2. C. Vann Woodward, *Origins of the New South, 1877–1913* (1951; rpt., Baton Rouge: Louisiana State University Press, 1971), 171–2.

3. Osterweis, *Myth of the Lost Cause*. For a civil-religion angle, see Wilson, *Baptized in Blood*. In a more critical vein, Gains Foster argues that bitter sectionalism did not really characterize the majority of postwar southerners. See Foster, *Ghosts of the Confederacy*. A more recent book in this vein is Goldfield, *Still Fighting the Civil War*. Historians of the Lost Cause myth are indebted to an earlier generation of historians who studied the New South, particularly C. Vann Woodward, who, in his 1951 *Origins of the New South*, noted the irony that "along with the glittering vision of a "metropolitan" and industrial South to come there developed a cult of archaism, a nostalgic vision of the past" (142–74). See also Paul Gaston, *The New South Creed: A Study in Southern Mythmaking* (New York: Knopf, 1970).

4. The most influential example of this kind of scholarship is Blight, *Race and Reunion*. Blight argues that reunion was accomplished at the expense of justice for African Americans. See also Silber, *Romance of Reunion*, which analyses gendered as well as radicalized components of the reunion process, but focuses on the northern perspective. Edward Blum argues that white northern Protestant clergy came to favor reunion with southerners over a program of aid to southern African Americans (*Reforging the White Republic*). See also Fahs and Waugh, eds., *Memory of the Civil War in American Culture*. Other historians have

questioned the extent and depth of postwar reunion. See Neff, *Honoring the Civil War Dead*, and Janney, *Remembering the Civil War.*

5. E. P. Phelps to Matthew Simpson, December 19, 1860, Matthew Simpson Papers, Library of Congress, Manuscript Collection.

6. "Juntus," "New York Correspondence," Louisville *Western Recorder*, February 4, 1860.

7. W. W. Whipple to "the Rev. Secries. of the A.H.M.S.," September 1857, American Home Mission Society Papers—Missouri, Library of Congress, Manuscript Division.

8. Davis, *Methodist Unification*, 1.

9. The material for this paragraph is drawn from Balmer and Fitzmier, *Presbyterians*, 97–110.

10. William Brackney, *Baptists in North America: An Historical Perspective* (Malden, Mass.: Blackwell Publishing, 2006), 107–11.

11. Ibid., 112.

12. Copeland, *Southern Baptist Convention and the Judgment of History*, 49–51; 57–60. In 1972, the American Baptist Convention again changed its name to become the American Baptist Churches in the United States of America (ABC/USA). Northern Baptists continued to struggle. At the end of the twentieth century they were "no longer a majority denomination." See Brackney, *Baptists in North America*, 135.

BIBLIOGRAPHY

MANUSCRIPT COLLECTIONS

Central Methodist University, Missouri United Methodist Archives, Fayette, Mo.

Autobiographies.

Central Methodist Biographies File.

Jacob Lanius Correspondence.

Edwin Robinson [David Ross] Papers.

Emory University, Manuscripts and Rare Books Library (MARBL), Atlanta

John McClintock Papers.

Methodist Leaders Miscellany.

James Osgood Andrew Papers.

Joshua Soule Papers.

Filson Historical Society, Louisville, Ky.

Cleveland Family Papers.

Thomas Horace Cleland Papers.

Nelson N. Fuller Papers.

Grigsby Collection.

Edmund T. Halsey Papers.

Samuel Haycraft, Jr. Journal.

Joyes Family Papers.

John McClintock Papers.

William Thomas McElroy Papers.

Samuel S. Miner Papers.

Stuart Robinson Papers.

Winn-Cook Family Papers.

Library of Congress, Manuscript Division, Washington, D.C.

American Home Mission Society Papers.

Breckinridge Family; Robert Jefferson Breckinridge Papers.

Matthew Simpson Papers.

Edwin M. Stanton Papers.

Missouri Digital Heritage

Missouri's Union Provost Marshal Papers: 1861–1866.

Missouri Historical Society, St. Louis
Blow Family Papers.
Civil War Collection.
Charles Gibson Papers.
Love Papers.
David Rice McAnally Papers.
Berry Hill Spencer Correspondence.

Partee Center, William Jewell College, Liberty, Mo.
Caroline O. P. Moss Diary.
Partee Center Biographical File.

Presbyterian Historical Society, Philadelphia
Albert Barnes Papers.
Artemas Bullard Papers.
Robert Lewis Dabney Papers.
Ezra Stiles Ely Papers.
Jonathan Palmer Finley Diaries.
Robert W. Landis Papers.
Alexander Taggart McGill Papers.
Mitchell Family Papers.
Preston-Johnson Papers.

Princeton University, Rare Books and Manuscripts Library
Edward Ames Papers.
Charles Hodge Papers.

Southern Baptist Historical Library and Archives, Nashville
Ebenezer Lee Compere Papers.
Thomas Treadwell Eaton Papers.
Frost Papers.
Home Mission Board Executive Office Files.
Reuben Jones Papers.
Manly Collection of Manuscripts.
Manly Family Papers.

Southern Baptist Theological Seminary Archives, Louisville, Ky.
James P. Boyce Papers.
John A. Broadus Papers.

University of Kentucky, Special Collections, Manuscripts, Lexington
Breckinridge Family Papers.
Gunn Family Papers.
Thomas Henry Hines Papers.
Lyle Family Papers.
William M. Pratt Papers.
Preston-Johnson Papers.
Samuel R. Wilson Sermons.

Western Historical Manuscript Collection, University of Missouri, Columbia
Breckenridge Family Papers.
Henry R. Keeton Memoir.
Payne-Broadwell Papers.
Peter Goodman Rea Papers.
Frederick Starr, Jr. Papers.
Thomas Watt Ustick Papers.

Western Historical Manuscript Collection, University of Missouri, Kansas City
Jonathan B. Fuller Papers.
Missouri Collection.

DENOMINATIONAL MINUTES

Board of the Kentucky and Foreign Bible Society. General Association of Baptists in Kentucky.

Journal of the General Conference of the Methodist Episcopal Church.

Methodist Circuit Minutes, Central Methodist University Archives, Fayette, Mo.
Danville Circuit.
Grant City Circuit Springfield District.
Missouri Annual Conference.

"Minutes of Session, First Presbyterian Church of Louisville, Kentucky." Vol. 2. University of Kentucky, Lexington.

Minutes of the General Assembly of the Presbyterian Church in the Confederate States of America. Vol. 1 (1861–1864). Augusta, Ga.: Steam Power Press Chronicle and Sentinel.

Minutes of the General Assembly of the Presbyterian Church in the United States [South]. Vols. 1–6 (1865–1886). Augusta, Ga.: Constitutionalist Job Office; Jackson and Bell; Presbyterian Publishing House.

Minutes of the General Assembly of the Presbyterian Church in the United States of America [New

School]. Vols. 12–15 (1861–69). New York: Presbyterian Publication Committee.

Minutes of the General Assembly of the Presbyterian Church in the United States of America [Old School]. Vols. 16–18 (1861–1869). Philadelphia: Presbyterian Board of Publication.

Minutes of the General Assembly of the Presbyterian Church in the United States of America, New Series [North]. Vols. 1–9 (1870–1886). New York: Presbyterian Board of Publication.

Minutes of the General Association of Baptists in Kentucky. Louisville, Ky.: Geo. R. Montsarrat's Steam Power Press, 1845.

Minutes of the Kentucky Baptist Anniversaries. Louisville, Ky.: Geo. R. Montsarrat's Steam Power Press, 1845.

Presbytery Minutes, Presbyterian Historical Society, Philadelphia.

Ebenezer Presbytery.

Louisville Presbytery.

Missouri Presbytery.

Potosi Presbytery.

St. Louis Presbytery.

West Lexington Presbytery.

PERIODICALS

Baptist Banner and Western Pioneer (Louisville).

Baptist Home Mission Monthly (ABHMS).

Baptist Monthly.

Christian Advocate (St. Louis).

Christian Repository (Louisville).

Christian Repository and Family Visitor (Memphis).

Courier-Journal (Louisville).

Daily Courier (Louisville).

Daily Journal (Louisville).

Danville Quarterly Review.

Home and Foreign Journal (SBC).

Methodist Quarterly Review.

Missouri Baptist Journal (Palmyra).

Missouri Methodist.

Presbyterian Quarterly and Princeton Review.

Southern Baptist Review.

Southern Presbyterian (Columbia, S.C.).

Southern Presbyterian Review.

True Presbyterian (Louisville).

Western Baptist Review (Frankfort, Ky.).
Western Christian Advocate (Cincinnati).
Western Recorder (Louisville).

COURT DECISIONS

Bascom v. Lane. 2 F. Cas. 994 (1851).
Cummings v. The State of Missouri. 71 U.S. 277 (1866).
First Presbyterian Church of Louisville v. Watson. 77 Ky. 252 (1878).
Gibson et. al. v Armstrong. 46 Ky. 481 (1847).
Lewis v. Watson. 67 Ky. 228 (1868).
Sage, etc. v. Dillard, etc. 53 KY 340.
Smith v. Swormstedt. 22 F. Cas. 663 (1852). 57 U.S. 288 (1853).
State of Missouri ex rel. Watson v. Ferris. 45 Mo. 183 (1869).
Watson v. Jones. 80 U.S. 679 (1871).

OTHER PUBLISHED PRIMARY SOURCES

Adger, John. "The General Assembly of 1861." *Southern Presbyterian Review* 14 (1861): 296–348.

Alexander, R. W. *A Digest of the Acts and Proceedings of the General Assembly of the Presbyterian Church in the United States.* Richmond, Va.: Presbyterian Committee of Publication, 1888.

American Annual Cyclopedia and Register of Important Events of the Year 1865. Vol. 5. New York: Appleton and Co., 1869.

Bascom, Henry B. *Methodism and Slavery: With Other Matters in Controversy between the North and the South; Being A Review of the Manifesto of the Majority, in Reply to the Protest of the Minority, of the Late General Conference of the Methodist E. Church, in the Case of Bishop Andrew.* Frankfurt, Ky.: Hodges, Todd, and Pruett, 1845.

Beecher, Lyman. *A Plea for the West.* Cincinnati: Truman and Smith, 1835.

Birney, James G. *The American Churches, the Bulwarks of American Slavery.* Newburyport, Mass.: Charles Whipple, 1842.

Board of Trustees of the Western Baptist Theological Institute. "Reply to 'Brief Historical Sketch of the Western Baptist Theological Institute,' In Covington, Kentucky." 1850.

Correspondence Between the Conference Committees of the Presbyterian General Assemblies (North and South). St. Louis: Democrat and Printing Co., 1875.

Crooks, George R. *The Life of Bishop Matthew Simpson of the Methodist Episcopal Church.* New York: Harper and Brothers, 1890.

Du Bose, Horace M. *Life of Joshua Soule.* Nashville: Publishing House of the M.E. Church, South, 1911.

Duncan, Robert S. *A History of the Baptists in Missouri.* St. Louis, Mo.: Scammell and Co., 1883.

Dunn, William McKee. *Early History of Hanover College.* Madison, Ind.: Courier Co., 1883.

Elliott, Charles. *History of the Great Secession from the Methodist Episcopal Church.* Cincinnati: Swormstedt & Poe, 1855.

———, and Leroy Vernon. *South-Western Methodism: A History of the M.E. Church in the Southwest, from 1844–1864.* Cincinnati: Poe and Hitchcock, 1868.

Finley, James. *Sketches of Western Methodism.* Cincinnati: Methodist Book Concern, 1857.

Fuller, Erasmus Q. *An Appeal to the Records: A Vindication of the Methodist Episcopal Church.* Cincinnati: Hitchcock and Walden, 1876.

History of the Organization of the Methodist Episcopal Church, South, Comprehending all the Official Proceedings of the General Conference; the Southern Annual Conferences, and the General Convention; With Such Other Matters as Are Necessary to a Right Understanding of the Case. Nashville: William Cameron, 1845.

Hodge, Archibald A. *The Life of Charles Hodge.* New York: T. Nelson and Sons, 1881.

Johnson, Thomas Cary. "A History of the Southern Presbyterian Church." In *A History of the Methodist Church, South, the United Presbyterian Church, the Cumberland Presbyterian Church, and the Presbyterian Church, South in the United States.* New York, 1894.

———. *The Life and Letters of Benjamin Morgan Palmer.* 1906. Reprint. Edinburgh, Scotland: Banner of Truth Trust, 1987.

———. *The Life and Letters of Robert Lewis Dabney.* Richmond, Va.: Presbyterian Committee of Publication, 1903.

Leftwich, William M. *Martyrdom in Missouri.* 2 vols. St. Louis, Mo.: S.W. Book & Pub. Co., 1870.

Lewis, W. H. *The History of Methodism in Missouri for a Decade of Years from 1860–1870.* Vol. 3. Nashville: Publishing House of the M.E. Church, South, 1890.

Magie, David. *Memorial Sermon of the Late Frederick Starr, Jr.* Rochester, N.Y., 1867.

Marlay, John F. *The Life of the Reverend Thomas A. Morris, D.D.* Cincinnati: Hitchcock and Walden, 1875.

Marshall, John A. *American Bastille: A History of the Arbitrary Arrests and Imprisonment of American Citizens in the Northern and Border States, On Account of Their Political Opinions, During the Late Civil War, Together With a Full Report of the Illegal Trial and Execution of Mrs. Mary E. Surratt, By a Military Commission, and a Review of the Testimony, Showing Her Entire Innocence.* Philadelphia: T. W. Hartley & Co., 1884.

Matlack, Lucius C. *The Antislavery Struggle and Triumph in the Methodist Episcopal Church.* New York: Phillips and Hunt, 1881.

McCarter, J. Mayland. *Border Methodism and Border Slavery.* Philadelphia: Collins, 1858.

McPheeters, Samuel B., et. al., *A Correspondence Between Some of the Members of the Pine Street Presbyterian Church and Its Pastor.* St. Louis, Mo., 1862.

A Memorable Historical Document: Its Antecedents and Its Outcome: The Declaration and Testimony. 1867. Presbyterian Historical Society.

Myers, Edward. *The Disruption of the Methodist Episcopal Church, 1844–1846.* Nashville: A. H. Redford, 1875.

Nevin, Alfred, ed. *Encyclopedia of the Presbyterian Church in the United States of America, Including the Northern and Southern Assemblies.* Philadelphia: Presbyterian Encyclopedia Publishing Co., 1884.

Peck, Thomas E. *A Memorial of the Life and Labors of the Rev. Stuart Robinson.* 1882.

Presbyter. *Reunion Overture of the Northern General Assembly to the Southern Presbyterian Church, Considered: or the Records of the Northern O.S. Assembly, from A.D. 1861 to 1869, Reviewed.* Jackson, Miss.: Clarion Steam Printing Establishment, 1870.

Presbyterian Committee of Publication. *Memorial Addresses Delivered before the General Assembly of 1886, on Occasion of the Quarter-Centennial of the Organization of the Southern Assembly, in 1861.* Richmond, Va., 1886.

Redford, Albert Henry. *The History of Methodism in Kentucky.* Vol. 4. Nashville: Southern Methodist Publishing House, 1870.

———. *History of the Organization of the Methodist Episcopal Church, South.* Nashville: Southern Methodist Publishing House, 1871.

Riley, Benjamin Franklin. *A History of the Baptists in the Southern States East of the Mississippi.* Philadelphia: American Baptist Publication Society, 1898.

Robinson, Stuart. *An Appeal to the Christian Public.* Louisville, Ky.: Hanna & Co., 1862.

———. *The Presbyterian System of Government; and the Issues Between the General Assembly and the Synod of Kentucky.* Louisville, Ky.: Harney, Hughes & Co., 1867.

———. *Speech of Dr. Stuart Robinson Before the Southern Presbyterian Assembly in Advocacy of the General Presbyterian Alliance.* 1875.

———. "To The Presbyterian People of Kentucky." Pamphlet. [1865].

Simpson, Matthew. *A Hundred Years of Methodism.* New York: Nelson and Phillips, 1879.

Spencer, John Henderson. *A History of Kentucky Baptists.* Vol. 1. Cincinnati: J. R. Baumer, 1885.

Stanton, Robert L. *The Church and the Rebellion: A Consideration of the Rebellion Against the Government of the United States; and the Agency of the Church, North and South in Relation Thereto.* New York: Derby and Miller, 1864.

Stevens, John. *Brief Historical Sketch of the Western Baptist Theological Institute.* Cincinnati: Queen City Press, 1850.

Third or Walnut Street Presbyterian Church, Louisville, Ky. Jurisdiction of Federal and State Courts—Civil vs. Ecclesiastical Courts—Rights on Church Property, &c.: Fulton et al., *Plaintiffs against Farley* et al., *Defendants Louisville Chancery Court. Opinion of Special*

Chancellor A. Barnett, Member of the Louisville Bar, October 1869. Louisville, Ky.: Courier-Journal Job Department, 1869.

U.S. War Department. *Official Records of the Union and Confederate Armies.*

Waugh, Lorenzo. *Autobiography of Lorenzo Waugh.* Oakland, Calif.: Pacific Press, 1883.

———. *A Candid Statement of the Course Pursued by the Preachers of the Methodist Episcopal Church South, in Trying to Establish Their New Organization in Missouri.* Cincinnati: J. A. & U. P. James, 1848.

Williams, Alvin Peter. *An Essay on the Missouri Test Oath. Position of the Baptist Denomination of Missouri, On Said Oath.* 1868.

Wilson, Samuel R. *The Causes and Remedies of Impending National Calamities. An Address.* Cincinnati: J. B. Elliott, 1860.

———. *Reply to the Attack of the Rev. R. J. Breckinridge, D.D., LL.D. upon the Louisville Presbytery.* Louisville, Ky.: Hanna and Duncan, 1865.

Woods, Neander M. "Our Redeemer's Prayer for Christian Unity." In *Southern Presbyterian Pulpit: A Collection of Sermons by Ministers of the Southern Presbyterian Church.* Richmond, Va.: Presbyterian Committee of Publication, 1896.

Yeaman, William Pope. *A History of the Missouri Baptist General Association.* Columbia, Mo.: Press of E. W. Stephens, 1899.

SECONDARY SOURCES

Adams, Elizabeth. "Divided Nation, Divided Church: The Presbyterian Schism, 1837–1838." *Historian* 54 (1992): 683–96.

Agnew, Peter W. "'Methodists, to the Rescue!': Thomas Emerson Bond and Separation from the Methodist Episcopal Church, 1840–1848." *Methodist History* 27 (1989): 133–50.

Albritton, James McLean. "Slavery, Secession, and the Old School Presbyterians." *Southern Historian* 21 (2000): 25–39.

Ames, John T. "The Establishment of Fraternal Relations Between the Presbyterian Churches, U.S., and U.S.A." PhD diss., Duke University, 1970.

Andreason, Byron C. "As Good a Right to Pray: Copperhead Christians on the Civil War Homefront." PhD diss., University of Illinois at Urbana-Champagne, 1998.

———. "Civil War Church Trials: Repressing Dissent on the Northern Home Front." In *An Uncommon Time: The Civil War and the Northern Home Front,* ed. Paul A. Cimbala and Randall M. Miller, 214–42. New York: Fordham University Press, 2002.

———. "Proscribed Preachers, New Churches: Civil Wars in the Illinois Protestant Churches During the Civil War." *Civil War History* 44 (1998): 194–211.

Apperson, George M. "Presbyterians and Radical Republicans: President Lincoln, Dr. McPheeters, and the Civil War in Missouri." *American Presbyterians* 73 (1995): 239–50.

Arenson, Adam. *The Great Heart of the Republic: St. Louis and the Cultural Civil War.* Cambridge, Mass.: Harvard University Press, 2011.

Aron, Stephen. *American Confluence: The Missouri Frontier from Borderland to Border State.* Bloomington: Indiana University Press, 2006.

———. *How the West Was Lost: The Transformation of Kentucky from Daniel Boone to Henry Clay.* Baltimore: Johns Hopkins University Press, 1999.

Ash, Stephen. *Middle Tennessee Society Transformed, 1860–1870: War and Peace in the Upper South.* Baton Rouge: Louisiana State University Press, 2011.

———. *When the Yankees Came: Conflict and Chaos in the Occupied South, 1861–1865.* Chapel Hill: University of North Carolina Press, 1995.

Astor, Aaron. "The Crouching Lion's Fate: Slave Politics and Conservative Unionism in Kentucky." *Register of the Kentucky Historical Society* 110 (2012): 293–326.

———. *Rebels on the Border: Civil War, Emancipation, and the Reconstruction of Kentucky and Missouri.* Baton Rouge: Louisiana State University Press, 2012.

Auslander, Mark. *The Accidental Slaveholder: Revisiting a Myth of Race and Finding an American Family.* Athens: University of Georgia Press, 2011.

Baker, Robert Andrew. "Relations Between Northern and Southern Baptists." PhD diss., Yale University, 1948.

Balmer, Randall. *Blessed Assurance: A History of Evangelicalism in America.* Boston: Beacon Press, 1999.

———. *The Making of Evangelicalism: From Revivalism to Politics and Beyond.* Waco, Tex.: Baylor University Press, 2010.

———. and John R. Fitzmier. *The Presbyterians.* Westport, Conn.: Greenwood Press, 1993.

Barclay, Thomas S. "The Test Oath for the Clergy in Missouri." *Missouri Historical Review* 18 (1924): 345–81.

Bergeron, Paul H., ed. *The Papers of Andrew Johnson, Volume 8, May–August 1865.* Knoxville: University of Tennessee Press, 1989.

———. *The Papers of Andrew Johnson, Volume 9, September 1865–January 1866.* Knoxville: University of Tennessee Press, 1991.

Bergman, William H. *The American National State and the Early West.* New York: Cambridge University Press, 2012.

Berlin, Ira. *Many Thousands Gone: The First Two Centuries of Slavery in North America.* Cambridge, Mass.: Harvard University Press, 1998.

Blair, William. *With Malice toward Some: Treason and Loyalty in the Civil War Era.* Chapel Hill: University of North Carolina Press, 2014.

Blight, David W. *Race and Reunion: The Civil War in American Memory.* Cambridge, Mass.: Harvard University Press, 2001.

Blum, Edward. *Reforging the White Republic: Race, Religion, and American Nationalism, 1865–1898.* Baton Rouge: Louisiana State University Press, 2005.

———. and W. Scoot Poole, eds. *Vale of Tears: New Essays on Religion and Reconstruction*. Macon, Ga.: Mercer University Press, 2005.

Blumhofer, Edith, ed. *Religion, Politics, and the American Experience: Reflections on Religion and American Public Life*. Tuscaloosa: University of Alabama Press, 2002.

Boman, Dennis K. *Lincoln and Citizens' Rights in Civil War Missouri*. Baton Rouge: Louisiana State University Press, 2011.

Bowler, Kate. *Blessed: A History of the American Prosperity Gospel*. New York: Oxford University Press, 2013.

Brackney, William. *Baptists in North America: An Historical Perspective*. Malden, Mass.: Blackwell Publishing, 2006.

Brewer, W. M. "Lincoln and the Border States." *Journal of Negro History* 34 (1949): 46–72.

Brodrecht, Grant. "'Our Country': Northern Evangelicals and the Nation in the Civil War and Reconstruction." PhD diss., Notre Dame University, 2008.

Brown, Candy Gunther. *The Word in the World: Evangelical Writing, Publishing, and Reading in America*. Chapel Hill: University of North Carolina Press, 2004.

Browning, Judkin. "'Bringing Light to our Land . . . When She Was Dark as Night': Northerners, Freedpeople, and Education during Military Occupation in North Carolina, 1862–1865." *American Nineteenth Century History* 9 (2008): 1–17.

———. *Shifting Loyalties: The Union Occupation of Eastern North Carolina*. Chapel Hill: University of North Carolina Press, 2011.

Buck, Paul. *The Road to Reunion, 1865–1900*. Boston: Little, Brown and Co., 1937.

Bucke, Emory S., ed. *The History of American Methodism*. 3 vols. New York: Abingdon Press, 1964.

Burke, Diane Mutti. *On Slavery's Border: Missouri's Small Slaveholding Households*. Athens: University of Georgia Press, 2010.

Burton, Joe W. *Road to Recovery: Southern Baptist Renewal Following the Civil War*. Nashville: Boardman Press, 1977.

Bushman, Richard. *Refinement of America: Persons, Houses, Cities*. New York: Vintage Books, 1992.

Butler, Jon. "Jack-in-the-Box Faith: The Religion Problem in Modern American History." *Journal of American History* 90 (2004): 1357–78.

Carney, Charity R. *Ministers and Masters: Methodism, Manhood, and Honor in the Old South*. Baton Rouge: Louisiana State University Press, 2011.

Carwardine, Richard. *Evangelicals and Politics in Antebellum America*. Knoxville: University of Tennessee Press, 1997.

Chesebrough, David B. *Clergy Dissent in the Old South, 1830–1865*. Carbondale: Southern Illinois University Press, 1996.

———. ed. *"God Ordained This War": Sermons on the Sectional Crisis*. Columbia: University of South Carolina Press, 1991.

———. "A Holy War: The Defense and Support of the Confederacy by Southern Baptists." *American Baptist Quarterly* 6 (1987): 17–30.

Clossman, Richard H. "Antebellum Dream of a St. Louis Baptist Minister—'But We Are Now Two Parties.'" *American Baptist Quarterly* 22 (2003): 33–51.

Coffman, Elesha J. *The Christian Century and the Rise of the Protestant Mainline*. New York: Oxford University Press, 2013.

Copeland, E. Luther. *The Southern Baptist Convention and the Judgment of History: The Taint of an Original Sin*. New York: University Press of America, 1995.

Coulter, E. Merton. *Civil War and Readjustment in Kentucky*. Chapel Hill: University of North Carolina Press, 1926.

Cox, LaWanda. *Lincoln and Black Freedom*. Columbia: University of South Carolina Press, 1981.

Crooks, George R. *The Life of Bishop Matthew Simpson of the Methodist Episcopal Church*. New York: Harper & Brothers, 1890.

Crowther, Edward. *Southern Evangelicals and the Coming of the Civil War*. Lewiston, N.Y.: Edwin Mellen Press, 2000.

Curry, Richard O., ed. *Radicalism, Racism, and Party Realignment: The Border States During Reconstruction*. Baltimore: Johns Hopkins University Press, 1969.

Daly, John Patrick. *When Slavery Was Called Freedom: Evangelicalism, Proslavery, and the Causes of the Civil War*. Lexington: University Press of Kentucky, 2002.

Davis, J. Treadwell. "Obstacles to Reunion of the Presbyterian Church, 1868–1888." *Virginia Magazine of History and Biography* 63 (1955): 28–39.

———. "The Presbyterians and the Sectional Conflict." *Southern Quarterly* 8 (1970): 117–33.

Davis, Morris L. *The Methodist Unification: Christianity and the Politics of Race in the Jim Crow Era*. New York: New York University Press, 2008.

DeRogatis, Amy. *Moral Geography: Maps, Missionaries, and the American Frontier*. New York: Columbia University Press, 2003.

Doherty, Robert W. "Social Bases for the Presbyterian Schism of 1837–1838: The Philadelphia Case." *Journal of Social History* 2 (1968): 69–79.

Duncan, Richard R. "Maryland Methodists and the Civil War." *Maryland Historical Magazine* 59 (1964): 350–68.

Dunham, Chester Forrester. *The Attitude of the Northern Clergy Toward the South, 1860–1865*. Toledo, Ohio: Gray Co., 1942.

Dvorak, Katherine. *African-American Exodus: The Segregation of the Southern Churches*. Brooklyn, N.Y.: Carlson Pub., 1991.

Earle, Jonathan, and Diane Mutti Burke, eds. *Bleeding Kansas, Bleeding Missouri: The Long Civil War on the Border*. Lawrence: University Press of Kansas, 2013.

Eighmy, John Lee. "The Baptists and Slavery: An Examination of the Origins and Benefits of Segregation." *Social Science Quarterly* 49 (1968): 666–73.

———. *Churches in Cultural Captivity: A History of the Social Attitudes of Southern Baptists.* Knoxville: University of Tennessee Press, 1987.

Eslinger, Ellen. "The Evolution of Racial Politics in Early Ohio." In *The Center of a Great Empire: The Ohio Country in the Early American Republic*, ed. Andrew Cayton and Stewart Hobbs, 86–87. Athens: Ohio University Press, 2005.

Etcheson, Nicole. *Bleeding Kansas: Contested Liberty in the Civil Was Era.* Lawrence: University Press of Kansas, 2004.

———. *The Emerging Northwest: Upland Southerners and the Political Culture of the Old Northwest, 1787–1861.* Bloomington: Indiana University Press, 1996.

———. "The Great Principle of Self-Government: Popular Sovereignty and Bleeding Kansas." *Kansas History* 27 (2004): 14–29.

Fahs, Alice, and Joan Waugh, eds. *The Memory of the Civil War in American Culture.* Chapel Hill: University of North Carolina Press, 2004.

Farmer, James Oscar, Jr. *The Metaphysical Confederacy: James Henley Thornwell and the Synthesis of Southern Values.* Macon, Ga.: Mercer University Press, 1986.

Faust, Drew Gilpin. *This Republic of Suffering: Death and the American Civil War.* New York: Vintage Books, 2009.

Fehrenbacher, Don, ed. *Abraham Lincoln: Speeches and Writings, 1832–1858.* New York: Library of America, 1989.

———. ed. *Abraham Lincoln: Speeches & Writings, 1859–1865.* New York: Library of America, 1989.

Fellman, Michael. *Inside War: The Guerrilla Conflict in Missouri During the American Civil War.* New York: Oxford University Press, 1989.

Fields, Barbara Jeanne. *Slavery and Freedom on the Middle Ground: Maryland during the Nineteenth Century.* New Haven, Conn.: Yale University Press, 1985.

Finck, James. *Divided Loyalties: Kentucky's Struggle for Armed Neutrality in the Civil War.* El Dorado Hills, Calif.: Savas Beatie, 2012.

Findlay, James. "The SPCTEW and Western Colleges: Religion and Higher Education in Mid–Nineteenth Century America." *History of Education Quarterly* 17 (1977): 31–62.

Finke, Roger, and Rodney Stark. *The Churching of America, 1776–1990: Winners and Losers in our Religious Economy.* New Brunswick, N.J.: Rutgers University Press, 1992.

Finnie, Gordon. "The Antislavery Movement in the Upper South Before 1840." *Journal of Southern History* 35 (1969): 319–42.

Fisher, Noel C. *War at Every Door: Partisan Politics and Guerrilla Violence in East Tennessee.* Chapel Hill: University of North Carolina Press, 1997.

Fitz, Christian G. *American Sovereigns: The People and America's Constitutional Tradition Before the Civil War.* New York: Cambridge University Press, 2008.

Foner, Eric. *Free Soil, Free Labor, Free Men: The Ideology of the Republican Party Before the Civil War.* New York: Oxford University Press, 1995.

———. *Politics and Ideology in the Age of the Civil War.* New York: Oxford University Press, 1980.

———. *Reconstruction: America's Unfinished Revolution, 1863–1877.* New York: Harper and Row, 1988.

———. "Reconstruction Revisited." *Reviews in American History* 10 (1982): 82–100.

Ford, Bridget. "Beyond Cane Ridge: The 'Great Western Revivals' in Louisville and Cincinnati, 1828–1845." *Ohio Valley History* 8 (2008): 17–37.

———. "Black Spiritual Defiance and the Politics of Slavery in Antebellum Louisville." *Journal of Southern History* 78 (2012): 69–106.

———. *Bonds of Union: Religion, Race, and Politics in a Civil War Borderland.* Chapel Hill: University of North Carolina Press, 2016.

Ford, Lacy. *Deliver Us from Evil: The Slavery Question in the Old South.* New York: Oxford University Press, 2009.

Foster, Gains M. *Ghosts of the Confederacy: Defeat, the Lost Cause, and the Emergence of the New South, 1865–1913.* New York: Oxford University Press, 1987.

Freidel, Frank. "General Orders 100 and Military Government." *Mississippi Valley Historical Review* 32 (1946): 541–56.

Gardner, Robert C. *Decade of Debate and Division: Georgia Baptists and the Formation of the Southern Baptist Convention.* Macon, Ga.: Mercer University Press, 1995.

Gaston, Paul. *The New South Creed: A Study in Southern Mythmaking.* New York: Knopf, 1970.

Genovese, Eugene. *A Consuming Fire: The Fall of the Confederacy in the Mind of the White Christian South.* Athens: University of Georgia Press, 1998.

———. *The Slaveholders' Dilemma: Freedom and Progress in Southern Conservative Thought, 1820–1860.* Columbia: University of South Carolina Press, 1992.

Geiger, Mark. *Financial Fraud and Guerrilla Violence in Missouri's Civil War, 1861–1865.* New Haven, Conn.: Yale University Press, 2010.

Gerteis, Louis. *Civil War St. Louis.* Lawrence: University Press of Kansas, 2001.

Gienapp, William. "Abraham Lincoln and the Border States." *Journal of the Abraham Lincoln Association* 13 (1992): 13–46.

Gilliam, Will D., Jr. "Robert J. Breckinridge: Kentucky Unionist." *Register of the Kentucky Historical Society* 69 (1971): 362–85.

Gjerde, Jon and S. Deborah Kang. *Catholicism and the Shaping of Nineteenth-Century America.* New York: Cambridge University Press, 2012.

Goen, C. C. *Broken Churches, Broken Nation: Denominational Schisms and the Coming of the American Civil War.* Macon, Ga.: Mercer University Press, 1985.

Goldfield, David. *America Aflame: How the Civil War Created a Nation.* New York: Bloomsbury Press, 2011.

———. *Still Fighting the Civil War: The American South and Southern History.* Baton Rouge: Louisiana State University Press, 2002.

Gordon, Ralph C. "Nashville and the U.S. Christian Commission in the Civil War." *Tennessee Historical Quarterly* 55 (1996): 98–111.

Gordon, Sarah Barringer. *The Mormon Question: Polygamy and Constitutional Conflict in Nineteenth-Century America.* Chapel Hill: University of North Carolina Press, 2002.

Gourley, Bruce. *Diverging Loyalties: Baptists in Middle Georgia During the Civil War.* Macon, Ga.: Mercer University Press, 2011.

Graf, LeRoy P., ed. *The Papers of Andrew Johnson, Volume 7, 1864–1865.* Knoxville: University of Tennessee Press, 1986.

Graham, Preston D., Jr. *A Kingdom Not of This World: Stuart Robinson's Struggle to Distinguish the Sacred from the Secular during the Civil War.* Macon, Ga.: Mercer University Press, 2002.

Gruenwald, Kim M. *River of Enterprise: The Commercial Origins of Regional Identity in the Ohio Valley, 1790–1850.* Bloomington: Indiana University Press, 2002.

Guétin, Nicole. *Religious Ideology in American Politics: A History.* Jefferson, N.C.: McFarland & Co., 2009.

Hall, Joseph H. *Presbyterian Conflict and Resolution on the Missouri Frontier.* Lewiston, N.Y.: Edwin Mellen Press, 1987.

Hamburger, Philip. *Separation of Church and State.* Cambridge, Mass.: Harvard University Press, 2002.

Hammond, John Craig. *Slavery, Freedom, and Expansion in the Early American West.* Charlottesville: University Press of Virginia, 2007.

Handy, Robert T. *A Christian America: Protestant Hopes and Historical Realities.* New York: Oxford University Press, 1971.

———. *Undermined Establishment: Church-State Relations in America, 1880–1920.* Princeton, N.J.: Princeton University Press, 1991.

Hanley, Mark Y. *Beyond a Christian Commonwealth: The Protestant Quarrel with the American Republic, 1830–1860.* Chapel Hill: The University of North Carolina Press, 1994.

Hansen, Klaus J. "The Millennium, the West, and Race in the Antebellum American Mind." *Western Historical Quarterly* 3 (1972): 373–90.

Harlow, Luke E. "The Long Life of Proslavery Religion." In Gregory Downs and Kate Masur, eds. *The World the Civil War Made.* Chapel Hill: University of North Carolina Press, 2015.

———. "Religion, Race, and Robert J. Breckinridge: The Ideology of an Antislavery Slaveholder, 1830–1860." *Ohio Valley History* 6 (2006): 1–24.

———. *Religion, Race, and the Making of Confederate Kentucky, 1830–1880.* New York: Cambridge University Press, 2014.

Harper, Keith. "Downwind from the New England Rat: John Taylor, Organized Missions, and the Regionalization of Religious Identity on the American Frontier." *Ohio Valley History* 9 (2009): 25–42.

Harrell, David Edwin, Jr. *Quest for a Christian America: The Disciples of Christ and American Society to 1866*. Nashville: Disciples of Christ Historical Society, 1966.

Harris, Troy. "Neutral Principles of the Law and Church Property in the United States." *Journal of Church and State* 30 (1988): 515–31.

Harris, William C. *Lincoln and the Border States: Preserving the Union*. Lawrence: University Press of Kansas, 2011.

Harrold, Stanley. *Border War: Fighting over Slavery before the Civil War*. Chapel Hill: University of North Carolina Press, 2009.

Harvey, Paul. *Redeeming the South: Religious Cultures and Racial Identities among Southern Baptists, 1865–1925*. Chapel Hill: University of North Carolina Press, 1997.

Haselby, Sam. *The Origins of American Religious Nationalism*. New York: Oxford University Press, 2015.

Hatch, Nathan. *The Democratization of American Christianity*. New Haven, Conn.: Yale University Press, 1989.

———. "The Puzzle of American Methodism." *Church History* 63 (1994): 175–89.

Hempton, David. *Methodism: Empire of the Spirit*. New Haven, Conn.: Yale University Press, 2005.

Holifield, E. Brooks. *Theology in America: Christian Thought from the Age of the Puritans to the Civil War*. New Haven, Conn.: Yale University Press, 2003.

Horn, Stanley Fitzgerald. "Nashville During the Civil War." *Tennessee Historical Quarterly* 4 (1945): 3–22.

Horsman, Reginald. *Race and Manifest Destiny: The Origins of American Racial Anglo-Saxonism*. Cambridge, Mass.: Harvard University Press, 1981.

Howard, Victor B. *Evangelical War Against Slavery and Caste: The Life and Times of John G. Fee*. Selinsgrove, Pa.: Susquehanna University Press, 1996.

Howe, Daniel Walker. *What Hath God Wrought: The Transformation of America, 1815–1848*. New York: Oxford University Press, 2007.

Howe, Mark DeWolfe. *The Garden and the Wilderness: Religion and Government in American Constitutional History*. Chicago: University of Chicago Press, 1965.

Hutter, Liz. "Ho for Salt River!" *Common Place* 7 (2007): www.common-place.org/vol-07/no-3/hutter/.

Hyman, Harold Melvin. *Era of the Oath: Northern Loyalty Tests During the Civil War and Reconstruction*. Philadelphia: University of Pennsylvania Press, 1954.

Irons, Charles F. *The Origins of Proslavery Christianity: White and Black Evangelicals in Colonial and Antebellum Virginia*. Chapel Hill: University of North Carolina Press, 2008.

James, William C. "A History of the Western Baptist Theological Institute." *Publications of the Kentucky Baptist Historical Society* 1 (1905): 31–100.

Janet, Richard J. "Prayer and Politics: General Fasts in the Early American Republic." *Mid-America* 67 (1985): 97–107.

Janney, Caroline. *Remembering the Civil War: Reunion and the Limits of Reconciliation.* Chapel Hill: University of North Carolina Press, 2013.

Johnson, Curtis D. *Redeeming America: Evangelicals and the Road to Civil War.* Chicago: Ivan R. Dee, 1993.

Johnson, Paul. *A Shopkeeper's Millennium: Society and Revivals in Rochester, New York, 1815–1837.* New York: Hill and Wang, 1978.

Johnson, Walter. *River of Dark Dreams: Slavery and Empire in the Cotton Kingdom.* Cambridge, Mass.: Harvard University Press, 2013.

Jones, Donald G. *The Sectional Crisis and Northern Methodism: A Study in Piety, Political Ethics, and Civil Religion.* Metuchen, N.J.: Scarecrow Press, 1979.

"Judicial Intervention in Disputes Over the Use of Church Property." *Harvard Law Review* 75 (1962): 1142–86.

Kaufman, Jason. *For the Common Good? American Civic Life and the Golden Age of Fraternity.* New York: Oxford University Press, 2002.

Kedro, Milan. "The Civil War's Effect upon an Urban Church: The St. Louis Presbytery under Martial Law." *Missouri Historical Society Bulletin* 27 (1971): 173–93.

Klement, Frank L. *Dark Lanterns: Secret Political Societies, Conspiracies, and Treason Trials in the Civil War.* Baton Rouge: Louisiana State University Press, 1984.

———. *The Limits of Dissent: Clement L. Vallandigham and the Civil War.* Lexington: University Press of Kentucky, 1970.

Klingaman, David C. and Richard K. Vedder, eds. *Essays in Nineteenth Century Economic History: The Old Northwest.* Athens: Ohio University Press, 1975.

Kohl, Martha. "Enforcing a Vision of Community: The Role of the Test Oath in Missouri's Reconstruction." *Civil War History* 40 (1994): 292–307.

Kutler, Stanley. "Reconstruction and the Supreme Court: The Numbers Game Reconsidered." *Journal of Southern History* 32 (1966): 42–58.

Lambert, Byron C. *The Rise of the Anti-Mission Baptists: 1800–1840.* New York: Arno Press, 1980.

Lee, Jacob. "'Between Two Fires': Cassius M. Clay, Slavery, and Antislavery in the Kentucky Borderlands." *Ohio Valley History* 6 (2006): 50–70.

———. "Unionism, Emancipation, and the Origins of Kentucky's Confederate Identity." *Register of the Kentucky Historical Society* 111 (2013): 199–233.

Lehmann, Frederick. "Edward Bates and the Test Oath." *Missouri Historical Society Collections* 4 (1923): 389–401.

Lewis, Patrick. *For Slavery and Union: Benjamin Buckner and Kentucky Loyalties in the Civil War.* Lexington: University Press of Kentucky, 2015.

Loetscher, Lefferts A. *A Brief History of the Presbyterians.* 3rd ed. Philadelphia: Westminster Press, 1978.

Loveland, Anne. *Southern Evangelicals and the Social Order, 1800–1860.* Baton Rouge: Louisiana State University Press, 1980.

Mackey, Thomas C. "Not a Pariah, but a Keystone: Kentucky and Secession." In *Sister States, Enemy States: The Civil War in Kentucky and Tennessee*, ed. Kent T. Dollar, Larry H. Whiteaker, and W. Calvin Dickinson. Lexington: University Press of Kentucky, 2009.

Maddex, Jack P. "From Theocracy to Spirituality: The Southern Presbyterian Reversal on Church and State." *Journal of Presbyterian History* 54 (1976): 438–57.

Maffly-Kipp, Laurie. "The Burdens of Church History." *Church History* 82 (2013): 353–67.

Marsden, George. *The Evangelical Mind and the New School Presbyterian Experience*. New Haven, Conn.: Yale University Press, 1970.

Marshall, Anne. *Creating a Confederate Kentucky: The Lost Cause and Civil War Memory in a Border State*. Chapel Hill: University of North Carolina Press, 2010.

Mason, Patrick. *The Mormon Menace: Violence and Anti-Mormonism in the Postbellum South*. New York: Oxford University Press, 2011.

Masters, Frank M. *A History of the Baptists in Kentucky*. Louisville: Kentucky Baptist Historical Society, 1953.

Matthews, Donald. "The Second Great Awakening as an Organizing Process, 1780–1830: An Hypothesis." *American Quarterly* 21 (1969): 23–43.

———. *Slavery and Methodism: A Chapter in American Morality, 1780–1845*. Princeton, N. J.: Princeton University Press, 1965.

McArthur, Marcus. "'Sent into a Land of Strangers': The Banishment of Reverend Berry Hill Spencer." *Missouri Historical Review* 106 (2011): 14–31.

———. "'There Can Be No Neutral Ground': Samuel B. McPheeters and the Collision of Church and State in St. Louis, 1860–1864." *Journal of Presbyterian History* 89 (2011): 16–26.

———. "Treason in the Pulpit: The Problem of Apolitical Preaching in Civil War Missouri." *Journal of Church and State* 54 (2011): 545–66.

McCaslin, Richard B. *Tainted Breeze: The Great Hanging at Gainesville, Texas, 1862*. Baton Rouge: Louisiana State University Press, 1994.

McKenzie, Robert Tracy. *Lincolnites and Rebels: A Divided Town in the American Civil War*. New York: Oxford University Press, 2006.

———. *One South or Many?: Plantation Belt and Upcountry in Civil War-Era Tennessee*. New York: Cambridge University Press, 1994.

McKivigan, John. "The American Baptist Free Mission Society: Abolitionist Reaction to the 1845 Baptist Schism." *Foundations* 21 (1978): 240–355.

———. "The Battle for the Border State Soul: The Slavery Debate in the Churches of the Border Region." *Ohio Valley History* 12 (2012): 48–71.

———. *The War against Proslavery Religion: Abolitionism and the Northern Churches, 1830– 1865*. Ithaca, N.Y.: Cornell University Press, 1984.

McKnight, Brian. *Contested Borderland: The Civil War in Appalachian Kentucky and Virginia*. Lexington: University Press of Kentucky, 2006.

McLeister, Ira Ford, and Roy Stephenson Nicholson. *History of the Wesleyan Methodist Church of America*. Marian, Ind.: Wesleyan Methodist Publishing Association, 1959.

McPherson, James. *Battle Cry of Freedom: The Civil War Era*. New York: Oxford University Press, 1988.

Melton, J. Gordon. *A Will to Choose: The Origins of African-American Methodism*. Lanham, Md.: Rowman & Littlefield, 2007.

Michaelsen, Scott, and David E. Johnson, eds. *Border Theory: The Limits of Cultural Politics*. Minneapolis: University of Minnesota Press, 1997.

Miller, Randall, Harry Stout, and Charles Regan Wilson, eds. *Religion and the American Civil War*. New York: Oxford University Press, 1998.

Montgomery, William. *Under Their Own Vine and Fig Tree: The African-American Church in the South, 1865–1900*. Baton Rouge: Louisiana State University Press, 1993.

Moore, R. Laurence. *Religious Outsiders and the Making of Americans*. New York: Oxford University Press, 1986.

Moore, Wilton P. "Union Army Provost Marshals in the Eastern Theater." *Military Affairs* 26 (1962): 120–26.

Moorhead, James. *American Apocalypse: Yankee Protestants and the Civil War*. New Haven, Conn.: Yale University Press, 1978.

———. "Between Progress and Apocalypse: A Reassessment of Millennialism in American Religious Thought, 1800–1880." *Journal of American History* 71 (1984): 524–42.

———. "The 'Restless Spirit of Radicalism': Old School Fears and the Schism of 1837." *Journal of Presbyterian History* 78 (2000): 19–33.

Morrison, Michael A. *Slavery and the American West: The Eclipse of Manifest Destiny and the Coming of the Civil War*. Chapel Hill: University of North Carolina Press, 1997.

Morrow, Ralph E. *Northern Methodism and Reconstruction*. East Lansing: Michigan State University Press, 1956.

Najar, Monica. "'Meddling With Emancipation': Baptists, Authority, and the Rift over Slavery in the Upper South." *Journal of the Early Republic* 25 (2005): 157–86.

Neely, Jeremy. *The Border Between Them: Violence and Reconciliation on the Kansas-Missouri Line*. Columbia: University of Missouri Press, 2011.

Neely, Mark E., Jr. *The Fate of Liberty: Abraham Lincoln and Civil Liberties*. New York: Oxford University Press, 1991.

Neff, John. *Honoring the Civil War Dead: Commemoration and the Problem of Reconciliation*. Lawrence: University Press of Kansas, 2005.

Niebuhr, H. Richard. *Christ and Culture*. New York: Harper & Row, 1951.

Noll, Mark A. *America's God: From Jonathan Edwards to Abraham Lincoln*. New York: Oxford University Press, 2002.

———. *The Civil War as a Theological Crisis*. Chapel Hill: University of North Carolina Press, 2006.

———. ed. *Religion and American Politics from the Colonial Period to the 1980s*. New York: Oxford University Press, 1990.

Noonan, John T., Jr. *The Believers and the Powers that Are: Cases, History, and Other Data Bearing on the Relation of Religion and Government.* New York: Macmillan, 1987.

Nord, David Paul. "The Evangelical Origins of Mass Media in America." *Journalism Monographs* 88 (1984): 1–30.

———. *Faith in Reading: Religious Publishing and the Birth of Mass Media in America.* New York: Oxford University Press, 2004.

———. "Religious Reading and Readers in Antebellum America." *Journal of the Early Republic* 15 (1995): 241–72.

Norwood, John Nelson. *The Schism in the Methodist Episcopal Church, 1844: A Study of Slavery and Ecclesiastical Politics.* Alfred, N.Y.: Alfred Press, 1923.

Oakes, James. *Freedom National: The Destruction of Slavery in the United States, 1861–1865.* New York: W. W. Norton, 2013.

Oshatz, Molly. *Slavery and Sin: The Fight against Slavery and the Rise of Liberal Protestantism.* New York: Oxford University Press, 2011.

Osterweis, Rollin G. *The Myth of the Lost Cause, 1865–1900.* Hamden, Conn.: Archer Books, 1973.

Parker, Harold M., Jr. "The Synod of Kentucky: From Old School Assembly to the Southern Church." *Journal of Presbyterian History* 41 (1963): 14–36.

———. *The United Synod of the South: The Southern New School Presbyterian Church.* New York: Greenwood Press, 1988.

Parrish, William E. *Missouri Under Radical Rule, 1865–1870.* Columbia: University of Missouri Press, 1965.

Perry, Jeffrey Thomas. "'Courts of Conscience': Local Law, the Baptists, and Church Schism in Kentucky, 1780–1840." *Church History* 84 (2015): 124–58.

Perry, Lewis, and Matthew C. Sherman. "'What Disturbed the Unitarian Church in This Very City?': Alton, the Slavery Conflict, and Western Unitarianism." *Civil War History* 54 (2008): 5–34.

Phillips, Christopher. *The Civil War in the Border South.* Santa Barbara, Calif.: Praeger, 2013.

———. "The Crime Against Missouri: Slavery, Kansas, and the Cant of Southernness in the Border West." *Civil War History* 48 (2002): 60–81.

———. *The Rivers Ran Backward: The Civil War and the Remaking of the American Middle Border.* New York: Oxford University Press, 2016.

Porterfield, Amanda. *Conceived in Doubt: Religion and Politics in the New American Nation.* Chicago: University of Chicago Press, 2012.

Posey, Walter B. "The Baptists and Slavery in the Lower Mississippi Valley." *Journal of Negro History* 41 (1956): 117–30.

Potter, David. *The Impending Crisis.* New York: Harper and Row, 1976.

Potts, David B. "American Colleges in the Nineteenth Century: From Localism to Denominationalism." *History of Education Quarterly* 11 (1971): 363–80.

Power, Richard Lyle. *Planting Corn Belt Culture: The Impress of the Upland Southerner and Yankee in the Old Northwest.* Indianapolis: Indiana Historical Society, 1953.

Price, Barton E. "*The Central Christian Advocate* and the Quest for a Heartland Identity in American Methodism, 1852–1900." *Methodist History* 50 (2012): 196–211.

Purifoy, Lewis M. "The Southern Methodist Church and the Proslavery Argument." *Journal of Southern History* 32 (1966): 325–41.

Rable, George. *God's Almost Chosen Peoples: A Religious History of the American Civil War.* Chapel Hill: University of North Carolina Press, 2010.

Randall, James G. "Captured and Abandoned Property During the Civil War." *American Historical Review* 19 (1913): 65–79.

Reilly, Timothy F. "Benjamin M. Palmer: Secessionist Become Nationalist." *Louisiana History* 18 (1977): 287–301.

Richards, Leonard. *"Gentlemen of Property and Standing": Anti-Abolition Mobs in Jacksonian America.* New York: Oxford University Press, 1970.

Richardson, Joe M. *Christian Reconstruction: The American Missionary Association and Southern Blacks, 1861–1890.* Athens: University of Georgia Press, 1986.

Rolfs, David. *No Peace for the Wicked: Northern Protestant Soldiers and the American Civil War.* Knoxville: University of Tennessee Press, 2009.

Rose, Willie Lee. *Rehearsal for Reconstruction: The Port Royal Experiment.* Indianapolis, Ind.: Bobbs-Merrill, 1964.

Ryan, Mary. *Cradle of the Middle Class: The Family in Oneida County, New York, 1790–1865.* New York: Cambridge University Press, 1981.

Salafia, Matthew. *Slavery's Borderland: Freedom and Bondage along the Ohio River.* Philadelphia: University of Pennsylvania Press, 2013.

Scott, Sean. *A Visitation of God: Northern Civilians Interpret the Civil War.* New York: Oxford University Press, 2011.

Sehat, David. *The Myth of American Religious Freedom.* New York: Oxford University Press, 2011.

Sellers, Charles. *The Market Revolution: Jacksonian America, 1815–1846.* New York: Oxford University Press, 1994.

SenGupta, Gunja. *For God and Mammon: Evangelicals and Entrepreneurs, Masters and Slaves in Territorial Kansas, 1854–1860.* Athens: University of Georgia Press, 1996.

Shurden, Walter B., and Lori Redwine Varnadoe. "The Origins of the Southern Baptist Convention: A Historiographical Study." *Baptist History and Heritage* 37 (2002): 71–96.

Silber, Nina. *The Romance of Reunion: Northerners and the South, 1865–1900.* Chapel Hill: University of North Carolina Press, 1993.

Simkins, Francis B. "Robert Lewis Dabney, Southern Conservative." *Georgia Review* 18 (1964): 393–407.

Skocpol, Theda, Marshall Ganz, and Ziad Munson. "A Nation of Organizers: The Institutional Origins of Civic Voluntarism." *American Political Science Review* 94 (2000): 527–46.

Smith, Edward Conrad. *The Borderland in the Civil War.* 1927. Rpt. Freeport, N.Y.: Books for Libraries Press, 1969.

Smith, Jonathan Z. *Imagining Religion: From Babylon to Jonestown.* Chicago: University of Chicago Press, 1982.

Smith, R. Drew. "Popular Democracy Denied, Elite Dominion Preserved: Antebellum Southern Methodists and Abolitionist and Democratic Dissenters." *Southern Studies* 3 (1992): 305–19.

———. "Slavery, Secession, and Southern Protestant Shifts on the Authority of the State." *Journal of Church and State* 36 (1994): 261–76.

Snay, Mitchell. *Gospel of Disunion: Religion and Separatism in the Antebellum South.* Cambridge, U.K.: Cambridge University Press, 1993.

Stanley, Matthew. "'Purely Military Matters': John A. McClernand and Civil Liberties in Cairo, Illinois, in 1861." *Ohio Valley History* 8 (2008): 23–41.

Stiffler, Angela N. "Missouri Baptist Heritage: Caroline Moss." *Word and Way,* November 2005.

Stout, Harry. *Upon the Altar of the Nation: A Moral History of the American Civil War.* New York: Viking, 2006.

Stowell, Daniel W. *Rebuilding Zion: The Religious Reconstruction of the South, 1863–1877.* New York: Oxford University Press, 1998.

Sweet, William Warren. *Methodism in American History.* New York: Methodist Book Concern, 1933.

———. "The Methodist Episcopal Church and the Civil War." Ph.D. diss., University of Pennsylvania, 1912.

———. "Some Religious Aspects of the Kansas Struggle." *Journal of Religion* 7 (1927): 578–95.

Tuveson, Ernest Lee. *Redeemer Nation; The Idea of America's Millennial Role.* Chicago: University of Chicago Press, 1968.

Vander Velde, Lewis G. *The Presbyterian Churches and the Federal Union, 1861–1869.* Cambridge, U.K.: Oxford University Press, 1932.

Volkman, Lucas P. "Church Property Disputes, Religious Freedom, and the Ordeal of African Methodists in Antebellum St. Louis: *Farrar v. Finney* (1855)." *Journal of Law and Religion* 27 (2012): 83–139.

———. "Houses Divided: Evangelical Schisms, Society, and Law and the Crisis of the Union in Missouri, 1837–1876." PhD diss., University of Missouri, Columbia, 2012.

Waldstreicher, David. *In the Midst of Perpetual Fetes: The Making of American Nationalism, 1776–1820.* Chapel Hill: University of North Carolina Press, 1997.

Weaver, Douglas C. *In Search of the New Testament Church: The Baptist Story.* Macon, Ga.: Mercer University Press, 2008.

Weber, Jennifer L. *Copperheads: The Rise and Fall of Lincoln's Opponents in the North.* New York: Oxford University Press, 2006.

Weeks, Louis, and James C. Hickey. "'Implied Trust' for Connectional Churches: 'Watson v. Jones' Revisited." *Journal of Presbyterian History* 54 (1976): 459–70.

Wenger, Tisa. *We Have a Religion: The 1920s Pueblo Indian Dance Controversy and American Religious Freedom.* Chapel Hill: University of North Carolina Press, 2009.

Wesley, Timothy. *The Politics of Faith during the Civil War.* Baton Rouge: Louisiana State University Press, 2013.

West, Elliott. "Reconstructing Race." *Western Historical Quarterly* 34 (2003): 7–26.

Wheeler, Kenneth H. "Higher Education in the Antebellum Ohio Valley: Slavery, Sectionalism, and the Erosion of Regional Identity." *Ohio Valley History* 8, no. 1 (2008): 1–22.

White, Heather Rachelle. "'The Glory of Southern Christianity': Methodism and the Mission to the Slaves." *Methodist History* 39 (2001): 108–21.

White, Ronald Cedric. *A. Lincoln: A Biography.* New York: Random House, 2009.

Wigger, John. *Taking Heaven by Storm: Methodism and the Rise of Popular Christianity in America.* New York: Oxford University Press, 1998.

Williams, Michael, Sr. *Isaac Taylor Tichenor: The Creation of a Baptist New South.* Tuscaloosa: University of Alabama Press, 2005.

Wilson, Charles Regan. *Baptized in Blood: The Religion of the Lost Cause, 1865–1920.* Athens: University of Georgia Press, 1980.

———. "The Religion of the Lost Cause: Ritual and Organization of the Southern Civil Religion, 1865–1920." *Journal of Southern History* 46 (1980): 219–38.

Witt, John. *Lincoln's Code: The Laws of War in American History.* New York: Free Press, 2012.

Woodward, C. Vann. *Origins of the New South, 1877–1913.* Louisiana State University Press, 1971.

———. *Reunion and Reaction: The Compromise of 1877 and the End of Reconstruction.* Boston: Little, Brown and Co., 1951.

Wyatt-Brown, Bertram. *Lewis Tappan and the Evangelical War Against Slavery.* Cleveland: Press of Case Western Reserve University, 1969.

Zeuner, Robert W. "The Appeal to Caesar: A History of the Methodist Church Property Case of 1849." *Methodist History* 8 (1969): 3–16.

INDEX

Note: page numbers in *italics* refer to illustrations; those followed by "n" indicate endnotes.